D0875295

Circulation of News in the Third World

A Study of Asia

CIRCULATION OF NEWS IN THE THIRD WORLD
A Study of Asia

by
Wilbur Schramm
and
Erwin Atwood

Communication Studies Series
The Chinese University Press
Hong Kong

International Standard Book Number: 962-201-238-8

Communication Studies Series
are issued by the Centre for Communication Studies
The Chinese University of Hong Kong

Typesetting by Mandarin Photo Typesetting Co., Hong Kong
Printing by Speed Printing Company Limited, Hong Kong

CONTENTS

Part One

Background

I. WHY THIS STUDY

No thoughtful observer, whether he comes from the Third World where three fourths of the world's people live, or from one of the industrialized nations where most of the advanced communication technology and the transnational media have their homes, can be completely content with the present international circulation of information. It is unevenly distributed. Its quality and reliability are sometimes suspect. And it is contributing less than the state of the art should be able to contribute to world peace and understanding and social and economic improvement.

For most of the last two decades international information has been the subject of a truculent debate, in and out of UN and Unesco committees and conferences, in which spokesmen for the Third World have usually been cast in the role of accusers, and spokesmen for the "First" World (meaning Western Europe, North America, Japan, and a few other countries) as defenders. The "Second" World, so called, (Eastern Europe and the Soviet Union) has tried to stay out of the line of fire but has in general supported the complaints in order to embarrass the capitalist countries of the First World.

Increasingly this debate has come to be between spokesmen for the Third World and spokesmen for the United States. The U.S. got into this position because at the end of World War II, when Europe and Japan were rebuilding their devastated industries, American science and industry were in position to launch a network of communication satellites, create a gigantic data processing industry, and offer films, broadcast programs and news services at favorable rates throughout the developing world where such things were in short supply. As new countries emerged from colonialism with a spirit of nationalism and militancy, many of them, even though they had gladly accepted these American services, began to question them as manifestations of "neo-colonialism" and of the economic inequity which provides an average per capita income of over $2,000 in the industrialized countries but less than $200 in the developing countries. Therefore, a "New World Information Order" came to be seen as an integral part of the "New World Economic Order" which was relied upon to remove some of the existing inequities.

Jonathan Gunter in a perceptive article in the *Journal of Communication* (Gunter, 1978) has stated three respects in which the Third World sees the present world information order as a threat:

- the threat to "national sovereignty" implied by U.S. preeminence in computers, remote-sensing, and communication technology – and, we might add, Western ownership of most of the international news channels.

- the threat of "cultural imperialism" reflected in U.S. export of publications, films, and television.

- the threat of "bias" in Western news agency coverage of foreign affairs. (Gunter, p. 160)

Thus the "New World Information Order" is seen as including at least three kinds of information – data processing and transmission; entertainment; and news. It includes the relation of content to ownership of technology, and the relation of government control to private control. In this book we are going to concentrate on the news, but let us not lose sight of the fact that the debate over news is part of a larger debate.

The full implications of the Western lead in computers and data processing (in an Age of Information) are just beginning to be understood, but for a long time many Third World countries have been dissatisfied with the I.T.U. policy of assigning radio spectrum frequencies and satellite parking spaces on a "first come, first served" basis. Most of these have been taken by the industrialized countries because they are now prepared to use them. The threat of cultural invasion – cultural "imperialism" in debating terms – has long seemed very real to Third World countries. The mere possibility of satellite broadcasting over national borders without "prior consent" by governments was sufficient to bring about a confrontation in the UN in the course of which the United States cast a lone vote against any such government control, and 100 other nations voted on the side of prior consent. Remote sensing from satellites has looked to countries without satellites like an invasion of privacy and national sovereignty. And a longtime uneasiness over the cultural impact of Western entertainment materials on developing countries came to a head with a study by Nordenstreng and Varis (1975) which measured the proportion of different countries' broadcasts that were imported from outside, and, not surprisingly, found that most of the imports came from the West. Where resources and expertise are scarce, it is cheaper to import programs than to make local ones of comparable quality. It should be noted, however, that many scholars from outside the Third World also have been concerned about the cultural baggage carried by Western entertainment. An example is Elihu Katz's article, *"Can Authentic Cultures Survive Mass Media?"* (Katz, 1977).

Increasingly the great debate on a New World Information Order has focussed on international circulation of the news, and in particular on the four large Western news agencies – Reuter, Agence France Presse, the Associated Press, and United Press International – which supply the bulk of foreign news to both industrialized countries and the Third World.

Around this topic the governments, the agencies, and the journalists have danced a *pas de trois.* None of the four Western international agencies is government-owned, and only one of them (AFP) receives any substantial amount of government subsidy. All of them, American agencies in particular, are suspicious of any governmental control over the flow of information. The First Amendment to the U.S. Constitution and a host of supplementary laws stand witness to this viewpoint. On the other hand, the typical Third World country is likely to feel that information is not something to be protected from government but simply another tool for development and survivial, to be guided by government. Where human needs have already largely been satisfied, where a government is secure and economic development is no longer a chief need, a free flow of information from many sources can be permitted and people can be allowed to choose what they want from that flow. But in a developing country where survival of a government may be at stake and where development is the chief order of business, governments feel that people should be given not just the information they want but the information their leaders think they *need.* It is fair to say, we think, that many of the journalists in developing countries share with Western journalists a concern over access to the news, and that Third World journalists are more likely to be concerned with the news coming into their countries over the agency wires than with the news going out. But nevertheless the journalists frequently share with their governments in the Third World a resentment over the way their countries are being reported to the world and the small proportion of news attention they get compared to that given to large industrialized nations like the United States. Thus a sense of hurt pride is combined with a feeling that information is not being used to the fullest extent to help a country overcome great obstacles and attain its chosen goals. And it is frustrating to a Third World country to know what it can do about the situation because the facilities of international communication are out of their hands.

Some of the complaints of Third World information spokesmen concerning the international news agencies have been expressed eloquently by Mustapha Masmoudi, who was Secretary of State for Information in Tunisia and first President of the Inter-governmental Coordinating Council for Information of the Non-Aligned Countries, and is currently Tunisia's Permanent Delegate to Unesco. Mr. Masmoudi has written:

> Almost 80 per cent of the world news flow emanates from the major transnational news agencies; however, they devote only 20 to 30 per cent of news coverage to the developing countries, despite the fact that the latter account for almost three-quarters of mankind. (172-173)

> By transmitting to the development countries only news processed by them, that is, news they have filtered, cut, and distorted, the transnational media impose their own way of seeing the world upon the developing countries . . . moreover (they often) present those communities – when indeed they do show interest in them – in the most unfavorable light, stressing crises, strikes, street demonstrations, putsches, etc., or even holding them up to ridicule. (174)

> Even important news may be deliberately neglected by the major media in favor of other information of interest only to public opinion in the country to which the media in question belong. Such news is transmitted to the client countries and is indeed practically imposed on them, despite the fact that readers and listeners in these countries have no interest therein . . . Their news coverage is designed to meet the national needs of their countries of origin. (Masmoudi, 1975, pp. 184-185)

He points out also that the major transnational agencies monopolize among them the major share of human and material potential for long-range communication of news, whereas almost a third of the developing countries do not yet have even a single national agency. What does the right of access to news sources mean in that situation, he asks; since "Right of access essentially benefits only those who have the resources to obtain and impart information" (*ibid.*, 173). Other representatives for Third World viewpoints on international news have for the most part followed these arguments: there is an imbalance in the circulation of the news, a Western bias in its presentation, inequity in access to news channels, and a failure to present news over international channels that would be most useful to Third World countries.

What would Masmoudi like to see done about this situation? Here is part of his prescription for a New World Information Order that applies to international news circulation:

> (The developed countries must) help "decolonize" information by taking a more objective approach to the aspirations and concerns of the developing nations, while at the same time eschewing all incitement to hatred or racial, religious, political, or any other kind of discrimination, and all initiatives liable to misrepresent, distort, or show in an unfavorable light the measures taken by the developing countries. (180)

> (The developed countries must) help establish a balance in the information flow by devoting more space in newspapers and in radio and television programs to news concerning developing countries. (180)

> (The developed countries must) ensure that, prior to each mission, special correspondents acquire as comprehensive a knowledge as possible of the countries to which they are sent, so as to be able to assess problems and concerns correctly and not use merely the sensational or anecdotal aspect of events, refrain from hasty judgments, free themselves of any distorting ideological lens through which they might be tempted to judge events and people, guard against all bias and prejudice, and endeavor to ensure that their conclusions correspond to reality. (*ibid.*, 180-182)

It is important to point out that during the last decade Western news agencies and Western newsmen in general have become a great deal more appreciative of these Third World points of view. For example in March 1979, Clayton Kirkpatrick, editor of the *Chicago Tribune*, said some things to a symposium, later printed by the U.S. Association for Education in Journalism that would hardly have been expected a decade earlier. "On this issue of the Third World and the coverage it receives," he said, "I think we can concede at the outset that there is an imbalance. I think we can concede . . . that there is bias in the reporting from the Third World. I think we can concede that the Western news agencies do dominate this field. And it is a matter of no satisfaction to most of us in our profession . . . I don't think the Western news agencies want monopoly. All they want is access." (Kirkpatrick, 1979, pp. 11, 15). Whereas Western newsmen at first strongly opposed the idea of a Third World news pool, they have now come to accept it, and have in general approved of the idea that there should someday be a Third World news agency or agencies, regional or world wide. Indeed the United States, through Ambassador John Reinhardt, head of the U.S. delegation to the 1976 Unesco general conference, offered help "through bilateral and multilateral channels, both private and government" to states that need such help in developing their own news media. Western newsmen have agreed strongly also on the need for objectivity in covering foreign countries, and the need to send out correspondents well-prepared for their assignments in a culture different from their own. But they have insisted vigorously on their own right of free access to foreign news sources; that is to say, they have not wanted news filtered to them through Third World government gatekeepers.

Indeed, American newsmen have been prepared by their own history to be sympathetic to many of the Third World objections concerning the Western news agencies. D.R. Mankekar, Chairman of the Coordinating Council of the Non-Aligned News Agencies Pool, at one point in the long debate reminded American journalists of something Kent Cooper had written in recalling his long term as General Manager of the Associated Press. This was when the AP was still mostly a national agency, while a European news cartel, headed by the Reuter agency, controlled the flow of news into and out of the United States. Cooper wrote in his history of the Associated Press:

> So Reuters decided what news was to be sent from America. It told the world about Indians on the war path in the West, lynchings in the South, and bizarre crimes in the North. The charge for decades was that nothing creditable to America was ever sent. Business men criticized the Associated Press for permitting Reuters to belittle America abroad . . .

> (On the other hand) their (the cartel's) own countries were always glorified. This was done by reporting great advances at home in (European) civilizations, the benefits of which would, of course, be bestowed on the world. (Cooper, 1942, p.4)

Simply substitute "developing countries" where Cooper referred to "America", said Mankekar, and Cooper could be speaking for the Third World today. His American audience got the idea.

In recent years the Western position on the news agency portion of the New Information Order debate has grown more conciliatory, and the Third World position more understanding of the requirements for international news circulation. But the debate has so far been conducted largely on matters of principles. The chief need now is to supplement it with some solid information on *practice.* Precisely what *is* happening in the international circulation of information? This is what we are going to try to supply in the following pages.

We are going to focus on the flow of news into and out of the Third World, especially the performance of the four Western international news agencies. That means that, no matter how much we should like to, we are not going to talk about the problems inherent in the inequities of facility ownership, the "threats to national sovereignty" implied by the Western lead in data processing and communication technology and the ability to broadcast and observe from satellites, or the "cultural imperialism" ascribed to the sale of American entertainment materials abroad. We are going to concentrate on the news. That is quite enough for one study. Within this limited area we are going to try to provide some light where there has been mostly heat – that is, to provide some concrete information about news circulation as it presently exists, its strengths and its shortcomings. What are the international agencies actually carrying? How does their coverage of the Third World compare with their coverage of the First World? What kinds and amounts of news are they providing to Third World daily newspapers? A number of statements have been made, in the course of debate, about the adequacy or inadequacy of international news circulation that can and should be checked. Here are a few examples:

> (The transnational news agencies) devote only 20 to 30 per cent of their news coverage to the developing countries. (Masmoudi, *ibid.,* 172-173)

> For those who question the validity of the Third World countries' argument about imbalance in flow of news from their part of the world, I will refer to a Unesco study estimating the input of Third World news into the total world circulation to be 15% while world news emanating from Paris, London, and New York was 90%. (El-Sherif, 1978, p. 3)*

> . . . the wires from the Western news agencies contain little information relevant to development needs. (Gunter, *ibid.*, p. 167, quoting "Third World spokespersons.")

Similiar statements have been made about the inordinate amount of attention said to be given to sensational news (crime, disaster, civil disorder, and the like), the way that Third World leaders are presented, the relative amounts of "positive" and "negative" news from the Third World, and so forth. Statements like these may be true, but they should not be allowed to stand without evidence.

Furthermore, the international news agencies need to be seen as part of the larger pattern of news circulation – the flow of news from event to reader. What kind of news does a medium in a Third World country find worth publishing about its own country? How many of these local stories do the wires export, and what kind of stories do they select from the ones available? What news about *other* Third World countries do the newspapers of the Third World take from the wires? And finally, what do Third World people seem to want to read in the news? When this larger pattern is set forth clearly we shall be in position to perceive more clearly the deficiencies within it, and the extent to which its component parts are meeting the needs they are intended to meet.

We are going to try to answer some of these questions and others of the same kind in the belief that it will be helpful in the formation of policy to know what is actually happening, in relation to what policy makers think *should* happen. That is the purpose of the next several hundred pages.

---

* We do not know this Unesco study which thus allocates 105 per cent of the news, but can at least measure the existing proportions of news.

II. HOW THE STUDY WAS DONE

Design

The study was planned to include five components of measurement and analysis:

1. Local and national news content of 18 Asian daily newspapers. One English language and one native language daily for each of nine countries, during one week in December, 1977.

2. Content of the international news agencies wire services delivered to Asian clients during the same week in December, 1977. All their news from whatever source or region was to be coded, but particular attention was to be paid to their coverage of Asian Third World news as compared with the local and national news found in the Asian dailies mentioned above.

3. Foreign news content of the 18 Asian dailies, with particular reference to what was selected from the international wires.

4. Readership of a sample – the number depending on what we could afford – of the Asian dailies.

5. Asian news in a sample of First World dailies – number again dependent upon finances.

Thus it was hoped to obtain some factual information on the flow of news in Asia from events to readers, from international wires to newspapers and readers, and the two-way circulation between developing and industrialized countries.

How the Project Was Supported

It is necessary to admit that the study was underfinanced. In candid moments we estimated that if we were doing a comparable study in the United States we should put a price tag of $100,000 on it. Actually we had about $4,000 in outside support – $2,500 contributed by the World Press Freedom Committee, the remainder by the Edward R. Murrow Center for Public Diplomacy, at Tufts University. The entire contribution of the Committee was used to pay for readership interviews on one newspaper in the Philippines. The problem was, therefore, to stretch a very small sum, by using other resources and contributed time and services, to cover as much as possible of an ambitious design.

The two chief investigators contributed all their time, as did the heads of cooperating organizations – Professor Timothy L.M. Yu, Director of the Center for Communication Studies at the Chinese University of Hong Kong, Dr. Gloria Feliciano, Dean of the Institute of Mass Communication at the University of the Philippines, and Dr. Jack Lyle, Director of the East-West Communication Institute, a division of the East-West Center in Honolulu. Schramm drew on other research funds and on personal funds to cover some of the expenditures. The three institutions where extensive computer work was done – Southern Illinois University, the East-West Center, and the Chinese University of Hong Kong – did this work without cost to the project. The international news agencies furnished their wire copy free of charge, and some of the newspapers also contributed their copies. Advanced students at the Chinese University were trained to code news copy. At least one secretary at the Chinese University learned to punch cards and operate a computer as an extraordinary part of her regular job during the project. A great deal of research time and skill was contributed, and when work was paid for, it was usually done by individuals deeply interested in the project who let personal interest rather than economics guide their rates of payment.

By stretching resources in these ways we were able to analyze about two and one half million words of news, in seven languages; make about seven hundred interviews with readers, editors, government information officers, and scholars; and perform a number of statistical operations including factor analysis.

We were *not* able, however, to do certain tasks envisaged in the design. We did study the content of 19 Asian daily newspapers, but were unable to study two papers, one in English, one in a native language, for each country. We followed the two-paper design for India, Korea, Hong Kong, Malaysia, Singapore, Iran*, and the Philippines, but either because of the difficulty in finding coders with the necessary

* The two Iranian papers became available to us about a year after we started work on the other data. Therefore, they are included in most of the Appendix tables, but not in all the qualitative comparisons or all the tabulations in the text.

language skills or the difficulty of obtaining suitable newspapers, coded only English language newspapers for Thailand and Sri Lanka and a native language paper for Indonesia. In both India and the Philippines, for reasons that will be explained later, we studied a third paper also.

We were unable furthermore, to make studies of readership in each country, as we had hoped to do. We feel that it is important to learn a great deal more about the reading of news in Asia, but the costs made it impossible for us to do so in the course of this study. Unless interview costs are contributed, a readership study in Asia is likely to cost between $4,000 and $5,000. We had barely enough funding even with the kind and helpful cooperation of the Institute of Mass Communication, at the University of the Philippines, to do *one* such study. We had hoped, at the least, to go to such a country as Malaysia and do a comparative readership study of an English and a native-language newspaper, but costs and time were against us. We had to settle for one readership study, of the *Bulletin Today,* in Manila. Further studies of readership in Asia are future agenda.

Nor were we able to do any new research on news content and news reading in Western countries. Fortunately, this was not missed so much as it might have been, because some data are already available there. In the United States, for example, we have a number of newspaper readership studies, from the 1930's and 40's; and Pinch conducted in December, 1977 some content studies of five American prestige papers and also of a small sample of Third World newspapers from Africa, Latin America, the Middle East, and Asia (Pinch, 1978). His categories and coding methods do not fit precisely with ours, but some interesting comparisons are possible.

The shortage of current financing had another undesirable effect: the study took longer. Preliminary reports were available within a few months of each piece of field work or content coding, as promised, but this main report has had to wait until the two chief investigators could take time from other duties to finish it. Therefore we are reporting the results two years after the data were gathered, rather than as early as we had hoped to do.

The experience with this study shows what an enormous amount of research can be done without much money if people are sufficiently motivated, but it also demonstrates what cannot be done without a certain basic level of funding.

The Newspapers and the News Agency Wires

We coded the following Asian daily newspapers (see Appendix for detailed information about the papers):

Hong Kong
- Sing Tao Jih Pao (Chinese language)
- South China Morning Post (English)

India
- Ananda Bazar Patrika, Calcutta (Bengali)
- Amrita Bazar Patrika, Calcutta (English)
- Statesman, Calcutta and New Delhi (English)

Indonesia
- Kompas, Jakarta (Indonesian)

Iran
- Ettelaat, Tehran (Farsi language)
- Kayhan International, Tehran (English)

South Korea
- Dong-a Ilbo, Seoul (Korean)
- Korea Times, Seoul (English)

Malaysia
- Nanyang Siang Pau, Kuala Lumpur (Chinese)
- New Straits Times, Kuala Lumpur (English)

Philippines
- Bulletin Today, Manila (English)
- Philippine Daily Express, Manila (English)
- Pilipino Express, Manila (Tagalog language)

Singapore
- Sing Chew Jit Poh (Chinese)
- Straits Times (English)

Sri Lanka
- Ceylon Daily News, Columbo (English)

Thailand
- Bangkok Post, Bangkok (English)

We have already indicated why we represented three countries with only one paper each. Some explanation is called for as to why we included a third paper for India and the Philippines. The third Indian paper was added when we discovered, to our surprise, that *Ananda Bazar Patrika,* the largest newspaper in India, was averaging at that time only about one foreign Third World news item per day. We hastily added another Indian daily while we looked into the question of whether this pattern of news selection possibly represented an atypical time, for *Ananda,* or an atypical newspaper for India. The third Philippine paper was added when the readership study was conducted, some months after the content studies. We could not afford to do the readership research, as we had hoped to do, during the week of the content studies. Therefore the figures on the content of *Bulletin Today* are not included in the large tables of Asian dailies for the test week in December, 1977. The content figures from *Ananda* are also omitted from the large tables because we doubt that they are representative.

Most of these dailies would be regarded as prestige papers of their countries. Additional information on them will be found in the appendix.

We coded the following international news wires, in each case the *Asian* wire which was supposedly the one seen by the Asian newspapers we studied:

Agence France Presse (headquarters in Paris)
Associated Press (New York)
Reuter (London)
United Press International (New York)

Much to our regret we were unable to obtain copies of Tass, the Soviet news wire, for that week. This may be a matter of largely academic interest beacuse we found very few items in our 17 papers that credited Tass as their source, but we regretted, nevertheless, that we could not include the fifth wire. Our study, therefore, concentrates on the relation of the *Western* international news agencies to Asian news. This is the relationship that has caused the most heat.

We also obtained and coded a complete file of Hsinhua (the New China News Agency) wire for the test week, partial files of Antara from Indonesia, and samples of several other national wires as well as such news services as those of the *New York Times,* the *Washington Post* and *Los Angeles Times,* and the *Asian Depthnews.*

For newspapers and wire services alike we obtained files for the week of December 4 through 10, Sunday through Saturday, of 1977. An exception, of course, is the *Bulletin Today,* of Manila, which was not included in the December content study but was the subject of a readership study on September 14, 1978. These, along with a number of talks with editors and information officials, and the approximately 500 reader interviews in the Philippines, were the raw materials of our study.

Coding the Content

The coders, who were either graduate students, academic staff members, or news professionals, were trained on sample newspapers until they achieved 92 per cent agreement (on all except two categories which, as will be explained, were discarded). Then each newspaper was read and coded by one coder and gone over again by a second coder. All cases where the two coders could not agree were then re-examined and adjudicated by one of the chief investigators.

Each news story, commentary, editorial, and news picture was coded on the following categories in addition to the name of the newspaper or news agency, the date, and a serial number for the story:

Short title (usually the headline)
Page number
Length in column inches
Words or picture
Domestic, news or commentary, foreign, or both
Region or regions referred to (e.g., Asia, Africa, etc.)
Country or countries referred to
Category of news (for list of categories, see below)
Source, if given (e.g., Reuter, paper's own correspondent, etc.)
Notes (features of the story which justified special attention, if any)

Two additional decisions were originally required by the code sheet. These were between "hard" and "soft" news, and "good" and "bad" news. The latter, especially, has had a great deal of attention during the international news debate, but we were unable to obtain sufficient agreement among coders to justify us in considering the results reliable. Therefore, we discarded those two items.

The actual coding was done chiefly by number (e.g., for countries or news categories) which the coders could easily learn and which could be transferred speedily to IBM cards.

Here is the list of news categories which we used:

1. Military, political violence
2. Foreign relations
3. Domestic, political
4. Economic
5. Science, health
6. Education
7. Accident, disaster
8. Crime, judicial
9. Energy, environment
10. Human rights
11. Sports
12. Art, culture
13. Human interest
14. Religion
15. Other

The great bulk of the stories, as will become evident, were codable in the categories 1 through 4, 7 and 8, and sports (number 11). Anyone wishing to scan an Asian daily's content hurriedly could use those seven content categories only, without losing too much. In the final analysis, we recorded the material into 12 rather than 15 categories, as explained in Appendix E.

With these categories as with others in the code, it was necessary to define boundaries as carefully as possible and to give the coders some experience in which they could compare their coding decisions and arrive at agreement. For statistical reasons we did not permit double coding; that is, for example a story about an accident resulting from a crime was coded either accident or crime depending on what the news emphasized.

The Readership Study

The readership survey was conducted on September 14, 1978. Ideally it should have been during the December week of the content studies, but at that time we had no funds for a field survey.

We followed the recommendation of the Institute of Mass Communication at the University of the Philippines in the choice of the paper – the *Bulletin Today.* The staff of the Institute also designed the sample, which was by quotas within areas selected randomly but closely proportionate to the circulation of the newspaper. Thus roughly three fifths of the sample were to be in metropolitan Manila, two fifths outside the metropolitan region. The sample was to total 500 adults. Actually our interviewers completed 296 interviews within the metropolitan district, 185 outside. The respondents were to be equally distributed between males and females. Actually, 250 of the completed interviews turned out to be with males, 231 with females.

The interviewers, who were advanced students in journalism, went through training sessions at the university. On the day of the survey, between early afternoon and midevening (the *Bulletin* is a morning paper) each interviewer went to his or her assigned area, and leafed through a clean copy of the paper with each respondent, asking what stories the respondent had read on each page and how far he or she had read in that story. To keep the answers "honest", questions checking up on what the respondent remembered about the content of the story were asked frequently in the first minutes of the interview. The interviewer drew a line down the column to indicate how far the respondent had read. At the end of the interview some brief demographic information was also collected on a sheet attached to the newspaper. This information included address, sex, age (within decades), education, occupation, and estimated time spent that day on the paper.

While the interviewers were in the field, the newspaper was coded for content exactly as the other Asian dailies had been. When the survey was completed, the information from the 481 copies of the newspaper was transferred to coding sheets and prepared for computer analysis. Factor analysis of these data were later conducted, under Atwood's supervision.

The Qualitative Studies

It was apparent from the time the study was planned that computer tables or statistical tests would not answer all the questions worth asking about the circulation of Third World news in Asia. In fact, many of the criticisms of wire coverage or fairness of news handling were the kind that required critical reading of the news itself and discriminations of the kind made more easily by a human computer than an electronic one.

Therefore, we planned and, so far as possible, carried out a series of qualitative studies based on reading news copy and describing gatekeeper performance in a way that our computer codes would hardly permit. Among the qualitative studies we projected were these:

1. The quality and extent of coverage of development news, both by the news wires and newspapers.

2. The focus of attention of newspapers in different parts of Asia. That is, would dailies in East Asia be likely to cover the news in Western Asia, and vice versa? In the circulation of news does Asia operate like more than one region?

3. How some of the most important stories during the test week were handled by the wires and by different papers? Examples were the crash of a hijacked airplane in Malaysia, the Tripoli meeting, the great cyclone in India, the trial of Aquino in the Philippines, the trial of Bhutto in Pakistan.

4. What image of different countries emerged from the week's news? We felt that cases worth studying as examples would be the news from the People's Republic of China, a smaller country like Malaysia, and a country like India which is remote from the great East Asia news centers.

5. What image of certain national leaders emerged from the wire news and newspaper coverage outside their own countries? Suharto in Indonesia, Mrs. Gandhi and Desai in India, Castro in Cuba, and Sadat in Egypt seemed examples worth studying.

6. How did the content of national wires relate to international coverage? Hsinhua, from China, was the only national wire of which we had a complete file, and we did analyze it closely. The larger question of relation of national wires to news agency and newspaper content is one that is worth studying but will have to be put off to a later time.

The Analysis

Data from the content and readership studies were transferred as quickly as possible to IBM cards and later to tapes, computer analyzed, and tabulated. A number of the tables that resulted will be seen in the following pages. In addition to the usual statistical tests where appropriate, a number of correlations were completed, and the readership data were reduced also by factor analysis.

A Note on the Participants in the Study

The data for this study were gathered and the preliminary coding and analysis accomplished while the two senior authors were at the Chinese University of Hong Kong – Schramm as Aw Boon Haw Professor of Communication for 14 months in 1977 and 1978, Atwood as Visiting Professor of Communication, on leave from Southern Illinois University, for the first five months of 1978. Because we were in Asia, we worked in Asia, but that explanation ignores the advantages of facilities, language skills, and experience with Asian journalism available to us in the University and in Hong Kong around the University. We could never have done the same amount of research on Third World news if we have been at our homes in the United States in 1977 and 1978.

Schramm was primarily responsible for the design, the content coding, and the readership field study. Atwood was primarily responsible for computer analysis and tabulation. They shared the task of interpretation.

At the Chinese University, Professor Timothy L.M. Yu, Director of the Center for Communication Studies, was a valuable source of advice on selection of Asian papers and locating coders with the needed language skills. He also made the resources of the Center generously available, and himself participated in the coding. Other members of the Center staff who were active in the study were Mansoon Chow, Leonard Chu, and Mei-fung Ying. Among the advanced students who worked on the coding and the qualitative studies were Clara King-wah Chan, Paul Siu-nam Lee, Hau-yeung Leung, and Chee-kong Yeung. Elsewhere in Hong Kong important parts of the non-English language coding were done by Virginia Casino, Tain-tain Chu, and S. Kamaluddin.

At the University of the Philippines, Dean Gloria Feliciano made the resources of the Institute of Mass Communications available for the readership study, and assembled a large staff of competent interviewers. The sampling, supervision of interviewers, and preliminary hand transfer of data were in charge of her two able research assistants, Marilou de Ocampo, and Eleanor Bacquiran.

At Southern Illinois University, where Dr. Atwood was working on computer tabulation and factor analysis, he had the assistance of Dr. Sunshine C. Kuang and Dr. Naiim Badii.

At the East-West Center, Dr. Jack Lyle, Director of the East-West

Communication Institute, made the resources of that organization available where needed in the course of the study, and permitted Dr. Schramm to spend a large share of his time for several months completing the work. Of special help in completing the Chinese-language coding was Dr. Georgette Wang, a research associate in the Institute.

Scores of others, too many to mention here, contributed advice and helped smooth the way toward the final product.

III. THE WEEK

The week of December 4 through 10, the one chosen for our major content study, was a fairly typical news week in Asia.

It began with a shocking event – the crash of a hijacked airplane, killing all its passengers, in Malaysia on the way to the Singapore airport. Throughout the world, but particularly in Asia, this generated a large amount of copy. Throughout the world, however, Third World news was dominated by the Tripoli meeting of Arab countries opposed to President Sadat's initiative toward Israel. This meeting was winding down, but President Sadat's initiative continued, and continued to be covered. Thus Asia, during that week, probably received more news than usual from the Middle East.

Political violence was under way in many places throughout the world from the horn of Africa to the southern Philippines. The full dimensions of an earlier disaster, the overwhelming storm in India that left 8,000 bodies behind it, were becoming apparent, but got surprisingly little coverage. Politics were heated in a number of Asian countries; these were covered locally but surprisingly seldom in other countries. Mrs. Gandhi and Prime Minister Desai were competing for votes in a by-election in Southern India. A national commission in India was investigating Mrs. Gandhi's conduct as prime minister, and Mrs. Gandhi was attacking the commission. President Marcos was preparing for a referendum in the Philippines and considering the case of Aquino who was appealing a death penalty. The new government in Pakistan was deciding what to do about Bhutto, a former prime minister who was also under sentence of death. President Suharto faced student demonstrations.

Textile-producing nations were negotiating for higher quotas. Sports matches and tournaments went on as usual. The King of Thailand was celebrating his fiftieth birthday. China was quiet, but apparently restudying its economic policy, looking toward the Fifth Party Congress. A parade of diplomats moved through the region, visiting their opposite numbers. Appropriately for the timing of the study, a conference sponsored by Unesco was meeting in Columbo to discuss how to improve news exchange in the Third World. We are sorry to say that this meeting was little covered in Asian newspapers.

If there was one uncommon feature in Asian news during the week of December 4-10, in addition to the airplane disaster, it was the absence of any very exciting news from the industrialized countries. Apart from that it was a week much like all weeks in Asian Third World news.

Part Two

Mainly Quantitative Questions

IV. THE BASIC PATTERN OF NEWS FLOW

More potentially newsworthy events occur in any country than reporters can write or newspapers of that country can publish. The country's newspapers publish more news than the international wires can pick up and export. The wires carry more than their clients in foreign countries can print. And these client newspapers print more news than their readers can read. Thus there is a declining gradient from the number of newsworthy events to the number of items read by any individual reader.

At every stage along that pathway stand gatekeepers. A reporter in Country A must select from among the events that come to his attention the ones he thinks are most worthy of being written that day as news. (It is unnecessary to say that *all* the newsworthy events may not come to his attention.) His editor, looking at all the copy written by all his reporters must then decide which ones he feels are most deserving of going into the paper's newshole on that particular day. The correspondent of the news agency, looking at all the stories available in Country A, must decide which ones he wants to transmit to the news agency for its wire services. At some regional headquarters an editor of the news agency will then select from among the stories coming in to him from Countries A, B, C, and so forth, those that seem to him most deserving of going on the wire that day. When the wire news comes to a given newspaper in Country X, Y, or Z the telegraph editor of the newspaper, looking at all the news he has available, must decide which items he wants to set in print to fill the space he has available in that day's paper. As a news story moves along this pathway it tends to shrink. Editors cut the stories so as to get more news on the line. The choice is complicated, especially when the news reaches the newspaper, because the same events may be reported on several wires and perhaps also by correspondents; therefore the editor must decide not only what stories to print, but also what *version,* as well as *how much* of the story, to print. All these gatekeeper activities come to the reader in the form of a daily newspaper, and then the final gatekeeper must decide what news to read in the paper, and how far to read in each item.

This is one way to describe the pattern of flow: the likelihood of any given story remaining in the pipeline decreases as it passes each gatekeeper. But on the other hand, the totality of the news flow *increases.* Fewer stories from Country A survive in the pipeline, but to these are added stories from Countries B, C, D, and so forth. The news wire serves a number of clients; even though each selects only a portion of the wire content the total amount of news these client newspapers print is very large. And each newspaper has a number of readers, so that the amount of news read at the end of the pipeline is very large indeed.

That is to say, looked at in terms of any one particular news story, there is a declining gradient throughout the path of flow. Looked at in terms of the totality of news exposure, from originating countries to news agency wires to newspapers to readers, there is a rising gradient.

The purpose of this chapter is to put some hard figures on those gradients. How much of the news from a given country or countries is likely to reach the eyes and cortex of readers in other countries?

From News Source to Readers

The average Asian daily in our sample carried about 70 local and national stories on a given day. (There is no magic about this figure, inasmuch as there was considerable variation among papers. The precise figure, averaged over a representative sample of daily newspapers, was 71.2 stories; the range was from 40 to more than 100.)

How many of these 70 stories were transmitted to an international news agency we have no way of knowing, but we do know that approximately 4 stories from any one of the countries in our sample were likely to appear, on an average day, on one of the news wires. Inasmuch as we studied four international wires, we were likely to see about 16 stories on an average day concerning an average country in our Asian sample. However, these were not 16 *different* stories. The wires would agree on a number of the stories they felt worth exporting from a given country. Therefore, the four wires together would carry about 7 or 8 *different* stories from Country A.

A client newspaper, therefore, if it subscribed to all four of the Western wires, would be likely to have available about 10 per cent as many stories concerning Country A as would appear in one of the leading papers of Country A. If the client subscribed to only one of the four wires, it would be likely to have 5 or 6 per cent of the news that originally appeared in Country A. We are talking about number of stories, not length of stories. The news would be cut in length as it passed the gatekeepers; therefore, the client newspaper might receive only 1 or 2 per cent as many column inches as appeared originally in Country A.

A prestige newspaper will have other sources of foreign news in addition to the international news agencies. It may get some input from regional wires, from its own correspondents, from special news services (for example, the New York Times Service, the Washington Post-Los Angeles Times Services, the London Observer Foreign News Service, or *Depthnews*), or from reprints, or from its own staff members who can cover stories of foreign relations locally. Thus the input from the international wire will have to be further reduced by the newspaper in order to include some of the important foreign news from these other sources. We estimate that the amount of news from Asian Country A that actually appears in a leading daily of Asian Country X would be less than 2 per cent of the number of stories that originally appeared in Country A, less than 1 per cent in terms of space.

We come finally to the reader, who must take his choice from a generous coverage of his own country and a highly selected harvest of news from other countries. How much of this does he read? If we depend on our readership study of the *Bulletin Today*, we have to say that he does not read very much. The average readership found in that study was about 1 story out of 11 – 8.4 per cent. There was no great difference between the average readership overall of foreign and of domestic news.

Is this low readership representative of other Asian dailies? We have no comparable readership study in Asia, and for a comparison have to turn to First World countries. The most extensive sample of newspaper readership was the Continuing Study of Newspaper Reading which measured the readership of 130 dailies in the United States during the 1920s and the 1940s. (For a summary, see Swanson, 1951.) In these 130 dailies the average readership of news was about 20 per cent – 1 story out of 5.

The Pattern in Charts

For the sake of this exercise we are willing to assume that the average daily newspaper reading in Asia may be as much as twice that we found in the *Bulletin Today* — 1 story out of 5 rather than 1 out 10 or 11. If that is the case, then the average reader of a leading newspaper in Country X might actually read four tenths of one per cent, or a little less, as much news of Country A as originally appeared in Country A. That is about 3 stories a week.

Let us put that into a chart. Assume that:

The average Asian daily in our sample will carry 70 local and national stories on an average day.

The four international wires together will carry 7 of those stories.

A leading daily of another Asian country will carry 2 of the stories.

An average reader of this latter paper will read about 3 stories a week from the originating country – about 0.4 per cent.

Here is how that gradient looks:

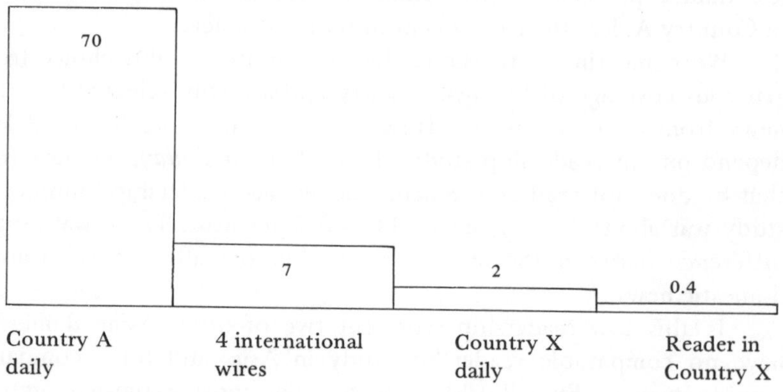

In practical terms, that means:

A leading Asian daily must carry 10 local and national stories in order to have a reasonable probability of getting one of them on one of the four international news agency wires.

This daily must carry *35* local and national stories in order to have a reasonable probability of getting one of them into a leading daily in another Asian country.

The same daily must carry *175* stories in order to have a reasonable probability of having one of them read by an average reader of a leading newspaper in another Asian country.

Note that we are talking about *Asian* dailies, and prestige papers and their readers. A Latin American daily, an African daily, or a Middle Eastern daily, would have to carry far more than 175 stories in order to reach an average Asian reader, as we shall see in the following chapters.

But let us look at the other side of the picture: the ascending gradient of total news flow from events to readers. Instead of considering only one average reader, let us add up some readership totals. To keep the chart within bounds, we shall calculate it for only eight Asian countries, and figure the flow of news at various stages in the pathway from one originating country to the other seven. Then we have this pattern:

The average Asian daily in our sample will carry *70* local and national stories.

Four international wires will deliver to seven other countries a total of *49* stories (7 x 7).

Twenty dailies in each of these seven other countries will carry an average of 2 stories each from the wires, or a total of 280 stories.

Supposing that each of these papers has an average of 30,000 readers, each of these readers will read 0.4 of a story from the originating country per day, or a total of 84,000 stories read.

This chart looks quite different from the other one:

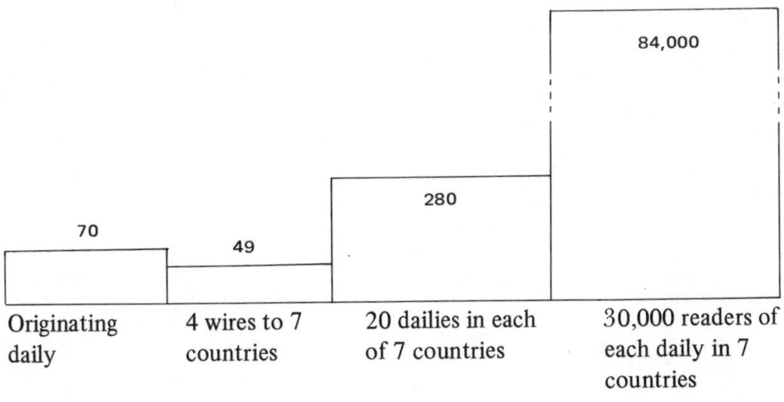

In other words, it is unlikely that any given reader in any given Third World country will read any given story about an event in another Third World country, unless it is a very newsworthy event indeed; but the total output of reading resulting from the news process in the Third World will be quite respectably large.

Summing Up

The implication of these figures is that in the Third World as elsewhere Country A makes more news than International News Agency B can possibly pick up; the international wires of B carry more news of A than the newspapers of Country C can reprint; and the newspapers of C in turn provide more news than their readers can read. Thus every item of news faces more and more competition from other stories and from other countries at every stage of the news process, and there is a very slight probability that any given news story from Country A will ever come to the eyes of a reader in Country C or D or E. But a few stories do survive this competition, pass all the gatekeepers, and reach the widespread audiences the process of news circulation makes possible. These tend to be the extraordinary stories – the crash of a hijacked jet rather than a thousand landings without incident, a famine rather than a good crop. And thus the news process itself makes it more difficult for even the best intentioned journalists to meet the needs so often expressed by critics, in the Third World and outside it, for more news of ordinary life, more "good" news, more development news that is encouraging or inspiring rather than sensational.

V. LOCAL AND NATIONAL NEWS IN THE THIRD WORLD DAILIES

The news process begins with reporters observing and sometimes photographing events, interviewing people, examining documents (such as police records or bureaucratic reports), scanning news releases, and then writing or telephoning news stories. The product of this activity is local stories in a newspaper or a broadcast, or copy delivered to a news agency.

Local Coverage

We are going to illustrate this local stage in the flow of Third World news by analyzing three Asian dailies: the old and respected *Statesman* of Delhi and Calcutta, which grew out of the English tradition of free press and fair comment; *Nanyang Siang Pau* Malaysia, the large and prosperous Chinese language daily of Kuala Lumpur; and the *Bulletin Today,* of Manila, one of the most respected newspapers in the Philippines. No two Asian dailies are precisely alike in their handling of the news, but these three papers give us a chance to observe the practice of prestige papers respectively in Southwest, Southeast and East Asia. The figures for *Bulletin Today* are for the one day when we studied it in connection with our readership survey; for the other two papers the figures are for an average day out of the week in which their content was measured.

Each of the dailies had some local important news to report during that time. In Malaysia it was the horrendous crash of a Malaysian Airlines plane that had been hijacked enroute to Singapore. In India it was the aftereffects of an abrupt change in government and the attempt to move out of the "Emergency" decreed by the previous regime. In the Philippines, although the news was somewhat muted, perhaps by the shadow of martial law, still there was a Muslim rebellion in the southern part of the country and, in the capital city, an appeal by President Marcos' chief rival against a death sentence.

Now, what news did these newspapers print?

What National News Did the Three Asian Dailies Carry?

Nanyang and the *Bulletin Today* are larger papers than the *Statesmen,* and carried more news items: 137 in *Nanyang,* 129 in *Bulletin*

Today, 103 in the *Statesman.* Of these, two thirds or more were, at least in part, local and national news. In the case of the *Statesman,* four fifths of the news dealt with India. Here are the figures for an average day in the three dailies.

	Statesman		**Nanyang**		**Bulletin Today**	
	Stories	*Proportion*	*Stories*	*Proportion*	*Stories*	*Proportion*
Domestic	77	74.8%	72	52.6%	70	54.3%
Both	8	7.8%	20	14.6%	23	17.8%
Foreign	18	17.5%	45	32.8%	36	27.9%

Thus the *Statesman* focused more of its attention on news of its own country than did the other two papers, but on the whole the pattern is quite similar.

Is this pattern typical also of other regions? We have very little comparative data to depend on, but Pinch studied the content of 12 non-Asian dailies in Africa, the Middle East, and Latin America, and four prestige papers in the United States. He does not divide the news as we do, into items dealing solely with the paper's own country, items solely about other countries, and items that deal with *both* the local and foreign countries, but simply gives a figure for the proportion of news about the "host country". This figure ranges, in his 12 developing country dailies, from 41.1 per cent in Mali to 86.2 per cent in Nigeria. A few examples: in Egypt he studied a paper that used 77.9 per cent for the "host country"; in Kenya, 59.2 per cent; in Peru, 74.0 per cent. Overall the 12 Third World dailies averaged about 65 per cent of their news stories devoted to their own countries. Four U.S. prestige papers he measured – the *New York Times,* the *Washington Post,* the *Los Angeles Times,* and the *Chicago Tribune* – all used between 70 and 80 per cent of their stories for their own country. The average was 77.3. Thus Asian dailies seem not to be significantly different from those of other countries in their attention to local news; newspapers all over the world are, first of all, *local* newspapers.

How Much Third World News?

How much of the content of these three Asian dailies is concerned with the Third World? Of course, all local stories would be Third World news; what we are really asking is how much of the foreign news is about the Third World?

12 out of 26 of the *Statesman's* foreign stories dealt with the Third World; 48 of 65 in *Nanyang;* 45 of 59 in the *Bulletin Today.* The proportions are, respectively, about 46 per cent, 74 per cent, and 76 per cent. Thus we can say that from half to three quarters of the foreign news in these Third World dailies deals also with the Third World. The overall content figures are as follows:

	Statesman		**Nanyang**		**Bulletin Today**	
	Stories	*Proportion*	*Stories*	*Proportion*	*Stories*	*Proportion*
Non-Third World	6	5.8%	17	12.4%	14	10.9%
Both	10	9.7%	14	10.2%	32	24.8%
Third World	87	84.5%	106	77.4%	83	64.3%

Thus the *Statesman* devotes a very high proportion of its news to the Third World, but this is mainly because it devotes a very high proportion of its news to India. The others carry more news both of Non-Third World and of other Third World countries.*

Pinch reports that the four U.S. prestige papers he studied carried an average of about 17 per cent of their news from the Third World. It is of interest, therefore, to ask what proportion of the news in these Third World dailies comes from the First and Second Worlds. We can arrive at that by tabulating their content by region, and using North America, Western Europe, and Eastern Europe to represent – approximately – the so-called First and Second worlds. Here are the pertinent figures:

	Statesman		**Nanyang**		**Bulletin Today**	
	Stories	*Proportion*	*Stories*	*Proportion*	*Stories*	*Proportion*
News content on North America, West Europe, and East Europe	11	10.7%	18	13.1%	22	17.1%

* We cannot use Pinch's figures for comparison here, because his proportions for host country plus First, Second and Third World news add up to more than 100 per cent, and must represent some double coding.

Therefore, it seems that prestige papers of Asia devote, if there is any significant difference, proportionately fewer stories to the industrialized countries than American papers devote to the Third World.*

Their Coverage by Regions

It may be interesting to look at the number of stories these three papers carry on different regions of the world:

	Statesman		Nanyang		Bulletin Today	
	Stories	*Proportion*	*Stories*	*Proportion*	*Stories*	*Proportion*
Asia	88	85.4%	107	78.1%	94	72.9%
Latin Am.	–	–	1	0.7%	2	1.6%
Africa	2	1.9%	1	0.7%	4	3.1%
Middle East	2	1.9%	10	7.3%	7	5.4%
North Am.	4	3.9%	8	5.8%	13	10.1%
West Eur.	6	5.8%	8	5.8%	8	6.2%
East Eur.	1	1.0%	2	1.5%	1	0.8%

It is interesting to compare this distribution of attention by region with that of a Western daily like the *Washington Post.* Let us take the average of three Third World dailies and set them beside the *Post's* distribution of regional news. In each case, the home region of the newspapers is omitted. The percentages are rounded out.

	Three Asian Dailies	Washington Post
Asia	–	25%
Latin Am.	4%	7%
Africa	9%	10%
Middle East	23%	17%
North Am.	31%	–
West Eur.	27%	29%
East Eur.	5%	11%
Intl. Orgs.	2%	1%

* The figures for the three Asian papers would be slightly – but only slightly larger – if we were to include also other countries that might be thought as belonging to the industrialized nations, for example Japan, Australia and New Zealand.

There is a great deal of similarity in the patterns. Substitute Asia in one pattern for North America in the other, and the resemblance comes clear. Just as the Asian newspapers give a high proportion of their attention to North America, so does the North American paper give a high proportion to Asia. Both give about the same degree of attention to Western Europe – a little over 25 per cent. The American daily pays more attention, as might be expected, to the Soviet Union and East Europe, but still considerably less than it pays to Western Europe. Both give a great deal of attention, in that particular week at least, to the Middle East. Each allocates about 10 per cent of its stories to Africa. And poor Latin America is the orphan of the foreign news editors, whether they are in the West or in Asia. It is the least covered of the regions.

In a later chapter we are going to review the coverage of different categories of news by all the Asian papers, so there is no use to anticipate here by giving similar figures for these three papers only. But let us illustrate, using the *Statesman,* the different categories of news represented by the domestic stories, the "both" stories (involving both the home country and one or more foreign countries), and foreign stories (exclusively about foreign countries). To make it easier to see the differences we shall give only percentages in this table:

Kinds of Content

Category	Percentage of Local Stories	"Both" stories	Foreign stories
1. Military, Political violence	0.6%	3.1%	8.9%
2. Foreign relations	0.3%	46.9%	35.4%
3. Domestic, political	27.2%	9.4%	15.2%
4. Economic	31.1%	–	13.9%
5. Science, health	0.9%	–	2.5%
6. Education	3.9%	–	–
7. Accident disaster	4.2%	3.1%	6.3%
8. Crime judicial	10.0%	3.1%	6.3%
9. Sports	12.6%	28.1%	3.8%
10. Culture	5.5%	6.3%	2.5%
11. Human interest	1.6%	–	2.5%
12. Other	1.9%	–	2.5%

Thus the bulk of local and national stories are domestic and political, or business and finance. Sizable proportions of the local news are crime and court trials and sports. On the other hand, almost half of the stories involving both the home country and a foreign country deal with foreign relations; these are the stories about diplomatic visits, treaties, agreements, international meetings and discussions. A sizable number of sports stories also deal with the home country and a foreign country; in the test week these would have included the cricket match between India and Australia, and the Asian basketball tournament in Malaysia. The largest proportion of exclusively foreign stories concerns the interrelation of foreign countries – for example, diplomats visiting, Egypt negotiating with Israel, and the like. Smaller but still significant proportions of the exclusively foreign news deal with domestic events in foreign countries, economic news (from Hong Kong, London and New York, amongst other places), and military preparations or political violence. Thus the pattern is like this:

News of	Is likely to come from		
Military and political violence			Foreign sources
Foreign relations		Joint sources	Foreign sources
Domestic and political developments	Local sources		Foreign sources
Economic developments	Local sources		Foreign sources
Crime and court trials	Local sources		
Sports	Local sources	Joint sources	

In reading this last summary table we must remember that it represents, in the *Statesman* especially, a great many more local stories than others, and more foreign stories than stories involving both the home country and foreign countries. Therefore, let us translate the percentages for different categories of news into the approximate number of stories in an average issue of the *Statesman:*

Category	Domestic	Both	Foreign	Total
1. Military, political violence	–	–	2	2
2. Foreign relations	–	4	7	11
3. Domestic, political	21	1	3	25
4. Economic	24	–	3	27
5. Science, health	1	–	–	1
6. Education	3	–	–	3
7. Accident, disaster	4	–	1	5
8. Crime, judicial	7	–	1	8
9. Sports	10	2	1	13
10. Culture	4	1	–	5
11. Human interest	1	–	–	1
12. Other	2	–	–	2
Total	77	8	18	103

What picture of an Asian Third World daily emerges from tables like the ones we have been reading? Half of the news hole is taken up with economic and domestic political news. Another quarter of the news is sports and foreign relations. Half of the remainder is crime and court trials, and accidents and disasters. (Even so, the 13 per cent of news stories that a paper like the *Statesman* allocates to crime and disaster is a bit less than American dailies give. Pinch figures that about 17 per cent of the news in the four U.S. prestige papers he measured were about crime and disaster. His comparable estimate for 16 Third World dailies was a little under 10 per cent.)

As in U.S. papers, three fourths or more of the news in these Asian Third World dailies is about their own countries. Most of their coverage of domestic politics, economic news, and sports comes from the local news, as does most of their crime news and their coverage of accidents and disasters. Most of their news of foreign relations and of military preparations and political violence, comes from the foreign news, not from their own country.

A Reader's View of Some Asian Dailies

The Straits Times

Let us try to put some flesh and blood – or, rather, ink and newsprint – on these numbers by briefly describing a few of the Asian dailies. We can begin with the one that is perhaps least local of all our sample, the *Straits Times,* of Singapore.

The *Times* is a large and prosperous newspaper. On the day we are going to talk about, Thursday, December 8, 1977, it had 34 pages, 10 columns to the page, with a very high proportion of advertising. By Thursday of the week, the crash of the hijacked airplane had moved off the front page, in fact all the way back to page 23. The main headline on page 1 were about the Middle East: "Sadat Warns Arab Hawks," and the sub-head, "Egypt closes Soviet consulates." This story was continued inside the paper, and altogether filled about 126 column inches. Another story about Saudi Arabia continuing its aid to Egypt ran beside the Sadat story, and several more stories on the aftermath of the Tripoli meeting were just inside the paper. Altogether the mideast situation got more than 300 inches in this one issue.

What Singapore news was on the front page? There was a story on Lee Kuan Yew, based on an interview with a *Newsweek* reporter. The question was whether there are enough "tough-minded, sensitive" men to take over from the present leadership when necessary. This story, with its continuation, took 40 column inches. There was also a story in which the Singapore Turf Club admitted it had paid off on the wrong horse on the preceding Sunday – 15 inches. There was a story about four Vietnamese suspected of hijacking and charged with bearing arms in a public place in Singapore – 27 inches, including inside continuation. There was a three-inch bulletin reporting some doubt that the initial flight of the supersonic Concorde between London and Singapore would take place. There was a half-inch weather forecast. And these were all the local items on the front page.

The next four pages were entitled "Around the World." One page picked up the Middle Eastern situation, another page the economic situation featuring Japan's new plans to cut its trade surplus, a third the Australian election outlook, and a fourth the Southeast Asia situation headlining a statement that Vietnam wanted to improve its ties within the region. Then came some local pages. Page 6: children in a crowded subdivision were going to be given study rooms in which to do their homework. A representative of the European Council was visiting Singapore officials. It was denied that Singapore was furnishing maps to Vietnam refugees. A paraplegic was accused of 15 instances of defrauding while on bail. Page 8 carried (in addition to comics like Blondie and Bringing up Father) a feature story on "lighter" jobs going to women, and a story about the sendoff planned for the Concorde – if it arrived. Page 9 featured two large headlines: a newsman complained of "excessive secrecy in the public sector," and police found the body of a 10-year-old girl stuffed into a manhole. The entire non-advertising portion of page 10 was taken up with a review of the state program for training premature school-leavers; the question was, will there be enough jobs for them when they are trained? Page 11 had a number of local stories; among them were plans for a scientific and cultural exchange with the Soviet Union, an appeal by a Soviet bank against a court decision, and a workman's fatal fall. Page 12 was mostly entertainment ads. Page 13 carried a large picture and story about a crane that had rammed into a Singapore storefront, and also stories about newly trained technicians finding jobs, and a girl whose decision to study advertising art had paid off in a good job. Page 14, the last page of the first section, carried the editorials. One editorial dealt with regional matters only: the visit of the Malaysian minister to Cambodia. A second dealt with OPEC. Other commentaries treated the worsening economic situation in the world and the problem of early retirement, both of which had obvious relevance to Singapore.

Then followed a page mostly of letters from readers, a page of stock and market reports, and six pages entitled "Across the Causeway", meaning the causeway between Singapore island and Malaysia. One page dealt mostly with the airplane crash and plans for burying the victims; the other had for its main story some of the apparent results of the Malaysian Foreign Minister's discussion with the Cambodian government. Three pages of sports come next, many of them local, but at least half from London (soccer and bowling), Manila (golf), and Kuala Lumpur (basketball). Page 28, the last page of section two, was used mostly for continuing stories from the front page, but also contained a story on Australia's decision to refuse entrance to Vietnamese refugees and a gloomy account of the U.S. decision not to build the new B-1 bomber.

The third section of the paper, six pages, was considerably more than 50 per cent advertising, with no local news. The content was largely features. There was a page on women in China, a story from Atlanta on a "super gonorrhea" which penicillin cannot cure, a story from London about a woman's frightening experience traveling with a murderer, a story from New York about a Eurasian woman author who has to her credit three husbands and 14 books.

Thus the *Straits Times* is regional rather than local in its orientation; and it keeps in close touch also with the Western world.

Nanyang Siang Pau

Nanyang Siang Pau, a principal Chinese language newspaper of Kuala Lumpur, is more locally oriented than the *Straits Times,* possibly because Malaysia is much larger and therefore has more local news to report than Singapore. *Nanyang* opens from what a Western reader would think of as the *back.* Page 2 is therefore a right-hand page, and page 3 a left-hand page. Its columns run horizontally, right to left, 18 to the page except when copy is set two columns or one and one-half columns wide. The issue of December 8 is 22 pages, and, like the *Straits Times,* is comfortably full of advertising.

By Thursday the news of the hijacked plane crash had cooled down. Almost the entire first page of Tuesday and Wednesday had been filled with the crash. On Thursday, however, the main headline was given to the Minister of Foreign Affair's visit to Cambodia to discuss relations between that nation and the ASEAN countries. As in the *Straits Times,* the Middle Eastern situation, and Secretary Vance's comments on his decision to visit that region, got the majority of front page space. The only important local story on the front page was the decision to bury all the plane victims in one place, because their bodies were so horribly mutilated. Page 2 picked up the airplane crash and the Middle East news again. The chief headlines on that page went to the Arab leaders and the oil situation, but there were a number of local stories also. The Prime Minister said the U.S. contemplated no limits on imported oil. The burial ceremony was to be arranged to satisfy the families of the crash victims. Malaysian Airlines changed its flight schedule. British experts arrived to study the crash. One of the victims had been happy about his "good luck" in getting a vacant seat on the doomed plane at the last minute before takeoff. Page 3 was more of the same. Politicians and passengers were arguing about tighter airport security. Two Japanese had almost boarded the doomed plane by mistake, but discovered their error just in time to get off. The investigation was focusing on three mysterious Asian youths as the possible hijackers. And four Vietnamese were convicted in court on a previous hijacking attempt. On page 4, readers learned that two lovers had leaped, hand in hand, to their death.

Then followed a page of Singapore news, and two pages of sports, with a great deal of attention to the Asian basketball tournament underway in Kuala Lumpur. A page of fiction came next, and then a page of miscellaneous feature material, followed by a page analyzing business, a page of news features on women, a highly detailed page on horseracing, and a page of features and advertising on jewelry. Thus pages 9 through 14 were all highly specialized or feature material.

Two unnumbered pages, designated a "supplement", immediately following page 14, were crowded with local news. There had been a fatal automobile accident. A salvage unit had been set up to care for possible flood victims. The head of state was back in the capitol after a visit. Long lines at the Immigration Bureau resulted from understaffing. The daughter of a well-known educator had been married. A co-op was offering a scholarship, and two state senators had allocated money for public construction. There was a feature on a youth training center. Clubs and schools were celebrating anniversaries. A peddler's union set up a co-op. And so forth.

Pages 15 and 16 are stocks and financial news. Local news picks up again on page 17 and 18. The Production Minister suggested a joint meeting between SEATO and the European Common Market. Two Muslim Party senators resigned. A conference on borders is to be held between Malaysia and Indonesia. A Chinese author's Who's Who is to be published in the Malaysian language. A plastic factory burns. Consumers were shocked at the increase in gas prices. The Vice Minister of Education announced that Chinese and Indonesian courses should be offered when 15 parents request them for their children. And so forth, through page 18. Part of page 18, and all of 19, are given to television, movies and other entertainment. The final page is local news again: the Central bank asks for bids; a committee for cultural development is to be set up; a regional effort to improve education is advocated by the Indonesian Minister of Education, the Malaysian Minister of Transportation urges SEATO to set up a joint port authority training program; and senior substitute teachers are to be admitted to special training courses. A three-color ad ends the Thursday paper.

The Statesman

The *Statesman* is the briefest and the most local of these three newspapers. It is 14 pages, 8 columns to the page on December 8, and favors small headlines. Alone of the three papers it fills its front page with its own local and national news. The only truly foreign story that makes page 1 is four column inches on Egypt closing the Soviet and other East Europe offices in Cairo. About one third of the page is taken up by reports on the Shah Commission, and Mrs. Gandhi's reactions; and there is another long story on Sanjay Gandhi's testimony before the Reddy Commission. Legislative matters are treated at some length: a new 42nd Amendment to the Constitution is being planned, and complete repeal of the Internal Security Act (by which Mrs. Gandhi managed the "Emergency") is being considered. Congress Party members walk out of the lower house of Parliament. A plan to revitalize the national press council has been completed. India's new High Commissioner in London is about to present his credentials to the Queen. And there are several stories about politics within the States. It is almost wholly, therefore, an Indian front page.

Pages 2 and 4 are taken up by notices and classified ads. The part of page 3 not filled by ads is Indian news: a picture of women counting the coins received in a charity donation campaign, three stories of police and court news, radio and TV programs, and brief art and music reviews. Page 5 is foreign news. The Kremlin is said to be divided over its China policy. The President of Zambia declines to participate in the Anglo-American plan for Rhodesia. Third World delegations are complaining about the cost of living in New York. And so forth. The small portions of pages 6 and 7 not filled with advertising are Indian news, the chief stories being an investigation of the Chief Minister of Karnataka State, and the fact that no applications had been received for the post of Mosquito Control Officer in Calcutta.

Page 8 carries the editorials, along with a four-inch story on Begin's recovery from an illness and some letters to the editor. The top editorial deals with India's need to generate more energy. There is an editorial on Japan's new economic policy, and an article on the economic relationships between Japan and the U.S. Another editorial deals with the problems of political negotiation, and a feature article is reprinted from the *Times* of London.

Page 9 is used for continuations from page 1, and a number of other Indian stories, including a weather chart. It has several stories of central and state government, and a summary of questions asked in Parliament. Eight inches are taken up with brief news bulletins – four from India, one each from Canada, Iran and the U.S. Pages 10 and 11 are mostly advertising, but about 7 inches on each page are used for brief news from India, including the tidings that 200,000 people, on the waiting list for telephones, can hope to get them within two years. Page 12 is sports, including a picture of "world series" cricket in which India has been participating in Sydney, and a lead-story about a football tournament in Bombay. Page 13 is business and finance, including markets, the Bombay stock exchange, and currency exchange rates. And the last page, 14, is taken up entirely by advertising and a 39-column-inch bylined story of a news-seeking trip to the Andaman and Nicobar islands. The report is not very favorable to government planning or administration.

Summing Up

This quick glance at a few Third World prestige papers reminds us not only how well some of these papers are doing their job, but also that the first job of a good newspaper is to report its own local and national news. Thus it is not surprising to discover that these Third World papers typically use between two thirds and three fourths of their news space for happenings in their own countries (or relations between their country and others). Papers like the *New York Times* and the *Washington Post* use an even higher proportion of their news for that purpose, and so do other Third World papers about which we have some information – from Kenya to Egypt to Peru. Four leading papers in the United States devote about one sixth of their space to the Third World; the three Third World papers analyzed in this chapter devote about one seventh of their space to North America, West Europe, and East Europe. All general newspapers try to meet the close-at-hand interests of their readers. Therefore it is interesting to see what kinds of news tend to be selected by these Third World dailies from foreign rather than local sources. They are news of military stirrings and political violence, foreign political developments (e.g., a new government), foreign economic developments (gold rises, the dollar falls). From both foreign and local sources come stories of the local country's relations with foreign nations, and sports.

VI. WHAT THE INTERNATIONAL NEWS WIRES CARRY

From newspaper such as those we have just been talking about, from correspondents in many countries, from exchange arrangements with national and regional wires, and from other sources, the four international news agencies that are owned in the West transmit about 919 stories, nearly 217,000 words, on their Asian wires during an average day. These figures are so large that they justify some talking about.

How Much News Do They Carry?

In the first place, there is a considerable variation among wires. Here are total stories and words for each of the wires on a representative day:

	Stories	Words
Wire A	197	48,503
Wire B	179	53,191
Wire C	291	70,854
Wire D	252	44,334
Four Wires	919	216,882

Thus the range is from 179 stories to 291, from 44,000 words to nearly 71,000. Wire D chooses to transmit a large number of fairly brief stories. Wire B seems to carry longer stories than the others: an average of 297 words each. Wire A's stories average 246 words, Wire C's 243, and Wire D's only 176.

Where Does the News Come From?

How many of these deal with the Third World? Almost exactly one half. Roughly one quarter of the wires is devoted to stories of the Third World alone, one quarter to stories of Third World combined with non-Third World countries, and one half to non-Third World countries alone. Here are detailed figures on the four wires combined, for one day, with the coverage figured in both number of stories and words. The numbers in parentheses are percentages of the total wire content.

	Stories	Words
Third World Countries only	216	49,425
	(23.5%)	(22.4%)
Third and non-Third	236	56,211
	(25.7%)	(25.5%)
Total concerned with Third World	452	105,636
	(49.2%)	(48.0%)
Non-Third World Countries Only	467	111,246
	(50.8%)	(52.0%)
Total	919	216,882

On the one hand, it may look like an imbalance that only one fourth of the wire content is devoted wholly to the Third World, where three fourths of the world's people are, and just under half to Third World countries in whole or in part. On the other hand, 105,000 words, 452 stories per day, is an enormous amount of news. This is the amount available to an Asian newspaper that subscribes to all four wires, as many of our Asian dailies do. Of course, if the newspaper takes less than one wire it receives less copy on the Third World. If it subscribes to one wire only, it has a choice that ranges from 82 to 159 stories per day, from 21,000 to 34,000 words. The average of the four wires is 113 stories, 26,400 words.

These figures will become more meaningful when, in the next chapter, we compare them with the amount and kinds of Third World news the Asian dailies actually carry. And it must be noted that in this chapter we are not talking about the *quality* of the news; these are purely *quantitative* measurements. Yet, the amount of Third World news on the wires per day is impressive.

Another question worth asking is how much of the international news agencies' Third World coverage on their Asian wires deals with Asia. The answer is, about three fifths of it. The difference between wires is not great: the highest proportion on a single wire is 60.5 per cent, the lowest 54.4 per cent. Here are the figures by region for an average day of the wires combined:

	Stories	Proportion
Asia	287	58.2%
Latin America	35	7.0%
Middle East	116	23.5%
Africa	56	11.3%

The attention given the Middle East undoubtedly reflects the potent events underway there at the time of our study. There is relatively little difference between the proportion of a regional stories that dealt with single countries and those that dealt with a combination of countries. The largest difference was in the Middle East, where 214 stories during the five days dealt with single countries, 249 with more than one country. This is not a great difference, but it has face validity, because most of the most newsworthy events at that time in the Middle East involved, at least by implication, international relations.

Let us not lose sight of the fact that, despite the large amount of coverage given to Asia, the wires still devoted more stories to the United States and Britain than to any other countries. In fact, the United States was the subject of almost as many stories as the entire Middle East, and more than twice as many as either Latin America or Africa. Here are some percentages of stories by country during the average day:

	Stories	Proportion
United States	204	22.2%
United Kingdom	62	6.7%
Japan	32	3.5%
West Germany	24	2.6%
U.S.S.R.	22	2.4%
Australia	22	2.4%
France	19	2.1%
Philippines	31	3.4%
Vietnam	31	3.4%
Malaysia	27	2.9%
China	23	2.5%
Pakistan	23	2.5%
Singapore	19	2.1%
Indonesia	10	1.1%
Egypt	38	4.1%

What Kinds of News?

Another comparison may be of interest at this point: the categories of Third World news carried by the wires and by the three Asian Third World dailies whose local news we analyzed in the preceding chapter. This is the local news only from those three newspapers, and therefore gives us some idea what the wires picked up as against what the local Third World newspapers publish about their own countries. We shall give percentages only:

		Three Asian Dailies	Four International Wires
1.	Military, political violence	1.1%	6.8%
2.	Foreign relations	7.0%	36.0%
3.	Domestic, political	15.4%	12.8%
4.	Economic	26.0%	12.3%
5.	Science, health	3.7%	0.7%
6.	Education	6.8%	0.4%
7.	Accident, disaster	7.3%	6.2%
8.	Crime, judicial	8.2%	3.3%
9.	Sports	15.1%	14.1%
10.	Culture	3.7%	0.7%
11.	Human Interest	1.8%	1.9%
12.	Other	3.9%	4.6%

The difference that jumps out from that table is in coverage of foreign relations. Obviously the wires feel more responsibility to cover that area than do the dailies: the wires must cover foreign relations for many countries whereas a national daily is responsible chiefly for the foreign relations of its own country. It is also worth noting that the chief preparations for war and incidents of political violence during that week were elsewhere than in India, Malaysia, and the Philippines; therefore it is not surprising that the wires would carry more of that kind of news than the dailies published. One of the more interesting comparisons, however, is the fact that the dailies actually published proportionally more news of crime and disaster than the wires. We shall make a broader comparison of crime and disaster coverage in the next chapter, but there is nothing in this comparison to indicate that the wires are overplaying the crime and disaster news they find in the local news coverage. On the other hand, there is a great deal more coverage of science, health, and education in the local news than on the wires. This is probably what would be called news of development, and suggests why the Third World countries feel that their development news is not being covered as fully by the international wires as it should be. In a later chapter we shall look in more detail at development news.

These represent some educated guesses as to what the wires pick up from the local news. In the next chapter we shall see what the dailies pick up from the wires.

Four Hours of an Asian Wire

But before turning to that, it may be helpful to look at the flow of news during a few hours on the Asian wire of one of the international news agencies. Let us look at the wire for Wednesday, December 7, which is the one most likely to be reflected in the dailies for December 8. The wire we are going to sample is the one called Wire C in the tables. This, you will remember, is the wire that carried the largest number of words but not the largest number of stories. Let us begin, say, about 1000 (10 am) by wire time. If we began with the start of the day, at 0001, Asia would be asleep and most of the news would probably be coming from Europe and the United States. But by 1000, Asia would have awakened and Asia news should be flowing. So this is a glance at the content of Wire C beginning at 10:00 am December 7.

The first story that comes over the wire is about the aftermath of the Tripoli meeting: King Hussein is visiting Syria in an attempt to alleviate the strained feelings between President Sadat and the other Arab governments. This story comes in three takes during the next 45 minutes. At 1011 it is interrupted for a brief note that Bobby Fisher, the former world chess champion, was to be arrested on a civil complaint. At 1012 attention shifts to the Malaysia plane crash. This story, too, comes in four short takes, totalling about 670 words, and the main news peg is that the plane's "black box" (the flight recorder) has not been found. At 1016 comes the Malaysia stock market, and at 1017 a note on NATO's attitude toward the proposed SALT treaty. At 1026 there is a paragraph that some of the Vietnamese refugee "boat people" are about to reach Darwin, where they will supposedly be turned back by Australian authorities. Just after that comes another take on the Hong Kong story that all policemen refuse to testify concerning an investigation of the department. The Singapore market prices come in at 1028. Then follows a story that the U.S. dollar has dropped in value on the French market. At 1035 editors learned that South Africa had banned a film. At 1038 the first paragraphs of a story on the World Golf Tournament begin to come in from Manila. This story, with a number of individual scores, comes in five takes, adding up to 600 words. Then:

1042 – Swiss girl wins cup in French skiing
1044 – Taiwan clam boat seized by Australian sea police
1046 – Hong Kong plans more diversification of products to combat competition from other countries
1051 – Russians win gymnastics in England
1053 – Australia plans to sell uranium to Finland
1057 – Mount Etna erupts in Sicily
1058 (and two takes after that) – Japan is making emergency plans

That ends the first hour.
After the Japanese story come these items:

1104 (and two later takes) – Davis Cup tennis, U.S. vs Australia
1119 – Laos and Vietnam sign youth agreement
1120 – Stock market prices from Japan
1121 – Wife of Thai rice merchant kidnapped
1124 (and two more takes) – Woman Guerrillas' leader surrenders in Indonesia
1129 (three takes) – Former Sri Lanka Prime Minister attacks new government
1137 – Rhodesian guerrillas kill whites
1142 – Switzerland elects a new President
1144 – Fraud punished in Russia
1146 – African wins boxing title in Ghana
1147 – Australian cricket
1151 – King Hussein visits Damascus
1153 (and two more) – Vance attends NATO meeting
1158 – Philippine army plans attack on Muslim rebels

During the 12 o'clock hour these stories came in:

1201 – Japan-Britain football
1208 – More British football results
1211 (and two more takes) – Begin speaks on Israel-Arab relations
1221 – Dutch urban guerrilla defends his conduct
1224 (plus two) – Hope for better U.S.-Turkey relations
1239 – U.S. dollar drops in U.K.
1250 – More British football
1254 – New road in Irian
1257 – Soviet cultural center in Cairo ordered to close

One more hour on the wire:

1300 – Australia-New Zealand yacht race
1306 – Another story on Hussein, this one about his plan to visit Egypt
1309 (and two later takes) – Expert says U.S. might lose next war if there is one
1320 (and three more takes) – Scores from Asian basketball tournament in Kuala Lumpur
1321 – Black leaders in Rhodesia reluctant to join talks
1330 – Indonesia and Malaysia plan joint border operation
1338 – NATO said to fear Soviet buildup
1342 – Weather
1346 – Philippine government signs trade treaty with East Germany
1351 – England appoints a cricket captain
1353 – Lee Kuan Yew meets with representative of European Economic Community
1356 – U.S. dollar stronger on German market
1358 – Australia defeats Japan in basketball
1358 – Hong Kong criticizes European Common Market for attitude toward trade

That ends the hour. During these four hours nearly 6,000 words of copy have come over the wire. Asian news dominated during this period; during the evening and the very early morning hours, there would have been less news about Asia. For the record, during these four hours wire C transmitted 31 different stories on Asia, 13 chiefly on

Western Europe, 7 on North America, 5 on the Middle East, 4 on Africa, 3 chiefly on East Europe, none on Latin America. Approximately 40 stories dealt chiefly with the Third World, a little more than half that many with non-Third World countries. Twelve stories dealt with foreign relation, 11 with sports, 10 with business and finance, 8 with military matters and political violence, 4 with crime, 3 with domestic politics (e.g., new Swiss President), and two with disasters (e.g., Mount Etna). The telegraph editors received something for nearly every section of their papers.

Summing Up

We have hurried through this survey of the content of the international news wires because it will become more meaningful in the next chapter when it can be compared with what the Asian dailies took from the wires. But even a quick look at these Asian wires of the four news agencies furnishes some rather unexpected information. They are carrying – or were in December 1977 – about 100,000 words, 450 stories, per day on the Third World. Most of the papers we studied subscribed to all or most of these wires; a paper that received only one wire would receive an average of about 25,000 words, a little over 100 stories. Just under half of the Asian wire content is devoted to the Third World and its relations with other countries; about 60 per cent of the news on the wire deals with Asia. The United States is the country most often mentioned in the news, and the U.K. is second, but the Philippines, Vietnam, Japan, and Egypt each get more than 3 per cent of the wire coverage, and Malaysia, China, Pakistan, and Australia, along with the Soviet Union, France, and West Germany were not far behind. There was a great variety in the wire news, as our examples indicate. Whether it was the kind of news Asian editors wanted we can tell more about in the following chapter, but it is clear that there was far more news on the wire than newspapers were likely to take off it.

VII. WHAT THE ASIAN DAILIES TAKE FROM THE INTERNATIONAL WIRES

An Example

Let us begin with the front page of the *Straits Times,* for December 8, 1977, as an example of how the Asian Third World newspapers make use of the international news wires.

The principal headline on that page, as we noted in Chapter V, is about the Middle East: "Sadat Warns Arab Hawks." The subtitle is, "Egypt Closes Soviet Consulates." This story, which fills more than 100 column inches, including a continuation on an inside page, is credited to the *New York Times* service and UPI, indicating that the editors combined material from those two sources. Next to it is a story from Nicosia to the effect that "Saudi Aid to Egypt To Go On" despite the opposition of other Arab states. This story comes from the AP. Under it is a one-inch bulletin from New York, on the Dow-Jones stock average; this comes from UPI. The front page pictures, filling a little over 30 column inches, are also credited to UPI. They show a 14-year-old Meo boy who killed two Pathet Lao soldiers in order to escape into Thailand. In the corner of the page is a three-inch bulltin in dark type, from London, warning that British Airways is ready to cancel the inaugural flight of the Concorde to and from Singapore if Malaysian objections cannot be overcome. This story is from Reuter. The other front page stories are apparently by the *Times'* own writers. Prime Minister Lee Kuan Yew is quoted at length in a by-lined story on the need of "tough-minded, sensitive men" to take over after the present administration. A second by-lined story reports that four Vietnamese, suspected of airplane hijacking, are to stand trial on a charge of carrying arms at the Singapore airport. A third story, without by-line, says that the Singapore Turf Club admits that it paid bets on the wrong horse during a recent race day. Still another front-page story summarizes a long by-line report on an inside page, from London, saying that a Malaysian psychiatrist had been awarded damages of about a million dollars for alleged surgical errors that caused him irreversible brain damage.

Thus five of the nine news items on page 1 are from the international news agency wires, three are by local writers (two with by-lines), and the ninth apparently from a London correspondent. Three of the four international wires are represented on the front page, and we have only to look as far as page 2 to discover that AFP also comes into the *Times* Office: there are two stories credited jointly to AFP, AP, and Reuter. Thus the *Straits Times* receives all four of the international wires, and at least one special news service – that of the *New York Times;* and its editors are not afraid to combine news from the different sources in a single story.

The *Straits Times* is an outstanding newspaper, and carries more foreign news than most of the others in our sample, but its use of the international news services is not unrepresentative. Three-fourths of its foreign news comes from the international news agencies, the rest of it from correspondents and special services.

The Average Asian Daily and the News Wires

To put figures like those in perspective, let us record that the average Asian daily in our sample* carries about 23 stories from other Third World countries (about 16 from other Third World countries only, 7 that combine the home country with other Third World countries) and about 18 stories from non-Third World countries. Bearing in mind that the average daily carries approximately 70 local stories, that makes a total of about 111 stories on an average day in an average paper.

Those figures mean that this mythical average Asian daily chooses 41 stories a day (23 concerning the Third World, 18 the non-Third) from the news agency wires and its other sources of foreign news.

What do we know about how many stories actually come from the wires? We were able to identify the sources of 83 per cent of the Third World foreign stories. Of these, 75.7 per cent came from one or more of the international news agencies. Disregarding stories from the paper's own staff (on events that could be covered locally) or the paper's own correspondents, 90 per cent of all the Third World foreign news (source

---

* When we speak of the "sample" in this chapter we are referring to 17 Asian dailies. *Ananda Bazar Patrika* was omitted from the sample because its very slight coverage of foreign Third World news left us uncertain how well the test week represented it, or how well it represented Asian dailies.

identifiable) not provided by the paper's own employees came from the international wires.

How about the sources of non-Third World news? We do not have as large a sample of non-Third World coding as of Third World, but the best estimate we can make is that the dependence on international wires for non-Third World news is between 85 and 90 per cent.

For Third World news, however, we have over 2,500 wire stories and more than 1,700 newspaper stories on which to calculate newspaper-wire relationships, and can estimate with some confidence. Here are the numbers of foreign Third World stories in the average daily, on the average wire, and on all four wires together:

	Average Newspaper	Average Wire	Total of Four Wires
Third World Foreign Only	15.8	55.9	223.4
Third World Home Country Combined with Others	7.3	46.1	184.4
Total	23.1	102.0	407.8

On an average day, therefore, the mythical average daily would be selecting 76 per cent of 23 Third World stories, or between 17 and 18 stories from the international wires. If it subscribed to one wire, it would be choosing, say, 17 out of 102 possible stories, or a little less than 18 per cent of the stories available to it. If it subscribed to all four wires it had about 408 stories to choose from, and would be selecting less than 5 per cent of the available items. Of course, 408 stories are not stories of 408 *different events*. They represent, perhaps, 200 different events because more than one wire will cover the same story. Therefore the daily will be selecting 17 out of 200, or about 9 per cent of the Third World news events available on the wires.

AVERAGE NUMBER OF DIFFERENT KINDS OF STORIES IN AN ASIAN DAILY AND NUMBER OF EACH KIND COMING FROM INTERNATIONAL NEWS AGENCIES

	Number in Newspaper	*Number Coming from Wires*	*Total Number on Wires*	*Average on One Wire*
THIRD WORLD – local only	70			
THIRD WORLD – foreign and combined with Non-Third	23	17	408	102
NON-THIRD – WORLD Only	18	16	467	117
TOTAL	111	33	875	219

The great disparity between the number of news stories available on the wires and the number selected raises questions: Is this variety presented on the wires in order to meet differing needs of the Asian newspapers? More important, if Third World newsmen and information officials are not satisfied with the international news wires' coverage of the Third World, is there not enough leeway in the nine out of ten wire stories unused by any one paper to make possible some changes in the content?

Content: Wires vs. Newspapers

This is a good time to look at some of the differences in categories of news content between the Third World dailies and the international wires. Here is a comparison of the 17 newspapers and the four wires, for one day, in terms of the kinds of content represented in their Third World news:

One Day Comparisons

	17 Newspapers		Four News Wires	
Category	N	%	N	%
1. Military, political violence	45	5.4	74	8.1
2. Foreign relations	203	24.2	207	22.5
3. Domestic government, political	106	12.6	96	10.4
4. Economics	186	22.2	193	21.0
5. Science, health	11	1.3	20	2.2
6. Education	8	0.9	3	0.3
7. Accidents, disaster	45	5.4	42	4.6
8. Crime, judicial	54	6.4	54	5.9
9. Sports	97	11.6	147	16.0
10. Arts, culture	22	2.6	13	1.4
11. Human interest	43	5.1	23	2.5
12. Other	19	2.3	47	5.1
TOTAL	839	100.0	919	100.0

These percentages are more similar than one might expect. The wires gave somewhat less attention to foreign relations, which may be surprising since their outlook is on a great many different countries, and their clients represent single countries. The newspapers give slightly more attention to domestic politics and to economic stories, but this also is understandable. They also give somewhat more attention to human interest stories. The important conclusion from this table, therefore, is not the difference but rather the degree of similarity. Why are the proportions so similar? Is it because the wires are carrying the kind of content the newspapers want, or because the newspapers have to rely on the wires for so much of their outside Third World news? We can't answer that question from a table.

There is another comparison of content categories that is worth making. Suppose we take *all* the foreign news in the Asian newspapers and compare its content, dividing the news by Third and Non-Third focus, with the total content, similarly divided, of the international wires. We can do that for one day during the test week. A table in the appendix does it in considerable detail. Here are a few categories from that table, comparing the proportions of certain kinds of news found in stories of the Third World only, with proportions found in stories of combined Third and non-Third World countries, with proportions found in stories of *non*-Third World countries.

	Percentages for Composite Wire	**Percentages for Composite Daily**
Military, political violence		
Third World	28.4	35.6
Third and Non-Third	21.6	13.3
Non-Third	50.0	51.1
Foreign relations		
Third World	29.0	35.0
Third and Non-Third	58.0	56.1
Non-Third	13.0	8.9
Domestic, political		
Third World	43.8	38.7
Third and Non-Third	7.5	11.3
Non-Third	49.0	50.0
Economic		
Third World	18.8	26.9
Third and Non-Third	14.4	25.3
Non-Third	66.9	47.8
Accidents, Disasters		
Third World	31.0	37.8
Third and Non-Third	21.4	22.2
Non-Third	47.6	40.0
Crime, Judicial		
Third World	24.1	27.8
Third and Non-Third	5.6	11.1
Non-Third	70.4	42.3

Sports		
Third World	9.5	31.9
Third and Non-Third	20.4	30.6
Non-Third	70.1	37.5

That table seems to say: Both wires and dailies are interested in military and politically violent news, but the editors of the Third World papers are a bit more interested in *Third World* violence and military preparations than are the news wire editors. Concerning foreign relations, the same difference prevails: the newspapers give a higher proportion of their attention to *Third World* relations than do the wires. There is really very little difference between their distribution of attention to domestic political news. The figures on accidents and disasters make one wonder about the complaints that the wires carry too much of those kinds of news. We found (in the preceding chapter) that Asian dailies tend to carry a higher proportion of such news than do the international wires; this table shows that the dailies also carry a higher proportion of accidents and disasters from their own Third World. The same things are true of crime news. As for sports, it is clear that these stories are of strong national and regional interest: therefore the newspapers emphasize Third World sports rather than sports in the industrialized countries.

Wire Coverage by Regions and Countries

How about Third World news coverage by regions? Asian newspapers emphasize news from Asia. The regional patterns on the wires and in the newspapers, however, are very much the same, as these comparisons show:

Percentage of Third World Stories by Region

	Asia	*Latin America*	*Middle East*	*Africa*
17 Dailies	68.1%	4.0%	20.9%	7.0%
4 News Agencies	58.2%	7.0%	23.5%	11.3%

The news wires, in other words, emphasize Asia a little less on their Asian Wires, and the other regions a little more, than do the newspapers. But the agencies still draw nearly three fifths of their Third World stories from Asia.

Another way to compare the content of the wires with that of the Asian Third World dailies in our sample is in terms of their coverage of specific countries. Here is an ordered comparison of country coverage for 12 countries, each of which had substantial attention during the test week. The percentages are proportions of the total coverage given these 12 countries in the Third World news*, not of the total news content.

Countries	**Seventeen Daily Newspapers**		**Countries**	**Four International News Wires**	
	Stories	*%*		*Stories*	*%*
Malaysia	267	18.6	Egypt	288	14.7
Egypt	229	15.9	United States	286	14.6
United States	177	12.3	Philippines	189	9.7
China	153	10.6	Malaysia	179	9.2
Singapore	132	9.2	China	170	8.7
Philippines	82	5.7	Indonesia	145	7.4
Thailand	82	5.7	Thailand	138	7.1
Pakistan	74	5.1	India	135	6.9
India	69	4.8	Singapore	127	6.5
Indonesia	68	4.7	Pakistan	101	5.2
Vietnam	56	3.9	Vietnam	95	4.9
Japan	50	3.5	Japan	90	4.6

The newspapers and wires are as similar in their selection of types of news content as in their country coverage. The following table contains correlation coefficients between wires and dailies for numbers of stories in each category of content.

* Meaning that the United States and Japan would appear in this list only when combined with a Third World country in a news story.

Correlations[a] Between Content (12 Categories) of the Newspapers on Thursday, December 8, 1977 and the Wires on Wednesday, December 7, 1977.

	Wire					
Newspaper	*A*	*B*	*C*	*D*	*Compos-ite*	*Hsin hua*
Amrita Bazar Patrika	.48	.61	.53	.66	.63	.42
Bangkok Post	.71	.74	.71	.69	.72	.39
Ceylon Daily News	.59	.52	.49	.64	.57	.33[b]
Dong-a Ilbo	.72	.79	.76	.64	.83	.78
Ettelaat	.55	.45	.52	.50	.53	.42
Kayhan International	.74	.71	.62	.44	.60	.45
Korea Times	.55	.65	.61	.76	.69	.50
Kompas	.50	.53	.40	.68	.55	.48
Nanyang Siang Pau	.64	.69	.70	.77	.77	.51
New Straits Times	.73	.68	.71	.61	.71	.36[b]
Philippine Daily Express	.46	.43	.36[b]	.38	.38	.25[b]
Sing Chew Jit Poh	.52	.58	.58	.75	.59	.34[b]
Sing Tao Jih Pao	.35[b]	.38	.38	.46	.39	.16[b]
South China Morning Post	.69	.69	.66	.73	.76	.45
The Statesman	.52	.64	.60	.64	.65	.49
Straits Times	.56	.59	.55	.76	.60	.34[b]
Bulletin Today[c]	.44	.38	.36[b]	.20[b]	.17[b]	.54
Composite Paper	.69	.74	.66	.79	.76	.46

a) All correlations are tau and are significant at the .05 level unless otherwise noted.

b) Not significant at the .05 level.

c) Issue of *Bulletin Today* is for September 14, 1978.

This table represents the news wires for Wednesday, December 7, 1977, and the newspapers. for Thursday, December 8. While we cannot be completely sure of all the stories available to the papers at any given time, it seems likely that this one-day lag – bearing in mind that all except two of the 16 Asian dailies are morning papers* – will give us some idea of the impact of the wire services on news selection for the following issues of the newspapers.

These correlations and other data in this chapter indicate that the wires provide not only the bulk of foreign news for the newspapers, but also a pattern of coverage that most of the dailies seem to follow. The Asian papers did not use nearly all the wire material provided: their usage ranged from 15 stories (1.6 percent) by *Kompas* to 111 (12 percent) by the *South China Morning Post* and the *Straits Times.* But what they did use was quite similar in distribution of content to what they found on the wires. The correlation between content proportions on the composite newspaper and the composite news wire was .76, meaning that the wire content was apparently responsible for nearly 60 percent of the variance in the newspaper selection.

In reading the table, bear in mind that only correlations of .37 or over are statistically significant at the .05 level (that is, could have occurred by chance less than 5 out of 100 times). Therefore the size of the correlations is impressive.

We noted earlier that the two Indian papers, *Amrita Bazar Patrika* and the *Statesman,* tended to have the lowest association of all the dailies with the wires on country coverage for the week studied. This does not hold true for the one-day content category comparisons represented by the table we have just read. None of the coefficients for the two Indian papers is significantly lower than any of the other coefficients. Thus, so far as kinds of content are concerned, the Indian papers seem to follow the lead of the wires about as much as any of the other papers.

Do the Wires "Set the Agenda"?

The "gatekeepers" who select the types of news for the news agencies apparently help considerably to set the agenda for the "gatekeepers" who select the items for the newspapers. This finding seems to

* The *Philipino Express* was excluded from this analysis because it published only four wire stories (three of them sports) on December 8. The two evening papers are *Dong-a Ilbo* and *Ettelaat.*

fit with outcomes in the United States which show that daily newspaper wire editors tend to use whatever is supplied in about the same proportions as the wires provide, and thus that the primary editing decisions made by the news agencies are very influential on what finally comes to the readers.

There is a strong suggestion also that over time the content of the wires and papers does not vary greatly in content categories. The issue of the *Bulletin Today* examined in this readership study was published more than nine months after the other papers and the wires appeared. Yet, in only one instance (with Wire D) was a correlation less than statistically significant between the *Bulletin* and one of the international wires.

The following table indicates that a reader of any one of the Asian newspapers in our sample would have received about the same emphasis on kinds of news as a reader of any other of these papers. The composite news wire told the newspapers that the news of the day consisted of (1) foreign affairs, (2) economic news, (3) sports, and (4) domestic politics. The newspapers told their readers that the important categories of news that day were (1) foreign affairs, (2) economic news, (3) sports, or (4) domestic politics. Nine months later the *Bulletin Today* told its readers the important categories for another day were (1) economic news, (2) sports, (3) miscellaneous, and (4) foreign affairs. The readership followed that order quite closely. The readers' ranking was (1) economic news, (2) domestic politics, (3) sports, and (4) miscellaneous. Foreign affairs dropped into fifth place in the readership.

Rank Order of Content Categories by Frequency of Appearance on the Four International News Wires and in 18 Asian Daily Newspapers for All Countries for One Day and 42 Third World Countries for Five Days.

Content	*One Day*[a]		*Five Days*[b]	
Category	*Wires*	*Papers*	*Wires*	*Papers*
1. Military, political violence	5	6	5	5
2. Foreign relations	1	1	1	1
3. Domestic politics	4	3	4	4

Circulation of News in the Third World – A Study of Asia

Content	*One Day*[a]		*Five Days*[b]	
Category	*Wires*	*Papers*	*Wires*	*Papers*
4. Economics	2	2	2	2
5. Science, health	10	11	10	12
6. Education	12	12	12	11
7. Accidents, disasters	8	7	6	6
8. Judicial, crime	6	5	8	7
9. Sports	3	4	3	3
10. Arts, culture	11	9	11	10
11. Human interest	9	8	9	8
12. Other	7	10	7	9

a tau correlation between wires and papers for one day is 0.82. The one day for the wires is Wednesday, December 7, 1977; for the papers, Thursday, December 8, 1977.

b tau correlation between wires and papers for five days is 0.88. The five day period is December 5-9, 1977 for the wires and December 6-10, 1977 for the papers.

How should we interpret these findings?

One point of view would hold that the newspapers' "agenda" matches that of the news wires because the newspapers are almost totally dependent on the wires for their foreign news. However, this argument implies not only that the newspaper editors have almost no source of foreign news other than the wires but also that they accept the wires' example as to how much of each kind of news (content category) to print. If this is the case, then the newspaper editors are not editing but merely transporting the wire news to the printers.

Another point of view would imply that the wires are providing the newspaper editors pretty much what those editors want. Some support for this is found in the fact that, since the papers use so little of the total wire content, the editors could easily change the order of use of the content categories if the wire were not satisfying them. The wires do undoubtedly diverge from editors' preferences on individual stories, but, by and large, appear to provide the general kinds of news the papers seem to want.

It may be that underlying the whole question of "what's the news" is the question of the professionalization of journalism and the legitimization of news decision (see Tuchman, 1978, a and b). Newsmen define themselves, at least in part, by the kinds of decisions they make about what is news. If other newsmen are making the same kinds of decisions, that is, selecting the same events to be covered in the news, that encourages the newsman to believe that he is indeed a professional newsman.

Therefore, there is at least the appearance of agenda-setting influence in news selection from the wires to the newspapers to the readers.

Summing Up

The average Asian daily in our sample carried about 111 news stories per day. 70 of these were local and national only; 33 of the others came from the news wires. About 90 per cent of the foreign news published in these 18 Asian dailies, stories for which the source could be identified and which could not be covered locally, came from the four wires we have been studying. Looking at the wire content and the newspaper usage of that content, two striking conclusions emerge. One is the relatively small proportion of the wire copy that actually got into the newspapers. If a paper received only one wire it would be likely to use a little less than 18 per cent of the stories (and a smaller proportion of the words) available to it. If it received all four wires, it would be likely to select less than 5 per cent of the available items, about 9 per cent of the *different news events*, available on the wires. A second conclusion is the rather surprising similarity of the wire and the newspaper content, whether measured by types of news, regional coverage, or country coverage. Most of the correlations were in the 60's and 70's. This does not, of course, imply that the newspaper editors were completely satisfied with what they found on the wires. Another possible explanation would be that the newspapers had no other large sources of foreign news to rely on. And the wire do undoubtedly diverge from editors' preferences on individual stories rather than in types of content. But there is little reason to doubt that the wires have a great deal of influence in "setting the agenda" for the newspapers' presentation of foreign news.

VIII. WHAT PEOPLE READ IN AN ASIAN THIRD WORLD DAILY

We come now to the last step in the process described in Chapter IV. An average Asian daily in our sample publishes just over 70 stories from its own country on an average day. Four of those stories, on the average, reach one of the international news agency wires. Four such wires move through Asia, each carrying an average of four stories per day from each of a number of Asian countries. From the international wires that came into his office, an average editor selects an average of 33 stories for his own daily, plus perhaps 8 additional foreign stories from sources other than the international wires. Finally the end product of this flow, the stories that have survived the various gatekeepers along the way, comes to the reader in the form of a daily newspaper carrying an average of about 111 news items, and the reader must decide how many and which ones to read.

How much news and what kind of news *is* he likely to read?

We could answer that question with more confidence if we had a larger number of readership studies. If, for example, we had 130 readership studies of dailies, as the United States has in the Continuing Study of Newspaper Reading; if we had even six or eight readership studies of Asian newspapers from our sample, some in English, some in native languages – then we could speak in a louder voice about what Asian readers read. But we have only one such study, and it was not conducted during our test week in December, 1977. As explained in Chapter II we simply did not have the money or people to do readership studies at that time, nor to do a large number of studies later. Everything we say about readership in this chapter, therefore, depends on one study of the readers of one newspaper in Manila, in September of 1978.

The Manila Readership Study

Concerning the results of that study we are reasonably confident. The newspaper itself, the *Bulletin Today,* of Manila, is clearly a prestige paper. A study of DATA, INC. made in 1977 for the Philippine Mass Communication Research Society found that the *Bulletin Today* was read (during the previous week) by more people than read any other newspaper in Manila: 43 per cent as compared to 28 per cent for the nearest rival. It was described as the most popular among the newspapers. Readers mentioned especially its regular features, and many of them said it had more news, more complete news, and more up-to-date news reporting than other papers. Its sports coverage and its classified ads were also singled out for special praise. Thus we were able to study a leading paper and a large sample of its readers. Unfortunately it was only one paper, and we needed more.

On 14 September, 1978 the *Bulletin Today* carried 129 news items, 1,565 column inches of news. 70 of the stories (54 per cent) were about the Philippines, 23 about the Philippines *and* another country (18 per cent), and 36 (28 per cent) about foreign countries. 64 per cent were about Third World countries only, 25 per cent about Third and non-Third, and only 11 per cent about non-Third World countries only. 74 per cent of the news was about Asia. The largest number of stories by type (36 per cent) were economic; the second largest group (19 per cent) were sports. Just under 29 per cent of the stories could be classified as economic development. That was the kind of news the readers of *Bulletin Today* received on September 14, 1978, along with a large number of ads, several pages of features, and a number of comic strips. We described the content of the *Bulletin Today* in Chapter V; this is just to remind you.

We have also mentioned the most striking result of the study: the low average readership. The average reader read only 11 of 129 items – 8.4 per cent of the news content. This is less than half the average found in the 130 American studies we mentioned, and we suspect it is lower than the average for Asia; but we cannot prove that, for lack of comparable studies, nor can we explain why the *Bulletin's* readership should be so low. Readers told interviewers they spent an average of 30 minutes on the paper. This is about the average the world over. The urban readers estimated an average about 5 minutes higher than rural readers, and this too corresponds to other studies. But 30 minutes is a great deal more time than one needs to read 11 items. What else did they read, then? Our interviewers said they spoke of the comics, the classified ads, the movie and broadcast columns, and some of the other feature materials. Much of the use of the *Bulletin Today* must have been for purposes other than news. Is this typical of Asian readers, or is it specific to the Philippines, or to the *Bulletin?* Our observation in other countries lead us to doubt that such low reading of news is typical throughout Asia. Is the readership of the *Bulletin Today* affected in any way by knowledge of government restrictions on official news? We do not know, but it would be interesting to find out whether anything happens to readership when martial law is ended.

Reading: Third World, Foreign

In the following tables of readership of different types of news, "Average readership" means the *percentage of available news* of a given kind read by an average reader. "Average number of stories read" means the *number* of stories of a given kind read by an average reader. "Proportion of reading" describes how much of an average person's news reading was of a given class of news. Thus, for example, in the first table below, the average reader read 8.1 per cent of the foreign news; he read an average of 2.9 foreign stories; and this constituted 26.6 per cent of his entire news reading in the paper that day.

Type of News	Proportion of Stories	Average Readership	Average Number Stories Read	Proportion of Reading
Foreign	27.9%	8.1%	2.9	26.6%
Both	17.8%	9.4%	2.2	20.2%
Domestic	54.3%	8.3%	5.8	53.2%
Non-Third World	10.9%	6.5%	0.9	8.3%
Both	24.8%	9.6%	3.1	28.4%
Third World	64.3%	8.3%	6.9	63.3%

In this table the extraordinary features is how closely the proportion of reading follows the allocation of content. For example, 54 per cent of the stories were domestic, 53 per cent of the reading; 28 per cent of the stories were foreign, 27 per cent of the reading; 64 per cent of the stories were about Third World countries alone, 63 per cent of the reading; and so forth. It can be assumed that the editors are making a good guess as to the interest of their readers. A second thing to notice about the readership is that the *Bulletin's* readers, for one reason or another, tend to be likely to read stories that involve more than one country: note the readership of stories that involve "both" foreign and domestic news, and "both" Third and non-Third World countries.

Reading by Region

Let us look at readership by news of different regions.

Type of News	Proportion of Content	Average Readership	Average Number Stories Read	Proportion of Reading
Asia	72.9%	8.6%	8.1	74.3%
Latin America	1.6%	15.7%	0.3	2.8%
Africa	3.1%	12.7%	0.5	4.6%
Middle East	5.4%	14.0%	1.0	9.2%
North America	10.1%	5.6%	0.7	6.4%
Western Europe	6.2%	3.6%	0.3	2.8%
East Europe	0.8%	0.1%	–	–

Reading by Kind of News

Here is the readership by category of news:

Type of News	Proportion of Content	Average Readership	Average Number Stories Read	Proportion of Reading
Military, political strife	3.1%	1.0%	0.7	6.4%
Foreign relations	6.2%	8.8%	0.7	6.4%
Domestic political	5.4%	25.2%	1.8	16.4%
Economic	35.7%	6.6%	3.0	27.3%
Science, health	5.4%	4.5%	0.3	2.7%
Education	6.2%	5.9%	0.5	4.5%
Accident, disaster	1.6%	–	–	–
Judicial, crime	3.9%	5.3%	0.3	2.7%
Sports	19.4%	7.7%	1.9	17.3%
Culture	2.3%	–	0.1	1.0%
Human interest	1.6%	13.7%	0.3	2.7%
Other	9.3%	11.3%	1.4	12.7%

Compare readership with news space again. 74 per cent of the reading was of Asian news, and 73 per cent of the news stories were about Asia. On the other hand, 10 per cent of the printed news dealt with North America, 6 per cent with Western Europe, but only 6 and 3 per cent of the readership, respectively. The Middle East, however, is the subject of only 5 per cent of the news, but draws 9 per cent of the readership.

The *Bulletin's* readers are obviously interested in domestic and political news. But it is still more interesting to note that only 5 per cent of the stories in the paper dealt with domestic and political news. The opportunity to compare the proportion of news printed with the proportion read – to check the editor's judgment against the reader's taste – is tempting.

The editors guessed right on sports, on foreign relations, and in fact on most of the other categories except military and political strife and domestic and political news. In the former case, the reader (to say it simplistically) was twice as interested as the editor; in the latter, three times as interested.

Reading of Development News

Let us look also at the reading of development news.

Type of News	Proportion of Content	Average Readership	Average Number Stories Read	Proportion of Reading
Development news	28.7%	6.4%	2.4	22.0%
Not Development news	71.3%	9.3%	8.5	78.0%

These figures are important, because the *Bulletin's* editors were apparently making a serious effort to inform their readers about economic and social development. 29 per cent of all the stories in the paper concerned development. The readers, as the table shows were not quite that interested: their reading was 22%.

The third column in the preceding tables dealt with the number of stories read by an average reader. Let us summarize those results in a way that is easier to comprehend. We have said that the average reader of the *Bulletin* read 11 out of the 129 news stories in the *Bulletin Today?* Now, how were those stories divided by types of news?

The Average Reader

The average reader would read approximately –

- 6 domestic news stories, 3 foreign, and 2 a combination of domestic and foreign
- 8 stories about Asia, 1 about the Middle East, less than 1 about any other region
- 3 stories on economic and business news, 2 on domestic and political, 2 on sports, and the others scattered
- 2 or a little more on development, between 8 and 9 *not* development

Thus far we have been talking about "the average reader" as though all readers were the same. We know this is not the case, and the factor analyses to be presented later in this chapter will underline that. But how does reading differ with the characteristics of readers?

Here let us sum it up:

Reading by sex. Females read a bit less than males – about 8.9 stories compared to 12.8, on the average; 6.9 per cent average readership as compared to 9.9 per cent. Males are significantly more interested than females in foreign, Third World, and development news, and especially in news from North America and Western Europe. Females are somewhat more interested than males in domestic political news.

Reading by urban or rural residence. Urban reading is a little heavier than rural – 11.6 stories per person as against 9.9.

Reading by occupation. White collar workers read more than non-white collar workers, except in the case of sports news, where the heaviest reading is among unskilled workers.

Reading by education. The amount of reading rises uniformly with amount of education. This is notably true for development news, and news from the West.

Reading by age. Amount of reading tends to increase with age, as far as the decade of 40 to 50, and in some cases after that. An exception is sports news, where reading is heaviest among younger readers.

The Most-Read Stories

To get away from this emphasis on numbers and percentages, it may be useful to list the most read stories in the *Bulletin* on the day of the study. Here are the fifteen stories that were read by more than 100 (out of 481) readers each:

Title	Number of Readers	Percentage of Readership
New regulations on withholding-tax payments	315	65.5%
Marcos grants clemency to 432	225	47.0%
Korchnoi wins second chess game	220	45.7%
New weather disturbance forms	208	43.2%
Lunar eclipse visible Sunday	196	40.7%
Local basketball	186	38.7%
U.S. removes title of "base commander" from head of Clark AFB	149	31.0%
Flood control projects stopped	146	30.4%
Rebels control northern Nicaragua	139	28.9%
Measure presented to widen access of media to government information	112	23.3%
Opposition calls Iran's imposing of martial law illegal	107	22.2%
Camp David talks enter decisive stage	102	21.2%

Ministry of Education will regionalize payment of teachers	101	21.0%
Results of dirt slalom	101	21.0%
Trainer thinks Ali will regain title	101	21.0%

These 15 stories represent 46 percent of the total reading of the *Bulletin Today*. Half of all the reading of the paper was concentrated on 19 stories; the other half was spread over 110 stories. Obviously, a number of stories attracted very little reader attention, and a few attracted much.

Another interesting note is that 12 of the 15 most read stories began on the front page. In fact, 17 of the 20 stories with more than 15 percent readership, 22 of the 30 with more than 10 percent readership, all were front page stories. Thus news reading was heavily concentrated on a few stories and on page 1.

The most read story was one that touched every taxpayer: change in the income tax regulations. The second most read had to do with the release of a large number of political prisoners, all of whom were named in the story. The third was about the world championship match in chess, which was being played at that time in the Philippines – on neutral ground – and thus became local news as well as foreign news for Manila readers. The weather and lunar eclipse stories were very brief, appeared on page 1, and obviously affected everyone. The story about changing the title of the commander at Clark Air Force Base was particularly interesting in the Philippines because it amounted to the United States backing down from its control of Philippine bases. And any story about flood control raises memories of disastrous flooding in the Philippines. Each one of the top stories therefore had some particular reason for attracting readership.

Only five of the 15 top stories were wholly or in part concerned with foreign countries or foreign events: the readers of the *Bulletin Today* were distinctly more interested in domestic than in foreign news. Only two of the first 15 stories could be called "development"; that topic did not seem as attractive to readers as one might have expected. Four of the top 15 are sports news. Add that fact to the low interest in development news, and the apparent concentration on comics, features, and classified ads to the neglect of news, and one wonders how difficult it is going to be – if this pattern is at all representative of Asian reading – to bring to Third World people the news of national development they "need" to know.

Dimensions of News Reading as Seen by Factor Analysis

At this point a note of caution should be sounded. So far we have been talking about content of the news in terms of 12 categories. These categories are the *a priori* invention of newsmen and researchers who need some way to classify news content into identifiable groups of items. Although such labels are useful in comparing news across time and media, there is no reason to expect that readers of a newspaper will perceive the news in the same categories. In fact, there is good reason to suspect that they do not.

Since we have described the news wires and the daily newspapers in terms of *a priori* categories of news content, it may be instructive to try to find out something about how the readers of the *Bulletin Today* themselves classified the news items in the paper. We did not ask that question directly; indeed, it would take a long interview to do that, and would be very hard to put the questions in such ways as to obtain a valid answer. But we were able to analyze their reading patterns. All of us know that some members of a family are more likely than others to read sports, some more likely than others to read politics, and so forth. If we examine the reading patterns of the sports-interested persons we should expect to find that they read a number of sports stories; and the persons interested in politics read a number of political stories. But suppose that, instead of ourselves classifying the stories they read as sports or politics, or whatever, we were to find out what they actually *did* read and describe those groups of stories with whatever category names seem most appropriate?

This is why we applied factor analysis to the readership data. Factor analysis is described in Appendix E. It is essentially a mathematical device for grouping a number of items into clusters in terms of their resemblance on some chosen measure. In this case, we used it to find out what clusters of stories were read by the same people.

If there had been a perfect fit between the *a priori* content categories we used and the patterns of news interest that seemed to be reflected by their actual reading, we should have found 12 clusters (factors) of readership that we could have named military violence, domestic politics, and so forth. Actually we found only six distinct factors or clusters of stories in the readership patterns.

These can be seen in the table of factor loadings, Table D1 in the Appendix. Without going into the technical details of factor analysis, let us suggest that readers who are not trained in factor analysis look at the underlined numbers in the table. These are the stories that are closely related to one of the clusters which are represented at the top of the columns as Factors I, II, III, and so forth. The news stories in the *Bulletin Today* are listed, in headline form, at the left side of the table. You will see that 17 of the numbers are underlined under Factor I. The numbers represent the "factor loading": the higher the number the closer the relationship of this story to the others in the cluster. Thus 17 stories fit together into a cluster we call Factor I, and altogether six clear clusters, or dimensions of news, appear among the stories, which we have tried to describe by giving them the following names:

Dimension 1. International violence. 17 stories. Representative items: "200 Rhodesian blacks arrested," "Ethiopia criticizes China and CIA for arming insurgents."

Dimension 2. International economics. 9 stories. Representative: "ASEAN asked to set up pharmaceutical plant," "New crab industry."

Dimension 3. Sports. Representative: "Results of soccer tournament," "Results of dirt slalom."

Dimension 4. Finance/investment. 16 stories. Representative: "Capital inflow for development vital for Philippines," "Licensing of foreign technology transferred to industry secretary."

Dimension 5. Philippines general news. 29 stories. Representative: "Marcos grants clemency to 432," "Romulo restates civil rights position."

Dimension 6. Miscellaneous. 17 stories. Representative: "1,500 get medical aid from team in Cavite," "National quizbee starts."

Even a non-technical examination of these results will show that the readers of the *Bulletin Today* were not making the same distinctions among stories that we made in specifying the content categories *a priori.* "Economics," for instance, is a scholar's word. What we classified as economics the readers were likely to see as money or finance or investment, and to divide these items into foreign and domestic. "Foreign relations" is also a scholar's distinction; readers seemed to think of the foreign news items less in terms of international relations than in terms of the dynamic of the news, which, in those days as often since, has been violence or conflict. Thus, the same people who read "200 Rhodesian blacks arrested" were also likely to read foreign stories of conflict that had nothing to do with diplomacy or international violence, such as "Who is #1 – Borg or Connors?" (read also by the same persons as read sports, but even more heavily by readers of Dimension 1), and foreign stories of violence that had nothing to do with governments, such as "Boy forced to rape girl." In other words, the elements of violence and conflict seemed to fit together in these readers' perceptions with the element of foreignness, and governmental relations apparently played a rather minor part in the choice.

Furthermore, as we have suggested, readers of the *Bulletin Today* appeared to distinguish sharply between economic news dealing with the Philippines and economic news dealing with other countries. There was little overlap between the clusters we called "International Economics" and "Finance/Investment," the latter being mostly domestic news. Even within these clusters there were rather surprising differences from the *a priori* coding. Thus, eight of the nine stories that factored out as "International Economics" originally appeared in the *a priori* "Economics" category, but the ninth – a story of an insurance company being cleared of fraud charges – was classified by our coders as a legal and judicial story, whereas the readers apparently thought of it as a financial story.

These differences do not mean that one procedure is "right" and the other "wrong," or that what we find out by content analysis with a pre-constructed code is necessarily any less useful than what comes of factor analysis of readership. Each has its own usefulness. But it does indicate the danger of equating content analysis plus a readership survey with a map of motivations for reading any given kind of news content. And it points to the need of more studies of Third World reading and more detailed analysis of audience tastes, interests, and perceptions related to news.

From the factor analysis of these data we can make some inferences concerning the perceptions that must have led the *Bulletin's* readers to select one story rather than another. One was simply the location in the paper: the big news was likely to be on page 1. Another was foreign vs. domestic news, and reading of the paper was strongly skewed toward news of the Philippines. Another was "hard" news as opposed to "soft." For example, reading of the Philippine General News dimension was related negatively to reading of the "Miscellaneous" dimension. Both were chiefly domestic news, but one was hard news (like Marcos granting clemency to 432 prisoners) whereas the other was mostly news we should tend to call "soft," such as education, art, and science. Still another distinction may be between development and non-development news. Thus, readers of Finance/Investment news were unlikely to overlap with readers of other economic news, the reason perhaps being that Finance/Investment was heavily oriented to development, and the other not. But let us not make too much of these supposed psychological distinctions. The readership of the *Bulletin Today* was very low, and it represents one paper in one country on one day. More studies of the reasons for reading need to be made part of future research agenda in this field.

Types of Readers

Thus far we have been talking about dimensions of the news revealed by clustering the *stories* in some meaningful way. It is possible, by factor analysis, also to cluster the *readers* in terms of how much and what they read, and thus divide them into groups in which the members have similar news reading behavior. When we did this (the factor table and additional tables and description are in the Appendix) we found that a six-factor solution fit the reader data, although not the same six factors, of course, as we found by factor analyzing the stories. On the whole the result is somewhat more complicated than the other factor analysis.

The six types of readers we identified represent all except 12 of the 476 individuals on whom we had enough data to include in the analysis. The 12, most of whom read very little, seemed to be unrelated to any other groups or to each other. Therefore we discarded them in completing the analysis.

The other 464 readers, however, group themselves into clusters which are for the most part readily distinguishable in reading behavior. Distinguishable, that is, except in one respect: every cluster of readers read a great deal in the content dimension we previously called Philippine General News. Everyone read Philippine hard news, and there were no significant differences among the groups in how much or what kind of such news they read. However, in other respects they were more different.

In numbers, the reader groups were distributed as follows:

Type 1.	48	Type 4.	45
Type 2.	47	Type 5.	156
Type 3.	78	Type 6.	90

Type I readers were the heavy readers of the lot. Three-fourths of this group read more than 10 stories. This was twice as high a proportion as for any other group. Twenty-three percent of Type I readers actually read more than 50 of the 129 stories in the paper. They read heavily in every kind of news except sports, and they were the only type who read any considerable number of international and foreign stories. What were their demographic characteristics? A Type I reader tended to be older (85 percent of them were over 30), urban (77 percent) rather than rural, white collar in occupation (73 percent), and better educated (84 percent had at least a year in college).

A *Type II* reader turned out to be the lightest reader of the six. Whereas Type I readers as a group ignored only 2 of the 129 stories, Type II readers ignored *53*. Type II seems to focus on hard news — chiefly Philippine hard news — and to disregard the Philippine "soft" news of development. Type II is significantly different in age, occupation, and education from Type I, but not from Types III-VI.

A *Type III* reader was the second heaviest reader of the six. He tended to read, in addition to the Philippine hard news, all the International Economic stories and more Philippine development stories than could have happened by chance. There were no demographic characteristics that set Type III readers significantly apart except from Type I.

Type IV readers selected sports news oftener than any of the other types. They also read more International Violence stories than any other Type except I. They showed some tendency to reject development stories, foreign or domestic. Type IV readers tend to be younger than the average of the sample, contain proportionately more men (77 percent as compared to 50.5 for the whole sample), and include fewer college-educated persons.

Type V readers, representing the largest reader group, seemed systematically to reject only Philippine development stories, otherwise to read fairly evenly in all the news dimensions. A Type V reader is likely to be younger than average (for example, an average of 46 percent were under 31 years of age as compared to 15 percent for Type I).

A *Type VI* reader also reads fairly evenly in all except one news dimension. This is sports, which she – for the majority of Type VI members are women – tends to reject. There is also some indication that Type VI reads less than average in news of Philippine development.

These findings about what kinds of people read what kind and how much news fit well with other studies of readership. In Manila as elsewhere, readership increases with amount of education, with age (up to a certain point), with white collar education. There have been findings that urban dwellers read more than rural, and that men read more than women (particularly sports and politics), but these findings are not so clear in this factor analysis. Of course, it would be wrong to think that these demographic characteristics are the direct *cause* of the amount and kind of reading. They are interrelated; for example, more education usually is necessary for a white collar job, and more white collar jobs are available in the city than in the country. Furthermore, if education, age, occupation and other demographic characteristics really affect reading they must operate through values, interests, and knowledge they help to build up in the mind. It may seem, as suggested earlier, that we are approaching the problem through the back door by trying to infer why a person of a certain kind reads a certain kind of news instead of asking that person directly "Why did you read this story rather than these others?" But let us say again that this question is very hard to answer, and very hard to ask in such a way as to elicit a valid and meaningful response. A great deal more study of individual readers is required before we can be sure of these causal relationships. That, too, will be done in the future, but unfortunately not on the sample of readers interviewed in Manila in September 1978.

Summing Up

The results reported in this chapter are likely to be discouraging to many editors and critics. The question we should like to be able to answer, and cannot do so because we were able to make only one readership study, is whether the readership of the *Bulletin Today,* in Manila, on September 14, 1978 was typical of the reading of other papers in our sample. We suspect it was not typical. It was about half the percentage of readership found in 130 studies in the United States: the Manila figure was 8.4 per cent average readership, one story out of 11. Reading of domestic news was higher than foreign, reading of development stories lower than reading of other kinds of news. Reading was concentrated on front page stories, and after that there was some evidence that a number of readers skipped to the special pages, including features, comics, and classified ads. The average reader, selecting 11 stories, chose 6 domestic items, 3 foreign, and 2 a combination of domestic and foreign; 8 stories out of 11 about Asia, 1 about the Middle East, less than one about any other region; 3 stories of 11 on economic and business news, 2 on domestic and political, 2 on sports, the others scattered. Demographically reading was about like it is elsewhere in the world: higher with education, with white collar occupation, with urban residence, and (except for sports) with age as far as the decade of the 40's. Sophisticated factor analysis revealed that readers apparently saw the content-types of news somewhat differently from the types used by scholars, and also suggested six types of readers only one of which – older, better educated, and so forth – read much foreign or political news, or in fact read very heavily in any type of news except sports (where they were below the general average). As the list of best-read stories indicates, heavy reading was concentrated on a relatively few stories, largely of domestic importance, largely beginning on page 1. We make no claim that this pattern of reading is necessarily typical throughout the rest of our sample.

Part Three

Mainly Qualitative Questions

IX. THE COVERAGE OF DEVELOPMENT NEWS

In Chapter I we quoted three examples of statements made in the course of the debate on international circulation of information that, we thought, "can and should be checked". The last several chapters have thrown light on two of those examples – "(the news agencies) devote only 20 to 30 per cent of news coverage to the developing countries", and "a Unesco study estimating the input of Third World news into the total world circulation to be 15% while world news emanating from Paris, London, New York was 90%". It has become clear that those statements are at the least extremely dubious, or simply incorrect. The third item we quoted, however – "the wires from the Western news agencies contain little information relevant to development needs" – is a more difficult matter to adjudicate. We are going to try to do something about it in this chapter.

Some of the Problems

One of the most common complaints of Third World governments and journalists is that their "development news" does not get out of the country. Many of them complain also, and apparently with considerable justifications, that it is not circulated sufficiently *within* the country either.

By development news, these Third World spokesmen mostly mean "good" news. They are thinking of new factories, new housing, new agricultural projects, quotas exceeded, record crops, new educational opportunities, new scientific and technical discoveries, and other developments that will encourage the people of the country and stimulate them to work harder and to sacrifice immediate satisfactions for long-range achievements. Instead of this kind of "positive" news, the news director of an Asian Radio Television system said,

> "news film of catastrophes, political trouble, human suffering and misery is brought into the living room of Asian audiences night after night. By now an Asian viewer must be convinced that he is living in a much troubled world. He has yet to be exposed to the positive, or should I say the brighter side of things in his own continent such as news about improved living standards, better health facilities, greater

> spread of knowledge and perhaps even a little more happiness among Asia's teeming millions." (Ang, quoted by Sommerlad, 1978)

The lion's share of the blame for this situation in the last few years has fallen on the international news agencies owned in the West. Yet Fran Chopra, a distinguished Indian editor, who is himself highly critical of the Asian news that is available to Asians, says that "the fault is not entirely that of the western news agencies. The explanation lies in part, with the news values and selection criteria of the Asian media themselves."

Neither the pace of news itself nor the training of the typical newsman have been especially well suited to development news. News moves in a series of bulletins and retakes and revised leads and new bulletins, events piling on events so that an editor always has the sense of covering the world inadequately, always having to leave out items of importance, sometimes not able even to follow up events that he has already published to let his readers learn how the story "came out". The flow of news typically does not encourage the intellectual leisure an editor needs to sit back and analyze a pattern of events that must be interpreted in depth before it becomes truly meaningful. A newsman is typically trained to report events rather than to analyze situations. News is timely. It is a change in something; it can be dated and specified. A building burns. A bill is voted down or passed. An airplane falls, and either kills or does not kill its passengers. A new Supreme Court judge is appointed. A cyclone devastates the coast of south India. That is news; the newsman knows how to report it.

The news of development also sometimes moves that way – for example, a crop is found to be a world's record, or a great bridge is completed, or the first ship built in a new country is launched. But more often development news is important only because of its deeper meaning and implications. For example, China makes plans to upgrade its teaching of fourteen scholarly disciplines, a decision which may have great impact in a few years; but the news did not travel beyond China. India reports that the possibility of a regional "common market" is being discussed in South Asia, but until it actually happens it is important news only for its potential significance, and this requires the kind of investigation and analytical treatment for which most reporters are not prepared.

There is no doubt that news of development is in short supply in Asian newspapers, and yet the reason for it is probably more complex than shortcomings of the wire services. In order to find out something about just how the wires and the dailies are handling development news, we have selected 30 stories of development, from six countries – China, India, Sri Lanka, South Korea, the Philippines, and Indonesia. If we had to do it again, we should ask some of the editors and development agencies of these countries to identify, at the time, what they considered the most significant development events or topics that were available for coverage in each country during the week of December 4. It was impossible to ask them to make that decision some months after the time, and therefore we had to depend on items that were published in newspapers of these six countries or were carried on the national news agencies. The 30 stories we have chosen are not necessarily therefore the great development events of the week as seen from within the country, but they are certainly development news, they are of considerable potential interest, and most of them are the kind of "good" news that has been called for.

Thirty Development Stories and Their Coverage

These are the 30 stories we are going to trace through the news wires and the newspapers:

Development News

- from China
  1. The Ministry of Education announced plans for expanding and upgrading teaching and research in 14 scholarly disciplines.
  2. *People's Daily* editorializes on plans underway to speed up development in electronics.
  3. Local Hsinhua bookstores have already sold 450,000 textbooks for a new radio broadcast course in English language.
  4. A muscle relaxant has been discovered which is proving to be of great help in surgery.
  5. Two provinces – Heilungkiang and Kiangsi – have announced record harvests this year.
  6. Home-made small hydroelectric power systems have attracted world-wide attention to a small hilly county in Hupeh province.

7. A conference is to be held on mechanizing farms in China.
8. A national meteorological conference is being held in Peking.
9. *Red Flag* writes on plans adopted to revitalize industries in Shanghai.
10. A great many films that disappeared from the screens during the time of the Gang of Four have been rehabilitated and are again being shown.

- from India

11. A Hyderabad scientist shares the international Borlaug Award for his discoveries in improving food crops.
12. Loans and other assistance will be made available to stimulate the building of more houses.
13. Delhi will open 1,000 new centers for teaching literacy.
14. Delhi University will open again after long closure, indicating that the worst of national university troubles may be over.
15. The possibility of a regional "common market" is being discussed in South Asia.

- from Sri Lanka

16. A broad and sweeping new economic plan is announced in Parliament. This includes land reform (an acre for every landless rural family), abolition of most price controls, abolition of most controls on foreign exchange and imports, subsidies for tea planting, and abolition of free rice and sugar ration for families earning more than $300 a year.
17. The International Monetary Fund has made a grant for use in stimulating agriculture and industrial development in Sri Lanka.
18. The Asian Development Bank has made a loan to Sri Lanka to support an irrigation project, including the building of a 5,000-foot dam.

- from South Korea

19. Rice production for the year in South Korea is claimed as a world record. It is 35 per cent over the Korean average, and 15 per cent over the previous year.
20. The Government plans to stimulate industry by making foreign currency loans to elegible industries.

21. The Government is planning a new capital city, to be ready for occupancy in 10 to 15 years.

• from the Philippines

22. Study tours are being arranged for development specialists from the Philippines and other countries to observe the Barangay Movement.
23. Consultants say Philippines have been doing well under difficulties, but will need $1.4 billion in additional loans during the next two years.
24. Construction of a nuclear power plans on Bataan is being resumed, after stoppage for reconsideration.

• from Indonesia

25. The first quarter of the Brantas River redevelopment project has been completed.
26. Plans have been announced to modernize the old part of Jakarta harbor, thus increasing harbor capacity by 50 per cent.
27. The Government will make much more loan money available to help farmers.
28. Prolonged drought has threatened the rice crop, and measures are being taken to alleviate its effects.
29. Better manpower planning is said to be needed, because 40 per cent of young people of secondary school age are neither in school nor employed.
30. After 1980, 50 per cent of Indonesia's oil production is expected to come from the sea rather than the land.

These 30 items are about evenly divided among science and education (for example, new discovery in surgery, plans to revive 14 scholarly disciplines), agriculture (record harvests), and industry and commerce (Shanghai's industries to be revitalized, Jakarta's harbor to be modernized and enlarged). They range from a new national economic plan (Sri Lanka) to one city's opening a large number of new literacy centers (Delhi). They are about five to one about what governments are doing as compared to what the people are doing. Yet none of these distinctions seem to predict which items will be picked up and which will not, as the following tabulations indicate:

Thirty (30) Development Stories as Published by Four News Wires and Eighteen Dailies

Development Story (From China)	*Wire A*	*Wire B*	*Wire C*	*Wire D*	*Amrita Bazar Patrika*	*Ananda Bazar Patrika*	*Bangkok Post*	*Ceylon Daily News*	*Dong-a Ilbo*	*Ettelaat*	*Kayhan International*	*Kompas*	*Korea Times*	*Nanyang Siang Pau*	*New Straits Times*	*Philippine Daily Express*	*Pilipino Express*	*Sing Chew Jit Poh*	*South China Morning Post*	*Sing Tao Jih Pao*	*Statesman*	*Straits Times*
1. Education plans																						
2. Development of electronics		x	x	x				x					x	x					x			
3. 450,000 textbooks sold	x	x		x					x													x
4. New discovery for surgery				x										x								
5. Record harvests			x						x													
6. Electrical systems built																						
7. Mechanizing farms		x	x	x	x														x	x		
8. Meteorological conference	x			x																		
9. Develop Shanghai industry	x	x		x										x					x			
10. Films rehabilitated	x		x															x	x			

Development Story	*Wire A*	*Wire B*	*Wire C*	*Wire D*	*Amrita Bazar Patrika*	*Ananda Bazar Patrika*	*Bangkok Post*	*Ceylon Daily News*	*Dong-a Ilbo*	*Ettelaat*	*Kayhan International*	*Kompas*	*Korea Times*	*Nanyang Siang Pau*	*New Straits Times*	*Philippine Daily Express*	*Pilipino Express*	*Sing Chew Jit Poh*	*South China Morning Post*	*Sing Tao Jih Pao*	*Statesman*	*Straits Times*
(From India)																						
11. Prize to scientist																						
12. Stimulus to house building																						
13. New literacy centers																						
14. University opens again																						
15. Regional common market																						
(From Sri Lanka)																						
16. New economic package				x*	x										x							
17. IMF grant																						
18. Development bank loan																						
(From South Korea)																						
19. Record rice production	x		x				x												x			
20. Foreign currency loans																						

* One small, and negative, element of the plan only. See discussion of this in Chapter IX

(continued on next page)

Development Story	*Wire A*	*Wire B*	*Wire C*	*Wire D*	*Amrita Bazar Patrika*	*Ananda Bazar Patrika*	*Bangkok Post*	*Ceylon Daily News*	*Dong-a Ilbo*	*Ettelaat*	*Kayhan International*	*Kompas*	*Korea Times*	*Nanyang Siang Pau*	*New Straits Times*	*Philippine Daily Express*	*Pilipino Express*	*Sing Chew Jit Poh*	*South China Morning Post*	*Sing Tao Jih Pao*	*Statesman*	*Straits Times*
(South Korea cont.)																						
21. New capitol city																						
(From the Philippines)																						
22. Study tours to Barangay																						
23. $2.4 billion loans needed																						
24. Nuclear plant to be built																						
(From Indonesia)																						
25. Brantas River redevelopment																						
26. To modernize harbor																						
27. To help farmers				x			x															x
28. Problem of drought			x				x															
29. Work-school problem																						
30. Oil from the sea	x		x																			

WORDAGE CARRIED ON 30 DEVELOPMENT STORIES BY FOUR NEWS WIRES AND 18 DAILIES

Items	*Four Wires*		*16 Dailies*	
(From China)				
1. Education plans	0		0	
2. Development of electronics	960		1,350	
3. 450,000 textbooks sold	250		580	
4. New discovery for surgery	160		340	
5. Record harvests	80		240	
6. Electric systems built	0		0	
7. Mechanizing farms	790		1,030	
8. Meteorological conference	700		0	
9. Develop Shanghai industry	800		1,170	
10. Films rehabilitated	530		1,050	
		4,270		5,760
(From India)				
11. Prize to scientist	0		0	
12. Stimulus to house building	0		0	
13. New literacy centers	0		0	
14. University opens again	0		0	
15. Regional common market	0		0	
		0		0
(From Sri Lanka)				
16. New economic package	100		1,600	
17. IMF grant	0		0	
18. Development Bank loan	0		0	
		100		1,600
(From South Korea)				
19. Record rice production	330		220	
20. Foreign currency loans	0		0	
21. New capitol city	0		0	
		330		220
(From the Philippines)				
22. Study tours to Barangay	0		0	
23. $1.4 billion loans needed	0		0	
24. Nuclear plant to be built	0		0	
		0		0

(From Indonesia)				
25. Brantas River redevelopment	0		0	
26. To modernize harbor	0		0	
27. Help to farmers	160		200	
28. Problems of drought	250		240	
29. Work-school problem	0		0	
30. Oil from the sea	460		0	
		870		440
TOTAL:		5,570 words		8,020 words

What Stories Were Best Covered, and Why

It is interesting to try to analyze why some stories were picked up more often than others and why some were not picked up at all.

For one thing, it is clear that the stories from China fared better than those from any of the other countries. Why is this? The stories were not necessarily better. Rather, the reason must have been the size and strength of China, and the great interest it attracts throughout the world. One Asian editor remarked, about this, that when a lion turns his head toward you, it is more likely to attract your attention than is a dog barking at you. So when China talks of modernizing its electronics industry or mechanizing its farms, that may attract more interest than a broad national economic plan for a tiny country like Sri Lanka.

Furthermore, nine of the ten stories from China were carried by the Hsinhua (New China News Agency) wire. That means that they were promptly available to the four international news agencies, and to all the newspaper, news agency, and newsmagazine bureaus in Hong Kong, as well as elsewhere. And Hsinhua makes a special effort to cover development news. Thus it is not wholly surprising that the two development stories carried by the largest number of papers – the development of electronics, and the conference on mechanizing farms – were about China and had first been carried at length by Hsinhua. The only stories transmitted by as many as three of the four international agencies were all from China, and all appeared originally in the Hsinhua wire. These were the two stories mentioned above, plus the plans to rebuild Shanghai as a center of industry, and the sale of 450,000 textbooks for a radio course in English language.

Let us look for a moment at the stories that were not picked up at all, either by the international agencies or by any of the 16 dailies.

Some of these probably seemed to the average wire editor not broad enough in interest: They were not "gee whiz" stories (for example, the IMF grant to Sri Lanka, the study tours in the Philippines), or they were too local (the prize won by the Indian scientist, the loans for house building). Some of them may have seemed not timely enough: the new Korean capital city was a long way in the future; the Brantas River project was *one fourth* completed, not at some especially newsworthy point; the nuclear plant construction was merely *resumed,* rather than being started or completed. Some of them may have seemed to convey a strong tone of public relations or publicity (for example, the Hsinhua story that many observers were travelling to see what a county in Hupeh was able to do in building hydroelectric systems by its own efforts).

But a number of the untouched stories seem to be items that require more than routine reporting. The significance is not all there to be seen by the reporter or the reader. One can demur, of course, that there is deeper significance to be found in *any* news – even the arrest of a pickpocket, a fire resulting from an overheated stove, or an automobile collision. It might be quite possible, that is, to dig a little deeper and find out *why* the man had become a pickpocket, whether the number of pickpocket reports were increasing, whether there might be some special economic reasons behind them, and possibly whether the police were being paid protection money to turn their backs. One might dig into the story behind the story of the overheated stove, or inquire about the most frequent sites of automobile accidents and whether the roads or the lack of road signs or too much drinking before driving might be responsible. It is always possible to find significance even in a bulletin, but there are certain stories that call for special investigation and interpretation before they reveal their significance.

One of these is the story of China deciding to upgrade fourteen disciplines. That story is simply a generality unless one finds out what has been happening to scholarly disciplines in China during the Cultural Revolution (and in some cases, before that), what precisely is going to be done to upgrade them, what is the political significance of making these changes at the present time, and what is likely to be the effect on China's universities, the careers of its young people, and its economic development. In other words, it takes some investigation to write that story, whereas some of the other development stories on Hsinhua were ready to be published without additional work.

The story about the University of Delhi reopening is insignificant unless one puts it into the perspective of India's history of political unrest in the universities, and the numerous closures that had disrupted classes and careers. What does the reopening of the chief university in the capital city really mean – that some problems have been solved, that perhaps the troubled season is near an end, or merely that someone in the government thinks Delhi University has been punished enough?

So also with a number of other stories. The Development Bank loan to Sri Lanka is not much of a story by itself, but might become one if we were told what it is to accomplish – a large and imaginative irrigation and resettlement project. The fact that the Philippines are told they need $1.4 billion in loans during the next two years is not really an important development story unless one is told why they need it, what it is to be used for, and what it will mean to development of the national economy. Most development stories, that is to say, do not come directly off police blotters or releases: they require some investigation and interpretation. In some cases that can be done by the government that releases the story; in other cases, it requires journalists outside the government, within or without the country.

An example is the story of the new economic plan for Sri Lanka. This is a dramatic effort to breathe life and health back into a nation's economy. It is proposed to accomplish land reform by assuring that each landless rural family receives at least one acre. It is moving the country toward free trade by removing most restrictions on foreign currency and on imported goods, at the same time abolishing almost all price controls and warning local merchants that they can no longer expect to maintain artificially high prices. It provides subsidies for tea planting, and aims at increasing the incentives to produce more rice. These are, from the viewpoint of most Sri Lankans, positive steps, but there is also one negative element: the free rice and sugar ration are to be abolished for all families earning more than $300 a year, which means almost half the population. This obviously irritated almost half the population.

The only part of the new plan that was reported by the wires (*one* wire) was the single negative note: abolishing the free ration. This got

100 words on one of the international wires, and the news would probably not have been heard of in the newspaper if a writer for the London Observer Foreign News Service (OFNS) had not read the plan and written 800 words describing and interpreting it. This story was syndicated and reprinted entire by two newspapers, *Amrita* and the *New Straits Times.* It was no thanks to the four western news agencies, therefore, that a hundred thousand or so Asians outside of Sri Lanka heard about the economic development plan, and it would undoubtedly not have happened if a reporter able to see the larger significance of the plan had not happened upon it and written the story as it needed to be written.

Summing Up

On the whole, neither the international agencies nor the Asian dailies have any reason to be proud of their coverage of development news in Asia during the week of December 4. Only one story was printed in as many as four papers, one in three, five in two. The average wire carried six of the 30 development stories; the average daily, between one and two (outside their own country); six dailies, none at all. If the newspapers really want to exchange development news, they do not demonstrate it; and if they and the wires want the story of development adequately told, they do not seem to be using the best writers for the purpose.

In fact, this brief analysis of development news in Asia raises a serious question as to how well newsmen are prepared to cover the stories of development. We are not pointing a finger either at the news agency or the newspaper staffs alone. Those newsmen are obviously trained to cover politics and to report striking events and feature material. But are they prepared, either the news wire or the newspaper writers, with the economics and social understanding required to interpret development news in meaningful terms? And to what extent is the scarcity of development news on the Asian wires and especially in the Asian dailies due not so much to lack of interest on the part of readers as it is to lack of investigation and interpretation by news staffs? This raises a further question: whether an additional component in journalism education for today is not called for, and whether seminars, extension courses, and readings would not be useful for presently practicing journalists who have some responsibility for the news of economic and social development?

X. THE DISTRIBUTION OF COVERAGE: ASIA AS MORE THAN ONE NEWS REGION?

The amount and kind of coverage an event receives depends, in Asia as everywhere else, to no small degree on where the event happens. But location of a news event in Asia is especially significant because some characteristics of the news circulation make Asia look as though it were more than a single region. We can illustrate this by two parallel news developments that took place during the test week in opposite ends of the supposed region we are studying: Aquino's trial in the Philippines and Bhutto's trial in Pakistan.

The Aquino Story

On Monday, December 5, the retrial of Former Senator Benigno S. Aquino began before a military court in the Philippines. Aquino had long been a chief political rival of President Marcos and would probably have been the opposition candidate for the Presidency in 1973 had not Marcos imposed martial law a year earlier. Aquino had been charged with murder (of a village chief, some ten years ago) and subversion (against the present government). He was arrested, brought to trial, and condemned to death by a military tribunal. But the sentence had not been carried out, and during his five years in jail Aquino had been highly vocal. His protests against his conviction on what he called unjustified charges had attracted wide attention, particularly in the United States. Several members of the U.S. Congress had intervened informally. President Marcos agreed to reopen the case and allow Aquino to appeal the sentence.

Perhaps because of the international interest in the case, the international news agencies covered it in detail. In five days they carried nearly 9,000 words. The Asian dailies outside the Philippines carried somewhat less – about 7,000 words in total – but nevertheless more coverage than they gave to most of the other countries of Asia. 80 per cent of this coverage, however, was in the three countries of our sample nearest to the Philippines: Singapore, Malaysia and Hong Kong.

It may be interesting to review how the story developed during the week.

All the newspapers that covered the story depended upon the international wires for their information. The changes they made were chiefly to shorten the copy, combine takes, and sometimes polish up the lead after the scissors and paste job. Therefore, the story developed with the wires carrying reports mostly in the afternoon and evening, and the dailies (mostly morning) picking them up the next day. The courtroom session was on Monday; it came to newspapers readers on Tuesday. The decision of the Supreme Court to review the case was announced Wednesday and read in the newspapers on Thursday. And so forth.

The dailies stuck rather closely to the main facts, ignoring a number of possible digressions. One of these was an American civil rights lawyer named Davis who came supposedly as an observer, but offered his help to Aquino's defense. The offer was rejected. He observed the first day of the trial, and thereafter told reporters that the proceedings were a farce to which he could no longer remain neutral, and he was going home to stir up opposition to the trial. He got much more space on the wires than in the dailies. Another sidelight to the story was the refusal of Philippine authorities to permit the chairman of the Philippines Civil Liberties Union to board a plane for London even though he claimed he had valid travel papers. This man, Diokno, was a legal adviser to Aquino, and had been one of the politicians detained for a time when President Marcos proclaimed martial law. He was known as a highly vocal opponent of martial law. A third such sidelight was the first public address by the new American Ambassador to the Philippines, who said that the United States was pursuing a policy of preference toward societies that demonstrate respect for due process and free expression, and noted that the U.S. State Department had expressed concern over the death sentence passed on Aquino. This made at least one wire, but so far as we have been able to determine was not picked up by any of the dailies in our sample outside the Philippines.

Perhaps the most striking feature of the coverage of this story was the extent to which Aquino's ideas and protests were represented both by the wires and the newspapers. Aquino was apparently permitted to lecture the military court for two hours and a half, with reporters in the courtroom. He asked the court to search their consciences and decide whether they could really give him a fair retrial, after having once sentenced him to death. He said that at first he thought President Marcos was being merciful in reopening the case, but had now decid-

Before Dec. 5	Dec 5, Monday	Dec 6, Tuesday	Dec. 7, Wednesday	Dec. 8, Thursday
"Future" stories on coming retrial	*Aquino's day in court*	*Mostly statements for news media*	*Supreme Court decides to review the case*	
All wires carry something	Wire A 1,310 Wire B 1,850 Wire C 1,220 Wire D 860	Wire C 420 Wire D 270	Wire C 540 Wire D 160	
	– Bangkok Post 140			– Bangkok Post 100
	– S.C.M. Post 220	– S.C.M. Post 630	– S.C.M. Post 220 (+ pic 4½ x 5)	– S.C.M. Post 260
		– Sing Tao 430	– Sing Tao 370	
		– Nanyang 730		– Nanyang 240
	– New Straits Times 70			– New Straits Times 1,600 (+ 2 pic 1½ x 3)
	– Ceylon Daily News 130			
		– Straits Times 280		– Straits Times 1,680
		– Dong-a Ilbo 570		
	– Kayhan International 38	– Korea Times 160	– Korea Times 240 (+ pic 3 x 2½)	

ed it was merely a Machiavellian plot by the President. The phrase "Machiavellian plot" reappeared in most of the published account of the trial. So did Aquino's description of the retrial as a television show produced by the President.

Another striking feature was the concentration of coverage in Hong Kong, Singapore and Malaysia. About 80 per cent of the newspaper coverage was in five dailies in those three states. Indian papers did not touch it. The Indonesian paper did not touch it. The Sri Lanka paper said the trial was going to happen, then dropped it. *Kayhan International* carried only one story in which Aquino was mentioned. *Ettelaat,* the other Tehran paper, carried nothing on Aquino although it published a three-part interview with President Marcos (ignoring Aquino) on December 6, 7, and 8. The Korea papers carried Aquino's bitter courtroom words and a background story, but did not tell readers the concluding chapter: that the Supreme Court had agreed to review. Altogether eight out of 14 papers (omitting the local Philippine dailies) carried something on the story; five out of these eight took their readers through to the end, and informed them of the Supreme Court's decision.

What conclusions can we draw from this episode about the flow of Third World news in Asia? For one thing, even in a case where the human rights elements were as evident as this one, and where the facts were open and the accused allowed to speak for himself as fully as Aquino was, still the interest of Asian Third World dailies in the story was *less broad* than might have been expected. It was a story on which the wires provided a great deal more than the newspapers cared to use. But perhaps the most interesting thing of all is the apparent *localness* of interest. Four fifths of all the newspaper coverage, as we have said, was in Hong Kong, Singapore, and Malaysia, close neighbours of the Philippines. It did not seem like a particularly local story, but that is where the interest was concentrated.

Now let us look at the other news event.

The Bhutto Story

Zulfikar Ali Bhutto had been ousted as Prime Minister of Pakistan by Army Chief Zia, in a coup in July 1977. He was arrested, and charged with a number of criminal acts including the murder of a political opponent three years previously. Although Bhutto had been re-elected by a landslide vote four months before the coup, the opposition party had charged "massive and criminal rigging" of the election, and this set the stage for the coup and the trial. During the week of December 4, Bhutto's appeal against the murder charge was pending.

At the same time, General Zia, ruling under martial law, had decided to close the Urdu newspaper *Masawat,* owned by Bhutto and published by his wife. A number of journalists and printers from the paper's staff went on a hunger strike at the Press Club, protesting the closure of the paper. They tried to make it clear that their protest was not against the trial of Bhutto but merely against the attack on the press.

As so often happens, the active story pushed the pending story almost out of the news. On December 5, Wire C carried 170 words saying that police had arrested 21 of the strikers, including heads of the two unions, because the strike contravened martial law. On December 6, Wire D reported that the International Press Institute had cabled to the martial law administrator, protesting the closure of the paper (160 words). Wire D said on the same day (210 words) that "Pakistan's military rulers appeared ready to back down in their fight with detained journalists and printers who went on hunger strike." The Sind provincial government asked the martial law authorities to "give sympathetic attention" to the release of the arrested strikers – now numbering 26.

On December 7, however, Wire A reported the police had arrested five more hunger strikers; the total in jail was now 31 (120 words). The same wire (290 words) carried also a story on a new order by General Zia saying that anyone found guilty of malpractice in March 1977 elections would be disqualified from next year's elections. Thus a conviction on a criminal, financial, or political charge would disqualify Bhutto in the forthcoming elections.

On December 8, the Supreme Court handed down its decision on Bhutto's appeal. The grounds for his appeal had been that the trial judge should have been disqualified because he held a separate and concurrent position as election commissioner. This appeal was denied; "for reasons to be recorded later," the court said, there was no bar to the trial judge holding both appointments. This story ran 130 words (Wire C).

On December 8, also, the journalists called off their strike and it was announced the paper would be reopened. (It was forced to suspend publication again five months later.)

On December 9, a related story came over Wire D. Members of the banned National Awami Party – the opposition – who had been jailed by Bhutto on charges of killing a former home minister by a bomb explosion at the University of Peshawar, and of stirring up trouble among the Baluchistan tribesmen, would be released pending trial.

Thus there was not much coverage of Mr. Bhutto's case on the wires – about 1,500 words. Less than 10 per cent of it was about Bhutto himself.

The newspaper coverage was, comparatively, even less. It was restricted to India and Sri Lanka, Iran, Thailand and Korea. All the Southeast Asia papers ignored the story, even though *Nanyang Siang Pau* found space to report from Pakistan that a wildcat had "made off with a man's ear".

The *Statesman* said in 50 words, on December 6, that 20 journalists had been arrested, and on December 9 that the journalists had called off their strike (100 words). Also on December 9 it said that the hearing on Bhutto's petition had begun, and a day later that the appeal was denied (250 words).

The *Ceylon Daily News* reported on December 10 that Bhutto's appeal was denied, and mentioned the journalists' strike. The *Bangkok Post* carried two articles (340 words) on the hunger strike, *Dong-a Ilbo* 190 words on the strike, and the *Korea Times* an incidental mention of Bhutto (about 50 words).

Bhutto was mentioned in five stories in *Kayhan International,* each time referred to as the "deposed prime minister." All the items focused on the newsmen's strike. One noted that Bhutto was in jail, but none of them said why he was in jail, or how long he had been there, or whether he was going to come to trial. He was mentioned in two stories in *Ettelaat,* and Mrs. Bhutto in one. *Ettelaat* neglected to mention that he was in jail, though one story covered the arrest of 23 Bhutto followers for demonstrating in front of a court building. Total: 384 words.

It is perhaps worthy of note that whenever the wires mentioned the Bhutto case they seemed to feel the need to *explain what had happened,* and *why he was on trial.* Seeing how little attention he got in the press, that was not surprising.

The coverage of those two stories raises a number of questions. For one, why did Aquino get about six times as much coverage as Bhutto? Was one story intrinsically more interesting than the other; or is the Philippines, which proved throughout the study week to be a very live news center, simply more live in that respect than is Pakistan?

Why did the international wires actually carry more on these stories than the Asian dailies carried? But the most intriguing question of all is whether news interest in Asia is really as regional as these two stories indicate?

How Many News Regions?

Here is a chart of coverage of these stories by all the dailies represented in our sample which covered the stories at all. Of course the chart omits the countries where the events took place: therefore, this is coverage of *foreign* Third World news. The figures are the approximate number of words on each story during five days.

	AQUINO	BHUTTO
Singapore	1,960	
India		400
Malaysia	3,630	
Sri Lanka		70
Hong Kong	2,130	
Thailand	240	340
Korea	970	240
Iran	38	580

That chart suggests a region of news interest in the vicinity of the Subcontinent (represented here by India, Pakistan, Bangladesh, and Sri Lanka), and another interest region in Southeast Asia (represented here by the Philippines, Singapore, Indonesia, Malaysia and Hong Kong). There is another group of Third World countries (represented here by Thailand and the Republic of Korea) which belong to neither of the two principal regions, but sometimes cover the news of one, sometimes the other; in this case, of both. We cannot test this by any other pair of similarly appropriate and comparable items that occurred during the week of our test, but the pattern seems to hold. India and Sri Lanka are more likely to carry the news of the Western group of countries; Singapore, Kuala Lumpur, Hong Kong and Manila are more likely to carry the news of East Asia. This gives a certain advantage to East Asia, and perhaps helps to explain why Aquino got so much more coverage than Bhutto, for the East Asia countries have a number of the largest and most prosperous papers in Third World Asia. These papers typically have a large number of pages, large news holes, and large editorial staffs. They carry more news. But that does not explain why the story of Aquino hardly reached the Western tier of countries, and the story of Bhutto did not reach the Eastern tier.

Where does Iran fit in this regional picture? Clearly nearer the papers of India and Sri Lanka than those of Southeast Asia. It did cover the strike of journalists in support of Bhutto, although making little mention of Bhutto himself. It gave only 38 words to Aquino, which was 38 words more than other papers west of Thailand. But certain other characteristics of the Tehran papers – the lack of attention to any of the "big stories" from China, for example, the relatively scant coverage of the Subcontinent by the Farsi language paper, and the heavy coverage of the Middle East, makes one wonder whether Iran looks west rather than east for news, and really belongs to neither of the Asian news regions we have delineated.

Summing Up

We may be going too far in speaking of news "regions." What the data seem to show is two "centers" of news interest – one in Southeast and East Asia, the other in the Subcontinent. Around these are other countries with special or divided interests: Thailand, between the two centers; Iran with a special interest in the Middle East; Hong Kong with a special interest in China as well as its ties to Southeast and East Asia; Korea with its divided interests in the two centers and special interests in Japan and the West, not to mention North Korea. But the different treatments of the Bhutto and the Aquino story do tell us something important about the flow of Third World news in Asia.

XI. THE NEWS FROM TWO LARGE COUNTRIES: CHINA AND INDIA

Hsinhua's Part in China News Coverage

The news from China is a particularly interesting part of Asian news flow, both because of the importance of the country and because of its special definition of news and the controls it maintains upon the dissemination of news.

An examination of the flow of news from China properly begins with Hsinhua, the New China News Agency. This is not quite like any other news agency in the world. It is the chief supplier of news to all the media of China, from the *People's Daily* to the smallest commune newsheet. It publishes *Ts'en-Kao Hsiao-Hsi* (Reference News) which circulates somewhere between 8 and 10 million copies to Party leaders, cadre members, and others who are permitted to subscribe, and consequently has some right to be called the largest newspaper in China. But it resists being thought of as a national or "internal" news service. Its function, as described by Wang Chia-hua as early as 1957, is to "distribute news to the length and breadth of the world . . . the agency's early development into a world news agency is an urgent mission" (1957, p. 6). Presently it maintains perhaps as many as 100 bureaus in cooperative countries, staffed almost entirely by indigenous Chinese. More than 100 employees work in the Hong Kong Bureau; more remote offices may have only one or two persons. These offices receive the news service from Peking, make it available to subscribing newspapers and broadcasters, issue news releases when appropriate, and contribute to the flow of news from their regions back to Peking.

The Western concern for "all the news that's fit to print" is not very important to Hsinhua. For example, during the week when we analyzed the New China News Agency wire as it came through the Hong Kong Bureau, the other news agency wires and the newspapers were full of President Sadat's initiative and the Tripoli meeting that came in reaction to it. This subject was never mentioned directly by Hsinhua; even when they reported that King Hussein of Jordan visited both Egypt and Syria, they said that he talked with the leaders of those countries about "the situation" – never about *what* situation. In that same week the Asian papers, in particular, were pre-occupied with the crash of a hijacked airplane in Malaysia on its way to Singapore. Hsinhua carried not a word about this either, although it reported carefully the Asia men's basketball championship tournament from Malaysia.

What the Chinese tell their people through Hsinhua, and what is there made available for international wires and foreign newspapers, can therefore be understood only in terms of *why* they tell them what they do. Like many other Chinese media, Hsinhua is not intended to be essentially informative, but rather instrumental. It is expected to be an instrument of political policy and guidance. That is why it can take such a detached and timeless view of news-breaks and getting there first with the news, why it feels it can omit many of the chief stories that excite other news agencies, and why, perhaps more than any other wire service, it feels the need to concentrate on the Third World. Despite recent changes within China it is probably still true (and was certainly true in December, 1977) that Hsinhua's view of the world is essentially that of Mao in his theory of the "Three Worlds" (described in the *Peking Review,* 45, November 4, 1977, 10ff.) Mao revised the older concept of a capitalist world, a communist world, and a developing world, and asked his readers to think of the three divisions as:

1) A First World consisting of two "hegemonist" powers, the USSR and the U.S.
2) A Second World of powers like Europe and Japan, many of them affluent but none so hegemonistically inclined as the first two. "Second World" countries are consequently potential allies of the developing countries in their resistance to the allegedly war-mongering First World.
3) A Third World of developing countries whose hope lies in creating a united front against the First World, and developing their own military and economic power for self-defense and preservation.

Given this world view, we can assume, then, that Hsinhua's news selection must have related, at least in 1977, to instrumental goals like these:

1) The world must realize that the hegemonist powers are enemies of peace and independence. At the moment the USSR is the most dangerous country in the world, but a capitalistic

country like the U.S. is capable of being just as dangerous if the decay of its system drives it to desperate measures.

2) It is necessary for other countries to stand up to this First World, to develop economic and military strength to resist the First World and to cooperate – to face the First World with a United Front.
3) In this situation China should be seen as a friend and aider to all who seek peace and who wish to defend their independence and dignity.

These themes run through Hsinhua's news report. Given such a world view and such long term goals, it is not hard to see why the crash of an airliner does not fit into the Hsinhua news budget, or why the agency might prefer to say nothing about events in the Middle East that seem contrary to the idea of a united front; why Hsinhua is centered as much as it is upon the Third World (about 6,600 of its daily average 7,500 words are devoted to the Third World); or why news breaks, competition, even spectacular disasters or political maneuvers like those in the Middle East might seem unimportant at the moment. Better to wait and see how they fit into the Big Picture.

China is not an easy country for an international news agency or a foreign newspaper to cover, even since the country has opened its doors to them. Bureaus, correspondents, and stringers cannot be distributed over the country. Officials cannot be interviewed or quizzed at regular press conferences as easily as they can in many other countries. Attendance at conferences and official sessions is controlled, and plans for important meetings are often kept so far from the public eye that sometimes not even their dates are publicly known before the meetings take place. Policy is seldom announced openly until it has been known and put into effect within official circles. The news that Hsinhua exchanges with international news services and delivers to subscribing papers is thus important in what the world knows of China. We shall consider it along with the other channels as we examine the flow of news from China.

How Much News Comes out of China?

The flow of news outward from China is surprisingly large when one considers that what Chinese newsmen call "aberrations" and Western readers think of as some of the most exciting parts of their news – accidents, disasters, violence, crime, court trials – rarely appear in Chinese news*, and that many of the most interesting manifestations of the policy-making process – debates on national and provincial policy, confrontations of political personalities, and election campaigns – are typically conducted outside the public eye and only the results are announced.

Yet the Hsinhua wire available in Hong Kong carries just under 5,000 words about China on an average day. The average international wire provides about 1,300 words a day, although the range among wires is large – from 800 to 2,500. The 16 Asian dailies in our sample offered a total of about 17,300 words on an average day. Thus the average Asian daily (if there is such a thing) can be thought of as carrying about 1,100 words on China. Here, too, there is a wide range – from zero in *Ananda Bazar Patrika* and 100 in *Amrita* to nearly 4,000 in *Sing Tao Jih Pao,* of Hong Kong. Indeed, 40 per cent of all the China news published in the 16 Asian dailies in our sample was in the two large Hong Kong papers, *Sing Tao* and the *South China Morning Post.*

These word totals stand for an average of 18 stories on China per day in Hsinhua, 34 a day in the four international agencies (about 9 per day for the average wire), and 37 per day for the 16 papers (2 to 3 stories in an "average" paper). The range in number of stories was as wide as the range in words: from an average of 9 a day in the *South China Morning Post,* to less than one in the *Bangkok Post* and *Kompas,* and, of course, none in *Ananda.*

The pattern of news flow is thus parallel to the general pattern described in Chapter IV: descending by individual channel or media, but rising overall, as the following chart shows:

---

* The almost complete absence of crime and accidents in the news from China is all the more striking when we note that these two categories accounted for 11.4 percent of the total words on the four wires (Table B3) and 9.5 percent of the news during five days of 42 Third World countries (Table C3).

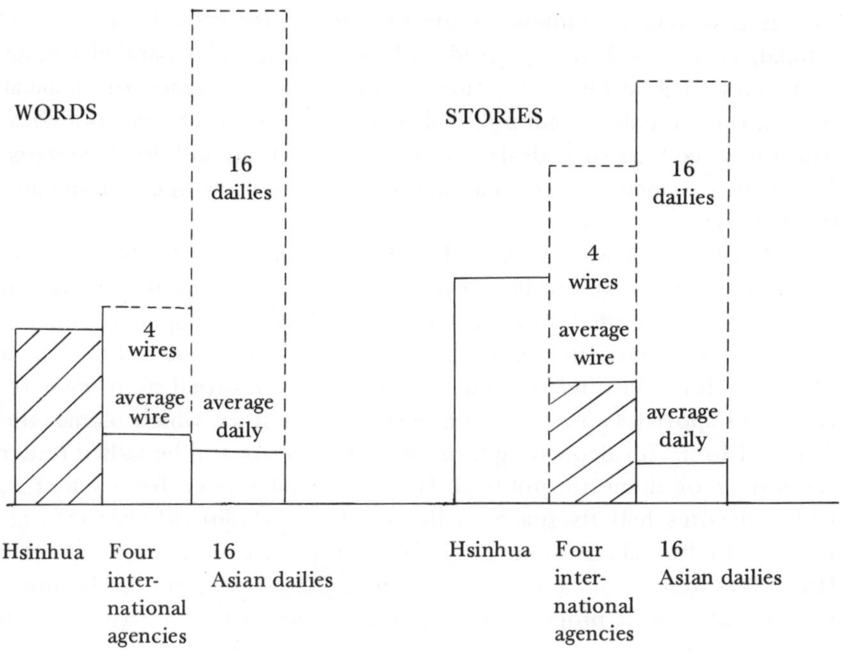

The Newspapers' Sources for the News from China.

Of the 167 separate stories on China in the Asian dailies, 85 per cent could be identified by source. The sources were almost exactly the same as for Third World news as a whole in these newspapers. 73 per cent of the stories on China (as compared to 76 per cent of all Third World news) came from one or more of the four international news agencies. 11 per cent were credited to a regional or national wire (including Hsinhua). 8 per cent came from a newspaper's own correspondents. 6 per cent was local coverage, and 1 per cent from reprints or special services.

The Kinds of News That Come from China.

The accompanying table tells us something about the kinds of news that flow from China through the wires and the newspapers. The largest part of it deals with foreign relations; for the most part this reports a seemingly endless stream of foreign visitors, official and unofficial, entertained or conferred with in Peking, and a parallel stream of Chinese friendship delegations, athletic teams, dance or musical groups, trade missions, and political representatives to foreign countries. Another large part of it deals with domestic politics and developments. Two other segments of considerable size have to do with economic and sports news.

When this flow is compared with the content of Hsinhua it must be remembered that the New China News Agency wire is not easy to code in the categories we have used for the Asian newspapers and the international wires. In a sense, *everything* on Hsinhua is political. Is a reception for a visiting volleyball team to be classified as foreign relations or sports? Is an economic development story which blames the "gang of four" for depressing farm or factory output to be tallied under economics or domestic politics? Is a memorial service for a scientist, which devotes half its space to listing the important officials who attended, to be called domestic politics or science or human interest? How does one code a long story on a British lecturer in London, praising the social program in China, or a report that a Swiss journal

News from China in Percent: Five Days

News Category	*Hsinhua*	*Four News Agencies*	*Seventeen Asian Dailies*	*All Third World Foreign News Agencies*	*All Third World Foreign News Dailies*
1. Military, political violence	0	4.3	0	7.0	6.6
2. Foreign relations	41.2	43.1	31.0	36.3	30.2
3. Domestic politics	1.9	14.7	24.8	11.0	11.5
4. Economic, social	15.7	16.4	12.4	15.5	17.8
5. Science, health	21.6	3.4	3.1	1.1	0.9
6. Education	5.9	3.4	3.9	0.4	1.0
7. Accidents, disasters	0	0	0	5.5	5.3
8. Crime, judicial	0	1.7	0	4.1	4.7
9. Sports	11.8	6.0	12.4	11.4	12.2
10. Art, culture	1.9	1.7	0.8	0.8	2.1
11. Human interest	0	2.6	7.8	2.0	3.9
12. Other	0	2.6	3.9	4.9	3.7
	100.0	100.0	100.0	100.0	100.0

has republished Mao's article on "Three Worlds"? Thus the differences between column 3 and the first two columns in the preceding table may be less important than they might seem.

The international wires and the newspapers follow the Chinese lead in reporting little or no crime or accident news, and a great deal of foreign relations news. They all report a substantial amount of sports. The chief differences are that the outside observers are more interested in domestic developments within China than the Chinese media present themselves as being, and that the kind of domestic news one finds in Hsinhua or the *People's Daily* tends to be news of development – economic, scientific and educational. Thus the wires, the dailies, and Hsinhua all devote somewhere near 40 per cent of their stories to domestic political, economic, scientific, and educational news. Outside observers are deeply interested in the currents of Chinese politics, and so doubtless are readers inside China, but the cadres read political news in the lists of officials who attend a meeting or a ceremony or a banquet, which the international wires and Asian dailies usually present as meetings or ceremonies or banquets. The outside readers are interested in stories of individuals in China, but news in China is not very often personalized. In Hsinhua, stories of individuals are usually presented in the form of development stories – for example, a review of the career of a worker who has invented a new cutting tool, or an account of high officials setting an example for others by doing manual labor in the fields, and consequently classified as economic rather than human interest.

When the news from China is compared with all Third World news on the international wires and in the papers (Columns 4 and 5 in the table), the chief differences, as we might expect, are seen to be the absence of news of military preparations and political violence, of crime and accidents. The amount of foreign relations news and sports are relatively the same. The absent categories in China news are replaced in the outside media by greater attention to domestic developments and news of economic development in China.

However, the concentration in Hsinhua and other Chinese media on news on economic growth, scientific and educational development, is not quite duplicated either by Third World news on the international wires or by Asian Third World newspapers outside China. Perhaps the best way to look at this is in terms of actual stories.

What Happens to the "Big News" from China?

We selected 20 stories which, on the basis of their play, might represent the "big news" of the week in China. These are listed in the accompanying chart. The first 10 fall into the classification of development – economic, scientific, and educational – and have already been treated in Chapter IX, so we shall not say much about them here. The next six are a sample of other news likely to be seen or heard in China – a memorial for a distinguished scientist, a Chinese airline diverting its flight schedule to save an ill passenger, two examples of international relations as practiced in Peking and two others of Chinese political and friendly delegations abroad. Finally, we have included four stories that did not appear in Hsinhua during the week we studied, but did get some play outside China. These included a crime story, which does not ordinarily fall within the net of news as officially defined by Hsinhua, although the *People's Daily,* before the week was over, felt it needed to defend a court's decision on executing some public officials; a story about China considering the purchase of jet fighters abroad, which also would not usually be reported in that context in China; the appointment of a new head of the New China News Agency, to which the Chinese news media, in their emphasis on collectivity rather than personality, would not be expected to give the same attention as would Western news media; and finally, an account of "rehabilitation" and return to the screen of a number of films that were banned during the Cultural Revolution. The chart shows which of these stories were picked up by each of the wires and the dailies.

Of all these stories the one most often picked up was about the presence of Chinese officials in Cambodia, conferring, being entertained, touring the provinces near Vietnam and near China. Three of the wires carried this story and seven of the dailies. The reason was obviously the implications for a possible confrontation of the Soviet Union and China – one backing Vietnam, the other Cambodia.

Of the ten stories specifically dealing with development, all were carried by Hsinhua, all except two by one or more of the international wires. The two not picked up by the wires were the account of the Ministry of Education making plans for the development of 14 academic disciplines neglected during the Cultural Revolution, and the account of many visitors going to see how one province had built its own hydro-

Coverage of Twenty Development Stories from China by Four International News Wires, Hsinhua, and Eleven Asian Daily Newspapers

Development Story	*Hsinhua*	*Wire A*	*Wire B*	*Wire C*	*Wire D*	*Amrita Bazar Patrika*	*Bangkok Post*	*Ceylon Daily News*	*Dong-a Ilbo*	*Kayhan International*	*Korea Times*	*Nanyang Siang Pau*	*Sing Chew Jit Poh*	*South China Morning Post*	*Sing Tao Jih Pao*	*Straits Times*
1. Ministry of Education makes plans for 14 disciplines	x															
2. Move to speed development in electronics	x		x	x	x			x			x	x		x		
3. 450,000 textbooks sold for radio English course	x	x	x		x				x			x				x
4. Discover new muscle relaxant for surgery	x				x						x					
5. Record harvest in northern provence	x			x												
6. Tungching's home-made hydro-electric power system	x															
7. National conference on mechanizing farms	x		x	x	x	x								x	x	
8. National meteorological conference	x	x			x											
9. Find much plant and animal life on high Tibetan plateau	x		x		x									x	x	
10. Plan to make more use of Shanghai's industries	x	x	x		x							x		x		

(continued on next page)

Non-Development Story	*Hsinhua*	*Wire A*	*Wire B*	*Wire C*	*Wire D*	*Amrita Bazar Patrika*	*Bangkok Post*	*Ceylon Daily News*	*Dong-a Ilbo*	*Kayhan International*	*Korea Times*	*Nanyang Siang Pau*	*Sing Chew Jit Poh*	*South China Morning Post*	*Sing Tao Jih Pao*	*Straits Times*
11. Mourn death of Wu Yu-shun, famous scientist	x		x	x	x							x		x		
12. Reception in Peking in honor of Thai King's birthday	x	x	x	x												
13. Plane diverts flight to save ill passenger	x		x	x										x		
14. Chinese officials in Cambodia	x	x	x		x		x		x			x	x	x	x	x
15. Chinese journalists traveling in Europe, Africa	x	x	x	x												
16. West German delegation in Peking	x	x	x	x	x									x		
17. China may buy jet fighters and Concorde					x			x		x				x		
18. New head of NCNA		x	x		x							x		x	x	
19. Teacher sentenced over student suicide				x	x											
20. 600 pre-Cultural Revolution films "rehabilitated"		x			x									x	x	

NOTE: Newspapers not included in this table carried none of the stories in this group.

electric power stations and the electric system they fed. The first of these was obviously important, but wire editors may have felt it was lacking in specifics. In the second, outside readers may have detected the tone of instruction rather than news: other communities and provinces were being told to follow the example of Tungching.

Although eight of the ten stories were available on at least one international wire, and five on an average wire, the Asian dailies showed less interest in them than might have been expected. Eighteen dailies carried a total of 14 Chinese development stories, an average of less than one per newspaper. Thus the pyramid of coverage is very steep: 10 development stories on Hsinhua, five on an average international wire, one in an average daily.

Words Carried on "Big News"

Story	*Hsinhua*	*Four Int'l Agencies*	*Eighteen Dailies*
1. Ministry of Education makes plans	300	0	0
2. Speed developments in electronics	630	941	1,341
3. 450,000 textbooks sold for radio course	180	248	565
4. New discovery for use in surgery	120	162	240
5. Record harvest in northern province	180	84	0
6. Home-made hydro-electric system	570	0	0
7. Conference on mechanizing farms	180	839	1,039
8. National meteorological conference	270	704	0
9. Much plant and animal life in high Tibet	540	1,786	756
10. Plan develop industries in Shanghai	1,140	796	1,176
11. Mourn death of famous scientist	900	447	1,021
12. Reception for Thai King's birthday	120	126	0
13. Plane diverts flight to save passenger	180	383	148
14. Chinese officials in Cambodia	510	1,117	1,912
15. Chinese journalists traveling	420	298	0
16. West German delegation in Peking	240	442	111
17. May buy jet fighters and Concorde	0	210	525
18. New head of NCNA	0	485	1,813
19. Teacher sentenced in suicide case	0	738	0
20. Films "rehabilitated" since Cultural Rev.	0	516	1,052
TOTAL	6,480	10,322	11,699

This is a pattern of news coverage we have seen before. Third World news from Asia is being covered more fully by the wires than by the daily newspapers, and there seems to be a wide divergence in taste and interest among the dailies as to what they choose to reprint from the wires.

On the 20 "big" stories (see the preceding table). Hsinhua carried a total of approximately 6,400 words, the four wires 10,000 (2,500 per average wire), and the dailies 11,500 (700 words per average paper).

The relative coverage of the ten development stories is not far different. Hsinhua carried 4,110 words, the four wires 5,560 (1,390 per wire), and the 16 dailies 5,117 words (320 per average paper). In fact, the relative interest of the newspapers seems a little lower in development news from China than in other news. The ratios can be expressed this way:

On 20 "big" stories from China.

Hsinhua carried *2.6* times as many words as the average international wire, which in turn carried *4.0* times as many as the average Asian daily in our sample.

On 10 "development" stories,

Hsinhua carried *3* times as many words as the average international wire, which in turn carried *4.9* times as many as the average Asian daily in our sample.

How Some Special Kinds of News Were Covered.

China's emphasis on development news is more than that of most Third World countries. However, certain other types of news are even more characteristic of China than of its neighbors. Two of these are the accounts of the parade of visitors – governmental and nongovermental – given official attention in Peking, and the parade of Chinese visitors, governmental and nongovernmental, through other countries. The international wires reported the visitors *to* Peking more faithfully than those *from* Peking, and the dailies covered neither group very fully but concentrated on *future* travels – "Teng to visit Burma", "Prime Minister invited to visit Peking".

The international wires covered more of the visits to Peking than might have been expected. Of *13* such Peking visitors or visiting groups reported by Hsinhua in the time when the wires would have had a chance to cover them, *9* were reported by the international agencies, a total of 15 times. These included the West German delegation (3 wires), a Romanian delegation (two wires each), and an Iranian volleyball team (entertained socially), an East German delegation, a Japanese military academy group, and two other Japanese friendship delegations (once each). Of 15 stories of Chinese travels in other countries carried by Hsinhua, however, only three were reported by the international agencies, a total of 10 separate times (6 of them on the Malaysian visits, 3 on the travels of the Chinese journalist delegation, and one on a friendship delegation in Benin). As indicated, these were not very popular with the dailies. Dailies carried an average of about two such stories each in the five days of the study.

One type of news of China more likely to be found in the outside dailies than in China itself, is the general review article on developments in China. This is particularly true of the papers in Hong Kong, which sits on the doorstep of China and has been the world headquarters of "China watchers". These newspapers, and some others in the sample, have special channels of information on China in addition to the international wires and Hsinhua. An example of the result is their attention to what is happening to Chinese films and dance programs, and political and social articles like "internal security tightens in Kwangtung", "China the principal source of heroin", "Hua actively builds up Hunan as a base", "Freedom of speech in China criticized by Canadian journalist", "Differences erupt in Chinese leadership", "Peking emphasis on Educational TV", "Purged leaders back in posts". These headlines are all from Hong Kong papers. Another kind of "China-watching" is represented by a headline from Korea which obviously did not come either from Hsinhua or the *People's Daily:* "Taipei says Teng Hsiao-Ping to be head of China".

How Was the News Edited?

As the Chinese news was edited and shaped, passing from first sources to the international wires to the newspapers, in general the changes were mostly to abbreviate the story and take out the elements that would be of less interest to an audience outside than inside China.

For example, Hsinhua carried 900 words on the memorial service for Professor Wu, who had a long and distinguished career and most recently had been Vice President of the National Academy of Science and a member of the Standing Committee of the National People's Congress. The Hsinhua story used almost half of its space to list the national leaders who presented wreaths and attended the memorial service. Wu's career was described briefly, and there were long quotes from the eulogy spoken by Fang Yi. Three international wires picked up the story, carrying a total of about 450 words. Thus the average wire story was about one-sixth the length of Hsinhua's account. Most of the names of dignitaries at the funeral were omitted, Wu's chief titles and positions were briefly listed, and a sentence or two were quoted from Fang's memorial address. Example:

> Fang said Wu "applied himself to science and technology with a strict and down-to-earth approach and passed on his knowledge earnestly. He trained a large number of scientific workers, some of whom have become well-known scientists in China and abroad."

In each of the international wire stories the name of at least one of China's top leaders was listed as attending the ceremony and/or presenting a wreath, but there were no such long lists as in Hsinhua. The *South China Morning Post* and *Nanyang Siang Pau* reprinted the story, the *Post* on the 9th, *Nanyang* on the 10th. They used wire copy with the change of only a few words, and the *Post* added a three column picture, about two inches high, of the memorial service.

The Shanghai story, however, was a bit different. It was based originally on an article in *Red Flag,* the Party's special magazine, written by Peng Fung, a member of the Politburo, and hence carrying the force of policy already decided upon. This story, too, was picked up by three of the international wires. In the case of the 16 "big stories", carried by Hsinhua, the Hsinhua account had usually been in advance of the international wires, suggesting that it might have been the source or one of the sources of the external wire report. The Hsinhua story on the development of Shanghai industry, however, came out only on December 10, whereas the wire stories were on December 8. Two of the wires quoted *Red Flag* as the source. The third wire attributed the story to "Hong Kong Communist newspapers", who in turn quoted Peng's article. It seems that in this case, at least, Hsinhua apparently made no effort to get there first with the news, and the editors were reading *Red Flag.*

Hsinhua, when it got around to carrying the story, carried a little over 1,100 words. The three wires that reported the story carried a total of 800 words. Three newspapers picked up the item, with a total of nearly 1,200 words. The two papers that depended all or mostly on the wires used the copy with little change. The way the *Morning Post* handled the copy illustrates the kinds of changes they did make. The *Post* changed "blue-print" (for Shanghai's development), as it appeared on the wire, to "plan". It added a new clause to explain the significance of the Gang of Four in the story. And it deleted a statement attributing part of the information to "a 200-word article broadcast by Radio Peking". Thus the alterations were minor.

Summing Up

The flow of news from China over the international wires to the daily newspapers of Asia can be summed up this way: The flow is larger than might be expected from the nature of news as conceived by and made available by the Chinese. The international news agencies are more likely to cover the big stories than are the dailies of Asia. Among the dailies there is the same diversity of interests and tastes in selecting news from China that they show in selecting other Third World news. They display less interest than might be expected in news of economic and social development. A distinctive feature of the flow of news of China, however, is the presence of "China watchers" on the outside who contribute from their own knowledge and their own sources to the news and its interpretation.

The Coverage of Indian News

India got somewhat less coverage than did China: on the international wires, 87 stories as against 116 in five days; in the Asian dailies, 71 stories as against 129.* Even so, a little over 3 per cent of

* This comparison of newspaper stories is not completely fair because it has to exclude two Indian papers with respect to Indian news, but include them for China. If two additional Asian dailies had been included at the rate of coverage of the other papers, the total for India would have been about 106 – still considerably less than China.

the stories on the four Asian wires, a little under 3 per cent of the stories in 13 dailies outside India, were Indian news. Judging from the play given news from India, Asian newspaper editors did not consider the week of December 4-10 a very exciting one in India. Yet interesting and important things were happening there.

The country was recovering from two disasters – the worst storm of the century had killed 8,000 people and caused enormous property damage; and an explosion at the nuclear heavy water plant in Baroda had put that plant out of action and raised suspicions of sabotage. Two important commissions were in session, hearing testimony, issuing statements and reports, and being discussed and challenged. These were the Shah Commission, investigating the "National Emergency" and the leadership of Indira Gandhi; and the Reddi Commission, investigating alleged illegal actions of former officials including Sanjay Gandhi. Parliament was in session, asking the sometimes newsworthy and often embarrassing questions that Indian parliaments ask, and being answered by top government officials. Politics were hot, with charges and counter-charges flying; and the ruling Janata Party, the old Congress Party, and Indira Gandhi's "New" Congress were gearing up for important state elections to come in early spring. England was playing Australia in cricket at Brisbane. And there was quite a lot of other news, including some spicy items like the arrest of 500 teachers who had been striking for higher pay, and publication followed by denial that Nehru had asked Lord Mountbatten to take charge of India after partition.

The range of coverage among news agencies and among Asian newspapers was not quite as large as we have seen it in some other cases. One wire gave India less than one per cent of its copy during the week; two others gave it nearly 5 per cent. This was a range of 2,700 to 17,000 words. One Asian daily carried nothing at all on India during the week; the *South China Morning Post,* on the other hand, had 15 stories, and the *New Straits Times* had 19. This meant about 5,000 words for the *Times,* and about 3,750 for the *Morning Post.* But the best way to get a sense of this varied and spotty coverage is to see how some of the big stories of the week were handled.

The Shah Commission. All the wires covered this story, but in different lengths and styles. One wire carried a single story of about 400 words, emphasizing the disclosure of secret intelligence documents implying that Mrs. Gandhi had put a number of her government colleagues under surveillance. A second wire also carried but one story, about 200 words, summing up testimony before the commission. A third wire covered the commission every day but emphasized rather what was happening outside the hearings than what happened inside. On Monday, this wire carried a denial by Mrs. Gandhi that she had caused any acts of violence; on Tuesday, the possibility that she might be made to testify, and the advice given to Congress members not to appear before the commission; on Thursday, Mrs. Gandhi's protest against the actions of the commission; and on Friday, a story that the commission definitely would call her to testify. On Wednesday and Friday, two stories of about 350 words each were devoted wholly to what happened at the hearings of the commission. The fourth wire carried about 1,400 words on the commission, reporting testimony, and about 1,200 words on attacks by Mrs. Gandhi and her allies on the commission. Total of the four wires: about 5,000 words.

The Reddi Commission. The Reddi Commission was reported regularly within India, although at much less length than the Shah Commission. Only one wire carried anything on it: 250 words on Sanjay Gandhi's denial that he used his government influence to further his business.

Parliament. Except on one wire, Parliament went largely unnoticed. Total coverage for the five days was about 500 words. Parliament was talking about violence at the textile mill, about an investigation of the Baroda explosion, a bill to reform the banking law (which was defeated in the upper house), and plans to recast the 42nd amendment to the Constitution in order to give more protection to freedom and human rights.

Politics. This obviously was hotter news within India than outside. If readers had heard about the political unrest in Karnataka and Andhra Pradesh, they might have been less surprised to read, in February, about the victory of Mrs. Gandhi's new Congress Party in those state elections. No specific wire coverage, December 5-9.

Crime and Disaster. Most of the hard news on the storm and the Baroda explosion had been reported before December 5. In India, the papers were concerned with what caused the nuclear plant to blow up, and with efforts to provide relief for the surviving victims of the storm. It was announced that India had raised rupees equivalent to some millions of dollars for relief, and that a government commission would investigate the explosion. The wires altogether carried about 900 words on the Baroda explosion, 600 on the aftermath of the cyclone. The coverage of the explosion was mostly about why it happened and the possibility of sabotage. The coverage of the storm was mostly about aid from the outside. Pakistan sent tents; Japan sent money; China sent sympathy. And Billy Graham got several hundred words of wire copy simply by touring the area. The principal crime story in India papers that week was a particularly ugly case of a riot, police action, and the murder of hostages. It was reported of two wires – about 200 words.

Cricket. Australia won the cricket match. It was by far the best covered Indian news of the week on the wires, although two wires did not touch it at all. No less than 45 per cent of one wire's total coverage of India that week, 30 per cent of the second wire, were cricket. Together the two wires carried about 9,000 words during the five days on the match in Brisbane.

Wire Coverage vs. Newspaper Coverage

One of the best-covered India stories of the week, by the wires, was Prime Minister Desai's plans to go to Nepal at the end of the week for an official visit. This was reported by every wire and got altogether 3,200 words. A trial on drug-selling charges got 650 words on the wires. The wires covered India's decision to contract with Britain to build cargo ships, the word that Air India would tighten security measures, a murder trial, prediction of an earthquake in northern India, the arrest of 500 teachers for picketing, and various other brief stories.

Some stories that got attention in India, but not on the wires, in addition to those mentioned, were the intended repeal of the Maintenance of Internal Security Act in order to eliminate vestiges of the "emergency" rule, the sudden death of one of India's most famous musicians Ustad Khan, a prediction that the Indian budget deficit might be ten times the expected amount, a series of cases of violent demonstrations by students resulting in openings and closings of universities, a somewhat startling statement by the chairman of the Communist Party of India congratulating Indira Gandhi on her emergency rule, a charge by Ananda Marg that foreign intelligence agencies are actually responsible for the political violence against diplomats for which the Marg has been blamed in Australia and elsewhere, and a

Story	*Wire A*	*Wire B*	*Wire C*	*Wire D*	*Bangkok Post*	*Ceylon Daily News*	*Dong-a Ilbo*	*Ettelaat*	*Kayhan International*	*Kompas*	*Korea Times*	*Nanyang Siang Pau*	*New Straits Times*	*Philippine Daily Express*	*Pilipino Express*	*Sing Chew Jit Poh*	*Sing Tao Jih Pao*	*South China Morning Post*	*Straits Times*
SHAH Commission	x	x	6x	7x		x			x				2x	x				2x	x
REDDI Commission		x											x						
BARODA Explosion	x		x	2x		x		x	2x	x	x		x	x		x			
Mill RIOT	x		2x	2x	x				x			x	2x	x		x			
P. M. to Nepal	x	x	2x	x														x	
CRICKET			5x	4x		2x			2x			x	2x					2x	
BASKETBALL	2x	2x	x	x	2x							x				x		x	
STORM VICTIMS	2x	3x	x	x						x							x	x	
TEACHERS Arrested			x			x							x						
MURDER Trial				x									x						
India at Sri Lanka MEETING				3x								x							

(Figure preceding x indicates number of stories during the five days)

NOTE: Newspapers not listed in this table carried none of these stories.

thoughtful analysis of what has happened to India's birth-control program.

If the wires made quite different choices within the news available in India, the newspapers were even more divergent. We have noted that one newspaper in the sample carried nothing at all on India during the five days studied. *Ettelaat* carried only 96 words. *Dong-a Ilbo* carried only 500 words, the *Philippine Daily Express* carried only 900 words, and the *Korea Times* only 1,100. The *Straits Times* carried 1,300, but the *New Straits Times* offered its readers 5,000!

The average of 15 Asian (non-Indian) newspapers during the five days was 5 to 6 stories. Overall, one third of the words were on sports.

Coverage of the big stories was quite irregular, also. Five of the thirteen newspapers reported the Shah Commission, six the Baroda explosion, five the big cricket match, and four the mill riot. The readers of these 13 newspapers had a chance to read a total of 1,800 words on the Shah Commission, 1,200 on the Baroda explosion, 600 on the mill riot, and just under 3,000 on the cricket match. Only one newspaper covered all four of those stories – the *New Straits Times.* The *South China Morning Post* covered three of the four, although at greater length.

What One Prestige Paper Carried on India

Since the *New Straits Times* carried the largest amount of copy on India, it may be interesting to review what it told its readers. It reported the Shah Commission at two points during the week: when the Congress Party told its members to boycott the hearings, and when the commission seemed "headed for a showdown" with Mrs. Gandhi about her summons to testify. The Baroda explosion was described as a "setback for India's fuel output". Readers were told about hostages being slain, and workers "dying in riot"; of a crime fancied up into a "chicken curry murder"; and about the 500 picketing teachers being arrested. The *Times* carried one story on the Reddi Commission: Sanjay Gandhi denied that he had exerted any undue influence. It carried also one story on parliament – the Janata Party had suffered its first legislative defeat (on the banking reform bill). The cricket match was fully reported, in addition to tennis, basketball, and hockey. Altogether, 43 per cent of the space devoted to India by the *Times* was about sports.

Coverage by Kinds of Content

Here is a table that compares the proportion of stories on India classifiable under twelve categories of content, for five days beginning December 6. The *Stateman* is included to represent local news judgment as compared with that of the news agencies and the Asian dailies.

Category of news	Local News in Statesman	Four News Wires	15 Asian Dailies
1. Military, political violence	0.6%	2.3%	5.6%
2. Foreign relations	0.3	2.3	7.0
3. Domestic, political	27.2	25.3	22.5
4. Economic	31.2	14.9	14.1
5. Science, health	0.9	3.4	1.4
6. Education	3.9	0	0
7. Accident, disaster	4.2	10.3	11.3
8. Crime, judicial	10.2	8.1	9.9
9. Sports	12.6	29.9	25.4
10. Culture	5.5	0	2.8
11. ·Human interest	1.0	2.3	0
12. Other	2.4	1.1	0

Three Chinese Language Newspapers on India

We asked a young Chinese scholar to read the three large Chinese dailies in East Asia – *Sing Chew Jit Poh* of Singapore; *Nanyang Siang Pau* of Malaysia; and *Sing Tao Jih Pao* of Hong Kong – for the entire week of December 4-10, and report to us on the picture of India he derived from that experience. Our intention was to see how India was reported in the non-English press. He reported with some surprise that the three papers had conveyed somewhat different impressions.

Eighteen items concerning India were printed in *Sing Chew* during the week. Only three of them were solely on India, and eight mentioned her only briefly. Most of them were given small headlines and carried on inside pages. There was one picture – the new Singapore Commissioner in the presence of Indian officials.

The bulk of the coverage was on sports. No fewer than 10 of the 18 stories reported India's (quite successful) performance in the Ninth

Asian Basketball Championship. The India players were described as strong and skillful, and it is noted that they won all their six games during the week.

In addition to the sports coverage, there was one story on crime, two on disasters, two on economic matters, one on domestic government, one on foreign relations.

The theme of economic and social troubles in India comes through clearly, he says. One of the sports stories reports that India has asked the sponsoring country of the Asian Women's Basketball Tournament to provide board and lodging in order that the Indian team might take part. A feature article on "The Green Revolution" cites India as an example of the failure of the revolution, and blames it on the caste system. The story about textile workers on strike killing five senior executives emphasizes acute labor problems. The report of Mrs. Gandhi's refusal to testify before the Shah Commission strengthens a reader's suspicions of wrongdoing, he says. And whereas one disaster (the explosion in the nuclear plant) indicates that India has made some scientific achievements, the other disaster (the cyclone) emphasizes that a large number of Indians are waiting to be fed, clothed, and sheltered.

As a whole, he said, the picture of India that emerged from *Sing Chew* was rather grim: a country that has little to boast of except basketball; its economy hampered by the social structure and stricken by disasters; and at a time of crisis deprived of political unity.

Nanyang Siang Pau carried 33 stories on India, 22 of them on sports, and many of them identical with those in *Sing Chew.* Of the stories not dealing with sports, four are on economic matters, two on violence, two on domestic government, one on international relations, one on crime. The sporting image of India comes through, as it did from *Sing Chew.* This is reinforced by three pictures of her participants in the basketball championship. The economic problem also comes through clearly. One story reports "50 million people undernourished," and notes that only this year is India able to produce enough cereal for local consumption.

However, a somewhat different theme also appears. This is India's international activity. She is reported as an active participant in the News Agencies Meeting, in Sri Lanka, suggesting that regional centers be created for gathering and disseminating Asian news. She is one of the countries negotiating with the EEC for new textile quotas. She is a force to be reckoned with in the future of the Indian ocean; Mrs. Gandhi's fall, the story says, may prove a handicap to Russian ambitions in that area. And India is described as the second most popular tour destination for Singaporeans.

Thus the portrait of India in *Nanyang,* our reader says, is upbeat more than down: active in sports, interesting to see, concerned with food, economic, and political problems, but not losing contact with other nations and demonstrating influence with them.

The large Chinese paper in Hong Kong, *Sing Tao Jih Pao,* carried only nine stories on India during the week. Three of them were on sports, two on economic matters, one on science, one on human rights, and one apparently written to encourage tourism.

One interesting characteristic of the *Sing Tao* coverage is that, except for the tourism pitch, none of the stories is solely about India. The country is always mentioned in connection with other countries, sometimes quite casually. A representative from Hong Kong is attending an international climatology meeting in India; India is one of the countries participating in or affected by Hong Kong's present negotiation with EEC and Canada on textiles. The British Prime Minister is planning a visit to Bangladesh, and India will be his next stop. India is *one* of the countries accused of violating human rights.

Thus India is seldom treated by itself. With the exception of the tourism story, which has a PR tone and seems to be meant to sell India as a tour destination for Buddhist pilgrims, India sits in the background while the spotlight of the news is on other countries. To *Sing Tao,* our reader concluded, India, in that week, did not seem very important.

Thus three papers, three pictures.

Summing Up

How shall we sum up this record of Indian news in Asia during the study week? Uneven. Spotty. Less than we might expect for the second largest country in the world. More coverage by the news agencies than their clients, the Asian newspapers, reflected. Much greater emphasis on Indian sports by the wires and the other Asian dailies than by Indian newspapers themselves. On the other hand, less coverage of Indian arts and culture, and of the very lively Indian political scene, than might have been expected. On the whole, an Indian editor, reading about his country in the newspapers of other Asian countries, might have had some doubts as to how fully and fairly India was being portrayed.

XII. COVERAGE OF TWO MAJOR EVENTS: THE PLANE CRASH AND THE TRIPOLI MEETING

Calendar of the Plane Crash Story

At about 8:35 in the evening of Sunday, December 4, a Boeing 737 of Malaysian Airlines crashed at Johore, Malaysia. All the 100 persons abroad were killed. The plane had apparently been hijacked on its way from Kuala Lumpur to Singapore. This was the most spectacular story of the week in Asia, and gives us a chance to see how Third World news channels handle a disaster story.

Let us begin with a calendar of the story as it developed. The plane, as we have said, fell late on December 4, not many hours before Monday morning papers had to go to press. As a matter of fact, rescue workers did not reach the crash site until after midnight. Monday, December 5, was used mostly for sorting out the facts: how many and who were aboard, had there or had there not been an explosion, who were the hijackers, what did the scene look like, and so forth. On Tuesday, December 6, attention shifted to the search for the cause of the crash. The identity of the hijackers was still a mystery. The "black box" – actually "boxes", the two recorders of cockpit conversation and navigation record – had still not been found. Human interest stories began to appear concerning victims, and also concerning lucky persons who had intended to be on the plane but were not. Malaysian Airline pilots threatened to strike because they suspected laxity in checking passengers for weapons. (The strike was called off). On Wednesday, December 8, plans were announced for burying the victims, and more human interest stories came to light. The "black box" was still missing. Friday, December 9, was the day of the funeral. Officials agreed that the cause of the crash would probably never be known with certainty. Malaysian Airlines promised tighter security measures at airports. That was the way the week of news developed.

Wire Coverage and Newspaper Coverage

Only one wire was available to us in the late hours of Sunday evening, because we were able to start service on the other three wires only at midnight Sunday. However, using that one wire for the first hours, and the full complement of wire services after 12 midnight, we can see how a story like this first comes to the newspapers of Asia.

The first bulletin we have seen came at 2140, Sunday the 4th. It came from Singapore and read:

> URGENT: A Malaysia Airlines plane crashed at the Jurong Industrial area here tonight, it was learned here today. It is understood that the plane, from Kuala Lumpur, was carrying about 90 passengers. No further details were available.

That was almost exactly one hour after the crash.

The second report came forty minutes later. This time, the exact number of passengers (93) and crew members (7) was reported. It was reported also that the plane was a Boeing 737 and "overflew Kuala Lumpur due to a technical fault". No mention of hijacking yet.

Short reports began to come at intervals of a few minutes. A Singapore police rescue squad was pushing to the scene. Then the word "hijack" first appears in the news. It was still in the stage of rumor. It is also reported that the general manager of Malaysia Airlines had left for Singapore to investigate the crash.

The first details on passengers aboard the unfortunate plane came about one and one half hours after the first bulletin. Readers were told that Malaysia's Minister of Agriculture and the Cuban Ambassador to Japan were thought to have been on the plane and were believed to have been killed in the crash.

These preliminary facts about the crash were all reported in takes of 100 words or less. The first major news-break came two hours after the first report. The wire carried a bulletin saying that according to Malaysian Airline source, the plane had been hijacked by (Japanese) Red Army men. Still in time for some Monday headlines.

About five hours after the crash, it was reported that the site had been located. Shortly after that, integrated stories of the accident began to come out, although still short of many of the essential details. Rescue workers had reached the crash site. There were no survivors. The rescue team could find only two complete bodies; the rest were torn into bits and pieces. Then the emphasis turned to confirming the names of the victims (among who were, indeed, the Cuban Ambassador, the Malaysian Minister, and a high official of the World Bank), and trying to find out reliable details of the cause. MAS denied earlier reports that

Red Army guerrillas had been involved, but the pilot was reported to have radioed the tower that he was in distress before the plane disappeared from radar screens.

During the first 24 hours, all the news agencies got correspondents to the site of the crash and carried stories about the scene. One wire warned editors (perhaps thinking of broadcasters who might tear off the copy and read it on the air without editing) that portions of its following report might be objectionable to some readers. The story began:

> There were no groans, no moans and no cries for help at Kampong Tanjung Kutang . . . There were no survivors . . . Hideously strewn here and there . . . were a hand, a leg, a head.

Another wire:

> The little fishing village on the Southern tip of Johore where the MAS Boeing 737 exploded in midair never looked like a crash scene at all . . . I and two other Singapore journalists reached a small clearing that made us wonder if someone had done up the place for the coming Christmas season.

Gradually during the following days the details were cleared up, and the story was carried through as competent newsmen do.

The casualty list was authenticated; some persons reported to have been on the stricken plane were found alive and at home, and others not so lucky were described in terms of their careers, their families, or some unhappy accident as to how they happened to be on that particular plane. The threatened strike of pilots over slack security was reported called off. Search for the flight recorder and other evidence of the cause of the crash continued, and speculation continued with it. On December 8 one wire reviewed all the evidence – how many hijackers and who they were (the general conclusion was that there was only one, identity unknown), whether a bomb exploded in the air (the general belief was that there was an explosion in the air), what actually happened in the last minutes of the flight, and so forth – and concluded that the mysteries surrounding the crash probably never would be dispelled.

The wires were really very similar in the coverage they gave the story. When they diverged, it was most often for feature reports (for example, describing the crash scene, the grief at the home of a victim, the jubilation at homes of persons who had *almost* been passengers on that plane, and so forth). They also had their own ideas as to what might have happened just before the crash. One wire quoted the *New Straits Times* as suggesting that the hijackers might have belonged either to the German Baeder-Meinhof terrorist gang or to the Indian Ananda Marg sect. Another wire quoted the *Malay Mail* in speculating that the hijackers might have carried explosives aboard to blow up the plane. Still a third wire suggested that Malaysian Communist terrorists may have been the hijackers: they may have got into a tussle with two bodyguards believed to have accompanied the Cuban Ambassador, said the bulletin, and the exchange of gunshots set off the explosion.

Three wires mentioned that American and British aviation experts were brought in to help investigate the cause of the disaster; the fourth wire did not. Only one wire covered the new Malaysian Airline security measures supposed to deal with hijackers, and the report that the International Airlines Pilots Association might publish a list of airports believed to be lax in security. Only one wire covered the mobbing of the airlines operations room in Kuala Lumpur by relatives seeking news of their loved ones who had been on the plane. Only one wire dealt with the subject of compensation for the families of the crash victims, and only one (not the same one) reported that the Australian Ambassador told the UN of the crash. But these were comparatively small details of difference in a pattern of coverage that was generally much the same from wire to wire.

Altogether about 25,000 words on the crash moved over the four international wires that week. The briefest coverage by an individual wire was about 4,000 words; the most extensive, more than twice that.

How did the newspapers handle the story?

Ten of the 16 dailies reported it on Monday, December 5. Three more (*Kompas,* of Jakarta, the *Korea Times* and *Dong-a Ilbo,* of Seoul) caught up with it on Tuesday the 6th. Three did not cover it at all. These were *Ananda Bazar Patrika* and *Amrita Bazar Patrika,* of Calcutta, and the *Pilipino Express,* of Manila.

The Monday headlines, with two exceptions, were large, and very much the same. Two dailies had the plane crashing into the sea (actually it fell into a mangrove swamp). Most mentioned the Japanese Red Army as hijackers (they went to press before that could be officially denied). Here were the headlines on December 5:

New Straits Times:	Hijack MAS Jet Crashes in Johore
Nanyang Siang Pau:	MAS Jet-Liner Crashed
Sing Chew Jit Poh:	MAS Jetliner hijacked by Japanese Red Army and crashed in Johore
Straits Times:	Hijacked MAS Plane Crashed
South China Morning Post:	Hijacked Plane Crashed in Sea
Sing Tao Jih Pao:	Malaysian Airliner Crashed near Singapore
Bangkok Post:	Hijacked Malay 737 Jet Crashes
Philippine Daily Express:	Malaysian Jet Hijacked
The Statesman:	Hijacked Boeing 737 Crashed
Ceylon Daily News:	Hijacked MAS Plane Crashed into Sea
Kayhan International:	100 killed as Blast Rocks Hijacked Jet

The coverage in Singapore and Malaysia was massive. For both these countries it was practically a local story, and they could use their own reporters and photographers. On the first day the *New Straits Times,* of Kuala Lumpur, devoted 84 column inches of the front page, and 13 more inches on the back page, to the story. *Nanyang Siang Pau,* also of Kuala Lumpur, carried four stories on the front page, a total of 66 column inches in addition to a picture. *The Straits Times,* of Singapore, carried 70 column inches on the front page, plus two pictures adding 75 square inches to the total. *Sing Chew Jit Poh,* of Singapore, carried a 61 column inch story on the front page, and six pictures totaling 64 square inches showing teams of rescue workers and police (not yet at the crash site).

On Tuesday, both the Chinese papers devoted their entire front pages to the story, along with considerable amounts of space inside the paper. *Nanyang* had a two-page center spread of pictures of the crash scene. *Sing Chew* used its entire back page for pictures. Both the English language papers used most of their front pages for the story, and the *Straits Times* carried a 100-square inch picture on its back page.

Thereafter, the coverage tapered off throughout the week, but the total amount of news that appeared on the crash, in the two Singapore and two Kuala Lumpur papers during the five days, is startling:

Nanyang Siang Pau – 1,018 column inches of copy, 1,206 square inches of photographs
New Straits Times – 498 column inches of copy, 706 square inches of photographs
Sing Chew Jit Poh – 892 column inches of copy, 767 square inches of photographs
Straits Times – 354 column inches of copy, 511 square inches of photographs

This is the equivalent of over 140,000 words, plus 3,190 square inches of pictures. Three thousand one-hundred ninety square inches is more than 10 full pages.

Coverage elsewhere, as might be expected, was less. It depended, except for local angles, on the news agencies. The following chart shows coverage outside Malaysia and Singapore:

Newspaper	**December**					
	5	6	7	8	9	10
South China Morning Post	X	X	X	X	X	X
Sing Tao Jih Pao	X	X	X	X		X
Bangkok Post	X	X	X	X	X	X
Philippine Daily Express	X	X	X	X		X
Ceylon Daily News	X	X		X		X
Kayhan Internatioal	X	X	X	X		
Kompas		X	X			
Korea Times		X	X			
Dong-a Ilbo		X	X			
Statesman	X				X	

Coverage in Hong Kong also was heavy. In Bangkok it was heavy, although with fewer pictures. Elsewhere, coverage was uneven. The regionality of news showed up dramatically. The *Ceylon Daily News* carried during the week a total of 26 column inches, no picture; *Dong-a Ilbo,* 24 inches of copy, no picture. Two of the Indian papers, as we have noted did not carry anything at all on it. The *Statesman* had a bulletin, one and one-half inches, on Monday. On Thursday it carried 3 inches, mentioning a denial by the Malaysian Home Minister that the Japanese Red Army had been involved. Total: 4½ inches of copy, no picture. The Malaysian papers carried about 60 times as many words, and the Singapore papers about 50 times as many words, as the Indian and Sri Lanka papers combined.

Of course, coverage tended to be heavier in countries that were either geographically or psychologically closer to the event. Secondly, it was heavier where the dailies could use their own staffers (as in Singapore and Malaysia), lighter where a newspaper had to depend on the wires, despite the fact that the wires covered the story well and fully. Why no more attention was paid to the story in India we do not know. Perhaps India was preoccupied with its own disasters.

Calendar of the Tripoli Story

The Tripoli meeting of Arab states opposed to President Sadat's initiative began before the week of our study, and almost all the news from it came in the first two days – December 5 and 6 for the news agencies, December 6 and 7 for the newspapers. When our week began, therefore, the conference was already winding down. The final arguments were recorded – Syria demurring from taking such a hard line, Iraq walking out because the line was not harder. The communique was announced, strongly condemning Sadat's diplomacy. The participating countries broke relationships with Egypt. President Sadat responded scornfully, closed the embassies of the Tripoli countries and sent their diplomats home. In turn, the Egyptian diplomats were sent back to Cairo. That was about all the hard news. After these two days the focus of attention turned away from Tripoli toward other events in the Middle East.

Wire Coverage and Newspaper Coverage

It is not always easy to separate news of the Tripoli meeting from news of related or parallel events. Countries like the U.S. and the U.S.S.R. were expressing their opinions on it. Whenever reporters found Vance or Began or other national leaders, they were always asked for an opinion. President Sadat was very much in the news. The news from Tripoli must therefore be read against the background of events in the Middle East and statements about those events, and it is extremely hard to separate background from foreground. Because of this we may have underestimated the total amount of space or words given to coverage of the Tripoli meeting, particularly by the wires.

Therefore, the amount of coverage on Tripoli is even more striking than the raw figures make it seem. In our sample of Asian dailies it was the most widely covered story, appearing in even more papers than did the crash of the hijacked plane. Sixteen of the 18 dailies carried it, all of them with the essential facts. In two days the four international wires carried nearly 20,000 words, the newspapers nearly 55,000. The

COVERAGE OF TRIPOLI STORY (in number of words)

Wires		*Newspapers*	
Wire A	5,540	Amrita Bazar Patrika	1,330
Wire B	3,570	Bangkok Post	2,040
Wire C	4,410	Ceylon Daily News	1,200
Wire D	5,830	Dong-a Ilbo	4,660
		Ettelaat	3,584
Total	19,350	Kayhan International	2,304
		Kompas	850
		Korea Times	3,710
		Nanyang Siang Pau	9,270
		New Straits Times	4,110
		Philippine Daily Express	1,840
		South China Morning Post	1,780
		The Statesman	2,750
		Straits Times	910
		Sing Chew Jit Poh	7,920
		Sing Tao Jih Pao	5,770
		Total	54,028

average was 4,840 per wire, 3,377 per paper. The fact that 14 newspapers would average 1,688 words per day on a story from a faraway region is, in view of other coverage we have reported, little short of phenomenal.

Why did the story draw so much coverage? It was, of course, the most newsworthy single event in the Third World outside Asia during the early part of that week. Television would provide special competition for newspapers on a story of this kind. Beyond that, it was Third World rather than Big Power news. And there may have been a still more subtle reason: the fact that this story, more than most others, seemed to provide a reason for interpretation and commentary.

On the wires, for example, the coverage was by no means limited to hard news of events. Several newspapers and commentators were quoted on the meaning of Tripoli. One wire carried almost a thousand words analyzing the rift among the Arab countries, and nearly 900 words of feature material on the meeting after it ended. Other wires carried interpretive and background material. The papers, also, seemed to feel that the story deserved editorial comment or background articles. No fewer than five newspapers published editorials on Tripoli during the two days when coverage was high, and two others carried general background articles on the Arab situation in general. A distinguished Asian editor remarked recently that Asian readers, unlike Western readers, do not keep up with daily events in the world and therefore need more background in order to understand events as they are reported. That is what was being provided in the coverage of the Tripoli meeting, and for the most part *not* being provided in the coverage of Asian development news. We return to a question previously asked: whether journalists on the whole are not better trained to analyze and interpret political than economic developments? Another question also comes up again: how adequate are the international wire services on stories like this? The airplane story, of course, was local for Singapore and Malaysia, but the other countries of Asia depended on the wire services for it. All the Asian dailies had to depend on the news agencies for the Tripoli story. Their heavy use of the news off the wires suggests that it must have met their needs.

XIII. THE OTHER NEWS FROM MALAYSIA

What Other News Was Available

The crash of the hijacked jetliner so dominated the news from Malaysia during the week of 4 December, 1977 that it might have seemed nothing else was happening. The disaster received enormous coverage – 25,000 words on the international news agency wires, 80,000 words in the two principal Kuala Lumpur papers alone, and considerable coverage in all except three of the other dailies in our sample. But what happened to the *other* news from Malaysia that week? Was it simply blotted out by the big story?

What else *did* happen in Malaysia that week? For one thing, there was a second airplane crash, but a very minor one, indeed, compared to the loss of the big passenger jet. The plane was an RAAF single-seater, and the pilot was saved. Considerably more important was a potential breakup of the National Front, a political coalition which had dominated politics in the country for some years. The Pan-Malayan Islamic Party was charged with defying the Front's leadership, and the supreme council of the Front was meeting to decide whether the Islamic Party should remain a member.

Among the crimes and court cases reported in the papers, the Bank Rakyat case stood out. This case resulted from the funding of a world title boxing match. Three men, including the former chief minister of Selangor, who was also chairman of Bank Rakyat, were found guilty of forging bank documents to raise money for the match. They appealed, but the result of that was a more severe rather than a lighter sentence.

Government officials were traveling in and out of the country on various missions. The King and Queen of Malaysia were visiting Selangor. The Foreign Minister went to Cambodia and Burma to explain the concept of ASEAN (the Association of Southeast Asia Nations) to those governments. The Deputy Minister of Primary Industries was off to Jakarta to attend a ministerial conference. The Minister of Primary Industries was just back from an international trade meeting in Geneva, much disappointed by what he called the "insincere attitude" of developed countries toward setting up an international commodities fund; he threatened to boycott such meetings in the future. The Deputy Law Minister was back from a twelve-day visit to Hong Kong, Singapore, Thailand, and the Philippines where he studied anti-drug efforts.

There were several interesting developments in education. The Education Ministry directed all schools to provide facilities for teaching Chinese or Tamil, in addition to the Malaysian tongue. It was decided to make Islamic studies a requirement in all teachers training colleges. The first convocation of the Universiti Teknoloji Malaysia was held amidst a magnificent display of Malay culture – and was boycotted by the *Chinese* students. And among other meetings underway, a regional educational conference on the problem of use of drugs was convened in Kuala Lumpur.

Some economic news was hopeful, some not. A few items: The sugar talks with Australia seemed to have been a failure. To preserve the natural environment, state governments agreed to establish permanent forest reserves. 54,000 million gallons of water were tapped from two dams to save paddy fields from drying up. A plan to fight pollution from palm oil mills was being put into effect. EEC had promised to help Malaysia find European trade partners. The finance Minister opened an international automobile exhibition. A modern tourist resort was to be built in Klang, and more room was being sought to expand Malaysia's two main ports.

And throughout the week, Malaysia was host to the ninth Asian Men's Basketball Championship.

Following the lead of the Malaysian papers, these might be selected as ten representative big stories of the week:

1. The MAS plane crash
2. The threatened breakup of the National Front
3. The Foreign Minister's visit to Cambodia and Burma
4. The Bank Rakyat case appeal
5. The Asian Basketball Championship
6. The RAAF jet crash
7. Visit of the King and Queen to Selangor
8. All schools directed to teach Chinese or Tamil
9. State governments agree to establish forest reserves
10. Cultural pomp at first convocation of the Technological University

How It Was Handled by the Wires and Newspapers

All the wires covered the jetliner crash, the foreign minister's visit, and the basketball tournament. Two wires in each case covered the National Front story, the Bank Rakyat case, and the RAAF jet crash. The last four stories did not appear on any of the wires, although some news not listed here *did* make the wires. The following chart illustrates the wire coverage, and also contains an estimate of wordage rounded to the nearest ten.

Story	Wire A	Wire B	Wire C	Wire D	Total Words
Jetliner Crash	X	X	X	X	24,540
Break in National Front			X	X	1,470
Foreign Minister's Visit	X	X	X	X	3,110
Bank Rakyat Case			X	X	740
Asian Basketball Championship	X	X	X	X	9,320
RAAF Jet Crash	X		X		570
King and Queen to Selangor					0
Schools to Teach Chinese or Tamil					0
Will Establish Forest Reserves					0
University Convocation					0
TOTAL					39,760

Let us say again that the figures above do not represent the entire news wires coverage from Malaysia that week. Some stories covered by the wires are not included in these ten. We shall mention some of them later.

	Bangkok Post	Ceylon Daily News	Dong-a Ilbo	Ettelaat	Kayhan International	Kompas	Korea Times	Philippine Daily Express	Sing Chew Jit Poh	Sing Tao Jih Pao	South China Morning Post	Statesman	Straits Times	Words
Jetliner Crash	x	x	x	x	x	x	x	x	x	x	x	x	x	91,204
Break in National Front									x	x	x		x	11,630
Foreign Minister's Visit	x						x				x		x	3,400
Bank Rakyat Case	x								x		x	x	x	9,143
Asian Basketball Championship	x	x	x			x	x	x	x		x		x	35,920
RAAF Jet Crash									x				x	1,200
King and Queen to Selangor														0
Schools to Teach Chinese or Tamil									x					1,767
Will Establish Forest Reserves														0
University Convocation														0
TOTAL														154,264

NOTE: Newspapers not listed carried none of these stories.

Now let us see how the daily newspapers handled this news. Three of the 14 papers outside Malaysia carried nothing whatsoever on Malaysia during the six days we analyzed. These were two of the Indian papers and the Philippine native language daily. All the others covered the crash, at levels varying from 50,000 words in the *Sing Chew,* of Singapore, to 250 words in the *Statesman,* of Calcutta. All but two of them covered the basketball tournament. The remainder of the coverage was spotty, as the preceding chart illustrates.

It is interesting to compare the relative amount of attention given by the wires and the papers to the different stories. The table follows is the percentage (of the total number of words) devoted to each story:

Percentage of words carried on the ten stories by:

Story	*Four International Wires*	*Sixteen Asian Dailies*
Jetliner Crash	61.7%	57.9%
Break in National Front	3.7%	7.8%
Foreign Minister's Visit	7.8%	2.3%
Bank Rakyat Case	1.9%	6.1%
Asian Basketball Championship	23.4%	24.0%
RAAF Jet Crash	1.4%	0.8%
King and Queen to Selangor	0.0%	0.0%
Schools to Teach Chinese or Tamil	0.0%	1.2%
Will Establish Forest Reserves	0.0%	0.0%
University Convocation	0.0%	0.0%
	(99.9%)	(100.1%)

The surprising thing is how close the wires and the newspapers came in their estimates of the relative value of the two most widely circulated stories. The dailies judged the possible breakup of the national coalition and the bank fraud case as a bit more important than did the wires, whereas the wires gave more attention to the foreign minister's trip than did the newspapers. Despite faithful coverage in Malaysia, neither the wires nor the newspapers paid much attention to the last four stories on the list, apparently considering them of chiefly local interest. The one exception was the Singapore Chinese paper which, probably thinking about its own Chinese audience, gave good play to the story about schools being required to offer work in Chinese. *Sing Tao* in Hong Kong did not pick up the story, nor did any of the other papers in the sample. Of course, the Singapore paper was close at hand; the faraway papers were dependent on the wires, and what the wires did not carry they could not carry either.

Although the crash and the basketball tournament monopolized the time, we have noted that the wires did carry stories other than those listed among the ten. There were several stories on whether the Concorde would be allowed to fly over Malaysian airspace to land in Singapore. As might be expected, this story won space in the Singapore papers, and was also used in the *South China Morning Post.* Several papers made brief mention of the "disappointment" over the treatment given Malaysia and other Asian countries at the European economic talks. A meeting was underway with Indonesia on border problems; there was discussion of joint training of customs officers and measures to be taken against smuggling. Negotiations on sugar prices were going on with Australia, and apparently failed. The regional meeting on drug use was reported on two wires. A heroin possessor was caned. In the midst of the men's basketball tournament, Malaysia was named as host of the women's basketball tournament also. The possibility of building factories for metal production was being studied. Southeast Asian countries were holding talks on rubber prices and other economic matters. There were reports of complaints against treatment of overseas Chinese in Malaysia, Indonesia, and the Philippines. These and a few other stories appeared on one or more wires, in addition to the daily reports of Malaysian rubber and tin prices, and the six stories from among the "ten".

Very few of them, however, got much attention in the dailies. The

Concorde matter was mentioned in several places, the regional economic meeting in at least one place in addition to Singapore, the regional meeting on drugs appeared in the *Straits Times,* the disappointment with economic treatment of Asian countries in several places, and several papers picked up a brief feature from one of the wires (during the preceding week) that a Muslim boy or girl might be sent to jail in Malaysia if caught stealing a kiss in public. So there was at least a chance to hear a bit more than the two large stories from Malaysia that week. But for most readers and most papers Malaysia appeared in the week of December 4 as the scene of a horrific crash of a hijacked jetliner, and the site of a large and exciting basketball tournament.

XIV. COVERAGE OF SOME NATIONAL LEADERS: GANDHI AND DESAI, SUHARTO, CASTRO

We thought it would be interesting to find out how the international news agencies and the Asian dailies covered some national leaders. The political leaders of France, England, and the United States, the home countries of the four international agencies, were not making news waves during our study week; it was therefore not a good week to examine their coverage. Of all the world's leaders, it was unquestionably Sadat who drew most attention from newsmen that week, and we have already suggested in Chapter XII the extensive coverage given his statements and actions. Throughout the rest of the week he continued to be quoted and reported, and there is little more to say than we have said about the coverage except that it was large and continuing. In Asia itself, however, there were some leaders in the news. Mrs. Gandhi and Prime Minister Desai were in less than friendly competition in India, with the political future of that country at stake. President Suharto was the object of repeated student demonstrations in Indonesia. The distribution and balance of Indian and Indonesian coverage would be interesting to look at. And for a Third World leader from outside Asia let us take Fidel Castro. He can hardly be thought of as a friend of the countries that own the international agencies; therefore, let us see how they handled his news during the week, and how it passed on into the Asian newspapers.

Two Portraits: Gandhi and Desai

During the week of December 4, Mrs. Gandhi was busy battling the Shah Commission. Mr. Desai was busy being Prime Minister. Or at least, that is the image that emerges from the news of the troubled situation in India. Yet always below the surface of these events is the reminder that the two were also battling each other, and Mrs. Gandhi's New Congress was battling the presently-in-power Janata Party.

It is interesting to watch the battle, round by round, in the international wire services:

December 4-5: Speaking to a symposium on "The relevance of Nehru today," Mrs. Gandhi denied that her opposition Congress Party was responsible for violent acts in the country. At her invitation, the

Party directed its members not to appear before the Commission. Wire D: 220 words.

December 5-6: The Shah Commission examined an intelligence report allegedly found in the office vacated by Mrs. Gandhi's secretary following the last election. The document indicated that the national intelligence bureau was keeping a close watch on some of Mrs. Gandhi's cabinet ministers who were believed not to be loyal to her. At another session of the Commission, several of the former cabinet ministers reported that Mrs. Gandhi did not consult her cabinet before declaring the state of emergency. The late President of India was reported to have signed the document although it was "constitutionally impermissable for him to do so without the advice of the Council of Ministers." On these two stories: Wire B, 820 words; Wire C, 340; Wire D, 80.

December 7: Mrs. Gandhi called the Shah Commission a "platform for malicious propaganda." She argued that no court sits in judgment on an Act of Parliament. The wire story said it looked as though Mrs. Gandhi and the Commission were headed toward a confrontation. *The Times of India,* in an editorial quoted by the wire, said that her argument may not be as flimsy as Mr. Justice Shah thinks, and could at least drag the case into the Supreme Court. On the same day, four New Congress politicians joined Mrs. Gandhi in refusing to appear before the Commission. On these events, two stories, Wire C, 590 words.

December 8: Jagjivan Ram, present defense minister and former member of Mrs. Gandhi's cabinet, testified before the commission about his movements being watched and his telephone tapped, during the Gandhi regime. The present Indian Ambassador to Moscow said he lost his government information job because he refused to let Sanjay Gandhi see in advance all news bulletins to be broadcast on All India Radio. Other cabinet ministers said they were not consulted on declaring the state of emergency. Three stories: Wire A, 290 words; Wire C, 290; Wire D, 300.

(Concurrently with these developments, it was reported that the former chief minister of Tamil Nadu and 23 of his supporters were released from jail, six weeks after their arrest on the charge of conspiring to murder Mrs. Gandhi when she came to Tamil Nadu for a political rally. Thousands cheered him when he came out of prison.)

December 9: One wire reported that (it was understood) the Shah Commission had definitely decided to summon Mrs. Gandhi formally to appear before it. Wire D, 260.

December 9: In her third letter in three weeks to the Shah Commission, Mrs. Gandhi protested against some remarks made about her by Charan Singh, home minister, and against the general procedures of the Commission. Two stories: Wire C, 290; Wire D, 260.

So much for the continuing battle between Mrs. Gandhi and the Commission. If a word count means anything, the score was approximately 2,400 for the Commission, 1,400 for Mrs. Gandhi. Now let us look at the coverage of Mr. Desai.

On December 6, he appeared before Parliament to answer questions on the Baroda nuclear plant explosion. He announced that a committee of experts was being appointed to investigate the cause of the explosion, and said that he did not suspect sabotage. Two stories: Wire C, 380; Wire D, 100.

On December 8, it was announced that the Prime Minister would leave on December 9 for a two-day visit to Nepal, to try to improve India's relations with that neighboring state. One Story: Wire C, 460.

On December 8, also, the Janata Party lost a vote in Parliament for the first time since it came to power nine months ago. The argument was on a measure which opponents felt went against the principle of nationalizing banks. Wire C, 170.

On December 9, Mr. Desai arrived in Nepal, and there were pleasant notes on his reception. He met the King, and held first official talks with the Prime Minister. No results were yet announced. Wire A, 160; Wire C, 290; Wire D, 350.

That adds up to about 4,000 words on the Gandhi-Shah story and 1,500 on Mr. Desai. So far as the wires tell the story, Mr. Desai is presented wholly in his official capacity: facing up to his country's problems, at home and abroad, and trying to get his bills through Parliament. Mrs. Gandhi is presented as an embattled, defiant woman, who feels she is being persecuted. The interesting feature of the coverage, however, is that, regardless of all the unpleasant facts being revealed before the Commission – spying on Cabinet ministers, forcing the declaration of a state of emergency through without consultation, trying to control the news bulletins that went on the air – nevertheless, the story is not told one-sidedly. She is quoted as often against the Commission as it is quoted against her. She defies the Commission, challenges its concept of its assignment, accuses it of being a vehicle for "malicious propaganda" rather than a legal body trying to establish truth and recommend justice. In other words, she is raising the question whether she is not being persecuted for political reasons, rather than criminal acts, and therefore should be an object of sympathy rather than blame. If anything, the wire editors are bending over backwards to treat her fairly.

But the portraits of these two people are clearer on the wires than in the newspapers.

Only four of the 15 dailies (omitting the Indian papers) covered these two people during our week. Four of the stories were in the *New Straits Times,* three on the *South China Morning Post,* two in *Kayhan International,* one in the *Straits Times* – all English-language papers, and all except *Kayhan* in Southeast Asia. The total was a little over 2,000 words.

On December 7, the *New Straits Times* told its readers about the New Congress members being told to boycott the Shah Commission. On December 8, it said that the Shah Commission was apparently headed for a showdown with Mrs. Gandhi – quoting some of what she said and some of the testimony, the most striking part of which was about the government intelligence agency spying on Mrs. Gandhi's cabinet members. 950 words. The one story on Desai came on 10 December, and told of the defeat of the Janata bill in Parliament. 410 words.

The *South China Morning Post* carried a story on December 9, focusing on the New Congress boycott of the Commission, and relating some of the facts that were coming out in testimony. On December 10, it said that Mrs. Gandhi remained defiant, despite the developments in the Commission, and quoted her protest against the threat that she might be arrested. Two stories: 740 words. The one mention of Desai came also on December 10, about 40 words, saying that he had arrived in Katmandu.

The *Straits Times* carried a brief story on December 8, built around the testimony that Mrs. Gandhi did not consult her cabinet before declaring a state of emergency. It was one column inch – about 30 words.

This was clearly a case in which the wire coverage was better overall than the newspaper coverage. The readers of the *New Straits Times* would have read a fairly adequate continuing story of the Shah-

Gandhi battle, and at least heard of some of Mr. Desai's troubles. The *South China Morning Post* also gave its readers some sense of what was going on, and mentioned Desai's visit to Nepal. The attention in the *Straits Times* was certainly minimal. In most others outside India: zero.

In other words, if our papers are representative examples, most Asian readers were not being shown *any* portraits of Mrs. Gandhi or Desai during the week of December 4.

The News Picture of Suharto

Bands of protesting students, rather than President Suharto, were the chief actors in the news from troubled Indonesia during the week of December 4.

Less than might have been expected was actually said about the President, either on the wires or in the newspapers. The emphasis was on the student demonstrations, although always with the President as implied target: for example, "pressures against the 12-year-old rule of President Suharto are mounting in Indonesia as students step up their campaign for clean government, fair law enforcement, and a more equal distribution of the nation's wealth" (Wire A, December 8). President Suharto was almost never quoted in answer to the students; usually Admiral Sudomo, the administrator of internal security, or "an official," commented on the protests. Yet an atmosphere of tension was building up in the student rhetoric: "We have reached the point of no return in our struggle to eliminate all those misdeeds and deviations." And the wire story quoted above, noted, almost as an aside, that "Students, with the backing of the army, spearheaded the movement to topple Sukarno in 1966."

All the wires were quite frank in reporting the rhetoric associated with the student demonstrations. For example, Wire C said that in a demonstration in Jogjakarta which ended in a confrontation with police, some students were reported to have worn teeshirts with the slogan, "Wanted – A New President for Indonesia." The same story said "Some 70 students from all over the country voiced strong criticism of President Suharto . . . Antara News Agency said one of the speakers at the meeting had said there were only three ways out of the present situation: constitutional reform, a coup d'etat, or a total 'cultural revolution'." Admiral Sudomo was quoted as commenting,

"This is normal"!

Along with the continuing student demonstrations, a dissenter named Sawito Kartiwibowo was on trial. He is a mystic and a devotee of the Javanese belief called Kebatinan, to which President Suharto himself adheres. The trial gave him an opportunity to voice his ideas and to call on President Suharto to resign and hand over the Presidency to the Vice-president. The trial attracted so much interest that loud-speakers were installed outside the courtroom to allow 2,000 more spectators to hear what Sawito had to say.

During this troubled week, President Suharto made two public appearances. On December 7 he opened a new road in Irian Java, saying the former Dutch colony had made more progress in 14 years of independence as a part of Indonesia than in 350 years of colonial rule. On December 8 he spoke at the dedication of a new oil field. He denied that large-scale social corruption was responsible for deterioration of the socio-economic situation in the country, but warned that people "must not have the wrong impression that Indonesia's oil is the answer for all development problems" (Wire D). Wire C took the same tone in reporting the speech: President Suharto "told Indonesians today that production of 1.6 million barrels of oil a day did not alone solve all the country's development problems . . . The national news agency Antara said the President's remark had been prompted by criticism that there was still a large number of unemployed in Indonesia . . . difficulties in promoting public education . . . a poor welfare system . . . despite increased earnings from oil. Criticism along these lines had in recent weeks come from student and youth organizations as well as from some sections of the armed forces and political establishment." Three of the international wires covered the oil field speech, and one the remarks at the road-opening. Altogether the wires devoted a little over 1,000 words directly to President Suharto, and about twice as much to the students demonstrations in which the President was a target rather than an actor.

When one turns from the wire coverage to the newspapers, the localness of Asian news interest is again apparent. Asia is a group of regions, rather than a region. Just as the East Asia papers paid little attention to the Bhutto story, so did the Western papers ignore the Suharto story. The dailies in our sample (omitting the Indonesian paper, of course) carried a little over 5,000 words on the Indonesia troubles during the week of December 4, but the coverage was concentrated on the East coast of Asia, and all except 300 words of it (which appeared in *Dong-a Ilbo,* of Seoul) were in Singapore, Malaysia, and Hong Kong.

The *South China Morning Post* printed just under 1,300 words, during the five days, on President Suharto and his troubles; the *New Straits Times,* about 650; *Nanyang Siang Pau,* 1,400; *Sing Chew Jit Poh,* just under 2,000; and the *Straits Times,* about 1,350. All these in three countries only.

In the second place, the newspapers appeared to be much more interested in the students than in what the President had to say about the protests. If the ratio of student coverage to Suharto coverage on the wires was two to one, in the newspapers it was nearer 10 to one. There was only one story that covered directly either of the President's speeches (*Sing Chew*). More typical were the big stories on December 9 in the *South China Morning Post,* "Restless Students Flay Suharto" (500 words), and the *New Straits Times,* "Students Step Up Anti-Suharto Drive" (900 words). The stories that let Suharto speak for himself were readily available on the wires, but the dailies preferred the student news. In other words, even more than the wires the newspapers chose to present the news of conflict.

An outside observer would call the coverage of the Indonesian situation on the wires better balanced than that in the newspapers. In the wires, President Suharto appears as a man in trouble, but concerned about the problems and trying to do something about them. In the papers he appears simply as a man in trouble. (And the story gets very little attention of any kind in more than half the dailies in our sample.) One of the best balanced treatments in the dailies took the form of an editorial in the *Straits Times,* on December 7. After pointing out that the trial of the mystic Sawito was proving an embarrassment to the President, the editorial continued:

> Even more disturbing to the authorities is the mounting wave of criticisms against the performance of the government spearheaded by university students who recently took to the streets in Jakarta, Bandung, and Surabaya to focus attention on the people's dissatisfaction and the current political and economic situation. So far government response to the student protests is increased vigilance by the military and security forces.

> In a country where the students have always played an active political role – they were in the vanguard in President Sukarno's ouster – and where they mirror the feeling of so much of the public, it will be well for the government to take quick and concrete measures to meet the grievances, where legitimate, of the people. No one doubts that Mr. Suharto will be re-elected to another term and it will be a sad day when the clamour of the disgruntled students reaches such a pitch as to obscure the very real achievements of the present administration especially in the economic field. To his credit, Mr. Suharto appears resolved not just to brush aside the criticisms but to tackle the sources of the students' dissatisfaction. He is wisely not taking his expected re-election for granted.

The Portrait of Castro

During the week of December 4, President Fidel Castro of Cuba was visited by two U.S. Congressmen who apparently carried him a message from President Carter, but departed without commenting either on the message or his reaction. President Castro also had a long interview, lasting until after midnight, with a group of newsmen. He was described as "visibly upset" by what Mr. Brezinski (U.S. Security Adviser) was reported to have said about Cuba's involvement in Africa. He said that Mr. Brezinski was "magnifying the problem" and "creating artificial barriers." He also gave an interview which the *New York Post* claimed as "exclusive," in which he said he was willing to meet President Carter at any time, but thought that meeting was unlikely to happen until Mr. Carter's second term.

Mr. Castro's relations with the United States, rather than the doings of the Cuban Legion in Africa, then, were the chief elements of his portrait as the wires brought it to Asia. The African ventures came into what was described as a "hard-hitting speech" by U.S. Ambassador Andrew Young to the United Nations, calling on Cuba and the U.S.S.R. to stop stirring up trouble in Africa.

There was also a feature story resurrected from the past. It was reported, and later confirmed, that Castro, as a young student at a private Catholic school in Cuba, had written to President Franklin D. Roosevelt, asking him for a souvenir ten dollar bill. He got no reply from FDR, and no ten dollar bill, but the American Ambassador in Havana wrote a polite and noncommital reply, which was posted on the school bulletin board. Castro told the reporters it made him "famous" with his schoolmates: he had an exchange with President Roosevelt!

Another story appeared that was not so funny. The FBI released a number of previously classified papers including one reporting that Castro had ordered the assassination of President John Kennedy. The origin of this allegation was supposed to have been the Spanish Intelligence Service. The Spanish Ambassador to Rome at that time, Senor Sanchez Bella, was reported to have shown the intelligence report in 1963 to an American columnist in Rome. Sanchez Bella denied this.

So the elements of Castro's portrait offered to Asia during the week of December 4 were really four: what he said through newsmen to the United States government about his ventures in Africa; what the United States representative to the United Nations said about Castro's policy with respect to Africa; the rumor about his relation to the assassination of President Kennedy; and the old feature story about his letter to FDR.

All these elements were covered by the wires, although no wire covered all of them. The total wire coverage ran just under 3,000 words. The late night interview and the *Post* interview, as might be expected, drew the most attention (about 1,000 words), Young's speech in the UN got about 600, and the rumor on the Kennedy assassination a little more. The old feature on the ten dollar bills got 300. There were also brief mentions of the visiting Congressmen.

Only a few newspapers carried any material. The *South China Morning Post* carried a little over 400 words and a picture on December 8. The story was headed "Castro: I'm Prepared to See Carter," and was put together from several wires, including material from the night interview and the visit of the Congressmen. Castro said the presence of his troops in Africa was not negotiable, but he was always willing to talk things over. The *SCMP* carried also nearly 400 words on Young's speech.

The *Philippine Daily Express* carried 410 words, using as the lead Castro's willingness to meet Carter.

The *Korea Times* published 320 words from the night interview, built on the lead that Castro would not withdraw his military advisers from Africa.

Both the Tehran papers covered the story of Castro's letter to

Roosevelt – *Kayhan International* in 164 words, *Ettelaat* in 30 column inches including 288 words of text, a large headline, and a photo reproduction of the letter. *Ettelaat* covered also Castro's interview with the *New York Post,* expressing his willingness to meet with Carter: 320 words.

The total coverage among the Asian dailies (five out of 18) was about 2,148. The word equivalent of the total space was about 2,800.

Castro's image, then, was both tough and conciliatory, for those in Asia who got to read about it. But not many seem to have had that privilege.

Summing Up

So we return to a theme we have heard before: There was greater richness available in the news than the readers of Asian dailies got to see. And by no stretch of reasoning or imagination can the blame for this be laid wholly upon the international news agencies.

Part Four

Concluding Comments

XV. SOME MODEST SUGGESTIONS

Let us return to the problem with which we began this book – dissatisfaction with the current circulation of information and the declared need of a "new world information order".

We have necessarily concentrated on only one part of that problem – the circulation of news. We have studied this on only one continent – Asia. And we have examined the flow of news into and among only the Third World countries of Asia.

It goes without saying, therefore, that we have not looked at the whole problem. We have said nothing, for example, about the circulation of entertainment in the form of films, television tapes, and music recordings; of the exchange of books and magazines; or of the flow of digital information to and from computers which, in size and cost, may soon be the largest component of the total circulation of information. We have said little about other developing regions of the world; thus we do not know whether the same patterns of news we have seen in Asia apply also to Africa, and, although we know something about the circulation of African news in Asia, we have very little information about Asian news in Africa. And we have not been able to examine in any detail the flow of Third World news into the industrial West, although we have assembled a great deal of information about the flow of news from the Western countries into Third World Asia.

Thus we have presented a study of Third World news on one continent. It is a continent, however, on which more than half of all the world's people live, and where all the principal objections to the present world information order have been raised eloquently and vigorously. In Asia, as in the rest of the Third World, the international news agencies have been at the center of the controversy over news, and we have kept them so, even while we tried to describe the larger pattern of which they are a part.

As we have worked through our data, certain conclusions have become clearer than they were when we started:

1. The circulation of news in Third World Asia cannot be understood or assessed wholly in terms of the international news agencies or any other single element in the process.

We assume this applies also to other regions of the Third World, but the only region about which we can speak confidently is Asia.

Pran Chopra, a wise and experienced Asian newsman, came to this same conclusion in a paper he wrote for the Unesco Colombo conference on the development of news agencies in Asia. He said:

> International news flows into, out of and within Asia are mainly supplied by the main western news agencies. But to the extent that in supplying Asian or non-Asian foreign news to Asian audiences the western news agencies are themselves guided by what they believe to be the need of their Asian customers, that is Asian news agencies and other Asian news media, an examination of the work and values of the western agencies inevitably merges into an examination of the news values, judgements, criteria, preferences of the journalists working in the Asian media.

Concerning the Asian media, he adds:

> In Asia, as anywhere else, a gate which frequently regulates the flow of news can be named "What Sells", and in Asia too that name carries both of its two meanings: which news will interest most readers, and also which news will make the newspaper or other media most attractive to the advertiser. Alongside this gate stands in Asia too a gate which can be named "Public Interest", that is not merely what will but what should interest the public, that is what is in its interest to know according to the judgement of the journalist. In Asia too, as much as in Europe, both these gates are suddenly, abruptly replaced by another gate, which is not only erected in and on the frontier of those countries, a gate which does not regulate the flow of information according to what interests most the readers but according to criteria quite unrelated to what the rest of the world understands by news values. This gate can be named "State Policy", meaning current policy on what should be told when, by whom, to whom, by what means and whether and how it should conform to facts . . . (Chopra, 1977, pp. 1,4)

Our conclusion, like that of Chopra, is that it is far too simple to approach the problem of news circulation by regarding the Asian media as the only aggrieved parties, and the international agencies as the sole offenders.

For one thing, that leaves out one of the most important elements in the process, the readers. Our greatest disappointment with the data we were able to put together is that it included only one readership study. We hope there will soon be more information on the reading of news in the Third World. The daily newspaper editor's perception of what readers *want*, and his or his government's perception of what they *need* to know, is basic to what a newspaper is going to carry. As Frank Giles, deputy editor of *The Times of London*, wrote last year: "In the last resort, it is readers who determine the character of newspapers, not proprietors and their whims, or even boards of managment in a monopoly position."* (Giles, 1978, p. 31) This is the case in Asia as in England, in the Third World as in the industrial world. In England the editor may have more degrees of freedom, but the *Times* of India and the *Straits Times* of Singapore must be as aware of their readers as is The *Times*.

In the preceding pages we have seen that the international news agency wires carry a great deal more foreign news – from the Third World as well as the industrial countries, from Asia as well as countries outside Asia, development news as well as other types of news – than even the most distinguished and prosperous dailies of Asia can or do print. The daily prints more – a great deal more – than any of its users read. Both the dailies and the readers have good reasons for making the decisions about news they do. The readers are understandably more likely to be interested in news that is psychologically and geographically near to them. The dailies therefore carry a great deal of local and national news, and have limited space for foreign wire news no matter how important it is by objective standards. They have limited staffs for rewriting and re-editing foreign news. If they publish in a language other than English their time is further limited by the problem of translation from the wires. They can seldom afford to send correspondents to foreign news centers. And they have pressures on them, from government or elsewhere, to publish this and not that, less of this, more of that.

The news agencies therefore operate under a number of restraints imposed by their clients and the clients' readers, and also by the nature

---

* Which echoes the conclusion of another European student of the media, John Whale, "The broad shape and structure of the press is determined by no-one but its readers." (Whale, 1977, p. 181)

of their task and their resources. They are trying to cover an almost infinite spectrum of events in a finite space. Gerald Long, the general manager of the Reuter agency, said recently, "We are sometimes accused of not doing what we have not set out to do. How can you give a complete picture of India, say, in 3,000 words a day? No, we're not and we can't . . . We must operate on the principle of news as exception. Reuters tries to give a fair picture, a rounded picture, but we can only send a limited amount, and we must be selective." (Long, quoted in Rosenblum, 1977, p. 16) Thus, although 34,000 words of foreign Third World news per day on the Reuter wire seems like a great deal, divide it by 120 countries and it comes out to less than 300 words per country per day. If India gets 300 words, some other countries will get nothing. If each of 17 major Third World countries of Asia got 3,000 words each, that would more than fill the news space available on an average international wire. Therefore, hard decisions must be made. The news agencies are driven toward defining news, in Long's words, as "exception" – that is, extraordinary events rather than ordinary ones, timely rather than timeless ones, not what a country is, but what unusual events are occurring there. We are not saying this is necessarily the ideal concept of news; it is simply the position to which the agencies are pushed by pressures of limited space, deadlines, and the perceived needs of their clients.

Our observation has been that the international news agencies do try to serve the needs of their clients in Asia as they see these needs. We saw repeated examples – the Indian cricket match in Australia is one – where wires carried long stories, although these could have been of interest only to India and a few other cricket countries. Strangely enough, this service is not by any means motivated wholly by commercial considerations. It is believed to be the case that all the international agencies lose money on their Asian news services. Only 1 per cent of the Associated Press budget comes from sale of the news wire in Asia. AP's foreign service is subsidized by its 1,700 U.S. subscribers. Reuter finds its financial service profitable, although its news service is not. As Jeremy Tunstall says, "The governmental spokesman who complains about the depredations of the Anglo-American news agencies is often unaware that the Central Bank across the street finds Reuters Economics Services indispensable." (Tunstall, 1978, p. 1) The agencies would be happy to break even on the cost of their Asian news wires: but what they really want is access to the news. They set out to cover the world. Their clients expect a world-wide service. Therefore they have every reason to try to stay in the good graces of the national agencies, newspapers, and broadcasting newsrooms they serve.

So we have to confess that we have not found any one villain or any one hero in this situation. It isn't a question of one or the other being solely at fault; the entire system is less than ideal. The international agencies have taken the brunt of criticism in the Third World probably not so much for what they have or have not done, but for what they *are:* like other transnational enterprises owned in the industrial countries, they are haves amidst have-nots, and they come from outside.

However, when one analyzes the performance of the international wires he comes to the conclusion that:

2. The international news agencies are probably doing a better job quantitatively than qualitatively.

An enormous amount of news is flowing over these wires – over 200,000 words a day, an average of 407 stories, on the Third World, a little more than that on non-Third World countries. The wires are more likely to carry news from one side of Asia to the other – for example, Indian news to the Philippines, Philippine news to India – than the dailies of the distant receiving countries are to print it. Even in the case of development news, where the international agencies have come in for harsh and not entirely undeserved criticism, the performance of the wires is no worse than that of the dailies, which are surprisingly uninterested in development news from outside their own countries. One of the most significant findings of this study has been the large amount of unused news on the wires. So far as quantity goes, the wires offer Asian editors and broadcasters a far more complete view of daily events in the world than the editors and broadcasters give their listeners.

It is simply not true that the transnational news agencies (at least insofar as their Asian wires are representative) "devote only 20 to 30 per cent of their news coverage to the developing countries" (as Masmoudi says); nearly 50 per cent of the Asian wires are devoted to developing countries. It is not true that Third World news is only 15 per cent of the output of the transnational agencies (as El-Sherif says, quoting a Unesco study); on the Asian wire, as we have said, it is nearly one half, and 58 per cent of the Third World news that comes to Asian clients is from Asia. It is not even true that they contain "little information related to development needs" (as Gunter says). Their development news service could certainly be improved qualitatively; but *quantitatively* – on these and other measures – they come out pretty well.

Quantitative measures are easy; qualitative ones are more difficult. It is in this latter area of performance that Western news agencies are most vulnerable. And in this area that the principal authors of this report feel least competent to judge performance because we too have come up through the Western tradition of news coverage and news writing, and the chief objections to the agencies' qualitative performance are that they apply Western news standards which are not entirely suitable in the Third World, and that they are not prepared to understand and interpret Third World cultures. For understandable reasons, therefore, we have been reluctant to analyze news stories line by line, an exercise that might better be undertaken jointly by Asian and Western newsman.

With the possible exception of development news, we have seen little reason to fault the international agencies for lack of professionalism in their Third World coverage. They seemed to us to do well on stories as different as the crash of a hijacked jet, the Tripoli meeting, Gandhi and Desai, and the news from China. In fact they looked better on these stories than most of the Asian newspapers did. Asian newsmen themselves, as V.G. Kulkarni said, do not "question the credibility or objectivity of established agencies who have more than a century's experience behind them". But he adds, "This is merely to state that their perceptions, like those of the people from other parts of the world, are tinted by their own societal values." (Kulkarni, 1977. p. 8)

Western journalists also recognize this problem. For example, here is Frank Giles, of *The Times*, whom we quoted earlier: "It is not the purpose of this report to get into the controversy about third world news agencies, and non-aligned news pools. But the arguments that have been advanced along these lines cannot be set aside. Reporting the developing world, with all its economic, social, political, ethnic and other problems, through the eyes and pen of the developed world is bound to be, for the most part, an unsatisfactory business, involving, at the worst, an incomplete or unsatisfactory picture. There is, of course, no such thing as 'objective' reporting; every writer and journalist will, to a certain degree, reflect his own personality and upbringing, his education, his cultural background, in assessing and describing the scene or situation which he has been sent to report upon." (Giles, 1979, p.22)

This is no less stern a judgment than that of many Asian newsmen themselves. Here is another quote from Kulkarni, who is an Asian newsman of long experience, and presently the senior editor of *Depthnews* and Hong Kong representative of the Press Foundation of Asia. He told the Columbo meeting on news agencies in Asia: "Western wire services do not make a secret of the fact that their coverage of the entire world is dictated by Western news values, tastes and demands of the audiences of the industrialized West. Moreover they are not in it for altruism or for any lofty ideals of East-West understanding. The agencies have to make money to foot their bills. The overwhelming part of their revenues come from the West. Those who pay the piper call the tune." (Kulkarni, 1977, p. 7)

Asian observers object to the unpleasant accounts of the Third World that Western concepts of news led the agencies to present. For example, here is the statement of an Asian news broadcaster, quoted by E.L. Sommerlad: (Audiences in Asia receive) "news films of catastrophes, political trouble, human suffering and misery . . . brought into the living room . . . night after night. By now an Asian viewer must be convinced that he is living in a much troubled world. He has yet to be exposed to the positive, or should I say the brighter side of things on his own continent such as news about improved living standards, better health facilities, greater spread of knowledge, and perhaps even a little more happiness among Asia's teeming millions." (Personal communication from Sommerlad, 1978).

In the voice of Dilip Mukerjee, another Asian newsman, this objection becomes almost a cry of pain:

> Our need is urgent and acute (says Mukerjee). We belong to societies which are in the process of restructuring and reshaping themselves. In our environment there is and there will be for a long time to come,

> much that is ugly and distasteful. If we follow the western norm, we will be playing up only those dark spots, and thus helping unwittingly to erode the faith and confidence without which growth and development are impossible. (Quoted in Tharoor, 1977, p. 29)

Thus the dissatisfaction of Asians with the international agencies is not only with the negative news that their Western news standards lead them to report, but also with their lack of response to what seems to Third World observers almost a duty to contribute to the growth and betterment of life in Third World countries. These points are made by Narinder K. Aggarwala, of the United Nations Development Program:

> The media, particularly the news agencies, will have to cure, at least partially, their all-pervasive obsession with so-called "action" or "spot" news, and not with "soft" or "development" news. Disasters, famines, corruption, wars, political intrigue, and civil disorders do make for action-packed and "sexy" copy while economic and social development is a very slow and, over short periods, an almost imperceptible process . . .
>
> The lack of a Third World perspective is obvious in the manner in which Western journalists, rightly or wrongly, discuss the problems, such as employment, food, population, etc., confronting the developing countries. Their reports, more often than not, either ignore or belittle the efforts of developing countries, to alleviate the problems, often against seemingly insurmountable odds. (Aggarwala, 1977, p. 181)

Aggarwala is talking about development news. But what exactly *is* development news? He answers that question straightforwardly:

> . . . Development news? An all-inclusive definition is not easy to provide. It is not identifical with "positive" news. In its treatment, development news is not different from regular news or investigative reporting. It can deal with development issues at micro and macro levels. In covering the development newsbeat, a journalist should critically examine, evaluate, and report the relevance of a development project to national and local needs, the differences between a planned scheme and its actual implementation, and the differences between its impact on people as claimed by the government officials and as it actually is.

> Development journalism is the use of all journalistic skills to report developmental processes in an interesting fashion. It may require high skills and hard work but the rewards of this kind of journalism can be tremendous. It could almost lead to the humanization of international news. It could help to lower the walls of intense suspicion and distrust that have arisen between Third World political leaders and the media. (Aggarwala, *ibid.*, p. 181)

This kind of reporting is not alien to Western news norms and practices. It does, however, make two requirements of the reporter: that he find time to do the investigation, and that he have sufficient knowledge of economics and related subjects to interpret development news in depth. It is not easy, working under the threat of wire or newspaper deadlines, to meet the first of these requirements, even if one can meet the second. Our observation has been that the second requirement is also in short supply. Thus it is no accident that the new economic plan in Sri Lanka should be covered in the first instance not by the wires nor by nearby newspapers, but rather by a writer for a British syndicated service who perceived the importance of the plan and had time to write 800 words on it. And it is less than surprising that development news within a culture foreign to the reporter should not always be reported in a manner satisfactory both to the culture where the news takes place and the culture represented by the reporter.

It is very difficult for outsider like us to put ourselves into the minds and values of Asian peoples in order to look at events from their viewpoint, and make a judgment from their standards on the quality and fairness of reporting on their cultures. We recognized our own failures in this respect and hesitated to make such judgments. What seems to us as, most importantly, *professional* news coverage, may often seem to the people of a Third World country as, most importantly, *foreign* news coverage. We did note with some interest that the prestige newspapers of Asia paid about as much attention to accidents, disasters, crimes, and judicial proceedings as the international wires did. We noted with some interest that development news was not as high priority with Asian readers as might have been expected in view of all that has written about the lack of it. We asked some Malaysians to criticize stories about Malaysia, Indians to criticize stories about India, Chinese to criticize stories about China, and so forth.

Most of them found things they did not like, but there was little generality in their critiques except the "bad news rather than good" objection, and the disparaging comment that "this reporter just doesn't know enough about Malaysia" or India, or whatever country was represented. There were few if any comments about the skill or the intended fairness and accuracy of the reporting. These qualitative criticisms are very hard for us to handle, just as they must be hard for the international agencies to respond effectively to. Yet they are legitimate, and we shall have a suggestion to make, later in this chapter, concerning what might be done about them.

A third conclusion follows from what we have been saying about qualitative considerations:

3. The Third World countries will probably never be satisfied with the quality of their own news coverage until they have their own news agency.

This is quite understandable. In Chapter I we quoted Kent Cooper's statement on how frustrated were Americans, a century ago, when U.S. news was prepared and circulated by a European cartel of news agencies. Lloyd Sommerlad spoke to the same point for Asians in a paper on "Free Flow of Information", written while he was still an active member of the Unesco communication staff. "So far as news is concerned," he said,

> the main problem is that selection and orientation or 'angling' is done in distant places by journalists who, even if reporting objectively, have news values which are not shared by their agency's Third World clients. Whatever the quality of big news agencies' services, there is a widespread resentment in many developing countries. Against their dependence on external organizations, in whose running they have no voice, who select news according to a foreign philosophy, and whom rightly or wrongly, they do not fully trust. (Sommerlad, 1977, p. 9)

Thus it is a problem on the one hand of discontent with the quality of some news selection and interpretation, on the other of hurt pride at not having the right to do anything about it. The somewhat ill-considered statement of the president of the Associated Press that "we are not going to cover Africa for the Africans" has been quoted again and again as an example of the big agencies' lack of concern with their Third World clients and news sources. We know from our experience with the data of this study that the quotation does not represent the agency attitude throughout the Third World. We have seen numerous occasions in which an agency provided special service to an Asian country (for example, the extensive coverage for India of the cricket match in Australia), and our observation has been that the agencies have been rather more concerned during the last few years than previously with the needs of their Asian clients. Yet the feeling to which we have referred is general in the Third World, and an example is this statement by the director of news and current affairs for the Nigerian Broadcasting Corporation. News flow, he said, was clearly not set up to benefit Africans.

> The prime object of each news agency's operations in Africa has been and still is the collection of news for distribution to the world market. Their only concern is to sell the composite news output of their organization to local news media. The special needs of the African mass media are given no, or at best secondary consideration, so far as African news is concerned. (Olasope, 1977, quoted by Hester, 1978, p.3)

That was a newsman, rather than a political person speaking. It is easy to imagine that the comments of Third World ministers and directors of national information might be less restrained than Mr. Olasope's.

Thus it is only reasonable to anticipate the formation of one or more Third World news agencies, able to represent Third World cultures and responsible to Third World nations if their performance is not satisfactory. Yet such an agency, or such agencies, are not going to come into existence quickly. The Third World "news pools" are merely interim devices looking toward full-fledged agencies some years in the future. To assemble the resources, the skills, and workable policies for such organizations will take some time. And the necessary financing is something most Third World countries do not now have.

It seems to us probable that the formation of regional Third World agencies will precede the creation of a worldwide Third World agency, if indeed such a worldwide agency ever comes into existence. We are talking about perhaps one hundred countries that could legitimately think of themselves as the Third World. A news agency trying to represent all those special needs and interests, would be a ponderous thing, difficult to manage and staff, and its output might seem little more satisfying to an individual country than the present output of the international agencies. Ideally, a country wants its own agency, as the U.S. does, and Britain and France do. Even an agency representing 17 or more nations in Asia would have a hard time satisfying all its owners, but that task would be a great deal easier for such a regional organization than for an organization required to represent *all* the developing regions of the world. We can foresee that the countries of Southeast and East Asia, and perhaps all of Asia, might feel able to join in such an undertaking, and it should not take too many years to bring it about.

During that interim period, however, and certainly before anything like a worldwide Third World news agency would seem to be possible, the Third World countries will have to continue to rely mostly on the international news agencies. In that period, considering present attitudes and the amount of unused news on the international wires, it should be possible to arrive at a meeting of minds on what the Third World countries of Asia most need and what the international news agencies can furnish. We shall have more to say about this.

It is obvious that any steps toward a regional or worldwide Third World news agencies will require a great deal of preparation. Funding will have to be assured and technical facilities provided. Less obvious, perhaps, are the requirements of providing trained and skilled staff, and deciding on a number of policy questions.

The working paper for the intergovernmental conference on communication policies in Asia and Oceania, sponsored by Unesco and held in Kuala Lumpur February 5-14, 1979, stated quite matter-of-factly a very big job remaining to be done:

> . . . for disseminating national information as well as for providing the supporting services for fast expanding international and national telecommunication networks, personnel requirements have had to be reassessed in all countries of the region . . . The demands of government alone have far outstripped the initial "stockpile" of experienced journalists and media men in many countries which had begun to develop their own communication systems soon after attaining independence. Training programs have not always been able to match the requirements

> – quantitatively or qualitatively.
> (There is a) critical shortage of relevant and suitable training and other reading materials, including manuals and textbooks . . . Although training centers have increased in number, many of them lack the necessary equipment and adequately trained staff . . . There are obviously not enough specialized teachers . . . (Unesco, 1979, p. 39)

The industrialized countries could obviously help with this job of training and preparation, and yet if possible the training should be conducted in the Third World countries so that the needs and restrictions can always be front and center in the course. As Giles said in his essay for the International Commission for the Study of Communication Problems, even if adequate amounts of training can be provided for journalists from the Third World, either within their own frontiers or abroad, "the question still remains as to the sort of training which is needed". (Giles, 1978, p. 21) Too many Asians, trained in journalism in countries like the United States, with the new technology of communication readily available and allowed to become accustomed to the Western norms of free press and criticism of government, have been frustrated when they went home, and in many cases have drifted away from the news media to better paying and less restrictive jobs in government service or public relations. Furthermore, the special needs of substantive knowledge for the writing of development news must be met. And it will not be sufficient to wait ten years until new classes of journalism students can be trained and put into jobs; it is necessary to offer the opportunity of additional and perhaps part-time training to journalists already on the job.

Beside tooling up for the job it will be necessary to establish policies concerning some delicate questions of operation. One of these is the extent to which the operators of a Third World agency will be free to choose what seem to them the most newsworthy events of the day, and the extent to which they will be expected to balance out the news coverage over all the sponsoring countries. A news agency owned by a number of sovereign states can hardly operate as it could with single ownership. A still more difficult problem will be the extent to which the agency will specialize in the kind of depth reporting, relatively timeless stories, rather than the "spot news", the stories of "exception", the striking and startling news events that fill so much space in the present international agencies. Some of the Asian newsmen with whom we have discussed this problem have tended to feel that providing interpretive stories which are less dependent on a particular time peg may be the most valuable service a Third World agency could perform, and one in which they could usefully supplement the Western wires. It remains to be seen how much the Asian news media will make use of interpretive stories in competition with spot news. The most difficult and important question of all, however, will probably be the relationship of governments to the news. If a Third World agency proves to be chiefly a vehicle for news which individual governments think should be carried, for their own reasons, its popularity and usefulness in other countries will be dubious. On the other hand, the most frequent complaint about present news circulation is that Third World governments and national policies are not being represented fairly and fully in the news that goes out from their countries. El-Sherif, who himself represents a Third World country and whom we have quoted before, sees "a new international communication order" in a perspective which, we fear, is idealistic rather than realistic, but is worth quoting because it meets both sides of the problem. Such a new order, in order to be fair and meaningful, he says, must

> take into consideration the valid arguments of both sides. It will have to cultivate in the developing countries an open-door policy toward news, it will have to struggle to lift all forms of censorship, and to guarantee the freedom of the mass media. It will also have to find the ways and means, and create the systems and lay down the principles, by which more news about the development processes of the Third World countries are projected in the media of the industrial world. (El-Sherif, 1978, p. 7)

Steps toward that kind of solution will probably be slow and hesitant. In the meantime, however, steps *can* be taken.

With those in view, we should like to make some modest suggestions.

1. *Dialogue between newsmen.* One of the most useful results of the debate over the international news agencies, has been to stimulate some frank talk between newsmen of the developing countries and newsmen of the so-called developed countries. We

wonder whether the time has not come to repeat in modern form something that the International Press Institute did in the 1950s. The IPI asked a few editors from non-Western countries to read the news of their countries that appeared in a few Western newspapers, and similarly a few western editors to read what a few non-Western papers were reporting about *their* countries, and in each case to comment on the fullness and fairness of the coverage. It is easier now to travel than it was in the 1950s, and it would seem to us that a modern version of the IPI experiment would be to bring together a group of outstanding editors from the Third and the non-Third Worlds, to talk about the coverage of their countries in each other's papers, after reading them for, say, a month before coming to the meeting. This should produce frank dialogue by well-known persons that would be reported widely, and could well be recorded on videotape for later use in meetings or training programs.

2. *Dialogue between news agencies and their users.* Bearing in mind that approximately nine-tenths of the news on the international wires does not get into the newspapers or news broadcasts of their Third World clients, we wonder whether anything could be done to establish a meeting of minds on how the content of the news services might be made more useful. As we have said, our observation has been that the agencies are seriously trying to meet the needs of their clients in Asia as well as their clients in the home country. At the same time, they are being criticized for Western news norms and styles, and for not paying enough attention to the interests of non-Western countries. There should be some leeway in that large amount of unused wire copy for change if the parties can decide on the change. Therefore, just as we suggested that editors might meet to talk over the coverage of their countries in each other's newspapers, so it would seem useful to have a series of meetings, under whatever auspices and in whatever style seemed most suitable, between agency news representatives and Third World news media representatives. And we should suggest that, just as the editors could profitably talk about the news contents of each other's newspapers, so the news agency people and the Third World news people might base their talks on a few days of the wire news file, so that they could cite specifics rather than generalities.

3. *Assistance in training staff for a Third World agency.* Roger Tatarian (1978) has advanced a plan by which Third and non-Third

World news agencies and newspaper might second able staff members for a period of a year or more to a proposed Third World news agency, to share their expertise, join in the necessary planning, and offer in-service training to the nucleus of a permanent staff. This plan has been well enough received to encourage us to believe that Western agencies and newspapers, at least, would be willing to cooperate in some form of assistance, whether sending staff members to help with a new agency or receiving Third World newsmen for experience with existing agencies. It is conceivable also that short courses might be arranged, within Asia or elsewhere, in which news agency staff members might share their experience with prospective staff of a Third World agency. Things like this would require some financing, but we have observed a highly positive attitude toward giving help in any reasonable way.

4. *Training writers for development news.* In the preceding pages we have several times mentioned the apparent scarcity of reporters and editors trained in the economics and political sociology necessary for writing with insight about economic and social development. Newsmen are much more likely to be trained to write about politics than economics, and about judicial and legislative matters than about development. One way, a slow but important way, toward increasing competence in development news within agency, newspaper, and broadcasting staffs is to add such a component of training to journalism curricula, both in developed and developing countries. Still another way is to prepare some readings, and where possible to offer evening or other extension teaching in the economics of development, with the course tailored specially to the *news* of development. These approaches are not expensive; we know from past experience how to do them, and it seems a pity, when there is a shortage of such training, not to make use of what we know about how to meet the need.

5. *Some studies of readers.* We hesitate to introduce a research topic here in the midst of these action suggestions, but, as we have said, we were loathe to rest what we had to say about newspaper readership in Asia on a single study. Readership studies are far from impractical; in countries like the United States they proved their value 30 years ago. Both editors and advertisers learned things they had hardly suspected about what people read, what kind of people read what kind of news or advertising, and how location or display affects the amount of reading. We suspect that at least a handful of such studies in Asia, and

at least a few more in other Third World regions, would be most illuminating to the individuals who handle the news.

6. *A suggestion about existing agencies.* We have said that Third World newsmen and government officials will probably never be satisfied with the circulation of news from their own countries until they have their own agency or agencies. We have also said that this is not likely to happen tomorrow. At the same time we have been making suggestions leading toward regional Third World agencies, and perhaps ultimately to a world-wide agency representing needs and interests of the Third World. Nothing we have said along that line should be interpreted to mean that we foresee the pending demise of the international agencies. Certainly the news media of Asia are now dependent upon these agencies, and will probably be so for the foreseeable future. Just as important is the fact that the Western countries are dependent upon them for knowledge of the Third World. At this time of all times, the Western countries need to widen and deepen the base of news on which they rest their understanding of the Third World. At this time in the world's history the "capacity to inform", as Tinbergen said, must be widened, not shrunk. "More attention must in future be focused on information and education," he said; it is a "survival fact that the claim of the whole is wider and deeper than the claim of any of its parts." (Tinbergen, quoted in McBride Commission Report, 1978, p. 62) The international channels of news are not merely information lines; they are lifelines! And therefore, it is for the good of all countries that the international circulation of news be as full and reliable as possible. On the one hand, let us hope that the Third World countries will do everything possible to maintain access to the news by the international carriers. On the other, let us hope that, in the words of a wise Third World spokesman who prefers to be nameless, we can learn to "approach other people and their cultures and traditions with tolerance, humility, open-mindedness and the willingness to learn".

Part Five

Appendix

APPENDIX A: The Newspapers, the News Agencies, the Countries

A1. THE NEWSPAPERS

HONG KONG

Sing Tao Jih Pao

Publisher: Sally Aw Sian. Editor: Chu Ting. Morning. Chinese language. Circulation: 100,000. 17 columns, 1.2 inches wide. Offset.

South China Morning Post

Publisher: G. A. Pilgrim. Editor: R. G. Hutcheon. Morning. English language. Circulation: 55,000. 9 columns, 1.5 inches wide. Offset.

INDIA

Amrita Bazar Patrika (Calcutta)

Publisher: P. K. Roy. Editor: Tusher Gouti Ghosh. Morning. English language. Circulation: 108,963. 8 columns, 4.87 cm. wide. Letterpress.

Ananda Bazar Patrika (Calcutta)

Publisher: Bapparditya Roy. Editor: Asoke Kumar Sakar. Morning. Bengali language. Circulation: 298,660. 8 columns, 4.85 cm. wide. Letterpress.

The Statesman (Calcutta and New Delhi)

Publisher: S. C. Bhattacharya. Editor: S. Nihal Singh. Morning. English language. Circulation: 173,000 (Delhi edition, 187,012). 8 columns, 4.85 cm. wide. Letterpress.

INDONESIA

Kompas (Jakarta)

Publisher: P. K. Ojong. Editor: Jakob Oetama. Morning. Indonesian language. Circulation: 260,000. 9 columns, 4.2 cm. wide. Offset.

IRAN

Ettelaat (Tehran)

Publisher: Farhad Masoudi. Editor: Hosein Bani-Ahmad. Afternoon. Farsi language. Circulation: 300,000. 10 columns, 3.5 cm. wide. Letterpress.

Kayhan International (Tehran)

Publisher: Mrs. Forough Mesbahzadeh. Editor: Kazem Zarnegar. Morning. English language. Circulation: 57,000. 8 columns, 4.5 cm. wide. Letterpress.

KOREA (SOUTH)

Dong-a Ilbo (Seoul)

Publisher: Lee Dong-woon. Editor: Koon Oh-ki. Afternoon. Korean language. Circulation: 800,000. 17 columns, 3 cm. wide. Letterpress.

Korea Times (Seoul)

Publisher: Chang Kang-jae. Editor: Chung Tae-yun. Morning. English language. Circulation: 50,000. 8 columns, 4.4 cm. wide. Letterpress.

MALAYSIA

Nanyang Siang Pau (Kuala Lumpur)

Publisher: Harry Toh Ching Kiong. Editor: Chu Chee Chuan. Morning. Chinese language. Circulation: 96,583 weekdays, 119,272 Sunday. 18 columns; page size: 52.7 cm. x 38 cm. Offset.

New Straits Times (Kuala Lumpur)

Publisher: New Straits Times Press. Editor: Lee Siew Yee. Morning. English language. Circulation: 320,000. 10 columns; page size: 56 cm. x 10 columns. Offset.

PHILIPPINES

Bulletin Today (Manila)

Publisher: Hans Menzel. Editor: Ben F. Rodriguez. Morning. English language. Circulation: 243,000 weekdays, 279,000 Sunday. 9 columns, 3.8 cm. wide. Letterpress and Offset.

Philippine Daily Express (Manila)

Publisher: Juan A. Perez, Jr. Editor: Enrique P. Romalduez. Morning. English language. Circulation: 55,000. 9 columns, 3.6 cm. wide.

Pilipino Express (Manila)

Publisher: Juan A. Perez, Jr. Editor: Enrique P. Romalduez. Morning. Tagalog language. Circulation: 42,173. 5 columns, 5 cm. wide. Offset.

SINGAPORE

Sing Chew Jit Poh

Publisher: Aw It Haw. Editor: Frank Wong Yut Wah. Morning. Chinese language. Circulation: 170,000. 18 columns, 2.8 cm. wide. Offset.

Straits Times

Publisher: The Straits Times Press. Editor: T. S. Khoo. Morning. English language. Circulation: 173,447. 10 columns, 3.8 cm. wide. Offset.

SRI LANKA

Ceylon Daily News (Columbo)

Publisher: Associated Newspapers of Ceylon. Editor: D. D. Wettasinghe. Morning. English language. Circulation: 55,000. 8 columns, 11.5 cm wide. Letterpress.

THAILAND

Bangkok Times (Bangkok)

Publisher: Post Publishing Company, Ltd. Editor: Michael J. Gorman. Morning. English language. Circulation: 21,000. 8 columns, 1.75 inches wide. Offset.

Sources of Information: For all papers except *Ettelaat* and *Kayhan International, Asian Press* and *Media Directory,* 1978 (approximately current with test week, December 4-10, 1977), published by the Press Foundation of Asia. For *Ettelaat* and *Kayhan International,* all data were obtained from copies of the papers published during the test week, except for estimates of circulation. Estimates of circulation were provided by a former publisher of the Kayhan Group. Estimates of circulation for *Dong-a Ilbo* and *Korea Times* provided by Young Myung-ko, Chief Editor, Hankook Ilbo, New York.

A2. THE FOUR INTERNATIONAL NEWS AGENCIES

	Associated Press (AP)	United Press International (UPI)	Reuters	Agence France Presse (AFP)
adquarters	New York	New York	London	Paris
mber of ountries served	108	92	147	152
mber of ıbscribers	1,320 newspapers; 3,400 U.S. broadcasters; 1,000 others	7,079 including 2,246 outside U.S.; 36 national news agencies	6,500 newspapers; 400 radio, TV stations	12,000 newspapers; 69 national agencies
mber of countries ›vered by bureaus ıd stringers	62 foreign bureaus	81 foreign bureaus	153 countries	167 countries; 108 foreign bureaus
mber of words sued daily on ırious wires, clusive	17 million	11 million plus 200 news pictures	1,500,000	3,350,000 plus 50 news pictures
mber of gular staff	2,400	1,823	2,000	1,990
mber of rrespondents foreign untries	559	578	350 plus 800 stringers	171 plus 1,200 stringers

URCE: Document prepared by Unesco for International Commission for the tudy of Communication Problems. Quoted in that Commission's publication, *he World of News Agencies,* Paris, Unesco, 1979, p.3.

A3. DATA ON ELEVEN ASIAN COUNTRIES WHOSE NEWSPAPERS FIGURE PROMINENTLY IN THIS STUDY

	Estimated population 1975 (000's)	*Inhabitants per km^2*	*Percent of population rural*	*Average GNP ($) per capita*	*Percent of population illiterate*	*Telephones per 100 inhabitants*	*Radio receivers per 1,000 inhabitants*	*TV receivers per 1,000 inhabitants*	*Newspaper circulation per 1,000*	*Newsprint used per inhabitant (km^2)*
China (People's Republic of)	838,803	87		380			16	0.4		1.3
Hong Kong	4,500	4,366		1,146	28.0	2.4	240	97	350	12.2
India	598,097	182	79.4	140	66.6	0.3	24	0.5	16	0.3
Indonesia	136,044	71	81.8	220	43.4	0.2	37	2.0		0.5
Iran	33,019	20	56.0	1,660	63.1	2.0	249	51	15	0.8
Korea (Republic of)	34,663	352	51.5	560	12.4	4.0	144	48	173	4.2
Malaysia	11,900	36		760	47.2		38	33	87	3.8
Philippines	42,513	142	68.2	380	17.4	1.2	44	17	18	1.6
Singapore	2,250			2,450	31.1	12.9	158	120	201	12.7
Sri Lanka	13,986	213	77.6	190	22.4	0.5	38		49	0.1
Thailand	41,869	81	86.8	350	21.4	0.7	131	17	24	1.5

SOURCES: *UN Statistical Yearbook,* 1976; *UN Demographic Yearbook,* 1975; *Unesco Statistical Yearbook,* 1976; *World Bank Atlas* (for GNP), 1972. Most of the estimates and measures, except GNP, are for about 1975.

APPENDIX B: The News for One Day

8. Approximate Number and Percentage of Words and Number and Percentage of Stories for All Countries by Areas of the World for Each of the Four International News Wires and Hsinhua for One Day, Wednesday, December 7, 1977.

9. Approximate Number and Percentage of Words and Number and Percentage of Stories for All Countries by Areas of the World for Each of 17 Asian Daily Newspapers for One Day, Thursday, December 8, 1977.

10. Approximate Number and Percentage of Words and Number and Percentage of Stories for All Countries by Five World Zones for Each of the Four International News Wires and Hsinhua for One Day, Wednesday, December 7, 1977.

11. Approximate Number and Percentage of Words and Number and Percentage of Stories for All Countries by Five World Zones for Each of 17 Asian Daily Newspapers for One Day, Thursday, December 8, 1977.

12. Zero-order Correlations (tau) Among Four International News Wires, Hsinhua and 16 Asian Daily Newspapers for One Day.

TABLE B1

Number and Percentage of References to Each Country, Alone and Combined with Other Countries, on the Four International News Wires and Hsinhua for One day, Wednesday, December 7, 1977.

Country		*Wire A*	*Wire B*	*Wire C*	*Wire D*	*Four Wires*	*Grand Total*	*Hsinhua*
Organizations								
alone	n	1	3	3	4	11		1
	%	11.1	100.0	42.9	50.0	40.7	27	100.0
							2.9	
combined	n	8	0	4	4	16		0
	%	88.9	0	57.1	50.0	59.3		0
Argentina								
alone	n	0	0	2	1	3		0
	%	0	0	66.7	100.0	75.0	4	0
							0.4	
combined	n	0	0	1	0	1		0
	%	0	0	33.3	0	25.0		0
Australia								
alone	n	1	4	12	5	22		1
	%	100.0	100.0	100.0	100.0	100.0	22	100.0
							2.4	
combined	n	0	0	0	0	0		0
	%	0	0	0	0	0		0
Canada								
alone	n	0	0	1	1	2		1
	%	0	0	100.0	100.0	100.0	2	100.0
							0.2	
combined	n	0	0	0	0	0		0
	%	0	0	0	0	0		0
East Europe								
alone	n	1	2	9	1	13		0
	%	100.0	100.0	100.0	100.0	100.0	13	0
							1.4	
combined	n	0	0	0	0	0		0
	%	0	0	0	0	0		0
France								
alone	n	0	2	8	9	19		0
	%	0	100.0	100.0	100.0	100.0	19	0
							2.1	
combined	n	0	0	0	0	0		0
	%	0	0	0	0	0		0

Table B1 continued

Country		Wire A	Wire B	Wire C	Wire D	Four Wires	Grand Total	Hsinhua
Israel								
alone	n	0	0	0	0	0		0
	%	0	0	0	0	0	0	0
							0.0	
combined	n	0	0	0	0	0		0
	%	0	0	0	0	0		0
Japan								
alone	n	6	8	9	9	32		0
	%	100.0	100.0	100.0	100.0	100.0	32	0
							3.5	
combined	n	0	0	0	0	0		0
	%	0	0	0	0	0		0
New Zealand								
alone	n	2	0	2	1	5		0
	%	100.0	0	100.0	100.0	100.0	5	0
							0.5	
combined	n	0	0	0	0	0		0
	%	0	0	0	0	0		0
West Europe								
alone	n	2	3	28	9	42		3
	%	100.0	100.0	96.6	100.0	97.7	43	100.0
							4.7	
combined	n	0	0	1	0	1		0
	%	0	0	3.4	0	2.3		0
Scandinavia								
alone	n	2	0	1	5	8		0
	%	100.0	0	50.0	100.0	88.9	9	0
							1.0	
combined	n	0	0	1	0	1		0
	%	0	0	50.0	0	11.1		0
South Africa								
alone	n	0	1	2	4	7		0
	%	0	100.0	66.7	66.7	70.0	10	0
							1.1	
combined	n	0	0	1	2	3		0
	%	0	0	33.3	33.3	30.0		0
United Kingdom								
alone	n	11	9	23	16	59		0
	%	100.0	100.0	92.0	94.1	95.2	62	0
							6.7	
combined	n	0	0	2	1	3		0
	%	0	0	8.0	5.9	4.8		0

Table B1 continued

Country		*Wire A*	*Wire B*	*Wire C*	*Wire D*	*Four Wires*	*Grand Total*	*Hsinhua*
United States								
alone	n	78	55	49	17	199		0
	%	97.5	100.0	96.1	94.4	97.5	204	0
							22.2	
combined	n	2	0	2	1	5		0
	%	2.5	0	3.9	5.6	2.5		0
U.S.S.R.								
alone	n	4	4	8	5	21		3
	%	100.0	100.0	100.0	83.3	95.5	22	100.0
							2.4	
combined	n	0	0	0	1	1		0
	%	0	0	0	16.7	4.5		0
West Germany								
alone	n	5	8	4	7	24		0
	%	100.0	100.0	100.0	100.0	100.0	24	0
							2.6	
combined	n	0	0	0	0	0		0
	%	0	0	0	0	0		0
Bangladesh								
alone	n	0	0	0	0	0		0
	%	0	0	0	0	0	3	0
							0.3	
combined	n	0	0	0	3	3		0
	%	0	0	0	100.0	100.0		0
Burma								
alone	n	0	0	0	0	0		0
	%	0	0	0	0	0	0	0
							0.0	
combined	n	0	0	0	0	0		0
	%	0	0	0	0	0		0
Cambodia								
alone	n	0	0	0	0	0		0
	%	0	0	0	0	0	1	0
							0.1	
combined	n	0	0	1	0	1		0
	%	0	0	100.0	0	100.0		0
China								
alone	n	0	3	3	5	11		4
	%	0	42.9	60.0	50.0	47.8	23	28.6
							2.5	
combined	n	1	4	2	5	12		10
	%	100.0	57.1	40.0	50.0	52.2		71.4

Table B1 continued

Country		*Wire A*	*Wire B*	*Wire C*	*Wire D*	*Four Wires*	*Grand Total*	*Hsinhua*
Hong Kong								
alone	n	2	0	6	1	9		0
	%	100.0	0	85.7	100.0	90	10	0
							1.1	
combined	n	0	0	1	0	1		0
	%	0	0	14.3	0	10.0		0
India								
alone	n	1	1	2	3	7		0
	%	100.0	100.0	50.0	50.0	58.3	12	0
							1.3	
combined	n	0	0	2	3	5		0
	%	0	0	50.0	50.0	41.7		0
Indonesia								
alone	n	3	0	3	2	8		0
	%	75.0	0	100.0	66.7	80.0	10	0
							1.1	
combined	n	1	0	0	1	2		0
	%	25.0	0	0	33.3	20.0		0
Iran								
alone	n	0	0	0	2	2		0
	%	0	0	0	100.0	50.0	4	0
							0.4	
combined	n	0	1	1	0	2		0
	%	0	100.0	100.0	0	50.0		0
Laos								
alone	n	1	0	0	1	2		0
	%	100.0	0	0	100.0	100.0	2	0
							0.2	
combined	n	0	0	0	0	0		0
	%	0	0	0	0	0		0
Malaysia								
alone	n	2	3	5	10	20		0
	%	100.0	75.0	83.3	66.7	74.1	27	0
							2.9	
combined	n	0	1	1	5	7		1
	%	0	25.0	16.7	33.3	25.9		100.0
Nepal								
alone	n	0	0	0	1	1		0
	%	0	0	0	100.0	100.0	1	0
							0.1	
combined	n	0	0	0	0	0		0
	%	0	0	0	0	0		0

Table B1 continued

Country		Wire A	Wire B	Wire C	Wire D	Four Wires	Grand Total	Hsinhua
North Korea								
alone	n	0	1	0	0	1		0
	%	0	50.0	0	0	50.0	2	0
							0.2	
combined	n	0	1	0	0	1		0
	%	0	50.0	0	0	50.0		0
Other Asian Countries								
alone	n	0	0	0	0	0		0
	%	0	0	0	0	0	0	0
							0.0	
combined	n	0	0	0	0	0		0
	%	0	0	0	0	0		0
Pakistan								
alone	n	4	5	5	5	19		0
	%	80.0	100.0	83.3	71.4	82.6	23	0
							2.5	
combined	n	1	0	1	2	4		0
	%	20.0	0	16.7	28.6	17.4		0
Philippines								
alone	n	1	3	4	4	12		0
	%	16.7	50.0	44.4	40.0	38.7	31	0
							3.4	
combined	n	5	3	5	6	19		0
	%	83.3	50.0	55.6	60.0	61.3		0
Singapore								
alone	n	2	1	3	2	8		0
	%	66.7	50.0	50.0	25.0	42.1	19	0
							2.1	
combined	n	1	1	3	6	11		0
	%	33.3	50.0	50.0	75.0	57.9		0
South Korea								
alone	n	0	0	0	1	1		0
	%	0	0	0	100.0	11.1	9	0
							1.0	
combined	n	2	6	0	0	8		0
	%	100.0	100.0	0	0	88.9		0
Sri Lanka								
alone	n	0	0	2	0	2		0
	%	0	0	100.0	0	40.0	3	0
							0.3	
combined	n	0	0	0	1	3		0
	%	0	0	0	100.0	60.0		0

Table B1 continued

Country		*Wire A*	*Wire B*	*Wire C*	*Wire D*	*Four Wires*	*Grand Total*	*Hsinhua*
Taiwan								
alone	n	0	2	1	3	6		0
	%	0	66.7	25.0	75.0	42.9	14	0
							1.5	
combined	n	3	1	3	1	8		0
	%	100.0	33.3	75.0	25.0	57.1		0
Thailand								
alone	n	2	2	3	4	11		0
	%	100.0	100.0	100.0	100.0	100.0	11	0
							1.2	
combined	n	0	0	0	0	0		0
	%	0	0	0	0	0		0
Vietnam								
alone	n	4	5	3	4	16		0
	%	57.1	55.6	50.0	44.4	51.6	31	0
							3.4	
combined	n	3	4	3	5	15		0
	%	42.9	44.4	50.0	55.6	48.4		0
Brazil								
alone	n	0	0	0	0	0		0
	%	0	0	0	0	0	4	0
							0.4	
combined	n	2	0	1	1	4		0
	%	100.0	0	100.0	100.0	100.0		0
Columbia								
alone	n	0	0	0	0	0		0
	%	0	0	0	0	0	1	0
							0.1	
combined	n	1	0	0	0	1		0
	%	100.0	0	0	0	100.0		0
Chile								
alone	n	0	0	0	0	0		0
	%	0	0	0	0	0	0	0
							0.0	
combined	n	0	0	0	0	0		0
	%	0	0	0	0	0		0
Cuba								
alone	n	0	0	0	1	1		0
	%	0	0	0	50.0	20.0	5	0
							0.5	
combined	n	1	0	2	1	4		0
	%	100.0	0	100.0	50.0	80.0		0

Table B1 continued

Country		*Wire A*	*Wire B*	*Wire C*	*Wire D*	*Four Wires*	*Grand Total*	*Hsinhua*
Mexico								
alone	n	0	0	1	0	1		0
	%	0	0	100.0	0	50.0	2	0
							0.2	
combined	n	0	1	0	0	1		0
	%	0	100.0	0	0	50.0		0
Other Latin Countries								
alone	n	0	1	5	3	9		1
	%	0	100.0	100.0	60.0	75.0	12	100.0
							1.3	
combined	n	1	0	0	2	3		0
	%	100.0	0	0	40.0	25.0		0
Peru								
alone	n	0	0	1	0	1		1
	%	0	0	100.0	0	100.0	1	100.0
							0.1	
combined	n	0	0	0	0	0		0
	%	0	0	0	0	0		0
Venezuela								
alone	n	0	0	0	0	0		0
	%	0	0	0	0	0	1	0
							0.1	
combined	n	1	0	0	0	1		0
	%	100.0	0	0	0	100.0		0
Algeria								
alone	n	0	0	0	0	0		0
	%	0	0	0	0	0	0	0
							0.0	
combined	n	0	0	0	0	0		0
	%	0	0	0	0	0		0
Egypt								
alone	n	1	1	2	0	4		0
	%	14.3	12.5	16.7	0	10.5	38	0
							4.1	
combined	n	6	7	10	11	34		1
	%	85.7	87.5	83.3	100.0	89.5		100.0
Iraq								
alone	n	0	0	0	1	1		0
	%	0	0	0	100.0	50.0	2	0
							0.2	
combined	n	0	1	0	0	1		0
	%	0	100.0	0	0	50.0		0

Table B1 continued

Country		Wire A	Wire B	Wire C	Wire D	Four Wires	Grand Total	Hsinhua
Jordan								
alone	n	1	0	1	1	3		0
	%	50.0	0	100.0	25.0	42.9	7	0
							0.8	
combined	n	1	0	0	3	4		0
	%	50.0	0	0	75.0	57.1		0
Libya								
alone	n	0	0	0	0	0		0
	%	0	0	0	0	0	2	0
							0.2	
combined	n	0	0	0	2	2		0
	%	0	0	0	100.0	100.0		0
Other Mideast Countries								
alone	n	3	1	4	2	10		1
	%	50.0	11.1	66.7	25.0	34.5	29	100.0
							3.2	
combined	n	3	8	2	6	19		0
	%	50.0	88.9	33.3	75.0	65.5		0
Saudi Arabia								
alone	n	2	0	0	2	4		0
	%	100.0	0	0	100.0	80.0	5	0
							0.5	
combined	n	0	0	1	0	1		0
	%	0	0	100.0	0	20.0		0
Syria								
alone	n	1	3	5	5	14		0
	%	33.3	60.0	71.4	83.3	66.7	21	0
							2.3	
combined	n	2	2	2	1	7		0
	%	66.7	40.0	28.6	16.7	33.3		0
Kenya								
alone	n	0	0	0	0	0		0
	%	0	0	0	0	0	1	0
							0.1	
combined	n	0	0	0	1	1		0
	%	0	0	0	100.0	100.0		0
Nigeria								
alone	n	0	0	0	1	1		0
	%	0	0	0	100.0	50.0	2	0
							0.2	
combined	n	1	0	0	0	1		0
	%	100.0	0	0	0	50.0		0

Table B1 continued

Country		*Wire A*	*Wire B*	*Wire C*	*Wire D*	*Four Wires*	*Grand Total*	*Hsinhua*
Uganda								
alone	n	1	0	0	0	1		0
	%	50.0	0	0	0	33.3	3	0
							0.3	
combined	n	1	0	1	0	2		0
	%	50.0	0	100.0	0	66.7		0
Other African Countries								
alone	n	4	0	14	9	27		5
	%	100.0	0	82.4	50.0	64.3	42	71.4
							4.6	
combined	n	0	3	3	9	15		2
	%	0	100.0	17.6	50.0	35.7		28.6
South Pacific								
alone	n	0	0	0	0	0		0
	%	0	0	0	0	0	7	0
							0.8	
combined	n	2	4	0	1	7		0
	%	100.0	100.0	0	100.0	100.0		0
Total								
alone	n	151	131	234	167	683		21
	%	76.6	73.2	80.4	66.3	74.3	919	60.0
							100.0	
combined	n	46	48	57	85	236		14
	%	23.4	26.8	19.6	33.7	25.7		40.0
Grand Total	n	197	179	291	252	919		35
	%	100.0	100.0	100.0	100.0	100.0		100.0

TABLE B2

Number and Percentage of References to Each Country, Alone and Combined with Other Countries, in Each of 17 Asian Daily Newspapers for One Day, Thursday December 8, 1977

Country		*Amrita Bazar Patrika* (1)	*Bangkok Post* (2)	*Ceylon Daily News* (3)	*Dong-a Ilbo* (4)	*Ettelaat* (5)	*Kayhan International* (6)	*Kompas* (7)	*Korea Times* (8)	*Nanyang Siang Pau* (9)	*New Straits Times* (10)	*Pilipino Express* (11)	*Philippine Daily Express* (12)	*Sing Chew Jit Poh* (13)	*Sing Tao Jih Pao* (14)	*South China Morning Post* (15)	*Statesman* (16)	*Straits Times* (17)	*Total*	*Grand Total*
Organizations																				
alone	n	0	0	0	0	1	2	0	1	0	0	0	2	2	0	0	0	2	10	
	%	0	0	0	0	100.0	100.0	0	100.0	0	0	0	66.7	100.0	0	0	0	50.0	58.8	17
																				2.0
combined	n	0	1	1	0	0	0	0	0	0	0	0	1	0	0	1	1	2	7	
	%	0	100.0	100.0	0	0	0	0	0	0	0	0	33.3	0	0	100.0	100.0	50.0	41.2	
Argentina																				
alone	n	0	0	0	0	0	0	0	0	0	0	0	0	0	0	1	0	0	1	
	%	0	0	0	0	0	0	0	0	0	0	0	0	0	0	100.0	0	0	100.0	1
																				0.1
combined	n	0	0	0	0	0	0	0	0	0	0	0	0	0	0	0	0	0	0	
	%	0	0	0	0	0	0	0	0	0	0	0	0	0	0	0	0	0	0	
Australia																				
alone	n	1	5	0	0	0	0	0	0	1	3	0	1	4	0	4	1	5	25	
	%	100.0	100.0	0	0	0	0	0	0	100.0	100.0	0	100.0	100.0	0	100.0	100.0	100.0	100.0	25
																				3.0
combined	n	0	0	0	0	0	0	0	0	0	0	0	0	0	0	0	0	0	0	
	%	0	0	0	0	0	0	0	0	0	0	0	0	0	0	0	0	0	0	
Canada																				
alone	n	0	1	0	0	0	0	0	0	0	1	0	1	0	0	2	0	0	5	
	%	0	100.0	0	0	0	0	0	0	0	100.0	0	100.0	0	0	100.0	0	0	100.0	5
																				0.6
combined	n	0	0	0	0	0	0	0	0	0	0	0	0	0	0	0	0	0	0	

Country		Amrita Bazar Patrika (1)	Bangkok Post (2)	Ceylon Daily News (3)	Dong-a Ilbo (4)	Ettelaat (5)	Kayhan International (6)	Kompas (7)	Korea Times (8)	Nanyang Siang Pau (9)	New Straits Times (10)	Pilipino Express (11)	Philippine Daily Express (12)	Sing Chew Jit Poh (13)	Sing Tao Jih Pao (14)	South China Morning Post (15)	Statesman (16)	Straits Times (17)	Total	Grand Total
East Europe																				
alone	n	0	0	0	0	0	1	0	0	0	0	0	0	0	0	0	1	0	2	
	%	0	0	0	0	0	100.0	0	0	0	0	0	0	0	0	0	100.0	0	40.0	5 0.6
combined	n	0	0	0	1	0	0	0	0	0	0	1	1	0	0	0	0	0	3	
	%	0	0	0	100.0	0	0	0	0	0	0	100.0	100.0	0	0	0	0	0	60.0	
France																				
alone	n	0	1	1	0	0	3	0	0	0	1	0	0	0	0	1	0	3	10	
	%	0	100.0	100.0	0	0	100.0	0	0	0	100.0	0	0	0	0	100.0	0	100.0	100.0	10 1.2
combined	n	0	0	0	0	0	0	0	0	0	0	0	0	0	0	0	0	0	0	
	%	0	0	0	0	0	0	0	0	0	0	0	0	0	0	0	0	0	0	
Israel																				
alone	n	0	0	0	0	0	0	0	0	0	0	0	0	0	0	0	0	1	1	
	%	0	0	0	0	0	0	0	0	0	0	0	0	0	0	0	0	100.0	100.0	1 0.1
combined	n	0	0	0	0	0	0	0	0	0	0	0	0	0	0	0	0	0	0	
	%	0	0	0	0	0	0	0	0	0	0	0	0	0	0	0	0	0	0	
Japan																				
alone	n	1	6	0	2	1	0	0	0	0	0	0	0	2	2	8	1	6	29	
	%	100.0	100.0	0	100.0	100.0	0	0	0	0	0	0	0	100.0	66.7	100.0	100.0	87.0	90.6	32 3.8
combined	n	0	0	0	0	0	0	0	0	0	1	0	0	0	1	0	0	1	3	
	%	0	0	0	0	0	0	0	0	0	100.0	0	0	0	33.3	0	0	14.3	9.4	
New Zealand																				
alone	n	0	1	0	0	0	0	0	0	0	0	0	0	0	0	1	0	1	3	
	%	0	100.0	0	0	0	0	0	0	0	0	0	0	0	0	100.0	0	100.0	75.0	4 0.5
combined	n	0	0	0	0	0	0	0	0	0	0	0	0	0	0	0	1	0	1	
	%	0	0	0	0	0	0	0	0	0	0	0	0	0	0	0	100.0	0	25.0	

Table B2 continued

Country		*Amrita Bazar Patrika* (1)	*Bangkok Post* (2)	*Ceylon Daily News* (3)	*Dong-a Ilbo* (4)	*Ettelaat* (5)	*Kayhan International* (6)	*Kompas* (7)	*Korea Times* (8)	*Nanyang Siang Pau* (9)	*New Straits Times* (10)	*Pilipino Express* (11)	*Philippine Daily Express* (12)	*Sing Chew Jit Poh* (13)	*Sing Tao Jih Pao* (14)	*South China Morning Post* (15)	*Statesman* (16)	*Straits Times* (17)	Total	Grand Total
Western Europe alone	n	0	6	1	0	2	1	1	0	1	0	0	3	0	1	5	0	5	26	
	%	0	100.0	100.0	0	66.7	100.0	100.0	0	100.0	0	0	100.0	0	100.0	100.0	0	83.3	81.3	32 3.9
combined	n	2	0	0	0	1	0	0	0	0	0	0	0	1	0	0	1	1	6	
	%	100.0	0	0	0	33.3	0	0	0	0	0	0	0	100.0	0	0	100.0	16.7	18.7	
Scandinavia alone	n	0	0	0	0	0	0	1	1	0	0	0	0	1	0	2	0	0	5	
	%	0	0	0	0	0	0	100.0	100.0	0	0	0	0	50.0	0	100.0	0	0	83.3	6 0.7
combined	n	0	0	0	0	0	0	0	0	0	0	0	0	1	0	0	0	0	1	
	%	0	0	0	0	0	0	0	0	0	0	0	0	50.0	0	0	0	0	16.7	
South Africa alone	n	0	1	0	0	0	0	0	1	1	0	0	2	1	0	1	0	1	8	
	%	0	100.0	0	0	0	0	0	100.0	100.0	0	0	100.0	100.0	0	100.0	0	100.0	100.0	8 0.9
combined	n	0	0	0	0	0	0	0	0	0	0	0	0	0	0	0	0	0	0	
	%	0	0	0	0	0	0	0	0	0	0	0	0	0	0	0	0	0	0	
United Kingdom alone	n	1	3	3	0	0	4	0	0	3	5	0	3	2	4	11	3	10	52	
	%	100.0	100.0	100.0	0	0	100.0	0	0	100.0	83.3	0	75.0	100.0	100.0	100.0	100.0	100.0	96.3	54 6.4
combined	n	0	0	0	0	0	0	0	0	0	1	0	1	0	0	0	0	0	2	
	%	0	0	0	0	0	0	0	0	0	16.7	0	25.0	0	0	0	0	0	3.7	
United States alone	n	3	14	1	5	4	21	1	6	5	6	0	4	3	7	19	4	11	114	
	%	100.0	100.0	100.0	41.7	100.0	100.0	100.0	66.7	100.0	75.0	0	57.1	100.0	87.1	100.0	100.0	91.7	87.0	131 15.6
combined	n	0	0	0	7	0	0	0	3	0	2	0	3	0	1	0	0	1	17	
	%	0	0	0	58.3	0	0	0	33.3	0	25.0	0	42.9	0	12.9	0	0	8.3	13.0	

Table B2 continued

Country		Amrita Bazar Patrika (1)	Bangkok Post (2)	Ceylon Daily News (3)	Dong-a Ilbo (4)	Ettelaat (5)	Kayhan International (6)	Kompas (7)	Korea Times (8)	Nanyang Siang Pau (9)	New Straits Times (10)	Pilipino Express (11)	Philippine Daily Express (12)	Sing Chew Jit Poh (13)	Sing Tao Jih Pao (14)	South China Morning Post (15)	Statesman (16)	Straits Times (17)	Total	Grand Total
U.S.S.R.																				
alone	n	1	1	0	3	1	2	0	0	0	2	0	1	0	1	2	0	0	14	
	%	100.0	100.0	0	100.0	100.0	100.0	0	0	0	100.0	0	100.0	0	100.0	100.0	0	0	93.3	15 1.8
combined	n	0	0	0	0	0	0	0	0	0	0	0	0	1	0	0	0	0	1	
	%	0	0	0	0	0	0	0	0	0	0	0	0	100.0	0	0	0	0	6.7	
West Germany																				
alone	n	0	1	0	0	2	6	0	0	3	2	0	1	1	0	1	0	0	17	
	%	0	100.0	0	0	100.0	85.7	0	0	100.0	100.0	0	50.0	100.0	0	100.0	0	0	89.5	19 2.3
combined	n	0	0	0	0	0	1	0	0	0	0	0	1	0	0	0	0	0	2	
	%	0	0	0	0	0	14.3	0	0	0	0	0	50.0	0	0	0	0	0	10.5	
Bangladesh																				
alone	n	0	0	0	0	0	0	0	0	0	0	0	0	0	0	0	1	0	1	
	%	0	0	0	0	0	0	0	0	0	0	0	0	0	0	0	100.0	0	100.0	1 0.1
combined	n	0	0	0	0	0	0	0	0	0	0	0	0	0	0	0	0	0	0	
	%	0	0	0	0	0	0	0	0	0	0	0	0	0	0	0	0	0	0	
Burma																				
alone	n	0	0	0	0	0	0	0	0	0	0	0	0	0	0	0	0	0	0	
	%	0	0	0	0	0	0	0	0	0	0	0	0	0	0	0	0	0	0	0 0.0
combined	n	0	0	0	0	0	0	0	0	0	0	0	0	0	0	0	0	0	0	
	%	0	0	0	0	0	0	0	0	0	0	0	0	0	0	0	0	0	0	
Cambodia																				
alone	n	0	1	0	0	0	0	0	0	1	1	0	0	0	0	0	0	0	3	
	%	0	100.0	0	0	0	0	0	0	100.0	100.0	0	0	0	0	0	0	0	100.0	3 0.4
combined	n	0	0	0	0	0	0	0	0	0	0	0	0	0	0	0	0	0	0	
	%	0	0	0	0	0	0	0	0	0	0	0	0	0	0	0	0	0	0	

Table B2 continued

Country		Amrita Bazar Patrika (1)	Bangkok Post (2)	Ceylon Daily News (3)	Dong-a Ilbo (4)	Ettelaat (5)	Kayhan International (6)	Kompas (7)	Korea Times (8)	Nanyang Siang Pau (9)	New Straits Times (10)	Pilipino Express (11)	Philippine Daily Express (12)	Sing Chew Jit Poh (13)	Sing Tao Jih Pao (14)	South China Morning Post (15)	Statesman (16)	Straits Times (17)	Total	Grand Total
China																				
alone	n	1	0	0	0	0	1	0	1	2	0	0	1	1	2	6	1	1	17	
	%	100.0	0	0	0	0	100.0	0	50.0	100.0	0	0	50.0	100.0	50.0	75.0	50.0	50.0	63.0	27
																				3.2
combined	n	0	0	1	1	0	0	0	1	0	0	0	1	0	2	2	1	1	10	
	%	0	0	100.0	100.0	0	0	0	50.0	0	0	0	50.0	0	50.0	25.0	50.0	50.0	37.0	
Hong Kong																				
alone	n	0	2	0	0	0	0	0	0	2	0	0	0	2	0	0	0	2	8	
	%	0	100.0	0	0	0	0	0	0	40.0	0	0	0	100.0	0	0	0	66.7	61.5	13
																				1.5
combined	n	0	0	0	0	0	1	0	0	3	0	0	0	0	0	0	0	1	5	
	%	0	0	0	0	0	100.0	0	0	60.0	0	0	0	0	0	0	0	33.3	38.5	
India																				
alone	n	0	1	2	0	0	2	1	0	1	4	0	1	1	0	2	0	1	16	
	%	0	33.3	100.0	0	0	66.7	100.0	0	100.0	100.0	0	100.0	50.0	0	50.0	0	50.0	64.0	25
																				3.0
combined	n	0	2	0	1	0	1	0	0	0	0	0	0	1	1	2	0	1	0	
	%	0	66.7	0	100.0	0	33.3	0	0	0	0	0	0	50.0	100.0	50.0	0	50.0	36.0	
Indonesia																				
alone	n	1	1	0	0	1	0	0	0	0	1	0	0	2	0	1	1	2	10	
	%	100.0	100.0	0	0	100.0	0	0	0	0	100.0	0	0	100.0	0	100.0	100.0	50.0	83.0	12
																				1.4
combined	n	0	0	0	0	0	0	0	0	0	0	0	0	0	0	0	0	2	2	
	%	0	0	0	0	0	0	0	0	0	0	0	0	0	0	0	0	50.0	16.7	
Iran																				
alone	n	0	0	0	0	1	3	0	0	0	0	0	0	0	0	0	1	0	5	
	%	0	0	0	0	7.1	20.0	0	0	0	0	0	0	0	0	0	100.0	0	20.0	25
																				3.0
combined	n	0	0	0	0	13	7	0	0	0	0	0	0	0	0	0	0	0	20	
	%	0	0	0	0	97.9	80.0	0	0	0	0	0	0	0	0	0	0	0	80.0	

Country		Amrita Bazar Patrika (1)	Bangkok Post (2)	Ceylon Daily News (3)	Dong-a Ilbo (4)	Ettelaat (5)	Kayhan International (6)	Kompas (7)	Korea Times (8)	Nanyang Siang Pau (9)	New Straits Times (10)	Pilipino Express (11)	Philippine Daily Express (12)	Sing Chew Jit Poh (13)	Sing Tao Jih Pao (14)	South China Morning Post (15)	Statesman (16)	Straits Times (17)	Total	Grand Total
Laos																				
alone	n	0	0	0	0	0	0	0	0	0	0	0	0	0	0	0	0	1	1	
	%	0	0	0	0	0	0	0	0	0	0	0	0	0	0	0	0	100.0	100.0	1
combined	n	0	0	0	0	0	0	0	0	0	0	0	0	0	0	0	0	0	0	0.1
	%	0	0	0	0	0	0	0	0	0	0	0	0	0	0	0	0	0	0	
Malaysia																				
alone	n	0	1	1	0	0	0	1	0	0	0	0	0	20	0	2	1	19	45	
	%	0	50.0	50.0	0	0	0	100.0	0	0	0	0	0	80.0	0	66.7	50.0	90.5	77.6	58
combined	n	0	1	1	0	0	0	0	0	0	0	0	1	5	1	1	1	2	13	6.9
	%	0	50.0	50.0	0	0	0	0	0	0	0	0	100.0	20.0	100.0	33.3	50.0	9.5	22.4	
Nepal																				
alone	n	1	0	0	0	0	0	0	0	0	0	0	0	0	0	0	0	0	1	
	%	100.0	0	0	0	0	0	0	0	0	0	0	0	0	0	0	0	0	100.0	1
combined	n	0	0	0	0	0	0	0	0	0	0	0	0	0	0	0	0	0	0	0.1
	%	0	0	0	0	0	0	0	0	0	0	0	0	0	0	0	0	0	0	
North Korea																				
alone	n	0	0	0	0	0	0	0	1	1	0	0	0	0	0	0	0	0	2	
	%	0	0	0	0	0	0	0	50.0	100.0	0	0	0	0	0	0	0	0	66.7	3
combined	n	0	0	0	0	0	0	0	1	0	0	0	0	0	0	0	0	0	1	0.4
	%	0	0	0	0	0	0	0	50.0	0	0	0	0	0	0	0	0	0	33.3	
Other Asian Countries																				
alone	n	0	0	0	0	1	0	0	0	0	0	0	0	0	0	0	0	0	1	
	%	0	0	0	0	50.0	0	0	0	0	0	0	0	0	0	0	0	0	20.0	5
combined	n	0	0	0	0	1	2	1	0	0	0	0	0	0	0	0	0	0	4	0.6
	%	0	0	0	0	50.0	100.0	100.0	0	0	0	0	0	0	0	0	0	0	80.0	

Table B2 continued

Country		*Amrita Bazar Patrika* (1)	*Bangkok Post* (2)	*Ceylon Daily News* (3)	*Dong-a Ilbo* (4)	*Ettelaat* (5)	*Kayhan International* (6)	*Kompas* (7)	*Korea Times* (8)	*Nanyang Siang Pau* (9)	*New Straits Times* (10)	*Pilipino Express* (11)	*Philippine Daily Express* (12)	*Sing Chew Jit Poh* (13)	*Sing Tao Jih Pao* (14)	*South China Morning Post* (15)	*Statesman* (16)	*Straits Times* (17)	Total	Grand Total
Pakistan alone	n	0	1	1	0	2	2	0	0	0	0	0	1	2	0	1	1	1	12	
	%	0	33.3	100.0	0	50.0	100.0	0	0	0	0	0	100.0	100.0	0	25.0	50.0	50.0	52.2	23 2.7
combined	n	0	2	0	0	2	0	0	0	0	2	0	0	0	0	3	1	1	11	
	%	0	66.7	0	0	50.0	0	0	0	0	100.0	0	0	0	0	75.0	50.0	50.0	47.8	
Philippines alone	n	0	1	1	0	1	0	0	0	2	1	0	0	2	0	3	0	2	13	
	%	0	100.0	100.0	0	100.0	0	0	0	66.7	33.3	0	0	66.7	0	75.0	0	50.0	59.1	22 2.6
combined	n	0	0	0	0	0	0	0	1	1	2	0	0	1	0	1	1	2	9	
	%	0	0	0	0	0	0	0	100.0	33.3	66.7	0	0	33.3	0	25.0	100.0	50.0	40.9	
Singapore alone	n	0	2	0	0	0	0	0	0	8	5	0	0	0	0	2	0	0	17	
	%	0	66.7	0	0	0	0	0	0	80.0	71.4	0	0	0	0	66.7	0	0	73.9	23 2.7
combined	n	0	1	0	0	0	0	0	0	2	2	0	0	0	0	1	0	0	6	
	%	0	33.3	0	0	0	0	0	0	20.0	28.6	0	0	0	0	33.3	0	0	26.1	
South Korea alone	n	0	1	0	0	0	0	0	0	0	0	1	1	0	0	0	0	0	3	
	%	0	33.3	0	0	0	0	0	0	0	0	100.0	100.0	0	0	0	0	0	23.1	13 1.5
combined	n	0	2	0	0	0	0	0	0	1	1	0	0	1	1	3	0	1	10	
	%	0	66.7	0	0	0	0	0	0	100.0	100.0	0	0	100.0	100.0	100.0	0	100.0	76.9	
Sri Lanka alone	n	1	0	0	0	0	1	0	0	1	0	0	0	1	0	0	0	1	5	
	%	100.0	0	0	0	0	100.0	0	0	100.0	0	0	0	100.0	0	0	0	100.0	83.3	6 0.7
combined	n	0	0	0	0	0	0	0	0	0	0	0	0	0	0	1	0	0	1	
	%	0	0	0	0	0	0	0	0	0	0	0	0	0	0	100.0	0	0	16.7	

Country		Amrita Bazar Patrika (1)	Bangkok Post (2)	Ceylon Daily News (3)	Dong-a Ilbo (4)	Ettelaat (5)	Kayhan International (6)	Kompas (7)	Korea Times (8)	Nanyang Siang Pau (9)	New Straits Times (10)	Pilipino Express (11)	Philippine Daily Express (12)	Sing Chew Jit Poh (13)	Sing Tao Jih Pao (14)	South China Morning Post (15)	Statesman (16)	Straits Times (17)	Total	Grand Total
Taiwan																				
alone	n	0	0	0	1	0	0	0	2	1	0	0	0	1	1	2	0	2	10	
	%	0	0	0	50.0	0	0	0	100.0	100.0	0	0	0	100.0	33.3	66.7	0	100.0	62.5	16
combined	n	0	1	0	1	0	0	0	0	0	0	1	0	0	2	1	0	0	6	1.9
	%	0	100.0	0	50.0	0	0	0	0	0	0	100.0	0	0	66.7	33.3	0	0	37.5	
Thailand																				
alone	n	0	0	0	0	0	1	0	0	2	2	1	1	3	2	4	0	1	17	
	%	0	0	0	0	0	100.0	0	0	100.0	66.7	100.0	100.0	100.0	100.0	100.0	0	100.0	89.5	19
combined	n	0	0	0	0	0	0	1	0	0	1	0	0	0	0	0	0	0	2	2.3
	%	0	0	0	0	0	0	100.0	0	0	33.3	0	0	0	0	0	0	0	10.5	
Vietnam																				
alone	n	0	0	0	2	0	0	1	1	2	1	0	0	1	0	4	0	2	14	
	%	0	0	0	100.0	0	0	100.0	100.0	66.7	100.0	0	0	100.0	0	100.0	0	100.0	93.3	15
combined	n	0	0	0	0	0	0	0	0	1	0	0	0	0	0	0	0	0	1	1.8
	%	0	0	0	0	0	0	0	0	33.3	0	0	0	0	0	0	0	0	6.7	
Brazil																				
alone	n	0	0	0	0	0	0	0	0	0	0	0	0	1	0	0	0	0	1	
	%	0	0	0	0	0	0	0	0	0	0	0	0	100.0	0	0	0	0	25.0	4
combined	n	0	0	0	0	0	1	0	0	0	0	0	1	0	1	0	0	0	3	0.5
	%	0	0	0	0	0	100.0	0	0	0	0	0	100.0	0	100.0	0	0	0	75.0	
Columbia																				
alone	n	0	0	0	0	0	1	0	0	0	0	0	0	0	0	0	0	0	1	
	%	0	0	0	0	0	100.0	0	0	0	0	0	0	0	0	0	0	0	100.0	1
combined	n	0	0	0	0	0	0	0	0	0	0	0	0	0	0	0	0	0	0	0.1
	%	0	0	0	0	0	0	0	0	0	0	0	0	0	0	0	0	0	0	

Table B2 continued

Country		Amrita Bazar Patrika (1)	Bangkok Post (2)	Ceylon Daily News (3)	Dong-a Ilbo (4)	Ettelaat (5)	Kayhan International (6)	Kompas (7)	Korea Times (8)	Nanyang Siang Pau (9)	New Straits Times (10)	Pilipino Express (11)	Philippine Daily Express (12)	Sing Chew Jit Poh (13)	Sing Tao Jih Pao (14)	South China Morning Post (15)	Statesman (16)	Straits Times (17)	Total	Grand Total
Chile																				
alone	n	0	0	0	0	0	0	0	0	0	0	0	0	0	0	0	0	0	0	
	%	0	0	0	0	0	0	0	0	0	0	0	0	0	0	0	0	0	0	0
combined	n	0	0	0	0	0	0	0	0	0	0	0	0	0	0	0	0	0	0	0.0
	%	0	0	0	0	0	0	0	0	0	0	0	0	0	0	0	0	0	0	
Cuba																				
alone	n	0	0	0	0	0	0	0	0	0	0	0	0	0	0	1	0	1	2	
	%	0	0	0	0	0	0	0	0	0	0	0	0	0	0	50.0	0	100.0	25.0	8
combined	n	0	0	0	0	1	1	0	1	0	1	0	1	0	0	1	0	0	6	0.9
	%	0	0	0	0	100.0	100.0	0	100.0	0	100.0	0	100.0	0	0	50.0	0	0	75.0	
Mexico																				
alone	n	0	0	0	0	0	0	0	0	0	0	0	0	0	0	0	0	0	0	
	%	0	0	0	0	0	0	0	0	0	0	0	0	0	0	0	0	0	0	1
combined	n	0	0	0	0	0	0	0	0	0	0	0	1	0	0	0	0	0	1	0.1
	%	0	0	0	0	0	0	0	0	0	0	0	100.0	0	0	0	0	0	100.0	
Peru																				
alone	n	0	0	0	0	0	0	0	0	0	0	0	0	0	0	0	0	0	0	
	%	0	0	0	0	0	0	0	0	0	0	0	0	0	0	0	0	0	0	0
combined	n	0	0	0	0	0	0	0	0	0	0	0	0	0	0	0	0	0	0	0.0
	%	0	0	0	0	0	0	0	0	0	0	0	0	0	0	0	0	0	0	
Venezuela																				
alone	n	0	0	0	0	0	0	0	0	0	0	0	0	0	0	0	0	0	0	
	%	0	0	0	0	0	0	0	0	0	0	0	0	0	0	0	0	0	0	0
combined	n	0	0	0	0	0	0	0	0	0	0	0	0	0	0	0	0	0	0	0.0

Country		Amrita Bazar Patrika (1)	Bangkok Post (2)	Ceylon Daily News (3)	Dong-a Ilbo (4)	Ettelaat (5)	Kayhan International (6)	Kompas (7)	Korea Times (8)	Nanyang Siang Pau (9)	New Straits Times (10)	Pilipino Express (11)	Philippine Daily Express (12)	Sing Chew Jit Poh (13)	Sing Tao Jih Pao (14)	South China Morning Post (15)	Statesman (16)	Straits Times (17)	Total	Grand Total
Other Latin Countries																				
alone	n	0	1	0	0	0	1	0	0	0	0	0	0	0	0	0	0	0	2	
	%	0	33.3	0	0	0	100.0	0	0	0	0	0	0	0	0	0	0	0	33.3	6
combined	n	0	2	0	0	0	0	0	0	0	1	0	0	0	0	1	0	0	4	0.7
	%	0	66.7	0	0	0	0	0	0	0	100.0	0	0	0	0	100.0	0	0	66.7	
Algeria																				
alone	n	0	0	0	0	0	0	0	0	0	0	0	0	0	0	0	0	0	0	
	%	0	0	0	0	0	0	0	0	0	0	0	0	0	0	0	0	0	0	0
combined	n	0	0	0	0	0	0	0	0	0	0	0	0	0	0	0	0	0	0	0.0
	%	0	0	0	0	0	0	0	0	0	0	0	0	0	0	0	0	0	0	
Egypt																				
alone	n	0	0	0	0	0	0	0	0	0	0	0	0	0	0	0	0	0	0	
	%	0	0	0	0	0	0	0	0	0	0	0	0	0	0	0	0	0	0	27
combined	n	3	1	2	3	1	2	0	2	1	1	0	1	2	2	1	1	4	27	3.2
	%	100.0	100.0	100.0	100.0	100.0	100.0	0	100.0	100.0	100.0	0	100.0	100.0	100.0	100.0	100.0	100.0	100.0	
Iraq																				
alone	n	0	0	0	1	0	0	0	0	0	0	0	0	0	0	0	0	0	1	
	%	0	0	0	100.0	0	0	0	0	0	0	0	0	0	0	0	0	0	50.0	2
combined	n	0	0	0	0	0	0	0	0	1	0	0	0	0	0	0	0	0	1	0.2
	%	0	0	0	0	0	0	0	0	100.0	0	0	0	0	0	0	0	0	50.0	
Jordan																				
alone	n	0	0	0	0	0	3	0	1	0	0	0	0	0	0	0	0	0	4	
	%	0	0	0	0	0	37.5	0	100.0	0	0	0	0	0	0	0	0	0	36.4	11
combined	n	0	0	0	0	0	5	0	0	0	0	0	0	1	1	0	0	0	7	1.3
	%	0	0	0	0	0	62.5	0	0	0	0	0	0	100.0	100.0	0	0	0	63.6	

Table B2 continued

Country		Amrita Bazar Patrika (1)	Bangkok Post (2)	Ceylon Daily News (3)	Dong-a Ilbo (4)	Ettelaat (5)	Kayhan International (6)	Kompas (7)	Korea Times (8)	Nanyang Siang Pau (9)	New Straits Times (10)	Pilipino Express (11)	Philippine Daily Express (12)	Sing Chew Jit Poh (13)	Sing Tao Jih Pao (14)	South China Morning Post (15)	Statesman (16)	Straits Times (17)	Total	Grand Total
Libya																				
alone	n	0	0	1	0	0	0	0	0	0	0	0	0	0	0	0	0	0	1	1
	%	0	0	100.0	0	0	0	0	0	0	0	0	0	0	0	0	0	0	100.0	0.1
combined	n	0	0	0	0	0	0	0	0	0	0	0	0	0	0	0	0	0	0	
	%	0	0	0	0	0	0	0	0	0	0·	0	0	0	0	0	0	0	0	
Saudi Arabia																				
alone	n	0	1	1	0	1	0	1	1	0	1	0	0	1	1	0	0	2	10	15
	%	0	100.0	100.0	0	50.0	0	100.0	50	0	100.0	0	0	100.0	100.0	0	0	100.0	66.7	1.8
combined	n	0	0	0	1	1	1	0	1	1	0	0	0	0	0	0	0	0	5	
	%	0	0	0	100.0	50.0	100.0	0	50.0	0	0	0	0	0	0	0	0	0	33.3	
Syria																				
alone	n	1	0	0	1	0	2	2	2	0	1	0	2	1	0	0	0	3	15	34
	%	100.0	0	0	100.0	0	40.0	66.7	100.0	0	25.0	0	100.0	50.0	0	0	0	75.0	44.1	4.1
combined	n	0	0	0	0	3	3	1	0	4	3	0	0	1	3	0	0	1	19	
	%	0	0	0	0	100.0	60.0	33.3	0	100.0	75.0	0	0	50.0	100.0	0	0	25.0	55.9	
Other Mideast Countries																				
alone	n	0	0	0	1	1	0	0	0	0	0	0	0	0	0	2	0	1	5	13
	%	0	0	0	100.0	50.0	0	0	0	0	0	0	0	0	0	100.0	0	50.0	38.5	1.5
combined	n	0	1	0	0	1	0	1	0	2	0	0	0	0	2	0	0	1	8	
	%	0	100.0	0	0	50.0	0	100.0	0	100.0	0	0	0	0	100.0	0	0	50.0	61.5	
Kenya																				
alone	n	0	0	0	0	0	0	0	0	0	0	0	0	0	0	0	0	0	0	1
	%	0	0	0	0	0	0	0	0	0	0	0	0	0	0	0	0	0	0	0.1
combined	n	0	0	0	0	0	0	0	0	0	1	0	0	0	0	0	0	0	1	
	%	[illegible]	[illegible]	[illegible]	[illegible]	[illegible]	[illegible]	[illegible]	[illegible]	[illegible]	100.0	0	0	0	0	0	0	0	100.0	

Country		Amrita Baz Patrika (1)	Bangkok Post (2)	Ceylon Daily News (3)	Dong-a Ilb (4)	Ettelaat (5)	Kayhan Internation (6)	Kompas (7)	Korea Time (8)	Nanyang Siang Pau (9)	New Straits Times (10)	Pilipino Express (11)	Philippine Daily Expre (12)	Sing Chew Jit Poh (13)	Sing Tao Jih Pao (14)	South China Morning Pos (15)	Statesman (16)	Straits Times (17)	Total	Grand Total
Nigeria																				
alone	n	0	0	0	0	0	0	0	0	0	0	0	0	0	0	0	0	0	0	
	%	0	0	0	0	0	0	0	0	0	0	0	0	0	0	0	0	0	0	0
combined	n	0	0	0	0	0	0	0	0	0	0	0	0	0	0	0	0	0	0	0.0
	%	0	0	0	0	0	0	0	0	0	0	0	0	0	0	0	0	0	0	
Uganda																				
alone	n	0	0	0	0	2	0	0	0	0	0	0	0	0	0	0	0	1	3	
	%	0	0	0	0	100.0	0	0	0	0	0	0	0	0	0	0	0	100.0	50.0	6
combined	n	0	0	1	0	0	0	0	0	0	1	0	1	0	0	0	0	0	3	0.7
	%	0	0	100.0	0	0	0	0	0	0	100.0	0	100.0	0	0	0	0	0	50.0	
Other African Countries																				
alone	n	1	0	1	0	2	0	2	1	1	0	0	1	0	0	3	2	2	16	
	%	25.0	0	100.0	0	50.0	0	100.0	33.3	33.3	0	0	100.0	0	0	100.0	66.7	100.0	51.5	31
combined	n	3	0	0	0	2	4	0	2	2	0	0	0	1	0	0	1	0	15	3.7
	%	75.0	0	0	0	50.0	100.0	0	66.7	66.7	0	0	0	100.0	0	0	33.3	0	48.4	
South Pacific																				
alone	n	0	0	0	0	0	0	0	0	0	0	0	0	0	0	0	0	0	0	
	%	0	0	0	0	0	0	0	0	0	0	0	0	0	0	0	0	0	0	2
combined	n	0	1	0	0	0	0	0	0	0	0	0	0	0	0	1	0	0	2	0.2
	%	0	100.0	0	0	0	0	0	0	0	0	0	0	0	0	100.0	0	0	100.0	
Totals																				
alone	n	13	53	14	16	21	59	11	21	36	37	2	26	55	21	91	21	89	586	
	%	61.9	87.9	60.0	51.6	44.7	66.7	73.3	67.7	63.2	64.9	50.0	65.0	77.5	53.8	82.0	75.0	80.2	69.8	839
combined	n	8	15	6	15	26	29	4	10	21	20	2	14	16	18	20	7	22	253	100.0
	%	38.1	22.1	40.0	48.4	55.3	33.3	26.7	32.3	36.8	35.1	50.0	35.0	22.5	46.2	18.0	25.0	19.8	30.2	
Grand Total	n	21	68	20	31	47	88	15	31	57	57	4	40	71	39	111	28	111	839	
	%	100.0	100.0	100.0	100.0	100.0	100.0	100.0	100.0	100.0	100.0	100.0	100.0	100.0	100.0	100.0	100.0	100.0	100.0	

TABLE B3

Approximate Number and Percentage of Words and Number and Percentage of Stories for Each Content Category for Each Wire Service and Hsinhua for One Day, Wednesday, December 7, 1977.

Content Category	*Wire A*	*Wire B*	*Wire C*	*Wire D*	*Four Wires*	*Hsinhua*
1. Military						
words	3,403	9,245	8,694	3,078	24,420	930
%	7.0	17.4	12.3	6.9	11.2	11.5
stories	11	17	29	17	74	4
%	5.6	9.5	10.0	6.7	8.1	11.4
2. Foreign relations						
words	12,341	8,256	11,424	14,040	46,061	4,410
%	25.4	15.5	16.1	31.7	21.2	54.4
stories	46	29	48	84	207	18
%	23.4	16.2	16.5	33.3	22.5	51.4
3. Domestic politics						
words	3,731	4,386	9,870	7,236	25,223	210
%	7.7	8.2	13.9	16.3	11.6	2.6
stories	13	15	33	35	96	2
%	6.6	8.4	11.3	13.9	10.4	5.7
4. Economics						
words	11,521	12,212	12,432	7,560	43,725	1,050
%	23.7	23.0	17.6	17.1	20.2	13.0
stories	46	53	54	40	193	4
%	23.4	29.6	18.6	15.9	21.0	11.4
5. Science						
words	1,558	1,505	588	810	4,461	240
%	3.2	2.8	0.8	1.8	2.1	3.0
stories	6	6	4	4	20	2
%	3.0	3.4	1.4	1.6	2.2	5.7
6. Education						
words	246	0	210	0	456	0

7. Accidents						
words	1,599	2,322	2,394	2,430	8,745	0
%	3.3	4.4	3.4	5.5	4.0	0
stories	8	9	7	18	42	0
%	4.1	5.0	2.4	7.1	4.6	0
8. Judicial						
words	4,059	3,827	7,182	810	15,878	0
%	8.4	7.2	10.1	1.8	7.3	0
stories	14	10	24	6	54	0
%	7.1	5.6	8.2	2.4	5.9	0
9. Sports						
words	5,412	6,708	12,180	5,130	29,430	750
%	11.2	12.6	17.2	11.6	13.6	9.3
stories	37	24	57	29	147	4
%	18.8	13.4	19.6	11.5	16.0	11.4
10. Arts, culture						
words	1,189	1,505	1,218	162	4,074	0
%	2.5	2.8	1.7	0.4	1.9	0
stories	4	3	5	1	13	0
%	2.0	1.7	1.7	0.4	1.4	0
11. Human interest						
words	246	946	756	1,296	3,244	0
%	0.5	1.8	1.1	2.9	1.5	0
stories	2	4	7	10	23	0
%	1.0	2.2	2.4	4.0	2.5	0
12. Other						
words	3,198	2,279	3,906	1,782	11,165	510
%	6.6	4.3	5.5	4.0	5.2	6.3
stories	9	9	21	8	47	1
%	4.6	5.0	7.2	3.2	5.1	2.9
TOTAL						
words	48,503	53,191	70,854	44,334	216,882	8,100
%	100.0	100.0	100.0	100.0	100.0	100.0
stories	197	179	291	252	919	35
%	100.0	100.0	100.0	100.0	100.0	100.0

TABLE B4

Approximate Number and Percentage of Words and Number and Percentage of Stories for Each Content Category for Each of 17 Asian Daily Newspapers for One Day, Thursday, December 8, 1977.

Newspaper	*Military, political violence* (1)	*Foreign relations* (2)	*Domestic Politics* (3)	*Economics* (4)	*Science, Health* (5)	*Education* (6)	*Accidents, disasters* (7)	*Judicial, Crime* (8)	*Sports* (9)	*Art, culture* (10)	*Human interest* (11)	*Other* (12)	*Total*
Amrita Bazar Patrika													
words	368	2,484	368	1,242	0	0	92	138	0	0	184	0	4,876
%	7.5	50.9	7.5	25.5	0	0	1.9	2.8	0	0	3.8	0	100.0
stories	3	7	2	6	0	0	1	1	0	0	1	0	21
%	14.3	33.3	9.5	28.5	0	0	4.8	4.8	0	0	4.8	0	100.0
Bangkok Post													
words	476	4,624	4,250	11,322	374	0	782	2,176	8,908	0	102	0	33,014
%	1.4	14.0	12.9	34.3	1.1	0	2.4	6.6	27.0	0	0.3	0	100.0
stories	2	8	11	18	1	0	3	7	17	0	1	0	68
%	2.9	11.7	16.2	26.5	1.5	0	4.4	10.3	25.0	0	1.5	0	100.0
Ceylon Daily News													
words	0	1,628	528	572	0	0	308	88	308	264	0	220	3,916
%	0	41.6	13.5	14.6	0	0	7.9	2.2	7.9	6.7	0	5.6	100.0
stories	0	7	3	4	0	0	2	1	1	1	0	1	20
%	0	35.5	15.0	20.0	0	0	10.0	5.0	5.0	5.0	0	5.0	100.0
Dong-a Ilbo													
words	1,900	8,930	950	3,515	0	0	0	570	2,850	0	475	1,900	21,090
%	9.0	42.3	4.5	16.7	0	0	0	2.7	13.5	0	2.3	9.0	100.0
stories	4	11	2	6	0	0	0	2	3	0	1	2	31
%	12.9	35.5	6.4	19.4	0	0	0	6.4	9.7	0	3.2	6.4	100.0
Ettelaat													
words	0	11,264	1,792	1,600	0	0	224	480	6,688	3,840	0	2,816	28,704
%	0	39.2	6.2	5.6	0	0	0.8	1.7	23.3	13.4	0	9.8	100.0
stories	0	15	4	6	0	0	2	1	10	5	0	4	47
%	0	31.9	8.5	12.8	0	0	4.3	2.1	21.3	10.6	0	8.5	100.0

Newspaper	Milita politi violen (1)	Forei relat (2)	Dome Politi (3)	Econ (4)	Scien Healt (5)	Educ (6)	Accid disas (7)	Judic Crim (8)	Sports (9)	Art, c (10)	Hum inter (11)	Other (12)	Total
Kayhan International													
words	2,272	11,552	1,280	5,120	512	0	256	1,600	5,952	7,680	576	768	37,568
%	6.0	30.8	3.4	13.6	1.4	0	0.7	4.3	15.8	20.4	1.5	2.0	100.0
stories	7	15	6	16	2	0	4	9	15	10	1	3	88
%	8.0	17.0	6.8	18.2	2.3	0	4.5	10.2	17	11.4	1.1	3.4	100.0
Kompas													
words	1,904	1,496	2,958	442	34	0	102	0	1.156	0	0	0	8,092
%	23.5	18.5	36.6	5.5	0.4	0	1.3	0	14.3	0	0	0	100.0
stories	1	4	3	2	1	0	3	0	1	0	0	0	15
%	6.7	26.6	20.0	13.3	6.7	0	20.0	0	6.7	0	0	0	100.0
Korea Times													
words	1,360	4,560	520	880	0	0	80	160	160	0	1.880	0	9,600
%	14.2	47.5	5.4	9.2	0	0	0.8	1.7	1.7	0	19.6	0	100.0
stories	3	16	3	4	0	0	1	1	1	0	2	0	31
%	9.7	51.6	9.7	12.9	0	0	3.2	3.2	3.2	0	6.4	0	100.0
Nanyang Siang Pau													
words	2,501	22,265	2,989	19,703	0	0	1,098	3,904	3,660	0	7,503	549	64,172
%	3.9	34.7	4.7	30.7	0	0	1.7	6.1	5.7	0	11.7	0.9	100.0
stories	4	19	7	13	0	0	1	3	4	0	5	1	57
%	7.0	33.3	12.3	22.8	0	0	1.8	5.3	7.0	0	8.8	1.8	100.0
New Straits Times													
words	578	6,120	4,658	6,290	0	306	408	4,420	3,502	680	374	714	28,050
%	2.1	21.8	16.6	22.4	0	1.1	1.5	15.6	12.5	2.4	1.3	2.5	100.0
stories	2	8	6	16	0	1	3	7	7	1	3	3	57
%	3.5	14.0	10.5	28.0	0	1.8	5.3	12.3	12.3	1.8	5.3	5.3	100.0
Pilipino Express													
words	0	770	0	0	0	0	0	0	805	0	0	0	1,575
%	0	48.9	0	0	0	0	0	0	51.1	0	0	0	100.0
stories	0	1	0	0	0	0	0	0	3	0	0	0	4
%	0	25.0	0	0	0	0	0	0	75.0	0	0	0	100.0
Philippine Daily Express													
words	272	5,406	1,190	2,482	612	782	1,020	306	9,690	170	0	0	21,930
%	1.2	24.7	5.4	11.3	2.8	3.6	4.7	1.4	44.2	0.8	0	0	100.0
stories	1	9	3	10	1	4	3	2	5	2	0	0	40
%	2.5	22.5	7.5	25.0	2.5	10.0	7.5	5.0	12.5	5.0	0	0	100.0

Table B4 continued

Newspaper	Military, political violence (1)	Foreign relations (2)	Domestic Politics (3)	Economics (4)	Science, Health (5)	Education (6)	Accidents, disasters (7)	Judicial, Crime (8)	Sports (9)	Art, culture (10)	Human interest (11)	Other (12)	Total
Sing Chew Jit Poh													
words	1,482	10,602	9,006	11,286	0	399	6,384	513	6,327	0	6,555	1,596	54,150
%	2.7	19.6	16.6	20.8	0	0.7	11.8	1.0	11.7	0	12.1	2.9	100.0
stories	2	12	12	15	0	1	7	2	9	0	10	1	71
%	2.8	16.9	16.9	21.1	0	1.4	9.9	2.8	12.7	0	14.1	1.4	100.0
Sing Tao Jih Pao													
words	1,426	8,742	2,852	7,006	310	0	930	1,178	0	186	2,356	0	24,986
%	5.7	35.0	11.4	28.0	1.2	0	3.7	4.7	0	0.7	9.4	0	100.0
stories	1	11	3	16	1	0	1	2	0	1	3	0	39
%	2.6	28.2	7.7	41.0	2.6	0	2.6	5.1	0	2.6	7.7	0	100.0
South China Morning Post													
words	2,775	8,843	7,696	3,367	444	0	1,443	2,072	3,700	444	925	407	32,116
%	8.6	27.5	23.9	10.5	1.4	0	4.5	6.5	11.5	1.4	2.9	1.3	100.0
stories	8	29	24	10	3	0	7	9	8	1	8	4	111
%	7.2	26.1	21.6	9.0	2.7	0	6.3	8.1	7.2	0.9	7.2	3.6	100.0
Statesman													
words	250	2,400	350	2,300	50	50	150	200	150	550	250	0	6,700
%	3.7	35.8	5.2	34.3	0.8	0.8	2.2	3.0	2.2	8.2	3.7	0	100.0
stories	3	6	3	6	1	1	1	2	2	1	2	0	28
%	10.7	21.4	10.7	21.4	3.6	3.6	3.6	7.1	7.1	3.6	7.1	0	100.0
Straits Times													
words	1,715	12,215	5,355	8,960	385	70	4,130	3,150	5,565	0	7,245	0	48,790
%	3.5	25.0	11.0	18.4	0.8	0.1	8.4	6.5	11.4	0	14.9	0	100.0
stories	4	25	14	38	1	1	6	5	11	0	6	0	111
%	3.6	22.5	12.6	34.2	0.9	0.9	5.4	4.5	9.9	0	5.4	0	100.0
TOTAL													
words	19,279	123,901	46,742	86,087	2,7 21	1,607	17,407	20,955	59,421	13,814	28,425	8,970	429,329
%	4.5	28.8	10.9	20.1	0.6	0.4	4.1	4.9	13.8	3.2	6.6	2.1	100.0
stories	45	203	106	186	11	8	45	54	97	22	43	19	839
%	5.4	24.2	12.6	22.2	1.3	0.9	5.4	6.4	11.6	2.6	5.1	2.3	100.0

Approximate Number and Percentage of Words and Number and Percentage of Stories for Each Country by Content Category for the Composite News Wire (excluding Hsinhua) for One Day, Wednesday, December 7, 1977.

Country	*Military, political violence* (1)	*Foreign relations* (2)	*Domestic Politics* (3)	*Economics* (4)	*Science, Health* (5)	*Education* (6)	*Accidents, disasters* (7)	*Judicial, Crime* (8)	*Sports* (9)	*Art, culture* (10)	*Human interest* (11)	*Other* (12)	*Total*
Organizations													
words	960	2,483	324	1,560	294	0	0	0	205	0	0	1,712	7,538
%	12.7	32.9	4.3	20.7	3.9	0	0	0	2.7	0	0	22.7	100.0
stories	3	9	2	5	1	0	0	0	1	0	0	6	27
%	11.1	33.3	7.4	18.5	3.7	0	0	0	3.7	0	0	22.2	100.0
Argentina													
words	42	0	0	0	0	0	96	0	84	0	0	0	222
%	18.9	0	0	0	0	0	43.2	0	37.8	0	0	0	100.0
stories	1	0	0	0	0	0	2	0	1	0	0	0	4
%	25.0	0	0	0	0	0	50.0	0	25.0	0	0	0	100.0
Australia													
words	0	108	2,914	926	0	0	0	0	1,562	0	360	0	5,870
%	0	1.8	49.6	15.8	0	0	0	0	26.6	0	6.1	0	100.0
stories	0	1	8	6	0	0	0	0	4	0	3	0	22
%	0	4.5	36.4	27.3	0	0	0	0	18.2	0	13.6	0	100
Canada													
words	0	0	0	0	0	0	108	0	252	0	0	0	360
%	0	0	0	0	0	0	30.0	0	70.0	0	0	0	100.0
stories	0	0	0	0	0	0	1	0	1	0	0	0	2
%	0	0	0	0	0	0	50.0	0	50.0	0	0	0	100.0
Eastern Europe													
words	0	210	378	1,066	84	0	653	0	512	0	0	546	3,449
%	0	6.1	11.0	30.9	2.4	0	18.9	0	14.8	0	0	15.8	100.0
stories	0	1	1	1	1	0	3	0	3	0	0	3	13
%	0	7.7	7.7	7.7	7.7	0	23.1	0	23.1	0	0	23.1	100.0
France													
words	0	126	1,191	354	0	0	54	168	702	462	216	210	3,483
%	0	3.6	34.2	10.1	0	0	1.6	4.8	20.2	13.3	6.2	6.0	100.0
stories	0	1	4	3	0	0	1	1	5	2	1	1	19
%	0	5.3	21.0	15.8	0	0	5.3	5.3	26.3	10.5	5.3	5.3	100.0

Table B5 continued

Country	Military, political violence (1)	Foreign relations (2)	Domestic Politics (3)	Economics (4)	Science, Health (5)	Education (6)	Accidents, disasters (7)	Judicial, Crime (8)	Sports (9)	Art, culture (10)	Human interest (11)	Other (12)	Total
Israel													
words	0	0	0	0	0	0	0	0	0	0	0	0	0
%	0	0	0	0	0	0	0	0	0	0	0	0	0
stories	0	0	0	0	0	0	0	0	0	0	0	0	0
%	0	0	0	0	0	0	0	0	0	0	0	0	0
Japan													
words	431	210	86	4,298	0	42	86	300	251	0	0	0	5,704
%	7.6	3.7	1.5	75.3	0	0.7	1.5	5.3	4.4	0	0	0	100.0
stories	2	1	1	21	0	1	1	3	2	0	0	0	32
%	6.3	3.1	3.1	65.6	0	3.1	3.1	9.4	6.3	0	0	0	100.0
New Zealand													
words	0	0	0	0	0	0	0	0	911	0	0	0	911
%	0	0	0	0	0	0	0	0	100.0	0	0	0	100.0
stories	0	0	0	0	0	0	0	0	5	0	0	0	5
%	0	0	0	0	0	0	0	0	100.0	0	0	0	100.0
Western Europe													
words	1,573	162	3,116	1,430	0	0	192	1,386	1,250	462	0	969	10,540
%	14.9	1.5	29.6	13.6	0	0	1.8	13.1	11.9	4.4	0	9.2	100.0
stories	6	2	10	7	0	0	2	4	6	1	0	5	43
%	14.0	4.6	23.2	16.3	0	0	4.7	9.3	14.0	2.3	0	11.6	100.0
Scandinavia													
words	0	234	438	0	0	0	162	0	594	164	0	0	1,592
%	0	14.7	27.5	0	0	0	10.2	0	37.3	10.3	0	0	100.0
stories	0	2	3	0	0	0	1	0	2	1	0	0	9
%	0	22.2	33.3	0	0	0	11.1	0	22.2	11.1	0	0	100.0
South Africa													
words	0	194	648	0	0	0	0	0	798	126	0	702	2,468
%	0	7.9	26.3	0	0	0	0	0	32.3	5.1	0	28.4	100.0
stories	0	2	2	0	0	0	0	0	2	1	0	3	10
%	[illegible]	[illegible]	[illegible]	[illegible]	[illegible]	[illegible]	[illegible]	0	20.0	10.0	0	30.0	100.0

Country	Military, political violence (1)	Foreign relations (2)	Domestic Politics (3)	Economics (4)	Science, Health (5)	Education (6)	Accidents, disasters (7)	Judicial, Crime (8)	Sports (9)	Art, culture (10)	Human interest (11)	Other (12)	Total
United Kingdom													
words	54	858	496	4,531	108	0	0	168	4,363	764	213	0	11,555
%	0.5	7.4	4.3	39.2	0.9	0	0	1.5	37.8	6.6	1.8	0	100.0
stories	1	7	2	19	1	0	0	1	26	3	2	0	62
%	1.6	11.3	3.2	30.7	1.6	0	0	1.6	41.9	4.8	3.2	0	100.0
United States													
words	8,152	1,629	4,450	13,547	2,757	246	1,728	10,301	6,888	1,729	1,286	1,874	54,587
%	14.9	3.0	8.1	24.8	5.0	0.5	3.2	18.9	12.6	3.2	2.4	3.4	100.0
stories	13	7	14	65	10	1	8	28	40	3	6	9	204
%	6.4	3.4	6.9	31.9	4.9	0.5	3.9	13.7	19.6	1.5	2.9	4.4	100.0
U.S.S.R.													
words	1,656	503	126	215	0	0	108	126	693	205	248	522	4,402
%	37.6	11.5	2.9	4.9	0	0	2.4	2.9	15.7	4.7	5.6	11.8	100.0
stories	5	3	1	1	0	0	1	1	5	1	2	2	22
%	22.7	13.6	4.5	4.5	0	0	4.5	4.5	22.7	4.5	9.1	9.1	100.0
West Germany													
words	1,239	626	162	3,212	0	0	0	492	1,168	0	84	0	6,983
%	17.7	9.0	2.3	46.0	0	0	0	7.0	16.7	0	1.2	0	100.0
stories	6	2	11	7	0	0	0	1	6	0	1	0	24
%	25.0	8.3	4.2	29.1	0	0	0	4.2	25.0	0	4.2	0	100.0
Bangladesh													
words	0	378	0	0	0	0	0	0	0	0	0	0	378
%	0	100.0	0	0	0	0	0	0	0	0	0	0	100.0
stories	0	3	0	0	0	0	0	0	0	0	0	0	3
%	0	100.0	0	0	0	0	0	0	0	0	0	0	100.0
Burma													
words	0	0	0	0	0	0	0	0	0	0	0	0	0
%	0	0	0	0	0	0	0	0	0	0	0	0	0
stories	0	0	0	0	0	0	0	0	0	0	0	0	0
%	0	0	0	0	0	0	0	0	0	0	0	0	0

Table B5 continued

Country	Military, political violence (1)	Foreign relations (2)	Domestic Politics (3)	Economics (4)	Science, Health (5)	Education (6)	Accidents, disasters (7)	Judicial, Crime (8)	Sports (9)	Art, culture (10)	Human interest (11)	Other (12)	Total
Cambodia													
words	0	0	0	0	0	0	0	0	0	0	0	168	168
%	0	0	0	0	0	0	0	0	0	0	0	100.0	100.0
stories	0	0	0	0	0	0	0	0	0	0	0	1	1
%	0	0	0	0	0	0	0	0	0	0	0	100.0	100.0
China													
words	516	1,817	612	471	162	0	0	0	0	0	280	301	4,159
%	12.4	43.7	14.7	11.3	3.9	0	0	0	0	0	6.7	7.2	100.0
stories	2	12	3	2	1	0	0	0	0	0	2	1	23
%	8.7	52.2	13.0	8.7	4.3	0	0	0	0	0	8.7	4.3	100.0
Hong Kong													
words	0	0	378	1,160	0	0	0	294	0	0	108	84	2,024
%	0	0	18.7	57.3	0	0	0	14.5	0	0	5.3	4.2	100.0
stories	0	0	1	5	0	0	0	2	0	0	1	1	10
%	0	0	10.0	50.0	0	0	0	20.0	0	0	10.0	10.0	100.0
India													
words	0	162	1,409	450	0	0	123	54	168	0	0	0	2,366
%	0	6.8	59.6	19.0	0	0	5.2	2.3	7.1	0	0	0	100.0
stories	0	1	5	3	0	0	1	1	1	0	0	0	12
%	0	8.3	41.7	25.0	0	0	8.3	8.3	8.3	0	0	0	100.0
Indonesia													
words	378	82	540	876	0	0	518	0	0	0	0	451	2,845
%	13.3	2.9	18.9	30.8	0	0	18.2	0	0	0	0	15.9	100.0
stories	1	1	2	2	0	0	3	0	0	0	0	1	10
%	10.0	10.0	20.0	20.0	0	0	30.0	0	0	0	0	10.0	100.0
Iran													
words	0	0	216	654	0	0	0	0	0	0	0	0	870
%	0	0	24.8	75.2	0	0	0	0	0	0	0	0	100.0
stories	0	0	1	3	0	0	0	0	0	0	0	0	4
%	0	0	25.0	75.0	0	0	0	0	0	0	0	0	100.0

Country	Military, political violence (1)	Foreign relation (2)	Domesti Politics (3)	Econom (4)	Science, Health (5)	Educati (6)	Acciden disasters (7)	Judicia Crime (8)	Sports (9)	Art, cul (10)	Human interest (11)	Other (12)	Total
Laos													
words	0	354	0	0	0	0	0	0	0	0	0	0	354
%	0	100.0	0	0	0	0	0	0	0	0	0	0	100.0
stories	0	2	0	0	0	0	0	0	0	0	0	0	2
%	0	100.0	0	0	0	0	0	0	0	0	0	0	100.0
Malaysia													
words	1,083	918	1,100	1,442	0	0	2,075	0	252	0	0	0	6,870
%	15.8	13.3	16.0	21.0	0	0	30.2	0	3.7	0	0	0	100.0
stories	4	5	5	6	0	0	6	0	1	0	0	0	27
%	14.8	18.5	18.5	22.2	0	0	22.2	0	3.7	0	0	0	100.0
Nepal													
words	0	378	0	0	0	0	0	0	0	0	0	0	378
%	0	100.0	0	0	0	0	0	0	0	0	0	0	100.0
stories	0	1	0	0	0	0	0	0	0	0	0	0	1
%	0	100.0	0	0	0	0	0	0	0	0	0	0	100.0
North Korea													
words	0	0	258	129	0	0	0	0	0	0	0	0	387
%	0	0	66.7	33.3	0	0	0	0	0	0	0	0	100.0
stories	0	0	1	1	0	0	0	0	0	0	0	0	2
%	0	0	50.0	50.0	0	0	0	0	0	0	0	0	100.0
Other Asian Countries													
words	0	0	0	0	0	0	0	0	0	0	0	0	0
%	0	0	0	0	0	0	0	0	0	0	0	0	0
stories	0	0	0	0	0	0	0	0	0	0	0	0	0
%	0	0	0	0	0	0	0	0	0	0	0	0	0
Pakistan													
words	0	500	1,646	211	0	0	43	546	1,194	539	0	0	4,679
%	0	10.7	35.2	4.5	0	0	0.9	11.7	25.5	11.5	0	0	100.0
stories	0	2	8	2	0	0	1	3	4	3	0	0	23
%	0	8.7	34.8	8.7	0	0	4.4	13.0	17.4	13.0	0	0	100.0

Table B5 continued

Country	Military, political violence (1)	Foreign relations (2)	Domestic Politics (3)	Economics (4)	Science, Health (5)	Education (6)	Accidents, disasters (7)	Judicial, Crime (8)	Sports (9)	Art, culture (10)	Human interest (11)	Other (12)	Total
Philippines													
words	1,572	2,129	708	925	0	0	0	462	1,966	0	0	0	7,762
%	20.3	27.4	9.1	11.9	0	0	0	6.0	25.3	0	0	0	100.0
stories	6	8	3	5	0	0	0	1	8	0	0	0	31
%	19.4	25.8	9.7	16.1	0	0	0	3.2	25.8	0	0	0	100.0
Singapore													
words	0	600	0	1,334	0	0	0	486	882	0	108	0	3,410
%	0	17.6	0	39.1	0	0	0	14.2	25.9	0	3.2	0	100.0
stories	0	4	0	9	0	0	0	1	4	0	1	0	19
%	0	21.0	0	47.4	0	0	0	5.3	21.0	0	5.3	0	100.0
South Korea													
words	301	2,187	0	0	0	0	0	0	172	0	0	0	2,660
%	11.3	82.2	0	0	0	0	0	0	6.5	0	0	0	100.0
stories	2	6	0	0	0	0	0	0	1	0	0	0	9
%	22.2	66.7	0	0	0	0	0	0	11.1	0	0	0	100.0
Sri Lanka													
words	0	480	462	0	0	0	0	0	0	0	0	0	942
%	0	51.0	49.0	0	0	0	0	0	0	0	0	0	100.0
stories	0	2	1	0	0	0	0	0	0	0	0	0	3
%	0	66.7	33.3	0	0	0	0	0	0	0	0	0	100.0
Taiwan													
words	84	492	1,039	0	473	168	0	0	451	0	0	0	2,707
%	3.1	18.2	38.4	0	17.5	6.2	0	0	16.6	0	0	0	100.0
stories	1	4	6	0	1	1	0	0	1	0	0	0	14
%	7.1	28.7	42.9	0	7.1	7.1	0	0	7.1	0	0	0	100.0
Thailand													
words	0	177	54	210	0	0	54	138	466	0	0	731	1,830
%	0	9.7	3.0	11.5	0	0	3.0	7.4	25.5	0	0	39.9	100.0
stories	0	2	1	1	0	0	1	2	3	0	0	1	11
	[illegible]	[illegible]	[illegible]	[illegible]	0	0	9.1	18.2	27.3	0	0	9.1	100.0

Country	Military, political violence (1)	Foreign relations (2)	Domestic Politics (3)	Economics (4)	Science, Health (5)	Education (6)	Accidents, disasters (7)	Judicial, Crime (8)	Sports (9)	Art, culture (10)	Human interest (11)	Other (12)	Total
Vietnam													
words	1,074	3,281	324	172	499	0	258	0	0	0	95	211	5,914
%	18.2	55.5	5.5	2.9	8.4	0	4.4	0	0	0	1.6	3.5	100.0
stories	4	16	1	1	4	0	1	0	0	0	2	2	31
%	12.9	51.6	3.2	3.2	12.9	0	3.2	0	0	0	6.5	6.5	100.0
Brazil													
words	0	149	0	0	0	0	0	84	82	0	0	0	315
%	0	47.3	0	0	0	0	0	26.7	26.0	0	0	0	100.0
stories	0	2	0	0	0	0	0	1	1	0	0	0	4
%	0	50.0	0	0	0	0	0	25.0	25.0	0	0	0	100.0
Columbia													
words	0	0	0	0	0	0	0	0	164	0	0	0	164
%	0	0	0	0	0	0	0	0	100.0	0	0	0	100.0
stories	0	0	0	0	0	0	0	0	1	0	0	0	1
%	0	0	0	0	0	0	0	0	100.0	0	0	0	100.0
Chile													
words	0	0	0	0	0	0	0	0	0	0	0	0	0
%	0	0	0	0	0	0	0	0	0	0	0	0	0
stories	0	0	0	0	0	0	0	0	0	0	0	0	0
%	0	0	0	0	0	0	0	0	0	0	0	0	0
Cuba													
words	546	324	0	0	0	0	0	328	0	0	0	0	1,198
%	45.6	27.0	0	0	0	0	0	27.4	0	0	0	0	100.0
stories	2	2	0	0	0	0	0	1	0	0	0	0	5
%	40.0	40.0	0	0	0	0	0	20.0	0	0	0	0	100.0
Mexico													
words	0	0	0	882	0	0	0	0	559	0	0	0	1,441
%	0	0	0	61.2	0	0	0	0	38.8	0	0	0	100.0
stories	0	0	0	1	0	0	0	0	1	0	0	0	2
%	0	0	0	50.0	0	0	0	0	50.0	0	0	0	100.0

Table B5 continued

Country	Military, political violence (1)	Foreign relations (2)	Domestic Politics (3)	Economics (4)	Science, Health (5)	Education (6)	Accidents, disasters (7)	Judicial, Crime (8)	Sports (9)	Art, culture (10)	Human interest (11)	Other (12)	Total
Peru													
words	0	0	0	126	0	0	0	0	0	0	0	0	126
%	0	0	0	100.0	0	0	0	0	0	0	0	0	100.0
stories	0	0	0	1	0	0	0	0	0	0	0	0	1
%	0	0	0	100.0	0	0	0	0	0	0	0	0	100.0
Venezuela													
words	0	123	0	0	0	0	0	0	0	0	0	0	123
%	0	100.0	0	0	0	0	0	0	0	0	0	0	100.0
stories	0	1	0	0	0	0	0	0	0	0	0	0	1
%	0	100.0	0	0	0	0	0	0	0	0	0	0	100.0
Other Latin Countries													
words	126	162	1,294	0	0	0	0	0	42	0	162	0	1,786
%	7.1	9.1	72.4	0	0	0	0	0	2.3	0	9.1	0	100.0
stories	1	1	8	0	0	0	0	0	1	0	1	0	12
%	8.3	8.3	66.7	0	0	0	0	0	8.3	0	8.3	0	100.0
Algeria													
words	0	0	0	0	0	0	0	0	0	0	0	0	0
%	0	0	0	0	0	0	0	0	0	0	0	0	0
stories	0	0	0	0	0	0	0	0	0	0	0	0	0
%	0	0	0	0	0	0	0	0	0	0	0	0	0
Egypt													
words	129	9,913	215	0	0	0	0	205	0	162	0	168	10,792
%	1.2	91.8	2.0	0	0	0	0	1.9	0	1.5	0	1.6	100.0
stories	1	33	1	0	0	0	0	1	0	1	0	1	38
%	2.6	86.8	2.6	0	0	0	0	2.6	0	2.6	0	2.6	100.0
Iraq													
words	0	0	0	0	0	0	0	0	399	0	0	0	399
%	0	0	0	0	0	0	0	0	100.0	0	0	0	100.0
stories	0	0	0	0	0	0	0	0	2	0	0	0	2
%	0	0	0	0	0	0	0	0	100.0	0	0	0	100.0

Country	Military, political violence (1)	Foreign relations (2)	Domestic Politics (3)	Economi (4)	Science, Health (5)	Educatio (6)	Acciden disasters (7)	Judicial, Crime (8)	Sports (9)	Art, cult (10)	Human interest (11)	Other (12)	Total
Jordan													
words	0	1,228	0	0	0	0	0	0	0	0	0	0	1,228
%	0	100.0	0	0	0	0	0	0	0	0	0	0	100.0
stories	0	7	0	0	0	0	0	0	0	0	0	0	7
%	0	100.0	0	0	0	0	0	0	0	0	0	0	100.0
Libya													
words	0	594	0	0	0	0	0	0	0	0	0	0	594
%	0	100.0	0	0	0	0	0	0	0	0	0	0	100.0
stories	0	2	0	0	0	0	0	0	0	0	0	0	2
%	0	100.0	0	0	0	0	0	0	0	0	0	0	100.0
Saudi Arabia													
words	0	421	0	0	0	0	82	0	0	0	84	0	587
%	0	71.7	0	0	0	0	14.0	0	0	0	14.3	0	100.0
stories	0	3	0	0	0	0	1	0	0	0	1	0	5
%	0	60.0	0	0	0	0	20.0	0	0	0	20.0	0	100.0
Syria													
words	727	5,782	0	0	0	0	0	0	0	0	0	0	6,509
%	11.2	88.2	0	0	0	0	0	0	0	0	0	0	100.0
stories	4	17	0	0	0	0	0	0	0	0	0	0	21
%	19.1	80.9	0	0	0	0	0	0	0	0	0	0	100.0
Other Mideast Countries													
words	820	1,436	588	424	0	0	2,609	0	1,441	0	0	366	7,684
%	10.7	18.7	7.6	5.5	0	0	34.0	0	18.7	0	0	4.8	100.0
stories	1	10	2	2	0	0	8	0	4	0	0	2	29
%	3.4	34.5	6.9	6.9	0	0	27.6	0	13.8	0	0	6.9	100.0
Kenya													
words	0	216	0	0	0	0	0	0	0	0	0	0	216
%	0	100.0	0	0	0	0	0	0	0	0	0	0	100.0
stories	0	1	0	0	0	0	0	0	0	0	0	0	1
%	0	100.0	0	0	0	0	0	0	0	0	0	0	100.0

Table B5 continued

Country	Military, political violence (1)	Foreign relations (2)	Domestic Politics (3)	Economics (4)	Science, Health (5)	Education (6)	Accidents, disasters (7)	Judicial, Crime (8)	Sports (9)	Art, culture (10)	Human interest (11)	Other (12)	Total
Nigeria													
words	0	123	0	54	0	0	0	0	0	0	0	0	177
%	0	69.5	0	30.5	0	0	0	0	0	0	0	0	100.0
stories	0	1	0	1	0	0	0	0	0	0	0	0	2
%	0	50.0	0	50.0	0	0	0	0	0	0	0	0	100.0
Uganda													
words	0	0	0	0	0	0	0	0	126	0	0	287	413
%	0	0	0	0	0	0	0	0	30.5	0	0	69.5	100.0
stories	0	0	0	0	0	0	0	0	1	0	0	2	3
%	0	0	0	0	0	0	0	0	33.3	0	0	66.7	100.0
Other African Countries													
words	2,957	3,419	1,090	1,554	84	0	54	82	360	0	0	1,324	10,924
%	27.1	31.3	10.0	14.2	0.8	0	0.5	0.7	3.3	0	0	12.1	100.0
stories	8	16	4	5	1	0	1	1	3	0	0	3	42
%	19.1	38.1	9.5	11.9	2.4	0	2.4	2.4	7.1	0	0	7.1	100.0
South Pacific													
words	0	893	0	473	0	0	0	0	473	0	0	0	1,839
%	0	53.6	0	25.7	0	0	0	0	25.7	0	0	0	100.0
stories	0	4	0	2	0	0	0	0	1	0	0	0	7
%	0	57.1	0	28.6	0	0	0	0	14.3	0	0	0	100.0
Total													
words	24,420	46,061	25,223	43,725	4,461	456	8,745	15,878	29,430	4,074	3,244	11,165	216,882
%	11.4	21.2	11.6	20.2	2.0	0.2	4.0	7.3	13.6	1.9	1.5	5.2	100.0
stories	74	207	96	193	20	3	42	54	147	13	23	47	919
%	8.1	22.5	10.4	21.0	2.2	0.3	4.6	5.9	16.0	1.4	2.5	5.1	100.0

TABLE B6

Approximate Number and Percentage of Words and Number and Percentage of Stories for Each Country by Content Category for Hsinhua for One Day, Wednesday, December 7, 1977.*

Country	*Military political violence* (1)	*Foreign relations* (2)	*Domestic Politics* (3)	*Economics* (4)	*Science Health* (5)	*Sports* (9)	*Other* (12)	*Total*
Organizations								
words	0	390	0	0	0	0	0	390
%	0	100.0	0	0	0	0	0	100.0
stories	0	1	0	0	0	0	0	1
%	0	100.0	0	0	0	0	0	100.0
Australia								
words	90	0	0	0	0	0	0	90
%	100.0	0	0	0	0	0	0	100.0
stories	1	0	0	0	0	0	0	1
%	100.0	0	0	0	0	0	0	100.0
Canada								
words	0	0	0	60	0	0	0	60
%	0	0	0	100.0	0	0	0	100.0
stories	0	0	0	1	0	0	0	1
%	0	0	0	100.0	0	0	0	100.0
Western Europe								
words	540	300	90	0	0	0	0	930
%	58.0	32.3	9.7	0	0	0	0	100.0
stories	1	1	1	0	0	0	0	3
%	33.3	33.3	33.3	0	0	0	0	100.0
U. S. S. R.								
words	300	0	0	0	0	330	0	630
%	47.6	0	0	0	0	52.4	0	100.0
stories	2	0	0	0	0	1	0	3
%	66.7	0	0	0	0	33.3	0	100.0
China								
words	0	1,830	120	990	240	210	0	3,390
%	0	54.0	3.5	29.1	7.1	6.2	0	100.0
stories	0	7	1	3	2	1	0	14
%	0	50.0	7.1	21.4	14.3	7.1	0	100.0
Malaysia								
words	0	0	0	0	0	120	0	120
%	0	0	0	0	0	100.0	0	100.0
stories	0	0	0	0	0	1	0	1
%	0	0	0	0	0	100.0	0	100.0
Peru								
words	0	120	0	0	0	0	0	120
%	0	100.0	0	0	0	0	0	100.0
stories	0	1	0	0	0	0	0	1
%	0	100.0	0	0	0	0	0	100.0

Table B6 continued

Country	*Military, political viloence* (1)	*Foreign relations* (2)	*Domestic politics* (3)	*Economics* (4)	*Science, health* (5)	*Sports* (9)	*Other* (12)	*Total*
Other Latin Countries								
words	0	0	0	0	0	90	0	90
%	0	0	0	0	0	100.0	0	100.0
stories	0	0	0	0	0	1	0	1
%	0	0	0	0	0	100.0	0	100.0
Egypt								
words	0	180	0	0	0	0	0	180
%	0	100.0	0	0	0	0	0	100.0
stories	0	1	0	0	0	0	0	1
%	0	100.0	0	0	0	0	0	100.0
Other Mideast Countries								
words	0	120	0	0	0	0	0	120
%	0	100.0	0	0	0	0	0	100.0
stories	0	1	0	0	0	0	0	1
%	0	100.0	0	0	0	0	0	100.0
Other African Countries								
words	0	1,470	0	0	0	0	510	1,980
%	0	74.2	0	0	0	0	25.8	100.0
stories	0	6	0	0	0	0	1	7
%	0	85.7	0	0	0	0	14.3	100.0
Total								
words	930	4,410	210	1,050	240	750	510	8,100
%	11.5	54.4	2.6	13.0	3.0	9.3	6.3	100.0
stories	4	18	2	4	2	4	1	35
%	11.4	51.4	5.7	11.4	5.7	11.4	2.9	100.0

* Countries and content categories not found on the Hsinhua file are excluded. See Table 7 for a complete list of countries and categories.

TABLE B7

Approximate Number and Percentage of Words and Number and Percentage of Stories for Each Country by Content Category for the Composite Asian Daily Newspaper for One Day, Thursday, December 8, 1977.

Country	*Military, political violence* (1)	*Foreign relations* (2)	*Domestic Politics* (3)	*Economics* (4)	*Science, Healt!* (5)	*Education* (6)	*Accidents, disasters* (7)	*Judicial, Crime* (8)	*Sports* (9)	*Art, culture* (10)	*Human interest* (11)	*Other* (12)	*Total*
Organizations													
words	280	467	0	3,698	0	34	0	0	3,400	0	456	1,596	9,931
%	2.8	4.7	0	37.2	0	0.3	0	0	34.2	0	4.6	16.1	100.0
stories	1	2	0	10	0	1	0	0	1	0	1	1	17
%	5.9	11.8	0	58.8	0	5.9	0	0	5.9	0	5.9	5.9	100.0
Argentina													
words	0	0	0	0	0	0	37	0	0	0	0	0	37
%	0	0	0	0	0	0	100.0	0	0	0	0	0	100.0
stories	0	0	0	0	0	0	1	0	0	0	0	0	1
%	0	0	0	0	0	0	100.0	0	0	0	0	0	100.0
Australia													
words	0	0	9,979	280	0	0	1,026	0	686	0	105	0	12,076
%	0	0	82.6	2.3	0	0	8.5	0	5.7	0	0.9	0	100.0
stories	0	0	19	1	0	0	1	0	2	0	2	0	25
%	0	0	76.0	4.0	0	0	4.0	0	8.0	0	4.0	0	100.0
Canada													
words	0	0	296	238	0	0	990	0	0	0	0	0	1,524
%	0	0	19.4	15.6	0	0	65.0	0	0	0	0	0	100.0
stories	0	0	1	1	0	0	3	0	0	0	0	0	5
%	0	0	20.0	20.0	0	0	60.0	0	0	0	0	0	100.0
Eastern Europe													
words	0	2,504	0	0	0	0	0	0	146	0	0	380	3,030
%	0	82.6	0	0	0	0	0	0	4.8	0	0	12.5	100.0
stories	0	2	0	0	0	0	0	0	2	0	0	1	5
%	0	40.0	0	0	0	0	0	0	40.0	0	0	20.0	100.0

Table B7 continued

Country	Military, political violence (1)	Foreign relations (2)	Domestic Politics (3)	Economics (4)	Science, Health (5)	Education (6)	Accidents, disasters (7)	Judicial, Crime (8)	Sports (9)	Art, culture (10)	Human interest (11)	Other (12)	Total
France													
words	0	0	256	35	0	0	275	556	0	264	0	37	1,423
%	0	0	18.0	2.5	0	0	19.3	39.1	0	18.6	0	2.6	100.0
stories	0	0	2	1	0	0	2	3	0	1	0	1	10
%	0	0	20.0	10.0	0	0	20.0	30.0	0	10.0	0	10.0	100.0
Israel													
words	0	0	0	0	0	0	0	0	0	0	200	0	200
%	0	0	0	0	0	0	0	0	0	0	100.0	0	100.0
stories	0	0	0	0	0	0	0	0	0	0	1	0	1
%	0	0	0	0	0	0	0	0	0	0	100.0	0	100.0
Japan													
words	397	703	1,983	9,030	0	0	0	71	306	0	0	185	12,675
%	3.1	5.5	15.6	71.2	0	0	0	0.6	2.4	0	0	1.5	100.0
stories	2	2	3	21	0	0	0	2	1	0	0	1	32
%	6.3	6.3	9.4	65.6	0	0	0	6.3	3.0	0	0	3.0	100.0
New Zealand													
words	0	0	148	140	0	0	0	0	270	0	0	0	558
%	0	0	26.5	25.1	0	0	0	0	48.4	0	0	0	100.0
stories	0	0	1	1	0	0	0	0	2	0	0	0	4
%	0	0	25.0	25.0	0	0	0	0	50.0	0	0	0	100.0
Western Europe													
words	1,079	460	4,423	1,445	385	0	139	238	1,000	0	0	148	9,317
%	11.6	4.9	47.5	15.5	4.1	0	1.5	2.6	10.7	0	0	1.6	100.0
stories	4	1	10	7	1	0	3	1	4	0	0	1	32
%	12.5	3.1	31.3	21.9	3.1	0	9.4	3.1	12.5	0	0	3.1	100.0
Scandinavia													
words	0	598	308	0	0	0	0	0	456	0	0	0	1,362
%	0	43.9	22.6	0	0	0	0	0	33.5	0	0	0	100.0
stories	0	2	3	0	0	0	0	0	1	0	0	0	6
%	0	33.3	50.0	0	0	0	0	0	16.7	0	0.	0	100.0

Table B7 continued

Country	Military, political violence (1)	Foreign relations (2)	Domestic Politics (3)	Economics (4)	Science, Health (5)	Education (6)	Accidents, disasters (7)	Judicial, Crime (8)	Sports (9)	Art, culture (10)	Human interest (11)	Other (12)	Total
South Africa													
words	366	0	1,574	0	0	0	0	0	476	0	0	0	2,416
%	15.1	0	65.2	0	0	0	0	0	19.7	0	0	0	100.0
stories	1	0	6	0	0	0	0	0	1	0	0	0	8
%	12.5	0	75.0	0	0	0	0	0	12.5	0	0	0	100.0
United Kingdom													
words	0	1,593	475	7,158	304	136	408	2,202	5,104	618	1,845	0	19,843
%	0	8.0	2.4	36.1	1.5	0.7	2.1	11.1	25.7	3.1	9.3	0	100.0
stories	0	4	3	24	3	1	1	3	9	2	4	0	54
%	0	7.4	5.6	44.4	5.6	1.8	1.8	5.6	16.7	3.7	7.4	0	100.0
United States													
words	2,078	7,106	1,761	21,488	1,722	0	670	8,435	4,698	5,446	8,919	453	62,776
%	3.3	11.3	2.8	34.2	2.7	0	1.1	13.4	7.5	8.7	14.2	0.7	100.0
stories	5	15	6	37	6	0	6	22	11	5	16	2	131
%	3.8	11.5	4.6	28.2	4.6	0	4.6	16.8	8.4	3.8	12.2	1.5	100.0
U.S.S.R.													
words	3,463	3,216	0	832	0	0	0	111	2,072	0	170	0	9,864
%	35.1	32.6	0	8.4	0	0	0	1.1	21.0	0	1.7	0	100.0
stories	6	3	0	1	0	0	0	2	2	0	1	0	15
%	40.0	20.0	0	6.7	0	0	0	13.3	13.3	0	6.7	0	100.0
West Germany													
words	2,836	0	0	448	0	136	0	291	3,126	1,096	0	1,825	9,757
%	29.1	0	0	4.6	0	1.4	0	3	32.0	11.2	0	18.7	100.0
stories	4	0	0	3	0	1	0	2	6	2	0	1	10
%	21.1	0	0	15.8	0	5.3	0	10.5	31.6	10.5	0	5.3	100.0
Bangladesh													
words	0	0	0	250	0	0	0	0	0	0	0	0	250
%	0	0	0	100.0	0	0	0	0	0	0	0	0	100.0
stories	0	0	0	1	0	0	0	0	0	0	0	0	1
%	0	0	0	100.0	0	0	0	0	0	0	0	0	100.0

Table B7 continued

Country	Military, political violence (1)	Foreign relations (2)	Domestic Politics (3)	Economics (4)	Science, Health (5)	Education (6)	Accidents, disasters (7)	Judicial, Crime (8)	Sports (9)	Art, culture (10)	Human interest (11)	Other (12)	Total
Burma													
words	0	0	0	0	0	0	0	0	0	0	0	0	0
%	0	0	0	0	0	0	0	0	0	0	0	0	0
stories	0	0	0	0	0	0	0	0	0	0	0	0	0
%	0	0	0	0	0	0	0	0	0	0	0	0	0
Cambodia													
words	0	4,647	0	0	0	0	0	0	0	0	0	0	4,647
%	0	100.0	0	0	0	0	0	0	0	0	0	0	100.0
stories	0	3	0	0	0	0	0	0	0	0	0	0	3
%	0	100.0	0	0	0	0	0	0	0	0	0	0	100.0
China													
words	0	5,413	4,047	102	0	0	0	0	2,213	444	3,561	0	15,780
%	0	34.3	25.6	0.6	0	0	0	0	14.0	2.8	22.6	0	100.0
stories	0	15	5	1	0	0	0	0	2	1	3	0	27
%	0	55.6	18.5	3.7	0	0	0	0	7.4	3.7	11.1	0	100.0
Hong Kong													
words	0	0	0	7,008	0	0	0	347	684	0	3,904	0	11,943
%	0	0	0	58.7	0	0	0	2.9	5.7	0	32.7	0	100.0
stories	0	0	0	8	0	0	0	2	1	0	2	0	13
%	0	0	0	61.5	0	0	0	15.4	7.7	0	15.4	0	100.0
India													
words	192	344	831	876	0	0	140	443	1,842	0	0	0	4,668
%	4.1	7.4	17.8	18.8	0	0	3.0	9.5	39.5	0	0	0	100.0
stories	1	2	5	4	0	0	3	4	6	0	0	0	25
%	4.0	8.0	20.0	16.0	0	0	12.0	16.0	24.0	0	0	0	100.0
Indonesia													
words	484	70	140	1,871	0	0	0	0	76.2	0	1,383	64	4,774
%	10.1	1.5	2.9	39.2	0	0	0	0	16.0	0	29.0	1.3	100.0
stories	3	1	1	2	0	0	0	0	2	0	2	1	12
%	25.0	8.3	8.3	16.7	0	0	0	0	16.7	0	16.7	8.3	100.0

Country	Military, political violence (1)	Foreign relations (2)	Domestic Politics (3)	Economics (4)	Science, Health (5)	Education (6)	Accidents, disasters (7)	Judicial, Crime (8)	Sports (9)	Art, culture (10)	Human interest (11)	Other (12)	Total
Iran													
words	0	672	0	672	0	50	0	512	3,744	4,288	0	0	9,938
%	0	6.8	0	6.8	0	0.5	0	5.1	37.7	43.1	0	0	100.0
stories	0	3	0	4	0	1	0	2	8	7	0	0	25
%	0	12.0	0	16.0	0	4.0	0	8.0	32.0	28.0	0	0	100.0
Laos													
words	1,120	0	0	0	0	0	0	0	0	0	0	0	1,120
%	100.0	0	0	0	0	0	0	0	0	0	0	0	100.0
stories	1	0	0	0	0	0	0	0	0	0	0	0	1
%	100.0	0	0	0	0	0	0	0	0	0	0	0	100.0
Malaysia													
words	1,091	2,576	6,189	3,763	0	469	11,030	1,807	2,346	0	5,921	0	35,192
%	3.1	7.3	17.6	10.7	0	1.3	31.3	5.1	6.7	0	16.8	0	100.0
stories	2	6	9	10	0	2	15	3	3	0	8	0	58
%	3.4	10.3	15.5	17.2	0	3.4	25.9	5.2	5.2	0	13.8	0	100.0
Nepal													
words	0	0	0	138	0	0	0	0	0	0	0	0	138
%	0	0	0	100.0	0	0	0	0	0	0	0	0	100.0
stories	0	0	0	1	0	0	0	0	0	0	0	0	1
%	0	0	0	100.0	0	0	0	0	0	0	0	0	100.0
North Korea													
words	0	80	730	0	0	0	0	0	0	0	0	0	810
%	0	9.9	90.1	0	0	0	0	0	0	0	0	0	100.0
stories	0	1	2	0	0	0	0	0	0	0	0	0	3
%	0	33.3	66.7	0	0	0	0	0	0	0	0	0	100.0
Other Asian Countries													
words	1,904	960	0	0	0	0	320	0	0	0	0	0	3,184
%	59.8	30.1	0	0	0	0	10.0	0	0	0	0	0	100.0
stories	1	1	0	0	0	0	3	0	0	0	0	0	5
%	20.0	20.0	0	0	0	0	60.0	0	0	0	0	0	100.0

Table B7 continued

Country	Military, political violence (1)	Foreign relations (2)	Domestic Politics (3)	Economics (4)	Science, Health (5)	Education (6)	Accidents, disasters (7)	Judicial, Crime (8)	Sports (9)	Art, culture (10)	Human interest (11)	Other (12)	Total
Pakistan													
words	0	1,151	1,388	232	0	0	0	0	4,641	0	0	438	7,850
%	0	14.7	17.7	2.9	0	0	0	0	59.1	0	0	5.6	100.0
stories	0	5	5	3	0	0	0	0	7	0	0	3	23
%	0	21.8	21.9	13.0	0	0	0	0	30.4	0	0	13.0	100.0
Philippines													
words	182	397	4,610	0	0	0	0	0	5,303	0	0	0	10,483
%	1.7	3.8	43.9	0	0	0	0	0	50.6	0	0	0	100.0
stories	2	3	10	0	0	0	0	0	7	0	0	0	22
%	9.1	13.6	45.5	0	0	0	0	0	31.8	0	0	0	100.0
Singapore													
words	0	2,196	0	11,374	0	306	1,098	3,904	1,574	0	1,708	889	23,049
%	0	9.5	0	49.3	0	1.3	4.8	16.9	6.8	0	7.4	3.9	100.0
stories	0	3	0	9	0	1	1	3	3	0	1	2	23
%	0	13.0	0	39.1	0	4.3	4.3	13.0	13.0	0	4.3	8.7	100.0
South Korea													
words	0	1,795	408	374	0	0	0	496	4,166	0	0	0	7,239
%	0	24.8	5.6	5.2	0	0	0	6.9	57.5	0	0	0	100.0
stories	0	6	1	1	0	0	0	1	4	0	0	0	13
%	0	46.1	7.7	7.7	0	0	0	7.7	30.8	0	0	0	100.0
Sri Lanka													
words	96	1,233	171	736	0	0	0	0	0	0	0	0	2,236
%	4.3	55.1	7.6	32.9	0	0	0	0	0	0	0	0	100.0
stories	1	3	1	1	0	0	0	0	0	0	0	0	6
%	16.7	50.0	16.7	16.7	0	0	0	0	0	0	0	0	100.0
Taiwan													
words	0	898	570	1,417	0	0	0	0	1,096	186	183	0	4,350
%	0	20.6	13.1	32.6	0	0	0	0	25.2	4.3	4.2	0	100.0
stories	0	6	1	5	0	0	0	0	2	1	1	0	16

Country	Military, political violence (1)	Foreign relations (2)	Domestic Politics (3)	Economics (4)	Science, Health (5)	Education (6)	Accidents, disasters (7)	Judicial, Crime (8)	Sports (9)	Art, culture (10)	Human interest (11)	Other (12)	Total
Thailand													
words	0	1,718	834	886	310	476	37	0	873	0	0	0	5,134
%	0	33.5	16.2	17.3	6.0	9.3	0.7	0	17.0	0	0	0	100.0
stories	0	6	3	4	1	1	1	0	3	0	0	0	19
%	0	31.6	15.8	21.0	5.3	5.3	5.3	0	15.8	0	0	0	100.0
Vietnam													
words	915	8,150	0	0	0	0	0	1,150	0	0	0	0	10,215
%	8.9	79.8	0	0	0	0	0	11.3	0	0	0	0	100.0
stories	1	12	0	0	0	0	0	2	0	0	0	0	15
%	6.7	80.0	0	0	0	0	0	13.3	0	0	0	0	100.0
Brazil													
words	0	0	0	3,806	0	0	0	0	0	0	0	0	3,806
%	0	0	0	100.0	0	0	0	0	0	0	0	0	100.0
stories	0	0	0	4	0	0	0	0	0	0	0	0	4
%	0	0	0	100.0	0	0	0	0	0	0	0	0	100.0
Columbia													
words	0	0	32	0	0	0	0	0	0	0	0	0	32
%	0	0	100.0	0	0	0	0	0	0	0	0	0	100.0
stories	0	0	1	0	0	0	0	0	0	0	0	0	1
%	0	0	100.0	0	0	0	0	0	0	0	0	0	100.0
Chile													
words	0	0	0	0	0	0	0	0	0	0	0	0	0
%	0	0	0	0	0	0	0	0	0	0	0	0	0
stories	0	0	0	0	0	0	0	0	0	0	0	0	0
%	0	0	0	0	0	0	0	0	0	0	0	0	0
Cuba													
words	544	2,300	0	0	0	0	35	296	0	0	0	0	3,175
%	17.1	72.4	0	0	0	0	1.1	9.3	0	0	0	0	100.0
stories	1	5	0	0	0	0	1	1	0	0	0	0	8
%	12.5	62.5	0	0	0	0	12.5	12.5	0	0	0	0	100.0

Table B7 continued

Country	Military, political violence (1)	Foreign relations (2)	Domestic Politics (3)	Economics (4)	Science, Health (5)	Education (6)	Accidents, disasters (7)	Judicial, Crime (8)	Sports (9)	Art, culture (10)	Human interest (11)	Other (12)	Total
Mexico													
words	0	0	0	0	0	0	0	0	4,318	0	0	0	4,318
%	0	0	0	0	0	0	0	0	100.0	0	0	0	100.0
stories	0	0	0	0	0	0	0	0	1	0	0	0	1
%	0	0	0	0	0	0	0	0	100.0	0	0	0	100.0
Peru													
words	0	0	0	0	0	0	0	0	0	0	0	0	0
%	0	0	0	0	0	0	0	0	0	0	0	0	0
stories	0	0	0	0	0	0	0	0	0	0	0	0	0
%	0	0	0	0	0	0	0	0	0	0	0	0	0
Venezuela													
words	0	0	0	0	0	0	0	0	0	0	0	0	0
%	0	0	0	0	0	0	0	0	0	0	0	0	0
stories	0	0	0	0	0	0	0	0	0	0	0	0	0
%	0	0	0	0	0	0	0	0	0	0	0	0	0
Other Latin Countries													
words	32	170	614	0	0	0	0	0	952	0	0	0	1,768
%	1.8	9.6	34.7	0	0	0	0	0	53.9	0	0	0	100.0
stories	1	1	2	0	0	0	0	0	2	0	0	0	6
%	16.7	16.7	33.3	0	0	0	0	0	33.3	0	0	0	100.0
Algeria													
words	0	0	0	0	0	0	0	0	0	0	0	0	0
%	0	0	0	0	0	0	0	0	0	0	0	0	0
stories	0	0	0	0	0	0	0	0	0	0	0	0	0
%	0	0	0	0	0	0	0	0	0	0	0	0	0
Egypt													
words	0	20,788	0	0	0	0	0	0	1,792	0	0	0	22,580
%	0	92.1	0	0	0	0	0	0	7.9	0	0	0	100.0
stories	0	26	0	0	0	0	0	0	1	0	0	0	27
%	0	96.3	0	0	0	0	0	0	3.7	0	0	0	100.0

Country	Military, political violence (1)	Foreign relations (2)	Domestic Politics (3)	Economics (4)	Science, Health (5)	Education (6)	Accidents, disasters (7)	Judicial, Crime (8)	Sports (9)	Art, cultur (10)	Human interest (11)	Other (12)	Total
Iraq													
words	0	488	0	0	0	0	0	0	665	0	0	0	1,153
%	0	42.3	0	0	0	0	0	0	57.7	0	0	0	100.0
stories	0	1	0	0	0	0	0	0	1	0	0	0	2
%	0	50.0	0	0	0	0	0	0	50.0	0	0	0	100.0
Jordan													
words	0	1,924	0	0	0	0	0	0	0	0	0	0	1.924
%	0	100.0	0	0	0	0	0	0	0	0	0	0	100.0
stories	0	3	0	0	0	0	0	0	0	0	0	0	3
%	0	100.0	0	0	0	0	0	0	0	0	0	0	100.0
Libya													
words	0	264	0	0	0	0	0	0	0	0	0	0	264
%	0	100.0	0	0	0	0	0	0	0	0	0	0	100.0
stories	0	1	0	0	0	0	0	0	0	0	0	0	1
%	0	100.0	0	0	0	0	0	0	0	0	0	0	100.0
Saudi Arabia													
words	0	1,628	0	4,766	0	0	0	0	0	0	0	2,384	8,778
%	0	18.5	0	54.3	0	0	0	0	0	0	0	27.2	100.0
stories	0	4	0	9	0	0	0	0	0	0	0	2	15
%	0	26.7	0	60.0	0	0	0	0	0	0	0	13.3	100.0
Syria													
words	160	26,007	0	0	0	0	0	0	0	0	0	0	26,167
%	0.6	99.4	0	0	0	0	0	0	0	0	0	0	100.0
stories	1	33	0	0	0	0	0	0	0	0	0	0	34
%	2.9	97.1	0	0	0	0	0	0	0	0	0	0	100.0
Other Mideast Countries													
words	403	10,050	0	1,159	0	0	998	96	0	352	0	320	13,378
%	3.0	75.1	0	8.7	0	0	7.5	0.7	0	2.6	0	2.4	100.0
stories	2	9	0	4	0	0	3	1	0	1	0	1	21
%	9.5	42.8	0	19.0	0	0	14.3	4.8	0	4.8	0	4.8	100.0

Table B7 continued

Country	Military, political violence (1)	Foreign relations (2)	Domestic Politics (3)	Economics (4)	Science, Health (5)	Education (6)	Accidents, disasters (7)	Judicial, Crime (8)	Sports (9)	Art, culture (10)	Human interest (11)	Other (12)	Total
Kenya													
words	0	0	0	0	0	0	204	0	0	0	0	0	204
%	0	0	0	0	0	0	100.0	0	0	0	0	0	100.0
stories	0	0	0	0	0	0	1	0	0	0	0	1	
%	0	0	0	0	0	0	100.0	0	0	0	0	0	100.0
Nigeria													
words	0	0	0	0	0	0	0	0	0	0	0	0	0
%	0	0	0	0	0	0	0	0	0	0	0	0	0
stories	0	0	0	0	0	0	0	0	0	0	0	0	0
%	0	0	0	0	0	0	0	0	0	0	0	0	0
Uganda													
words	0	700	1,462	374	0	0	0	0	0	1,056	0	252	3,844
%	0	18.2	38.0	9.7	0	0	0	0	0	27.5	0	6.6	100.0
stories	0	1	1	1	0	0	0	0	0	1	0	2	6
%	0	16.7	16.7	16.7	0	0	0	0	0	16.7	0	33.3	100.0
Other African Countries													
words	1,657	10,635	3,522	1,491	0	0	0	0	0	64	70	0	17,439
%	9.5	61.0	20.2	8.5	0	0	0	0	0	0.4	0.4	0	100.0
stories	5	12	5	7	0	0	0	0	0	1	1	0	31
%	16.1	38.7	16.1	22.6	0	0	0	0	0	3.2	3.2	0	100.0
South Pacific													
words	0	0	0	0	0	0	0	0	710	0	0	0	710
%	0	0	0	0	0	0	0	0	100.0	0	0	0	100.0
stories	0	0	0	0	0	0	0	0	2	0	0	0	2
%	0	0	0	0	0	0	0	0	100.0	0	0	0	100.0
Total													
words	19,279	123,901	46,742	86,087	2,721	1,607	17,267	20,955	59,421	13,814	28,425	8,970	429,329
%	4.5	28.8	10.9	20.1	0.6	0.4	4.1	4.9	13.8	3.2	6.6	2.1	100.0
stories	45	203	106	186	11	8	45	54	97	22	43	19	839
%	5.4	24.2	12.6	22.2	1.3	0.9	5.4	6.4	11.6	2.6	5.1	2.3	100.0

TABLE B8

Approximate Number and Percentage of Words and Number and Percentage of Stories for All Countries by Areas of the World for Each of the Four International News Wires and Hsinhua for One Day, Wednesday, December 7, 1977.

Wire Service	*Non-Third*	*Both*	*Third*	*Total*
Wire A				
words	27,224	12,341	8,938	48,503
%	56.1	25.4	18.4	100.0
stories	115	46	36	197
%	58.4	23.3	18.3	100.0
Wire B				
words	31,906	13,072	8,213	53,191
%	60.0	24.6	15.4	100.0
stories	98	48	33	179
%	54.4	26.8	18.4	100.0
Wire C				
words	36,456	14,868	19,530	70,854
%	51.5	21.0	27.5	100.0
stories	161	57	73	291
%	55.3	19.6	25.1	100.0
Wire D				
words	15,660	15,930	12,744	44,334
%	35.3	35.9	28.7	100.0
stories	93	85	74	252
%	36.9	33.7	29.4	100.0
Four Wires				
words	111,246	56,211	49,425	216,882
%	51.3	25.9	22.8	100.0
stories	467	236	216	919
%	50.8	25.7	23.5	100.0
Hsinhua				
words	2,100	3,150	2,850	8,100
%	25.9	38.9	39.2	100.0
stories	12	14	9	35
%	34.3	40.0	25.7	100.0
Total				
words	113,346	59,361	52,275	224,982
%	50.4	26.4	23.2	100.0
stories	479	250	225	954
%	50.2	26.2	23.6	100.0

TABLE B9

Approximate Number and Percentage of Words and Number and Percentage of Stories for All Countries by Areas of the World for Each of 17 Asian Daily Newspapers for One Day, Thursday, December 8, 1977.

Paper	*Non-third*	*Both*	*Third*	*Total*
Amrita Bazar Patrika				
words	828	2,438	1,610	4,876
%	17.0	50.0	33.3	100.0
stories	7	8	6	21
%	33.3	38.1	28.6	100.0
Bangkok Post				
words	22,202	5,882	4,930	33,014
%	67.3	17.8	14.9	100.0
stories	40	15	13	68
%	58.8	22.1	19.1	100.0
Ceylon Daily News				
words	924	1,452	1,540	3,916
%	23.6	37.1	39.3	100.0
stories	6	6	8	20
%	30.0	30.0	40.0	100.0
Dong-a Ilbo				
words	5,035	10,830	5,225	21,090
%	23.9	51.4	24.7	100.0
stories	10	15	6	31
%	32.3	48.4	19.4	100.0
Ettelaat				
words	5,248	19,520	3,936	28,704
%	18.3	68.0	13.7	100.0
stories	12	26	9	47
%	25.5	55.3	19.2	100.0
Kayhan International				
words	16,224	16,480	4,864	37,568
%	43.2	43.9	12.9	100.0
stories	42	29	17	88
%	47.7	33.0	19.3	100.0
Kompas				
words	102	2,584	5,406	8,092
%	1.3	31.9	66.8	100.0
stories	3	4	8	15
%	20.0	26.7	53.3	100.0
Korea Times				
words	3,480	3,360	2,760	9,600
%	36.3	35.0	28.7	100.0
stories	11	10	10	31
%	35.5	32.3	32.3	100.0
Nanyang Siang Pau				
words	10,614	22,204	31,354	64,172
%	16.5	34.6	48.9	100.0
stories	14	21	22	57
%	24.6	36.8	38.6	100.0

Table B9 continued

Paper	*Non-third*	*Both*	*Third*	*Total*
New Straits Times				
words	7,990	13,906	6,154	28,050
%	28.5	49.6	21.9	100.0
stories	20	20	17	57
%	35.1	35.1	29.8	100.0
Pilipino Express				
words	0	1,050	525	1,575
%	0	66.7	33.3	100.0
stories	0	2	2	4
%	0	50.0	50.0	100.0
Philippine Daily Express				
words	4,522	14,110	3,298	21,930
%	20.6	64.3	15.1	100.0
stories	16	14	10	40
%	40.0	35.0	25.0	100.0
Sing Chew Jit Poh				
words	13,965	13,680	26,505	54,150
%	25.8	25.3	48.9	100.0
stories	16	16	39	71
%	22.5	22.5	54.9	100.0
Sing Tao Jih Pao				
words	8,122	13,640	3,224	24,986
%	32.5	54.6	12.9	100.0
stories	15	18	6	39
%	38.5	46.2	15.4	100.0
South China Morning Post				
words	14,134	7,141	10,841	32,116
%	44.0	22.2	33.8	100.0
stories	58	20	33	111
%	52.3	18.0	29.7	100.0
Statesman				
words	3,250	2,600	850	6,700
%	48.5	38.8	12.7	100.0
stories	13	7	8	28
%	46.4	25.0	28.6	100.0
Straits Times				
words	17,290	12,495	19,005	48,790
%	35.4	25.6	39.0	100.0
stories	43	22	46	111
%	38.7	19.8	41.4	100.0
Total				
words	133,930	163,372	132,027	429,329
%	31.2	38.1	30.7	100.0
stories	326	253	260	839
%	38.8	30.2	31.0	100.0

TABLE B10

Approximate Number and Percentage of Words and Number and Percentage of Stories for All Countries by Five World Zones for Each of the Four International News Wires and Hsinhua for One Day, Wednesday, December 7, 1977

News Wire	*Non-Third*	*Asia*	*Latin America*	*Middle East*	*Africa*	*Total*
Wire A						
words	29,725	8,241	1,066	7,298	2,173	48,503
%	61.3	17.0	2.2	15.0	4.5	100.0
stories	123	40	6	20	8	197
%	62.4	20.3	3.0	10.2	4.1	100.0
Wire B						
words	32,307	10,664	1,290	7,955	1,075	53,191
%	60.6	20.0	2.4	15.0	1.0	100.0
stories	99	49	3	24	4	179
%	55.3	27.4	1.7	13.4	2.2	100.0
Wire C						
words	39,858	16,044	2,352	7,308	5,292	70,854
%	56.3	22.6	3.3	10.3	7.5	100.0
stories	173	62	10	28	18	291
%	59.5	21.3	3.4	9.6	6.2	100.0
Wire D						
words	17,874	15,660	918	6,102	3,780	44,334
%	40.3	35.3	2.1	13.8	8.5	100.0
stories	103	85	8	36	20	252
%	40.9	33.7	3.2	14.3	7.9	100.0
Four Wires						
words	119,664	50,609	5,626	28,663	12,320	216,882
%	55.2	23.3	2.6	13.2	5.7	100.0
stories	498	236	27	108	50	919
%	54.2	25.7	2.9	11.8	5.4	100.0
Hsinhua						
words	2,100	3,510	210	300	1,980	8,100
%	25.9	43.3	2.6	3.7	24.4	100.0
stories	9	15	2	2	7	35
%	25.7	42.9	5.7	5.7	20.0	100.0
Total						
words	121,764	54,119	5,836	28,963	14,300	224,982
%	54.1	24.0	2.6	12.9	6.4	100.0
stories	507	251	29	110	57	954
%	53.1	26.3	3.0	11.5	6.0	100.0

TABLE B11

Approximate Number and Percentage of Words and Number and Percentage of Stories for All Countries by Five World Zones for Each of 17 Asian Daily Newspapers for One Day, Thursday, December 8, 1977.

Newspaper	*Non-Third*	*Asia*	*Latin America*	*Middle East*	*Africa*	*Total*
Amrita Bazar Patrika						
words	1,380	1,334	0	1,242	920	4,876
%	28.3	27.4	0	25.5	18.9	100.0
stories	9	4	0	4	4	21
%	42.9	19.0	0	19.0	19.0	100.0
Bangkok Post						
words	22,270	8,534	986	1,224	0	33,014
%	67.5	25.8	3.0	3.7	0	100.0
stories	41	21	3	3	0	68
%	60.3	30.9	4.4	4.4	0	100.0
Ceylon Daily News						
words	1,012	1,012	0	1,408	484	3,916
%	25.8	25.8	0	36.0	12.4	100.0
stories	7	7	0	4	2	20
%	35.0	35.0	0	20.0	10.0	100.0
Dong-a Ilbo						
words	8,835	6,270	0	5,985	0	21,090
%	41.9	29.7	0	28.4	0	100.0
stories	18	6	0	7	0	31
%	58.1	19.3	0	22.6	0	100.0
Ettelaat						
words	5,472	1,600	960	16,832	3,840	28,704
%	19.1	5.6	3.3	58.6	13.4	100.0
stories	12	5	1	25	4	47
%	25.5	10.6	2.1	53.2	8.5	100.0
Kayhan International						
words	16,800	2,144	768	15,360	2,496	37,568
%	44.7	5.7	2.0	40.9	6.6	100.0
stories	41	11	4	26	6	88
%	46.6	12.5	4.5	29.5	6.8	100.0
Kompas						
words	102	3,570	1,496	0	2,924	8,092
%	1.3	44.1	18.5	0	36.1	100.0
stories	3	5	5	0	2	15
%	20.0	33.3	33.3	0	13.3	100.0
Korea Times						
words	4,480	1,160	160	2,480	1,320	9,600
%	46.7	12.1	1.7	25.8	13.7	100.0
stories	12	8	1	7	3	31
%	38.7	25.8	3.2	22.6	9.7	100.0

Table B11 *continued*

Newspaper	Non-Third	Asia	Latin America	Middle East	Africa	Total
Nanyang Siang Pau						
words	10,614	39,711	0	9,516	4,331	64,172
%	16.5	61.9	0	14.8	6.7	100.0
stories	14	31	0	9	3	57
%	24.6	54.4	0	15.8	5.3	100.0
New Straits Times						
words	11,696	8,772	850	5,066	1,666	28,050
%	41.7	31.3	3.0	18.1	5.9	100.0
stories	24	22	2	7	2	57
%	42.1	38.6	3.5	12.3	3.5	100.0
Pilipino Express						
words	770	805	0	0	0	1,575
%	48.9	51.0	0	0	0	100.0
stories	1	3	0	0	0	4
%	25.0	75.0	0	0	0	100.0
Philippine Daily Express						
words	11,390	2,720	5,202	2,006	612	21,930
%	51.9	12.4	23.7	9.2	2.8	100.0
stories	25	7	3	3	2	40
%	62.5	17.5	7.5	7.5	5.0	100.0
Sing Chew Jit Poh						
words	16,473	28,215	798	8,322	342	54,150
%	30.4	52.1	1.5	15.4	0.6	100.0
stories	19	44	1	6	1	71
%	26.8	62.0	1.4	8.4	1.4	100.0
Sing Tao Jih Pao						
words	8,804	6,448	1,860	7,874	0	24,986
%	35.2	25.8	7.4	31.5	0	100.0
stories	17	12	1	9	0	39
%	43.6	30.8	2.6	23.1	0	100.0
South China Morning Post						
words	14,356	14,504	1,480	814	962	32,116
%	44.7	45.2	4.6	2.5	3.0	100.0
stories	59	43	3	3	3	111
%	53.2	38.7	2.7	2.7	2.7	100.0
Statesman						
words	3,400	1,050	0	600	750	6,700
%	50.7	29.1	0	9.0	11.2	100.0
stories	14	9	0	2	3	28
%	50.0	32.1	0	7.1	10.7	100.0
Straits Times						
words	18,935	21,945	35	7,035	840	48,790
%	38.8	45.0	0.1	14.4	1.7	100.0
stories	49	46	1	12	3	111
%	44.1	41.4	0.9	10.8	2.7	100.0
Total						
words	156,789	150,694	13,099	87,260	21,487	429,329
%	36.5	35.1	3.1	20.3	5.0	100.0
stories	365	284	20	132	38	839
%	43.5	33.8	2.4	15.7	4.5	100.0

TABLE B12

Zero-order Correlations[a] (tau) Among Four International News Wires, Hsinhua, and 16 Asian Daily Newspapers[b] for One Day.

		News Wire					*16 Asian Daily Newspapers*															
		(1)	*(2)*	*(3)*	*(4)*	*(5)*	*(6)*	*(7)*	*(8)*	*(9)*	*(10)*	*(11)*	*(12)*	*(13)*	*(14)*	*(15)*	*(16)*	*(17)*	*(18)*	*(19)*	*(20)*	*(21)*
(1)	Wire A	—	86	77	66	61	48	71	59	72	55	74	50	55	64	73	46	52	35	69	52	56
(2)	Wire B		—	83	77	68	61	74	52	79	45	71	53	65	68	68	43	58	38	69	64	59
(3)	Wire C			—	66	53	53	71	49	76	52	62	40	61	70	71	36	58	38	66	60	55
(4)	Wire D				—	56	66	69	64	64	50	44	68	76	77	61	38	75	46	73	65	76
(5)	Hsinhua					—	42	39	32	78	42	45	48	50	51	36	25	34	16	45	49	34
(6)	Amrita Bazar Patrika						—	52	50	64	20	37	53	92	76	49	26	65	72	73	82	61
(7)	Bangkok Post							—	48	54	40	58	55	59	59	68	55	66	49	66	65	77
(8)	Ceylon Daily News								—	41	73	56	55	49	49	63	55	52	44	55	39	53
(9)	Dong-a Ilbo									—	45	56	39	71	73	66	29	54	35	67	71	48
(10)	Ettelaat										—	80	34	28	35	53	50	35	17	34	26	38
(11)	Kayhan International											—	33	41	41	57	49	36	31	47	47	41
(12)	Kompas												—	57	48	34	46	48	37	52	50	59
(13)	Korea Times													—	89	56	34	78	68	79	90	72
(14)	Nanyang Siang Pau														—	69	28	85	62	82	78	73
(15)	New Straits Times															—	46	73	46	68	55	69
(16)	Philippine daily Express																—	48	22	27	43	56
(17)	Sing Chew Jit Poh																	—	58	69	69	88
(18)	Sing Tao Jih Pao																		—	62	68	62
(19)	South China Morning Post																			—	73	67
(20)	Statesman																				—	73
(21)	Straits Times																					—

a. Correlations are computed across the 12 content categories. Decimals have been omitted. Underscored coefficients are not significant at the .05 level.

b. *Pilipino Express* omitted because only 4 stories were published on Thursday, December 8, 1977.

APPENDIX C: The News for Five Days

Table — Title

1. Number and Percentage of References to Each of 42 Third World Countries, Alone and Combined with Other Countries, on the Four International News Wires and Hsinhua for Five Days, December 5-9, 1977.

2. Number and Percentage of References to Each of 42 Third World Countries, Alone and Combined with Other Countries, in 17 Asian Daily Newspapers for Five Days, December 6-10, 1977.

3. Approximate Number and Percentage of Words and Number and Percentage of Stories for Each Content Category for Each International News Wire and Hsinhua for 42 Third World Countries for Five Days, December 5-9, 1977.

4. Approximate Number and Percentage of Words and Number and Percentage of Stories for Each Content Category for Each of 17 Asian Daily Newspapers for 42 Third World Countries for Five Days, December 6-10, 1977.

5. Approximate Number and Percentage of Words and Number and Percentage of Stories for Each of 42 Third World Countries by Content Category for the Composite News Wire (excluding Hsinhua) for Five Days, December 5-9, 1977.

6. Approximate Number and Percentage of Words and Number and Percentage of Stories for Each of 42 Third World Countries by Content Category for Hsinhua for Five Days, December 5-9, 1977.

7. Approximate Number and Percentage of Words and Number and Percentage of Stories for Each of 42 Third World Countries by Content Category for the Composite Asian Daily Newspaper for Five Days, December 6-10, 1977.

8. Approximate Number and Percentage of Words and Number and Percentage of Stories for 42 Third World Countries by Area of the World for Each of the Four International News Wires and Hsinhua for Five Days, December 5-9, 1977.

9. Approximate Number and Percentage of Words and Number and Percentage of Stories for 42 Third World Countries by Area of the World for Each of 17 Asian Daily Newspapers for Five Days, December 6-10, 1977.

10. Approximate Number and Percentage of Words and Number and Percentage of Stories for 42 Third World Countries by World Zones for Each of the Four International News Wires and Hsinhua for Five Days, December 5-9, 1977.

11. Approximate Number and Percentage of Words and Number and Percentage of Stories for 42 Third World Countries by World Zones for Each of 17 Asian Daily Newspapers for Five Days, December 6-10, 1977.

12. Zero-order Correlations (tau) Among Four International News Wires, Hsinhua, and 16 Asian Daily Newspapers (for 42 Third World Countries) for Five Days.

TABLE C1

Number and Percentage of References to Each of 42 Third World Countries, Alone and Combined with Other Countries, on the Four Internatioanl News Wires and Hsinhua for Five Days, December 5-9, 1977.

Country		*Wire A*	*Wire B*	*Wire C*	*Wire D*	*Four Wires*	*Grand Total*	*Hsinhua*
Bangladesh								
alone	n	0	2	3	2	7		1
	%	0	100.0	100.0	33.3	58.3	12	100.0
							0.6	
combined	n	1	0	0	4	5		0
	%	100.0	0	0	66.7	41.7		0
Burma								
alone	n	0	0	0	1	1		0
	%	0	0	0	100.0	100.0	1	0
							0.0	
combined	n	0	0	0	0	0		0
	%	0	0	0	0	0		0
Cambodia								
alone	n	0	0	1	1	2		
	%	0	0	50.0	100.0	66.7	3	0
							0.2	
combined	n	0	0	1	0	1		0
	%	0	0	50.0	0	33.3		0
China								
alone	n	8	9	12	27	56		26
	%	40.0	33.3	46.2	62.8	48.3	116	51.0
							5.8	
combined	n	12	18	14	16	60		25
	%	60.0	66.7	53.8	37.2	51.7		49.0
Hong Kong								
alone	n	8	0	30	2	40		0
	%	88.9	0	85.7	66.7	83.3	48	0
							2.4	
combined	n	1	1	5	1	8		0
	%	11.1	100.0	14.3	33.3	16.7		0
India								
alone	n	7	2	17	24	50		0
	%	77.8	33.3	51.5	61.5	57.5	87	0
							4.4	
combined	n	2	4	16	15	37		1
	%	22.2	66.7	48.5	38.5	42.5		100.0
Indonesia								
alone	n	15	3	12	23	53		0
	%	83.3	60.0	70.6	71.9	73.6	72	0
							3.6	
combined	n	3	2	5	9	19		1
	%	16.7	40.0	29.4	28.1	26.4		100.0

Table C1 continued

Country		Wire A	Wire B	Wire C	Wire D	Four Wires	Grand Total	Hsinhua
Iran								
alone	n	0	1	4	3	8		2
	%	0	50.0	80.0	42.9	50.0	16	100.0
							0.8	
combined	n	2	1	1	4	8		0
	%	100.0	50.0	20.0	57.1	50.0		0
Laos								
alone	n	1	0	1	1	3		1
	%	100.0	0	100.0	100.0	100.0	3	100.0
							0.1	
combined	n	0	0	0	0	0		0
	%	0	0	0	0	0		0
Malaysia								
alone	n	12	14	33	42	104		0
	%	75.0	77.8	80.5	75.0	78.3	131	0
							6.6	
combined	n	4	4	8	14	30		1
	%	25.0	22.2	20.0	25.0	21.7		100.0
Nepal								
alone	n	1	2	6	5	14		0
	%	100.0	100.0	100.0	83.3	93.3	15	0
							0.8	
combined	n	0	0	0	1	1		0
	%	0	0	0	16.7	6.7		0
North Korea								
alone	n	0	1	0	1	2		2
	%	0	20.0	0	33.3	22.2	9	66.7
							0.5	
combined	n	0	4	1	2	7		1
	%	0	80.0	100.0	66.7	77.8		33.3
Other Asian Countries								
alone	n	0	0	0	0	0		1
	%	0	0	0	0	0	4	100.0
							0.2	
combined	n	1	0	2	1	4		0
	%	100.0	0	100.0	100.0	100.0		0
Pakistan								
alone	n	5	9	19	10	43		4
	%	62.5	64.3	42.2	55.6	50.6	85	100.0
							4.3	
combined	n	3	5	26	8	42		0
	%	37.5	35.7	57.8	44.4	49.4		0

Table C1 continued

Country		Wire A	Wire B	Wire C	Wire D	Four Wires	Grand Total	Hsinhua
Philippines								
alone	n	11	12	27	27	77		0
	%	40.7	52.2	50.0	69.2	53.8	143	0
							7.2	
combined	n	16	11	27	12	66		0
	%	59.3	47.8	50.0	30.8	46.2		0
Singapore								
alone	n	9	11	20	8	48		0
	%	56.3	78.6	62.5	34.8	56.5	85	0
							4.3	
combined	n	7	3	12	15	37		0
	%	43.7	21.4	37.5	65.2	43.5		0
South Korea								
alone	n	8	3	2	10	23		3
	%	42.1	16.7	16.7	62.5	35.4	65	75.0
							3.3	
combined	n	11	15	10	6	42		1
	%	57.9	83.3	83.3	37.5	64.6		25.0
Sri Lanka								
alone	n	0	2	4	7	13		1
	%	0	50.0	66.7	58.3	54.2	22	100.0
							1.1	
combined	n	0	2	2	5	9		0
	%	0	50.0	33.3	41.7	45.8		0
Taiwan								
alone	n	2	2	4	9	17		0
	%	33.3	25.0	33.3	69.2	43.6	39	0.0
							2.0	
combined	n	4	6	8	4	22		0
	%	66.7	75.0	66.7	30.8	56.4		0
Thailand								
alone	n	13	15	17	30	75		2
	%	81.3	71.4	68.0	75.0	73.5	102	66.7
							5.1	
combined	n	3	6	8	10	27		1
	%	18.8	28.6	32.0	25.0	26.5		33.3
Vietnam								
alone	n	12	11	8	13	44		0
	%	52.2	64.7	40.0	52.0	51.8	85	0
							4.3	
combined	n	11	6	12	12	41		0
	%	47.8	35.3	60.0	48.0	48.2		0

Table C1 continued

Country		*Wire A*	*Wire B*	*Wire C*	*Wire D*	*Four Wires*	*Grand Total*	*Hsinhua*
Brazil								
alone	n	4	0	1	1	6		0
	%	57.1	0	33.3	33.3	40.0	15	0
							0.8	
combined	n	3	2	2	2	9		1
	%	42.9	100.0	66.7	66.7	60.0		100.0
Columbia								
alone	n	1	2	2	3	8		0
	%	50.0	100.0	100.0	100.0	88.9	9	0
							0.5	
combined	n	1	0	0	0	1		0
	%	50.0	0	0	0	11.1		0
Chile								
alone	n	1	0	1	1	3		0
	%	100.0	0	50.0	33.3	27.3	11	0
							0.6	
combined	n	0	5	1	2	8		0
	%	0	100.0	50.0	66.7	72.7		0
Cuba								
alone	n	1	3	2	1	7		0
	%	14.3	75.0	33.3	33.3	35.0	20	0
							1.0	
combined	n	6	1	4	2	13		1
	%	85.7	25.0	66.7	66.7	65.0		100.0
Mexico								
alone	n	1	1	1	0	3		2
	%	33.3	50.0	33.3	0	37.5	8	66.7
							0.4	
combined	n	2	1	2	0	5		1
	%	66.7	50.0	66.7	0	62.5		33.3
Other Latin America								
alone	n	4	7	16	9	36		3
	%	50.0	38.9	80	56.3	61.0	62	75.0
							3.1	
combined	n	4	11	4	7	26		1
	%	50.0	61.1	20.0	43.8	39.0		25.0
Peru								
alone	n	0	0	2	0	2		1
	%	0	0	66.7	0	66.7	3	100.0
							0.1	
combined	n	0	0	1	0	1		0
	%	0	0	33.3	0	33.3		0

Table C1 continued

Country		*Wire A*	*Wire B*	*Wire C*	*Wire D*	*Four Wires*	*Grand Total*	*Hsinhua*
Venezuela								
alone	n	2	0	2	2	6		2
	%	50.0	0	66.7	66.7	54.5	11	100.0
							0.6	
combined	n	2	1	1	1	5		0
	%	50.0	100.0	33.3	33.3	45.5		0
Algeria								
alone	n	0	0	0	1	1		0
	%	0	0	0	50.0	50.0	2	0
							0.1	
combined	n	0	0	0	1	1		0
	%	0	0	0	50.0	50.0		0
Egypt								
alone	n	6	3	6	4	19		1
	%	17.6	10.0	12.8	11.4	13.0	146	50.0
							7.4	
combined	n	28	27	41	31	127		1
	%	82.4	90.0	87.2	88.6	87.0		50.0
Iraq								
alone	n	1	0	1	4	6		1
	%	50.0	0	33.3	57.1	42.9	14	50.0
							0.7	
alone	n	1	2	2	3	8		1
	%	50.0	100.0	66.7	42.9	57.1		50.0
Jordan								
alone	n	3	1	6	5	15		0
	%	75.0	50.0	100.0	50.0	68.2	22	0
							1.1	
combined	n	1	1	0	5	7		0
	%	25.0	50.0	0	50.0	31.8		0
Libya								
alone	n	0	1	1	1	3		0
	%	0	50.0	100.0	33.3	37.5	8	0
							0.4	
combined	n	2	1	0	2	5		0
	%	100.0	50.0	0	66.7	62.5		0
Saudi Arabia								
alone	n	9	3	4	10	26		0
	%	100.0	60.0	33.3	83.3	68.4	38	0
							1.9	
combined	n	0	2	8	2	12		0
	%	0	40.0	66.7	16.7	31.6		0

Table C1 continued

Country		Wire A	Wire B	Wire C	Wire D	Four Wires	Grand Total	Hsinhua
Syria								
alone	n	12	12	22	28	74		1
	%	66.7	54.5	62.9	73.7	65.5	113	100.0
							5.7	
combined	n	6	10	13	10	39		0
	%	33.3	45.4	37.1	26.3	34.5		0
Other Mideast Countries								
alone	n	14	10	14	17	55		6
	%	58.3	40.0	73.7	53.1	55.0	100	75.0
							5.1	
combined	n	10	15	5	15	45		2
	%	41.7	60.0	26.3	46.9	45.0		25.0
Kenya								
alone	n	0	0	1	0	1		0
	%	0	0	50.0	0	50.0	3	0
							0.1	
combined	n	0	0	1	1	2		0
	%	0	0	50.0	100.0	50.0		0
Nigeria								
alone	n	0	0	0	1	1		0
	%	0	0	0	100.0	50.0	2	0
							0.1	
combined	n	1	0	0	0	1		
	%	100.0	0	0	0	50.0		0
Other African Countries								
alone	n	14	13	50	45	122		23
	%	50.0	40.6	72.5	65.2	61.6	198	63.9
							10.0	
combined	n	14	19	19	24	76		13
	%	50.0	59.4	27.5	34.8	38.4		36.1
Uganda								
alone	n	3	0	3	7	13		0
	%	42.9	0	75.0	87.5	65.0	20	0
							1.0	
combined	n	4	1	1	1	7		0
	%	57.1	100.0	25.0	12.5	35.0		0
South Pacific								
alone	n	3	2	1	2	8		0
	%	30	18.2	100.0	16.7	23.5	34	0.0
							1.7	
combined	n	7	9	0	10	26		0
	%	70	81.8	0	83.3	76.5		0

Table C1 continued

Country		*Wire A*	*Wire B*	*Wire C*	*Wire D*	*Four Wires*	*Grand Total*	*Hsinhua*
Total								
alone	n	173	196	356	388	1,115		83
	%	47.8	55.5	57.5	60.1	56.2	1,982	38.5
							100.0	
combined	n	·191	157	263	258	869		52
	%	52.2	44.5	42.5	39.9	43.8		61.5
Grand Total	n	364	353	619	646	1,982	1,982	135
	%	100.0	100.0	100.0	100.0	100.0	100.0	100.0

TABLE C2

Number and Percentage of References to Each of 42 Third World Countries, Alone and Combined with Other Countries, in 17 Asian Daily Newspapers for Five Days, December 6-10, 1977.

Country		*Amrita Bazar Patrika* (1)	*Bangkok Post* (2)	*Ceylon Daily News* (3)	*Dong-a Ilbo* (4)	*Ettelaat* (5)	*Kayhan International* (6)	*Kompas* (7)	*Korea Times* (8)	*Nanyang Siang Pau* (9)	*New Straits Times* (10)	*Pilipino Express* (11)	*Philippine Daily Express* (12)	*Sing Chew Jit Poh* (13)	*Sing Tao Jih Pao* (14)	*South China Morning Post* (15)	*Statesman* (16)	*Straits Times* (17)	Total	Grand Total
Bangladesh																				
alone	n	0	0	1	0	0	0	0	0	0	0	0	0	0	0		3	0	4	
	%	0	0	100.0	0	0	0	0	0	0	0	0	0	0	0	0	100.0	0	100.0	4
combined	n	0	0	0	0	0	0	0	0	0	0	0	0	0	0	0	0	0	0	0.2
	%	0	0	0	0	0	0	0	0	0	0	0	0	0	0	0	0	0	0	
Burma																				
alone	n	0	0	0	0	0	0	0	0	1	1	0	0	0	0	0	0	0	2	
	%	0	0	0	0	0	0	0	0	100.0	100.0	0	0	0	0	0	0	0	100.0	2
combined	n	0	0	0	0	0	0	0	0	0	0	0	0	0	0	0	0	0	0	0.1
	%	0	0	0	0	0	0	0	0	0	0	0	0	0	0	0	0	0	0	
Cambodia																				
alone	n	0	2	0	0	0	0	1	0	2	2	0	0	0	0	0	0	2	9	
	%	0	100.0	0	0	0	0	100.0	0	100.0	100.0	0	0	0	0	0	0	100.0	100.0	9
combined	n	0	0	0	0	0	0	0	0	0	0	0	0	0	0	0	0	0	0	0.5
	%	0	0	0	0	0	0	0	0	0	0	0	0	0	0	0	0	0	0	
China																				
alone	n	2	0	6	3	0	0	5	1	7	1	3	6	2	18	33	2	6	95	
	%	100.0	0	54.5	75.0	0	0	71.4	100.0	50.0	100.0	100.0	85.7	100.0	85.7	78.6	50.0	66.7	73.6	129
combined	n	0	0	5	1	0	1	2	0	7	0	0	1	0	3	9	2	3	34	6.4
	%	0	0	45.5	25.0	0	100.0	28.6	0	50.0	0	0	14.3	0	14.3	21.4	50.0	33.3	26.4	
Hong Kong																				
alone	n	1	10	0	0	0	0	0	0	11	4	0	1	6	0	0	0	11	44	
	%	100.0	90.9	0	0	0	0	0	0	64.7	100.0	0	50.0	100.0	0	0	0	73.3	77.2	57
combined	n	0	1	0	0	0	1	0	0	6	0	0	1	0	0	0	0	4	13	2.8
	%	[illegible]	[illegible]	[illegible]	[illegible]	[illegible]	[illegible]	[illegible]	[illegible]	[illegible]	[illegible]	[illegible]	[illegible]	[illegible]	[illegible]	[illegible]	[illegible]	[illegible]	[illegible]	

Country		Amrita Bazar Patrika (1)	Bangkok Post (2)	Ceylon Daily News (3)	Dong-a Ilbo (4)	Ettelaat (5)	Kayhan International (6)	Kompas (7)	Korea Times (8)	Nanyang Siang Pau (9)	New Straits Times (10)	Pilipino Express (11)	Philippine Daily Express (12)	Sing Chew Jit Poh (13)	Sing Tao Jih Pao (14)	South China Morning Post (15)	Statesman (16)	Straits Times (17)	Total	Grand Total
India																				
alone	n	0	2	5	0	1	5	1	1	2	11	0	2	1	1	7	0	6	45	
	%	0	50.0	71.4	0	100.0	62.5	100.0	33.3	66.7	78.6	0	50.0	50.0	33.3	58.3	0	75.0	63.4	71 3.5
combined	n	0	2	2	1	0	3	0	2	1	3	0	2	1	2	5	0	2	26	
	%	0	50.0	28.6	100.0	0	37.5	0	66.7	33.3	21.4	0	50.0	50.0	66.7	41.7	0	25.0	36.6	
Indonesia	n																			
alone	n	2	5	1	1	1	0	0	0	6	6	0	2	6	0	4	2	14	50	
	%	100.0	83.3	100.0	100.0	100.0	0	0	0	100.0	85.7	0	66.7	100.0	0	80.0	100.0	77.8	86.2	58 2.9
combined	n	0	1	0	0	0	0	0	0	0	1	0	1	0	0	1	0	4	8	
	%	0	16.7	0	0	0	0	0	0	0	14.3	0	33.3	0	0	20.0	0	22.2	13.8	
Iran																				
alone	n	0	0	0	0	5	5	3	0	0	0	0	0	0	0	1	1	0	15	
	%	0	0	0	0	12.2	18.5	100.0	0	0	0	0	0	0	0	100.0	50.0	0	19.7	76 3.8
combined	n	0	0	0	0	36	22	0	0	0	2	0	0	0	0	0	1	0	61	
	%	0	0	0	0	87.8	81.5	0	0	0	100.0	0	0	0	0	0	50.0	0	80.3	
Laos																				
alone	n	0	2	0	0	0	0	0	0	0	0	0	0	0	0	0	0	2	4	
	%	0	100.0	0	0	0	0	0	0	0	0	0	0	0	0	0	0	100.0	100.0	4 0.2
combined	n	0	0	0	0	0	0	0	0	0	0	0	0	0	0	0	0	0	0	
	%	0	0	0	0	0	0	0	0	0	0	0	0	0	0	0	0	0	0	
Malaysia																				
alone	n	1	7	5	1	2	1	6	7	0	0	0	3	74	5	14	2	99	227	
	%	100.0	70.0	83.3	50.0	66.7	50.0	100.0	87.5	0	0	0	50.0	81.7	71.4	93.3	66.7	94.3	87.6	259 12.9
combined	n	0	3	1	1	1	1	0	1	0	0	0	3	11	2	1	1	6	32	
	%	0	30.0	16.7	50.0	33.3	50.0	0	12.5	0	0	0	50.0	12.9	28.6	6.7	33.3	5.7	12.4	

Table C2 continued

Country		*Amrita Bazar Patrika* (1)	*Bangkok Post* (2)	*Ceylon Daily News* (3)	*Dong-a Ilbo* (4)	*Ettelaat* (5)	*Kayhan International* (6)	*Kompas* (7)	*Korea Times* (8)	*Nanyang Siang Pau* (9)	*New Straits Times* (10)	*Pilipino Express* (11)	*Philippine Daily Express* (12)	*Sing Chew Jit Poh* (13)	*Sing Tao Jih Pao* (14)	*South China Morning Post* (15)	*Statesman* (16)	*Straits Times* (17)	Total	Grand Total
Nepal																				
alone	n	2	0	1	0	0	0	1	0	0	0	0	0	0	0	2	1	0	7	
	%	100.0	0	33.3	0	0	0	100.0	0	0	0	0	0	0	0	100.0	50.0	0	70.0	10
combined	n	0	0	2	0	0	0	0	0	0	0	0	0	0	0	0	1	0	3	0.5
	%	0	0	66.7	0	0	0	0	0	0	0	0	0	0	0	0	50.0	0	30.0	
North Korea																				
alone	n	0	0	0	2	0	0	2	0	0	0	0	0	0	1	0	0	0	5	
	%	0	0	0	33.3	0	0	50.0	0	0	0	0	0	0	100.0	0	0	0	38.5	13
combined	n	0	0	0	4	0	0	2	0	1	0	0	1	0	0	0	0	0	8	0.6
	%	0	0	0	66.7	0	0	50.0	0	100.0	0	0	100.0	0	0	0	0	0	61.5	
Other Asian Countries																				
alone	n	0	0	1	0	2	1	0	0	0	0	0	0	0	1	1	0	0	6	
	%	0	0	50.0	0	50.0	12.5	0	0	0	0	0	0	0	50.0	100.0	0	0	28.6	21
combined	n	0	0	1	0	2	7	0	1	0	0	0	2	0	1	0	0	1	15	1.1
	%	0	0	50.0	0	50.0	87.5	0	100.0	0	0	0	100.0	0	50.0	0	0	100.0	71.4	
Pakistan																				
alone	n	1	5	5	2	9	5	3	1	2	3	0	3	5	3	2	7	3	59	
	%	25.0	62.5	55.6	100.0	64.3	55.6	100.0	100.0	66.7	42.9	0	100.0	100.0	100.0	28.6	63.6	75.0	63.4	93
combined	n	3	3	4	0	5	4	0	0	1	4	0	0	0	0	5	4	1	34	4.6
	%	75.0	37.5	44.4	0	35.7	44.4	0	0	33.3	57.1	0	0	0	0	71.4	36.4	25.0	36.6	
Philippines																				
alone	n	0	6	1	4	2	3	4	0	6	4	0	0	7	3	15	1	12	68	
	%	0	66.7	100.0	100.0	66.7	75.0	66.7	0	75.0	66.7	0	0	77.8	100.0	88.2	50.0	70.6	73.9	92
combined	n	1	3	0	0	1	1	2	1	2	2	1	0	2	0	2	1	5	24	4.6
	%	100.0	33.3	0	0	33.3	25.0	33.3	100.0	25.0	33.3	100.0	0	22.2	0	11.8	50.0	29.4	26.1	

Country		Amrita Bazar Patrika (1)	Bangkok Post (2)	Ceylon Daily News (3)	Dong-a Ilbo (4)	Ettelaat (5)	Kayhan International (6)	Kompas (7)	Korea Times (8)	Nanyang Siang Pau (9)	New Straits Times (10)	Pilipino Express (11)	Philippine Daily Express (12)	Sing Chew Jit Poh (13)	Sing Tao Jih Pao (14)	South China Morning Post (15)	Statesman (16)	Straits Times (17)	Total	Grand Total
Singapore																				
alone	n	0	2	1	0	0	0	0	2	60	32	1	2	0	3	8	0	1	112	
	%	0	66.7	50.0	0	0	0	0	100.0	85.7	91.4	100.0	100.0	0	60.0	88.9	0	50.0	84.9	132
combined	n	0	1	1	0	0	1	0	0	10	3	0	0	0	2	1	0	1	20	6.6
	%	0	33.3	50.0	0	0	100.0	0	0	14.3	8.6	0	0	0	40.0	11.1	0	50.0	15.1	
South Korea																				
alone	n	0	2	0	0	1	0	0	1	1	0	2	5	2	2	1	0	0	17	
	%	0	40.0	0	0	100.0	0	0	100.0	33.3	0	66.7	71.4	66.7	66.7	25.0	0	0	45.9	37
combined	n	0	3	1	0	0	0	0	0	2	·2	1	2	1	1	3	1	3	20	1.8
	%	0	60.0	100.0	0	0	0	0	0	66.7	100.0	33.3	28.6	33.3	33.3	75.0	100.0	100.0	54.1	
Sri Lanka																				
alone	n	2	0	0	1	1	2	0	0	3	1	0	1	2	0	0	1	3	17	
	%	66.7	0	0	100.0	100.0	100.0	0	0	60.0	100.0	0	100.0	100.0	0	0	100.0	100.0	77.3	22
combined	n	1	0	1	0	0	0	0	0	2	0	0	0	0	0	1	0	0	5	1.1
	%	33.3	0	100.0	0	0	0	0	0	40.0	0	0	0	0	0	100.0	0	0	22.7	
Taiwan																				
alone	n	0	1	0	2	0	0	5	0	4	0	0	1	1	7	4	0	2	27	
	%	0	50.0	0	66.7	0	0	100.0	0	100.0	0	0	100.0	100.0	58.3	66.7	0	66.7	67.5	40
combined	n	0	1	0	1	0	0	0	0	0	2	1	0	0	5	2	0	1	13	2.0
	%	0	50.0	0	33.3	0	0	0	0	0	100.0	100.0	0	0	41.7	33.3	0	33.3	32.5	
Thailand																				
alone	n	0	0	2	0	0	1	1	3	11	5	4	5	8	5	14	1	11	71	
	%	0	0	66.7	0	0	50.0	100.0	75.0	100.0	71.4	100.0	71.4	100.0	83.3	93.3	100	100	88.8	80
combined	n	0	0	1	0	0	1	0	1	0	2	0	2	0	1	1	0	0	9	4.0
	%	0	0	33.3	0	0	50.0	0	25.0	0	28.6	0	28.6	0	16.7	6.7	0	0	11.2	

Table C2 continued

Country		Amrita Bazar Patrika (1)	Bangkok Post (2)	Ceylon Daily News (3)	Dong-a Ilbo (4)	Ettelaat (5)	Kayhan International (6)	Kompas (7)	Korea Times (8)	Nanyang Siang Pau (9)	New Straits Times (10)	Pilipino Express (11)	Philippine Daily Express (12)	Sing Chew Jit Poh (13)	Sing Tao Jih Pao (14)	South China Morning Post (15)	Statesman (16)	Straits Times (17)	Total	Grand Total
Vietnam																				
alone	n	0	4	0	2	1	0	2	2	6	1	0	2	4	3	9	0	5	41	
	%	0	100.0	0	40.0	50.0	0	66.7	100.0	60.0	50.0	0	66.7	100.0	100.0	100.0	0	71.4	69.5	59
combined	n	1	0	1	3	1	2	1	0	4	1	0	1	0	0	0	1	2	18	2.9
	%	100.0	0	100.0	60.0	50.0	100.0	33.3	0	40.0	50.0	0	33.3	0	0	0	100.0	28.6	30.5	
Brazil																				
alone	n	1	0	0	0	0	0	0	0	0	0	0	0	1	0	1	0	1	4	
	%	100.0	0	0	0	0	0	0	0	0	0	0	0	100.0	0	50.0	0	50.0	36.4	11
combined	n	0	0	0	0	1	2	0	0	0	0	0	1	0	1	1	0	1	7	0.6
	%	0	0	0	0	100.0	100.0	0	0	0	0	0	100.0	0	100.0	50.0	0	50.0	63.6	
Columbia																				
alone	n	0	0	0	0	0	1	0	0	0	1	0	0	0	1	0	0	0	3	
	%	0	0	0	0	0	100.0	0	0	0	100.0	0	0	0	100.0	0	0	0	75.0	4
combined	n	0	0	0	0	0	0	0	0	0	0	0	1	0	0	0	0	0	1	0.2
	%	0	0	0	0	0	0	0	0	0	0	0	100.0	0	0	0	0	0	25.0	
Chile																				
alone	n	0	0	0	0	0	0	0	0	0	0	0	0	0	1	0	0	0	1	
	%	0	0	0	0	0	0	0	0	0	0	0	0	0	100.0	0	0	0	50.0	2
combined	n	0	0	0	0	0	1	0	0	0	0	0	0	0	0	0	0	0	1	0.1
	%	0	0	0	0	0	100.0	0	0	0	0	0	0	0	0	0	0	0	50.0	
Cuba																				
alone	n	0	0	0	2	0	0	0	0	0	0	1	2	1	1	2	0	1	10	
	%	0	0	0	100.0	0	0	0	0	0	0	100.0	66.7	100.0	50.0	66.7	0	50.0	50.0	20
combined	n	0	0	0	0	3	1	0	0	1	1	0	1	0	1	1	0	1	10	1.0
	%	0	0	0	0	100.0	100.0	0	0	100.0	100.0	0	[illegible]	0	[illegible]	[illegible]	0	[illegible]	[illegible]	

Country		*Amrita Bazar Patrika* (1)	*Bangkok Post* (2)	*Ceylon Daily News* (3)	*Dong-a Ilbo* (4)	*Ettelaat* (5)	*Kayhan International* (6)	*Kompas* (7)	*Korea Times* (8)	*Nanyang Siang Pau* (9)	*New Straits Times* (10)	*Pilipino Express* (11)	*Philippine Daily Express* (12)	*Sing Chew Jit Poh* (13)	*Sing Tao Jih Pao* (14)	*South China Morning Post* (15)	*Statesman* (16)	*Straits Times* (17)	*Total*	*Grand Total*
Mexico																				
alone	n	0	0	0	0	0	1	1	0	1	0	0	0	0	2	0	0	0	5	
	%	0	0	0	0	0	100.0	100.0	0	100.0	0	0	0	0	66.7	0	0	0	55.6	9
combined	n	0	1	0	0	0	0	0	0	0	0	0	1	0	1	1	0	0	4	0.5
	%	0	100.0	0	0	0	0	0	0	0	0	0	100.0	0	33.3	100.0	0	0	44.4	
Other Latin America																				
alone	n	1	1	1	1	0	0	2	0	0	0	0	0	1	0	3	2	0	12	
	%	100.0	16.7	50.0	100.0	0	0	66.7	0	0	0	0	0	33.3	0	75.0	100.0	0	37.5	32
combined	n	0	5	1	0	1	2	1	0	2	5	0	0	2	0	1	0	0	20	1.6
	%	0	83.3	50.0	0	100.0	100.0	33.3	0	100.0	100.0	0	0	66.7	0	25.0	0	0	62.5	
Peru																				
alone	n	0	0	0	0	0	0	0	0	0	0	0	0	0	0	0	1	0	1	
	%	0	0	0	0	0	0	0	0	0	0	0	0	0	0	0	100.0	0	100.0	1
combined	n	0	0	0	0	0	0	0	0	0	0	0	0	0	0	0	0	0	0	0.0
	%	0	0	0	0	0	0	0	0	0	0	0	0	0	0	0	0	0	0	
Venezuela																				
alone	n	0	0	0	0	0	0	1	0	0	0	0	1	0	0	0	0	0	2	
	%	0	0	0	0	0	0	100.0	0	0	0	0	100.0	0	0	0	0	0	50.0	4
combined	n	0	0	0	0	0	0	0	0	0	1	0	0	0	1	0	0	0	2	0.2
	%	0	0	0	0	0	0	0	0	0	100.0	0	0	0	100.0	0	0	0	50.0	
Algeria																				
alone	n	0	0	0	0	0	0	0	0	1	0	0	0	0	2	0	0	0	3	
	%	0	0	0	0	0	0	0	0	100.0	0	0	0	0	100.0	0	0	0	75.0	4
combined	n	0	0	0	0	0	1	0	0	0	0	0	0	0	0	0	0	0	1	0.2
	%	0	0	0	0	0	100.0	0	0	0	0	0	0	0	0	0	0	0	25.0	

Table C2 continued

Country		*Amrita Bazar Patrika* (1)	*Bangkok Post* (2)	*Ceylon Daily News* (3)	*Dong-a Ilbo* (4)	*Ettelaat* (5)	*Kayhan International* (6)	*Kompas* (7)	*Korea Times* (8)	*Nanyang Siang Pau* (9)	*New Straits Times* (10)	*Pilipino Express* (11)	*Philippine Daily Express* (12)	*Sing Chew Jit Poh* (13)	*Sing Tao Jih Pao* (14)	*South China Morning Post* (15)	*Statesman* (16)	*Straits Times* (17)	Total	Grand Total
Egypt																				
alone	n	0	1	0	0	1	0	0	0	3	1	0	2	6	0	0	1	3	18	
	%	0	16.7	0	0	9.1	0	0	0	42.9	20.0	0	33.3	60.0	0	0	33.3	20.0	15.9	113
combined	n	5	5	6	6	10	12	9	2	4	4	0	4	4	8	2	2	12	95	5.6
	%	100.0	83.3	100.0	100.0	90.9	100.0	100.0	100.0	57.1	80.0	0	66.7	40.0	100.0	100.0	66.7	80.0	84.1	
Iraq																				
alone	n	0	0	0	1	2	4	0	0	1	0	0	0	4	0	1	0	1	14	
	%	0	0	0	33.3	40.0	100.0	0	0	33.3	0	0	0	100.0	0	100.0	0	33.3	53.9	26
combined	n	0	1	0	2	3	0	1	0	2	0	0	0	0	1	0	0	2	12	1.3
	%	0	100.0	0	66.7	60.0	0	100.0	0	66.7	0	0	0	0	100.0	0	0	66.7	46.1	
Jordan																				
alone	n	0	1	2	1	0	0	1	1	0	0	0	1	0	0	0	0	2	9	
	%	0	100.0	100.0	100.0	0	0	100.0	100.0	0	0	0	100.0	0	0	0	0	100.0	69.2	13
combined	n	0	0	0	0	0	0	0	0	0	0	0	0	1	3	0	0	0	4	0.6
	%	0	0	0	0	0	0	0	0	0	0	0	0	100.0	100.0	0	0	0	30.8	
Libya																				
alone	n	0	0	1	0	0	1	0	0	0	0	0	1	0	0	0	0	1	4	
	%	0	0	100.0	0	0	50.0	0	0	0	0	0	100.0	0	0	0	0	100.0	57.1	7
combined	n	0	0	0	0	0	1	1	0	0	1	0	0	0	0	0	0	0	3	0.3
	%	0	0	0	0	0	50.0	100.0	0	0	100.0	0	0	0	0	0	0	0	42.9	
Saudi Arabia																				
alone	n	1	2	1	1	6	4	2	1	2	4	1	3	5	6	2	0	3	44	
	%	50.0	66.7	100.0	50.0	54.5	33.3	50.0	50.0	33.3	100.0	100.0	100.0	83.3	100.0	100.0	0	75.0	63.8	69
combined	n	1	1	0	1	5	8	2	1	4	0	0	0	1	0	0	0	1	25	3.4
	%	50.0	33.3	0	50.0	45.5	66.7	50.0	50.0	66.7	0	0	0	16.7	0	0	0	25.0	36.2	

Country		*Amrita Bazar Patrika* (1)	*Bangkok Post* (2)	*Ceylon Daily News* (3)	*Dong-a Ilbo* (4)	*Ettelaat* (5)	*Kayhan International* (6)	*Kompas* (7)	*Korea Times* (8)	*Nanyang Siang Pau* (9)	*New Straits Times* (10)	*Pilipino Express* (11)	*Philippine Daily Express* (12)	*Sing Chew Jit Poh* (13)	*Sing Tao Jih Pao* (14)	*South China Morning Post* (15)	*Statesman* (16)	*Straits Times* (17)	Total	Grand Total
Syria																				
alone	n	3	4	4	7	1	2	8	5	5	6	0	5	7	8	5	2	8	80	
	%	60.0	80.0	66.7	70.0	7.1	15.4	72.7	83.3	33.3	35.3	0	100.0	77.8	66.7	100.0	66.7	80.0	54.8	146 7.3
combined	n	2	1	2	3	13	11	3	1	10	11	0	0	2	4	0	1	2	66	
	%	40.0	20.0	33.3	30.0	92.9	84.6	27.3	16.7	66.7	64.7	0	0	22.2	33.3	0	33.3	20.0	45.2	
Other Mideast Countries																				
alone	n	1	0	1	2	12	12	2	1	2	3	0	1	2	1	5	0	4	49	
	%	100.0	0	33.3	40.0	66.7	42.9	100.0	50.0	28.6	100.0	0	100.0	100.0	25.0	71.4	0	66.7	54.4	90 4.5
combined	n	0	1	2	3	6	16	0	1	5	0	0	0	0	3	2	0	2	41	
	%	0	100.0	66.7	60.0	33.3	57.1	0	50.0	71.4	0	0	0	0	75.0	28.6	0	33.3	45.6	
Kenya																				
alone	n	0	0	0	0	0	0	0	0	0	0	0	0	0	0	0	0	0	0	
	%	0	0	0	0	0	0	0	0	0	0	0	0	0	0	0	0	0	0	2 0.1
combined	n	0	0	1	0	0	0	0	0	0	1	0	0	0	0	0	0	0	2	
	%	0	0	100.0	0	0	0	0	0	0	100.0	0	0	0	0	0	0	0	100.0	
Nigeria																				
alone	n	0	0	0	0	0	0	0	0	0	1	0	0	0	0	0	0	0	1	
	%	0	0	0	0	0	0	0	0	0	100.0	0	0	0	0	0	0	0	100.0	1 0.0
combined	n	0	0	0	0	0	0	0	0	0	0	0	0	0	0	0	0	0	0	
	%	0	0	0	0	0	0	0	0	0	0	0	0	0	0	0	0	0	0	
Uganda																				
alone	n	0	0	0	0	1	3	0	0	0	0	0	0	0	0	2	1	1	8	
	%	0	0	0	0	100.0	75.0	0	0	0	0	0	0	0	0	100.0	100.0	50.0	50.0	16 0.8
combined	n	0	0	1	0	0	1	2	0	0	2	0	1	0	0	0	0	1	8	
	%	0	0	100.0	0	0	25.0	100.0	0	0	100.0	0	100.0	0	0	0	0	50.0	50.0	

Table C2 continued

Country		*Amrita Bazar Patrika* (1)	*Bangkok Post* (2)	*Ceylon Daily News* (3)	*Dong-a Ilbo* (4)	*Ettelaat* (5)	*Kayhan International* (6)	*Kompas* (7)	*Korea Times* (8)	*Nanyang Siang Pau* (9)	*New Straits Times* (10)	*Pilipino Express* (11)	*Philippine Daily Express* (12)	*Sing Chew Jit Poh* (13)	*Sing Tao Jih Pao* (14)	*South China Morning Post* (15)	*Statesman* (16)	*Straits Times* (17)	Total	Grand Total
Other African Countries																				
alone	n	7	5	3	2	7	13	5	3	5	4	0	4	3	3	12	10	9	95	
	%	58.3	62.5	50.0	40.0	43.8	54.2	71.4	100.0	55.6	100.0	0	80.0	75.0	60.0	100.0	71.4	90.0	66.0	144
																				7.2
combined	n	5	3	3	3	9	11	2	0	4	0	0	1	1	2	0	4	1	49	
	%	41.7	37.5	50.0	60.0	56.3	45.8	28.6	0	44.4	0	0	20.0	25.0	40.0	0	28.6	10.0	34.0	
South Pacific																				
alone	n	0	0	0	0	0	0	0	0	0	2	0	2	0	0	1	0	1	6	
	%	0	0	0	0	0	0	0	0	0	66.7	0	66.7	0	0	50.0	0	25.0	40.0	15
																				0.7
combined	n	0	1	0	0	0	0	0	1	1	1	0	1	0	0	1	0	3	9	
	%	0	100.0	0	0	0	0	0	100.0	100.0	33.3	0	33.3	0	0	50.0	0	75.0	60.0	
Total																				
alone	n	25	62	42	35	55	64	56	29	142	93	12	55	148	77	149	38	212	1,294	
	%	56.8	62.6	53.8	55.7	36.2	36.6	66.7	71.7	67.3	65.6	80.0	67.1	85.1	64.7	78.8	66.7	78.2	64.6	
																				2,004
																				100.0
combined	n	19	37	36	29	97	111	28	12	69	49	3	27	26	42	40	19	59	710	
	%	43.2	37.4	46.2	45.3	63.8	63.4	33.3	29.3	32.7	34.5	20.0	32.9	14.0	35.3	21.2	33.3	21.8	35.4	
Grand Total	n	44	99	78	64	152	175	84	41	211	142	15	82	174	119	189	57	271	2,004	
	%	100.0	100.0	100.0	100.0	100.0	100.0	100.0	100.0	100.0	100.0	100.0	100.0	100.0	100.0	100.0	100.0	100.0	100.0	

TABLE C3

Approximate Number and Percentage of Words and Number and Percentage of Stories for Each Content Category for Each International News Wire and Hsinhua for 42 Third World Countries for Five Days, December 5-9, 1977.

Content Category	*Wire A*	*Wire B*	*Wire C*	*Wire D*	*Four Wires*	*Hsinhua*
1. Military						
words	7,954	5,504	14,826	7,128	35,412	330
%	7.6	5.4	9.1	4.8	6.8	1.0
stories	22	20	52	45	139	2
%	6.0	5.7	8.4	7.0	7.0	1.5
2. Foreign						
words	47,847	47,042	50,484	41,040	186,413	15,780
%	46.0	45.8	30.9	27.8	36.0	47.2
stories	171	144	197	207	719	66
%	47.0	40.8	31.8	32	36.3	48.9
3. Domestic						
words	10,537	10,492	21,840	652	66,521	1,350
%	10.0	10.2	13.4	60.0	12.8	4.0
stories	28	32	68	91	219	7
%	7.7	9.1	11.0	14.1	11.1	5.2
4. Economics						
words	8,897	11,524	18,228	25,002	63,651	5,370
%	8.5	11.2	11.2	16.9	12.3	16.1
stories	45	60	94	108	307	20
%	12.4	17.0	15.2	16.7	15.5	14.8
5. Science						
words	82	946	1,260	1,404	3,692	4,020
%	0.1	0.9	0.8	0.9	0.7	12.0
stories	1	4	7	10	22	13
%	0.3	1.1	1.1	1.5	1.1	9.6
6. Education						
words	0	301	168	1,566	2,035	870
%	0	0.3	0.1	1.1	0.4	2.6
stories	0	1	1	5	7	3
%	0	0.3	0.2	0.8	0.3	2.2
7. Accidents						
words	8,077	6,063	6,426	11,448	32,014	0
%	7.8	5.9	3.9	7.8	6.2	0
stories	28	23	25	33	109	0
%	7.7	6.5	4.0	5.1	5.5	0
8. Judicial						
words	6,027	1,505	5,208	4,536	17,276	0
%	5.8	1.5	3.2	3.1	3.3	0
stories	18	6	27	30	81	0
%	4.9	1.7	4.4	4.6	4.1	0

Table C3 continued

Content Category		Wire A	Wire B	Wire C	Wire D	Four Wires	Hsinhua
9.	Sports						
	words	9,061	10,492	31,290	22,248	73,091	3,090
	%	8.7	10.2	19.2	15.1	14.1	9.2
	stories	35	30	96	65	226	17
	%	9.6	8.5	15.5	10.1	11.4	12.6
10.	Arts, Culture						
	words	902	43	1,554	1,080	3,579	1,920
	%	0.9	*	1.0	0.7	0.7	5.8
	stories	3	1	5	6	15	5
	%	0.8	0.3	0.8	0.9	0.7	3.7
11.	Human Interest						
	words	41	2,709	5,376	1,944	10,070	180
	%	*	2.6	3.2	1.3	1.9	0.5
	stories	1	9	17	13	40	1
	%	0.3	2.5	2.7	2.0	2.0	0.7
12.	Other						
	words	4,674	6,149	6,594	6,642	24,059	510
	%	4.5	6.0	4.0	4.5	4.7	1.5
	stories	12	23	30	33	98	1
	%	3.3	6.5	4.9	5.1	4.9	0.7
Total							
	words	104,099	102,770	163,254	147,690	517,813	33,420
	%	100.0	100.0	100.0	100.0	100.0	100.0
	stories	364	353	619	646	1,982	135
	%	100.0	100.0	100.0	100.0	100.0	100.0

* Less than 0.10%

TABLE C4

Approximate Number and Percentage of Words and Number and Percentage of Stories for Each Content Category for Each of 17 Asian Daily Newspapers for 42 Third World Countries for Five Days, December 6-10, 1977.

Newspaper	*Military, political violence* (1)	*Foreign relations* (2)	*Domestic Politics* (3)	*Economics* (4)	*Science, Health* (5)	*Education* (6)	*Accidents, disasters* (7)	*Judicial, Crime* (8)	*Sports* (9)	*Art, culture* (10)	*Human interest* (11)	*Other* (12)	*Total*
Amrita Bazar Patrika													
words	644	7,958	2,714	1,472	0	0	92	0	828	184	230	138	14,260
%	4.5	55.8	19.0	10.3	0	0	0.7	0	5.8	1.3	1.6	1.0	100.0
stories	4	18	8	5	0	0	1	0	3	3	1	2	44
%	9.1	40.9	18.2	11.4	0	0	2.3	0	6.8	2.3	4.5	4.5	100.0
Bangkok Post													
words	1,190	11,968	2,856	8,432	0	0	4,862	1,190	6,902	0	4,216	918	42,534
%	2.8	28.1	6.7	19.8	0	0	11.4	2.8	16.2	0	9.9	2.2	100.0
stories	4	25	10	22	0	0	7	4	19	0	4	4	99
%	4.0	25.3	10.1	22.2	0	0	7.1	4.0	19.2	0	4.0	4.0	100.0
Ceylon Daily News													
words	4,576	9,020	1,100	1,980	176	0	1,364	0	5,016	3,432	264	660	27,588
%	16.6	32.7	4.0	7.2	0.6	0	4.9	0	18.2	12.4	1.0	2.4	100.0
stories	3	28	7	7	2	0	6	0	17	4	1	3	78
%	3.9	35.9	8.9	8.9	2.6	0	7.7	0	21.8	5.1	1.3	3.9	100.0
Dong-a Ilbo													
words	2,945	26,885	2,185	1,995	0	190	190	0	8,835	855	1,235	5,795	51,110
%	5.8	52.6	4.3	3.9	0	0.4	0.4	0	17.3	1.7	2.4	11.3	100.0
stories	4	33	7	4	0	1	1	0	9	1	2	2	64
%	6.2	51.6	10.9	6.2	0	1.6	1.6	0	14.1	1.6	3.1	3.1	100.0
Ettelaat													
words	6,496	63,200	4,704	6,280	1,632	1,728	384	2,240	19,680	4,960	0	3,712	114,944
%	5.7	55.0	4.1	5.4	1.4	1.5	0.3	2.0	17.1	4.3	0	3.2	100.0
stories	15	59	7	18	3	3	3	5	23	7	0	9	152
%	9.9	38.8	4.6	11.8	2.0	2.0	2.0	3.3	15.1	4.6	0	5.9	100.0

Table C4 continued

Newspaper	*Military, political violence* (1)	*Foreign relations* (2)	*Domestic Politics* (3)	*Economics* (4)	*Science, Health* (5)	*Education* (6)	*Accidents, disasters* (7)	*Judicial, Crime* (8)	*Sports* (9)	*Art, culture* (10)	*Human interest* (11)	*Other* (12)	*Total*
Kayhan International													
words	7,168	35,904	3,872	13,440	1,280	128	224	384	10,784	8,736	0	2,656	84,576
%	8.5	42.4	4.6	15.9	1.1	0.2	0.3	0.5	12.7	10.3	0	3.1	100.0
stories	24	53	11	34	3	1	5	6	16	11	0	11	175
%	13.7	30.3	6.3	19.4	1.7	0.6	2.9	3.4	9.1	6.3	0	6.3	100.0
Kompas													
words	1,904	6,392	2,958	1,156	68	0	1,462	272	3,774	1,428	0	0	19,414
%	9.8	32.9	15.2	6.0	0.4	0	7.4	1.4	19.4	7.4	0	0	100.0
stories	1	18	3	5	1	0	6	2	3	2	0	0	41
%	2.4	43.9	7.3	12.2	2.4	0	14.6	4.9	7.3	4.9	0	0	100.0
Korea Times													
words	1,040	10,840	3,840	3,200	240	0	1,480	280	2,840	40	1,240	840	25,880
%	4.0	41.9	14.8	12.4	0.9	0	5.7	1.1	11.0	0.2	4.8	3.2	100.0
stories	5	36	11	10	1	0	4	1	8	1	3	4	84
%	5.9	42.8	13.1	11.9	1.2	0	4.8	1.2	9.5	1.2	3.6	4.8	100.0
Nanyang Siang Pau													
words	8,784	57,462	8,784	70,821	0	915	11,468	17,934	12,871	5,978	30,134	2,379	227,530
%	3.9	25.3	3.9	31.1	0	0.4	5.0	7.9	65.7	2.6	13.2	1.0	100.0
stories	10	61	14	52	0	2	10	17	21	4	17	3	211
%	4.7	28.9	6.6	24.6	0	1.0	4.7	8.1	10.0	1.9	8.1	1.4	100.0
New Straits Times													
words	2,312	15,062	5,644	10,438	0	1,462	272	4352	14,008	1,190	3,162	918	58,820
%	3.9	25.6	9.1	17.7	0	2.5	0.5	7.4	23.8	2.0	5.4	1.6	100.0
stories	6	28	9	37	0	2	3	11	34	1	6	5	142
%	4.2	19.7	6.3	26.1	0	1.4	2.1	7.8	23.9	0.7	4.2	3.5	100.0
Pilipino Express													
words	0	1,050	0	420	0	0	0	490	2,415	0	0	245	4,620
%	0	22.7	0	9.1	0	0	0	10.6	52.3	0	0	5.3	100.0
stories	0	2	0	1	0	0	0	1	10.0	0	0	1	15
%	0	13.2	0	6.7	0	0	0	6.7	66.7	0	0	6.7	100.0

Newspaper	Military, political violence (1)	Foreign relations (2)	Domestic Politics (3)	Economic (4)	Science, Health (5)	Education (6)	Accidents disasters (7)	Judicial, Crime (8)	Sports (9)	Art, cultur (10)	Human interest (11)	Other (12)	Total
Philippine Daily Express													
words	476	11,288	442	5,948	0	884	2,244	1,122	11,254	782	68	612	35,020
%	1.4	32.2	1.3	16.7	0	2.5	6.4	3.2	32.1	2.2	0.2	1.7	100.0
stories	3	20	2	21	0	2	5	4	20	3	1	1	82
%	3.7	24.4	2.4	25.6	0	2.4	6.1	4.9	24.4	3.7	1.2	1.2	100.0
Sing Chew Jit Poh													
words	4,560	32,148	25,536	15,048	0	2,451	56,601	6,612	21,888	0	10,431	513	175,788
%	2.6	18.3	14.5	8.6	0	1.4	32.2	3.8	12.4	0	5.9	0.3	100.0
stories	9	34	29	26	0	3	25	5	24	0	17	2	174
%	5.2	19.5	16.7	14.9	0	1.7	14.4	2.9	13.8	0	9.8	1.1	100.0
Sing Tao Jih Pao													
words	2,232	32,488	17,174	18,910	2,728	0	6,758	496	682	310	2,232	5,394	89,404
%	2.5	36.3	19.2	21.1	3.1	0	7.6	0.6	0.8	0.3	2.5	6.0	100.0
stories	4	39	22	23	5	0	9	1	2	2	5	7	119
%	3.4	32.8	1.7	19.3	4.2	0	7.6	0.8	1.7	1.7	4.2	5.9	100.0
South China Morning Post													
words	8,214	21,238	16,243	7,992	666	407	1,887	2,294	5,661	444	3,589	1,554	70,189
%	11.7	30.3	23.1	11.4	0.9	0.6	2.7	3.3	8.1	0.6	5.1	2.2	100.0
stories	17	59	37	27	2	2	6	10	13	1	12	3	189
%	9.0	31.2	19.6	14.3	1.1	1.1	3.2	5.3	6.9	0.5	6.3	1.6	100.0
Statesman													
words	250	8,650	3,600	850	0	50	200	450	200	0	0	950	15,200
%	1.6	56.9	23.7	5.6	0	0.3	1.3	3.0	1.3	0	0	6.3	100.0
stories	3	24	12	6	0	1	2	5	1	0	0	3	57
%	5.3	42.1	21.1	10.5	0	1.7	3.5	8.8	1.7	0	0	5.3	100.0
Straits Times													
words	6,020	28,525	17,745	20,440	70	1,750	10,990	9,905	13,615	490	8,400	3,710	121,660
%	5.0	23.5	14.6	16.8	0.1	1.4	9.0	8.1	11.2	0.4	6.9	3.0	100.0
stories	15	69	42	59	1	3	14	22	22	3	8	13	271
%	5.5	25.5	15.5	21.8	0.4	1.1	5.2	8.1	8.1	1.1	2.9	4.8	100.0

Table C4 continued

Newspaper	*Military, political violence* (1)	*Foreign relations* (2)	*Domestic Politics* (3)	*Economics* (4)	*Science, Health* (5)	*Education* (6)	*Accidents, disasters* (7)	*Judicial, Crime* (8)	*Sports* (9)	*Art, culture* (10)	*Human interest* (11)	*Other* (12)	*Total*
Total													
words	58,811	380,078	119,397	188,650	6,860	9,965	100,478	48,021	141,253	28,829	65,201	30,994	1,178,537
%	5.0	32.2	10.1	16.0	0.6	0.9	8.5	4.1	12.0	2.5	5.5	2.6	100.0
stories	132	606	231	357	18	20	107	95	245	41	78	74	2,004
%	6.6	30.2	11.5	17.8	0.9	1.0	5.3	4.7	12.2	2.1	3.9	3.7	100.0

TABLE C5

Approximate Number and Percentage of Words and Number and Percentage of Stories for Each of 42 Third World Countries by Content Category for the Composite News Wire (excluding Hsinhua) for Five Days, December 5-9, 1977.

Country	*Military, political violence* (1)	*Foreign relations* (2)	*Domestic Politics* (3)	*Economics* (4)	*Science, Health* (5)	*Education* (6)	*Accidents, disasters* (7)	*Judicial, Crime* (8)	*Sports* (9)	*Art, culture* (10)	*Human interest* (11)	*Other* (12)	*Total*
Bangladesh													
words	0	419	869	108	0	0	0	0	0	0	0	0	1,396
%	0	30.0	62.3	7.7	0	0	0	0	0	0	0	0	100.0
stories	0	4	7	1	0	0	0	0	0	0	0	0	12
%	0	33.3	58.3	8.3	0	0	0	0	0	0	0	0	100.0
Burma													
words	0	0	0	0	0	0	0	0	180	0	0	0	180
%	0	0	0	0	0	0	0	0	100.0	0	0	0	100.0
stories	0	0	0	0	0	0	0	0	1	0	0	0	1
%	0	0	0	0	0	0	0	0	100.0	0	0	0	100.0
Cambodia													
words	0	162	0	126	0	0	0	0	0	0	0	168	456
%	0	35.5	0	27.6	0	0	0	0	0	0	0	36.8	100.0
stories	0	1	0	1	0	0	0	0	0	0	0	1	3
%	0	33.3	0	33.3	0	0	0	0	0	0	0	33.0	100.0
China													
words	1,108	6,019	4,900	4,454	753	1,543	0	906	632	529	442	634	21,920
%	5.1	27.5	22.4	20.3	3.4	7.0	0	4.1	2.9	2.4	2.0	2.9	100.0
stories	5	50	17	19	4	4	0	2	7	2	3	3	116
%	4.3	43.1	14.7	16.4	3.4	3.4	0	1.7	6.0	1.7	2.6	2.6	100.0
Hong Kong													
words	0	0	1,289	4,362	0	0	126	1,381	168	714	318	630	8,988
%	0	0	14.3	48.5	0	0	1.4	15.4	1.9	7.9	3.5	7.0	100.0
stories	0	0	4	22	0	0	2	8	1	3	4	4	48
%	0	0	8.3	45.8	0	0	4.2	16.7	2.1	6.3	8.3	8.3	100.0

Table C5 continued

Country	Military, political violence (1)	Foreign relations (2)	Domestic Politics (3)	Economics (4)	Science, Health (5)	Education (6)	Accidents, disasters (7)	Judicial, Crime (8)	Sports (9)	Art, culture (10)	Human interest (11)	Other (12)	Total
India													
words	190	378	5,319	1,825	408	0	1,158	1,406	9,893	0	312	301	21,190
%	0.9	1.8	25.1	8.6	1.9	0	5.5	6.6	46.7	0	1.5	1.4	100.0
stories	2	2	22	13	3	0	9	7	26	0	2	1	87
%	2.3	2.3	25.3	14.9	3.4	0	10.3	8.1 .	29.9	0	2.3	1.1	100.0
Indonesia													
words	1,258	1,618	4,521	2,825	108	324	727	432	962	162	486	2,455	15,878
%	7.9	10.2	28.5	17.8	0.7	2.0	4.6	2.7	6.1	1.0	3.1	15.5	100.0
stories	5	8	14	15	1	2	6	4	8	1	2	6	72
%	6.9	11.1	19.4	20.8	1.4	2.8	8.3	5.6	11.1	1.4	2.8	8.3	100.0
Iran													
words	108	54	354	1,054	0	0	0	0	210	0	0	84	1,864
%	5.8	2.9	19.0	56.5	0	0	0	0	11.3	0	0	4.5	100.0
stories	2	1	3	6	0	0	0	0	3	0	0	1	16
%	12.5	6.3	18.8	37.5	0	0	0	0	18.8	0	0	6.3	100.0
Laos													
words	0	354	252	0	0	0	0	0	0	0	0	0	606
%	0	58.4	41.6	0	0	0	0	0	0	0	0	0	100.0
stories	0	2	1	0	0	0	0	0	0	0	0	0	3
%	0	66.7	33.3	0	0	0	0	0	0	0	0	0	100.0
Malaysia													
words	1,422	4,986	4,515	5,855	0	0	12,214	2,718	1,789	162	336	675	34,639
%	4.1	14.4	13.0	16.9	0	0	35.3	7.8	5.2	0.5	1.0	1.9	100.0
stories	6	28	14	28	0	0	36	7	7	1	1	3	131
%	4.6	21.4	10.7	21.4	0	0	27.5	5.3	5.3	0.8	0.8	2.3	100.0
Nepal													
words	0	4,686	0	0	0	0	0	0	0	0	0	0	4,686
%	0	100.0	0	0	0	0	0	0	0	0	0	0	100.0
stories	0	15	0	0	0	0	0	0	0	0	0	0	15
%	0	100.0	0	0	0	0	0	0	0	0	0	0	100.0

Country	Military, political violence (1)	Foreign relations (2)	Domestic Politics (3)	Economics (4)	Science, Health (5)	Education (6)	Accidents, disasters (7)	Judicial, Crime (8)	Sports (9)	Art, culture (10)	Human interest (11)	Other (12)	Total
North Korea													
words	0	1,095	690	420	0	0	0	0	0	0	301	0	2,506
%	0	43.7	27.5	16.8	0	0	0	0	0	0	12.0	0	100.0
stories	0	3	2	3	0	0	0	0	0	0	1	0	9
%	0	33.3	22.2	33.3	0	0	0	0	0	0	11.1	0	100.0
Other Asian Countries													
words	0	357	126	0	0	0	0	0	0	0	0	0	483
%	0	73.9	26.1	0	0	0	0	0	0	0	0	0	100.0
stories	0	3	1	0	0	0	0	0	0	0	0	0	4
%	0	75.0	25.0	0	0	0	0	0	0	0	0	0	100.0
Pakistan													
words	0	1,486	4,239	735	336	0	770	672	10,035	0	688	1,895	20,856
%	0	7.1	29.3	3.5	1.6	0	3.7	3.2	48.1	0	3.3	9.1	100.0
stories	0	9	17	7	1	0	4	4	33	0	2	8	85
%	0	10.6	20.0	8.2	1.2	0	4.7	4.7	38.8	0	2.4	9.4	100.0
Philippines													
words	4,146	6,718	9,097	3,745	0	0	1,270	1,928	13,414	205	0	2,339	42,861
%	9.7	15.7	21.2	8.7	0	0	3.0	4.5	31.3	0.5	0	5.5	100.0
stories	17	25	22	25	0	0	12	6	28	1	0	7	143
%	11.9	17.5	15.4	17.5	0	0	8.4	4.2	19.6	0.7	0	4.9	100.0
Singapore													
words	318	1,394	966	9,343	0	0	2,538	1,164	1,992	546	1,914	1,152	21,327
%	1.5	6.5	4.5	43.8	0	0	11.9	5.5	9.3	2.6	9.0	5.4	100.0
stories	2	7	2	51	0	0	1	5	6	1	4	6	85
%	2.4	8.2	2.4	60.0	0	0	1.2	5.9	7.1	1.2	4.7	7.1	100.0
South Korea													
words	301	8,692	582	1,231	0	0	129	1,686	2,802	0	0	623	16,046
%	1.9	54.2	3.6	7.7	0	0	0.8	10.5	17.5	0	0	3.9	100.0
stories	3	30	3	7	0	0	1	5	14	0	0	3	65
%	3.1	46.2	4.6	10.8	0	0	1.5	7.7	21.5	0	0	4.6	100.0

Table C5 continued

Country	Military, political violence (1)	Foreign relations (2)	Domestic Politics (3)	Economics (4)	Science, Health (5)	Education (6)	Accidents, disasters (7)	Judicial, Crime (8)	Sports (9)	Art, culture (10)	Human interest (11)	Other (12)	Total
Sri Lanka													
words	0	1,815	894	366	270	0	0	126	54	259	216	807	4,800
%	0	37.8	18.6	7.6	5.6	0	0	2.6	1.1	5.4	4.5	16.8	100.0
stories	0	6	4	2	2	0	0	1	1	2	1	3	22
%	0	27.3	18.2	9.1	9.1	0	0	4.5	4.5	9.1	4.5	13.6	100.0
Taiwan													
words	84	1,627	2,962	0	473	168	0	172	2,960	0	270	0	8,716
%	1.0	18.7	34.0	0	5.4	1.9	0	2.0	34.0	0	3.1	0	100.0
stories	1	11	17	0	1	1	0	1	6	0	1	0	39
%	2.6	28.2	43.6	0	2.6	2.6	0	2.6	15.4	0	2.6	0	100.0
Thailand													
words	4,090	1,887	1,882	8,483	216	0	928	1,725	5,536	0	649	2,374	27,690
%	14.8	6.8	6.8	30.6	0.8	0	3.4	6.2	20.0	0	2.3	8.6	100.0
stories	13	14	5	17	2	0	5	14	18	0	3	11	102
%	12.7	13.7	4.9	16.7	2.0	0	4.9	13.7	17.6	0	2.9	10.8	100.0
Vietnam													
words	1,182	11,545	618	787	661	0	0	258	0	0	1,031	820	16,920
%	7.0	68.3	3.7	4.7	3.9	0	0	1.5	0	0	6.1	4.9	100.0
stories	5	56	2	6	5	0	0	1	0	0	4	6	85
%	5.9	65.9	2.4	7.1	5.9	0	0	1.2	0	0	4.7	7.1	100.0
Brazil													
words	577	149	0	533	0	0	0	84	1,686	0	0	0	3,029
%	19.0	4.9	0	17.6	0	0	0	2.8	55.7	0	0	0	100.0
stories	3	2	0	3	0	0	0	1	6	0	0	0	15
%	20.0	13.3	0	20.0	0	0	0	6.7	40.0	0	0	0	100.0
Columbia													
words	0	390	442	108	0	0	425	0	164	0	0	0	1,529
%	0	25.5	28.9	7.1	0	0	27.8	0	10.7	0	0	0	100.0
stories	0	2	2	1	0	0	3	0	1	0	0	0	9

Table C5 continued

Country	Military, political violence (1)	Foreign relations (2)	Domestic Politics (3)	Economics (4)	Science, Health (5)	Education (6)	Accidents, disasters (7)	Judicial, Crime (8)	Sports (9)	Art, culture (10)	Human interest (11)	Other (12)	Total
Chile													
words	0	809	0	216	0	0	0	0	126	0	0	1,480	2,631
%	0	30.7	0	8.2	0	0	0	0	4.8	0	0	56.3	100.0
stories	0	3	0	2	0	0	0	0	1	0	0	5	11
%	0	27.3	0	18.2	0	0	0	0	9.1	0	0	45.5	100.0
Cuba													
words	1,489	2,102	0	498	0	0	6,044	328	0	0	0	0	10,460
%	14.2	20.1	0	4.8	0	0	57.8	3.1	0	0	0	0	100.0
stories	4	7	0	2	0	0	6	1	0	0	0	0	20
%	20.0	35.0	0	10.0	0	0	30.0	5.0	0	0	0	0	100.0
Mexico													
words	0	782	0	882	0	0	82	0	559	0	425	0	2,730
%	0	28.6	0	32.3	0	0	3.0	0	20.5	0	15.6	0	100.0
stories	0	3	0	1	0	0	1	0	1	0	2	0	8
%	0	37.5	0	12.5	0	0	12.5	0	12.5	0	25.0	0	100.0
Peru													
words	0	84	0	294	0	0	0	0	0	0	0	0	378
%	0	22.2	0	77.8	0	0	0	0	0	0	0	0	100.0
stories	0	1	0	2	0	0	0	0	0	0	0	0	3
%	0	33.3	0	66.7	0	0	0	0	0	0	0	0	100.0
Venezuela													
words	0	369	0	328	0	0	0	218	920	0	0	0	1,835
%	0	20.1	0	17.9	0	0	0	11.9	50.1	0	0	0	100.0
stories	0	2	1	0	0	0	0	2	6	0	0	0	11
%	0	18.2	0	9.1	0	0	0	18.2	54.5	0	0	0	100.0
Other Latin Countries													
words	4,729	3,128	3,141	432	215	0	0	258	3,303	0	792	1,389	17,387
%	27.2	18.0	18.1	2.5	1.2	0	0	1.5	19.0	0	4.6	8.0	100.0
stories	13	11	17	1	1	0	0	1	11	0	2	5	62
%	21.0	17.7	27.4	1.6	1.6	0	0	1.6	17.7	0	3.2	8.1	100.0

Table C5 continued

Country	Military, political violence (1)	Foreign relations (2)	Domestic Politics (3)	Economics (4)	Science, Health (5)	Education (6)	Accidents, disasters (7)	Judicial, Crime (8)	Sports (9)	Art, culture (10)	Human interest (11)	Other (12)	Total
Algeria													
words	0	0	324	270	0	0	0	0	0	0	0	0	594
%	0	0	54.5	45.5	0	0	0	0	0	0	0	0	100.0
stories	0	0	1	1	0	0	0	0	0	0	0	0	2
%	0	0	50.0	50.0	0	0	0	0	0	0	0	0	100.0
Egypt													
words	296	36,604	2,326	754	0	0	0	205	3,419	162	342	456	44,565
%	0.7	82.1	5.2	1.7	0	0	0	0.5	7.7	0.4	0.8	1.0	100.0
stories	2	124	4	3	0	0	0	1	4	1	2	4	146
%	1.4	84.9	3.4	2.1	0	0	0	0.7	2.7	0.7	1.4	2.7	100.0
Iraq													
words	490	43	0	0	0	0	0	108	2,241	786	0	0	3,668
%	13.4	1.2	0	0	0	0	0	2.9	61.1	21.4	0	0	100.0
stories	2	1	0	0	0	0	0	1	8	2	0	0	14
%	14.3	7.1	0	0	0	0	0	7.1	57.1	14.3	0	0	100.0
Jordan													
words	0	5,751	0	0	0	0	0	0	0	54	0	0	5,805
%	0	99.1	0	0	0	0	0	0	0	0.9	0	0	100.0
stories	0	21	0	0	0	0	0	0	0	1	0	0	22
%	0	95.5	0	0	0	0	0	0	0	4.5	0	0	100.0
Libya													
words	164	1,748	0	0	0	0	0	0	164	0	0	0	2,076
%	7.9	84.2	0	0	0	0	0	0	7.9	0	0	0	100.0
stories	1	6	0	0	0	0	0	0	1	0	0	0	8
%	12.5	75	0	0	0	0	0	0	12.5	0	0	0	100.0
Saudi Arabia													
words	276	9,552	0	1,666	0	0	82	42	0	0	84	0	11,702
%	2.4	81.6	0	14.2	0	0	0.7	0.4	0	0	0.7	0	100.0
stories	2	24	0	9	0	0	1	1	0	0	1	0	38
%	5.3	63.2	0	23.7	0	0	2.6	2.6	0	0	2.6	0	100.0

Country	Military, political violence (1)	Foreign relations (2)	Domestic Politics (3)	Economic (4)	Science, Health (5)	Education (6)	Accidents, disasters (7)	Judicial, Crime (8)	Sports (9)	Art, cultur (10)	Human interest (11)	Other (12)	Total
Syria													
words	1,159	39,028	0	168	0	0	0	0	0	0	0	486	40,841
%	2.8	95.6	0	0.4	0	0	0	0	0	0	0	1.2	100.0
stories	7	102	0	2	0	0	0	0	0	0	0	2	113
%	6.2	90.3	0	1.8	0	0	0	0	0	0	0	1.8	100.0
Other Mideast Countries													
words	1,922	8,076	2,213	1,689	0	0	4,611	423	2,977	0	642	642	23,195
%	8.3	34.8	9.5	7.3	0	0	19.9	1.8	12.8	0	2.8	2.8	100.0
stories	9	45	6	8	0	0	15	2	9	0	2	4	100
%	9.0	45.0	6.0	8.0	0	0	15.0	2.0	9.0	0	2.0	4.0	100.0
Kenya													
words	0	216	0	0	0	0	168	0	2,856	0	0	0	3,240
%	0	6.7	0	0	0	0	5.2	0	88.1	0	0	0	100.0
stories	0	1	0	0	0	0	1	0	1	0	0	0	3
%	0	33.3	0	0	0	0	33.3	0	33.3	0	0	0	100.0
Nigeria													
words	0	123	0	54	0	0	0	0	0	0	0	0	177
%	0	69.5	0	30.5	0	0	0	0	0	0	0	0	100.0
stories	0	1	0	1	0	0	0	0	0	0	0	0	2
%	0	50.0	0	50.0	0	0	0	0	0	0	0	0	100.0
Uganda													
words	108	438	0	756	0	0	108	576	516	0	0	2,714	5,216
%	2.1	8.4	0	14.5	0	0	2.1	11.0	9.9	0	0	52	100.0
stories	1	4	9	1	0	0	1	3	3	0	0	7	20
%	5.0	20.0	0	5.0	0	0	5.0	15.0	15.0	0	0	35.0	100.0
Other African Countries													
words	9,994	18,910	16,772	4,546	84	0	300	460	1,590	0	822	1,719	55,197
%	18.1	34.3	30.4	8.2	0.2	0	0.5	0.8	2.9	0	1.5	3.1	100.0
stories	35	70	47	21	1	0	3	3	9	0	3	6	198
%	17.7	35.4	23.7	10.6	0.5	0	1.5	1.5	4.5	0	1.5	3.0	100.0

Table C5 continued

Country	Military, political violence (1)	Foreign relations (2)	Domestic Politics (3)	Economics (4)	Science, Health (5)	Education (6)	Accidents, disasters (7)	Judicial, Crime (8)	Sports (9)	Art, culture (10)	Human interest (11)	Other (12)	Total
South Pacific													
words	0	2,820	270	1,809	168	0	334	0	2,016	0	0	216	7,633
%	0	36.9	3.5	23.7	2.2	0	4.4	0	26.4	0	0	2.8	100.0
stories	0	14	1	8	1	0	2	0	6	0	0	2	34
%	0	41.2	2.9	23.5	2.9	0	5.9	0	17.6	0	0	5.9	100
Total													
words	35,412	186,413	66,521	63,651	3,692	2,035	32,014	17,276	73,091	3,579	10,070	24,057	517,813
%	6.8	36.0	12.8	12.3	0.7	0.4	6.2	3.3	14.1	0.7	1.9	4.6	100.0
stories	139	719	219	307	22	7	109	81	226	15	40	98	1,982
%	7.0	36.3	11.0	15.5	1.1	0.4	5.5	4.1	11.4	0.8	2.0	4.9	100.0

TABLE C6

Approximate Number and Percentage of Words and Number and Percentage of Stories for Each of 42 Third World Countries by Content Category for Hsinhua for Five Days, December 5-9, 1977.

Country	*Military, political violence* (1)	*Foreign relations* (2)	*Domestic Politics* (3)	*Economics* (4)	*Science, Health* (5)	*Education* (6)	*Sports* (9)	*Art, culture* (10)	*Human interest* (11)	*Other* (12)	*Total*
China											
words	0	4,860	120	3,060	3,789	870	870	690	0	0	14,250
%	0	34.1	0.8	21.5	26.5	6.1	6.1	4.8	0	0	100.0
stories	0	21	1	8	11	3	6	1	0	0	51
%	0	41.2	1.9	15.7	21.6	5.9	11.8	1.9	0	0	100.0
India											
words	0	180	0	0	0	0	0	0	0	0	180
%	0	100.0	0	0	0	0	0	0	0	0	100.0
stories	0	1	0	0	0	0	0	0	0	0	1
%	0	100.0	0	0	0	0	0	0	0	0	100.0
Indonesia											
words	0	0	0	240	0	0	0	0	0	0	240
%	0	0	0	100.0	0	0	0	0	0	0	100.0
stories	0	0	0	1	0	0	0	0	0	0	1
%	0	0	0	100.0	0	0	0	0	0	0	100.0
Iran											
words	0	270	0	0	0	0	180	0	0	0	450
%	0	60.0	0	0	0	0	40.0	0	0	0	100.0
stories	0	1	0	0	0	0	1	0	0	0	2
%	0	50.0	0	0	0	0	50.0	0	0	0	100.0
Laos											
words	0	90	0	0	0	0	0	0	0	0	90
%	0	100.0	0	0	0	0	0	0	0	0	100.0
stories	0	1	0	0	0	0	0	0	0	0	1
%	0	100.0	0	0	0	0	0	0	0	0	100.0

Table C6 continued

Country	Military, political violence (1)	Foreign relations (2)	Domestic Politics (3)	Economics (4)	Science, Health (5)	Education (6)	Sports (9)	Art, culture (10)	Human interest (11)	Other (12)	Total
Malaysia											
words	0	0	0	0	0	0	120	0	0	0	120
%	0	0	0	0	0	0	100.0	0	0	0	100.0
stories	0	0	0	0	0	0	1	0	0	0	1
%	0	0	0	0	0	0	100.0	0	0	0	100.0
North Korea											
words	0	120	0	0	0	0	240	0	0	0	360
%	0	33.3	0	0	0	0	66.7	0	0	0	100.0
stories	0	2	0	0	0	0	1	0	0	0	3
%	0	66.7	0	0	0	0	33.3	0	0	0	100.0
Other Asian Countries											
words	0	0	0	0	0	0	180	0	0	0	180
%	0	0	0	0	0	0	100.0	0	0	0	100.0
stories	0	0	0	0	0	0	1	0	0	0	1
%	0	0	0	0	0	0	100.0	0	0	0	100.0
Pakistan											
words	0	420	0	0	0	0	0	90	0	0	510
%	0	82.4	0	0	0	0	0	17.6	0	0	100.0
stories	0	3	0	0	0	0	0	1	0	0	4
%	0	75.0	0	0	0	0	0	25.0	0	0	100.0
South Korea											
words	0	0	720	0	0	0	600	0	0	0	1,320
%	0	0	54.5	0	0	0	45.5	0	0	0	100.0
stories	0	0	2	0	0	0	2	0	0	0	4
%	0	0	50.0	0	0	0	50.0	0	0	0	100.0
Sri Lanka											
words	0	150	0	0	0	0	0	0	0	0	150
%	0	100.0	0	0	0	0	0	0	0	0	100.0
stories	0	1	0	0	0	0	0	0	0	0	1
%	0	100.0	0	0	0	0	0	0	0	0	100.0

Table C6 continued

Country	*Military, political violence* (1)	*Foreign relations* (2)	*Domestic Politics* (3)	*Economics* (4)	*Science, Health* (5)	*Education* (6)	*Sports* (9)	*Art, culture* (10)	*Human interest* (11)	*Other* (12)	*Total*
Thailand											
words	0	150	90	0	0	0	270	0	0	0	510
%	0	29.4	17.7	0	0	0	52.9	0	0	0	100.0
stories	0	1	1	0	0	0	1	0	0	0	3
%	0	33.3	33.3	0	0	0	33.3	0	0	0	100.0
Brazil											
words	0	0	0	150	0	0	0	0	0	0	150
%	0	0	0	100.0	0	0	0	0	0	0	100.0
stories	0	0	0	1	0	0	0	0	0	0	1
%	0	0	0	100.0	0	0	0	0	0	0	100.0
Cuba											
words	0	240	0	0	0	0	0	0	0	0	240
%	0	100.0	0	0	0	0	0	0	0	0	100.0
stories	0	1	0	0	0	0	0	0	0	0	1
%	0	100.0	0	0	0	0	0	0	0	0	100.0
Mexico											
words	0	0	0	180	120	0	0	0	180	0	480
%	0	0	0	37.5	25.0	0	0	0	37.5	0	100.0
stories	0	0	0	1	1	0	0	0	1	0	3
%	0	0	0	33.3	33.3	0	0	0	33.3	0	100.0
Peru											
words	0	120	0	0	0	0	0	0	0	0	120
%	0	100.0	0	0	0	0	0	0	0	0	100.0
stories	0	1	0	0	0	0	0	0	0	0	1
%	0	100.0	0	0	0	0	0	0	0	0	100.0
Venezuela											
words	0	0	0	390	0	0	0	0	0	0	390
%	0	0	0	100.0	0	0	0	0	0	0	100.0
stories	0	0	0	2	0	0	0	0	0	0	2
%	0	0	0	100.0	0	0	0	0	0	0	100.0

Table C6 continued

Country	Military, political violence (1)	Foreign relations (2)	Domestic Politics (3)	Economics (4)	Science, Health (5)	Education (6)	Sports (9)	Art, culture (10)	Human interest (11)	Other (12)	Total
Other Latin Countries											
words	0	1,140	240	0	0	0	90	210	0	0	1,680
%	0	67.9	14.3	0	0	0	5.4	12.5	0	0	100.0
stories	0	1	1	0	0	0	1	1	0	0	4
%	0	25.0	25.0	0	0	0	25.0	25.0	0	0	100.0
Egypt											
words	0	270	0	0	0	0	0	0	0	0	270
%	0	100.0	0	0	0	0	0	0	0	0	100.0
stories	0	2	0	0	0	0	0	0	0	0	2
%	0	100.0	0	0	0	0	0	0	0	0	100.0
Iraq											
words	0	240	0	0	0	0	390	0	0	0	630
%	0	38.1	0	0	0	0	61.9	0	0	0	100.0
stories	0	1	0	0	0	0	1	0	0	0	2
%	0	50.0	0	0	0	0	50.0	0	0	0	100.0
Syria											
words	0	0	0	0	0	0	90	0	0	0	90
%	0	0	0	0	0	0	100.0	0	0	0	100.0
stories	0	0	0	0	0	0	1	0	0	0	1
%	0	0	0	0	0	0	100.0	0	0	0	100.0
Other Mideast Countries											
words	120	1,240	0	0	0	0	0	0	0	0	1,410
%	8.5	91.5	0	0	0	0	0	0	0	0	100.0
stories	1	7	0	0	0	0	0	0	0	0	8
%	12.5	87.5	0	0	0	0	0	0	0	0	100.0
Other African Countries											
words	210	6,240	420	1,020	120	0	60	930	0	510	9,510
%	2.2	65.6	4.4	10.7	1.3	0	0.6	9.8	0	5.4	100.0
stories	1	22	3	5	1	0	1	2	0	1	36
[illegible]	[illegible]	[illegible]	[illegible]	[illegible]	2.8	0	2.8	5.5	0	2.8	100.0

Country	Military, political violence (1)	Foreign relations (2)	Domestic Politics (3)	Economics (4)	Science, Health (5)	Education (6)	Sports (9)	Art, culture (10)	Human interest (11)	Other (12)	Total
Total words	330	15,780	1,350	5,370	4,020	870	3,090	1,920	180	510	33,420
%	1.0	47.2	4.0	16.1	12.0	2.6	9.3	5.7	0.5	1.5	100.0
stories	2	66	7	20	13	3	17	5	1	1	135
%	1.5	48.9	5.2	14.8	9.6	2.2	12.6	3.7	0.7	0.7	100.0

* Countries and content categories not found on the Hsinhua file are excluded. See Table C5 for a complete list of countries and content categories.

TABLE C7

Approximate Number and Percentage of Words and Number and Percentage of Stories for Each of 42 Third World Countries by Content Category for the Composite Asian Daily Newspaper for Five Days, December 6-10, 1977.

Country	Military, political violence (1)	Foreign relations (2)	Domestic Politics (3)	Economics (4)	Science, Health (5)	Education (6)	Accidents, disasters (7)	Judicial, Crime (8)	Sports (9)	Art, culture (10)	Human interest (11)	Other (12)	Total
Bangladesh													
words	0	0	144	250	0	0	0	0	0	0	0	0	394
%	0	0	36.5	63.5	0	0	0	0	0	0	0	0	100.0
stories	0	0	3	1	0	0	0	0	0	0	0	0	4
%	0	0	75.0	25.0	0	0	0	0	0	0	0	0	100.0
Burma													
words	0	983	0	0	0	0	0	0	0	0	0	0	983
%	0	100.0	0	0	0	0	0	0	0	0	0	0	100.0
stories	0	2	0	0	0	0	0	0	0	0	0	0	2
%	0	100.0	0	0	0	0	0	0	0	0	0	0	100.0
Cambodia													
words	0	5,380	240	0	0	0	787	0	0	0	0	1,330	7,737
%	0	69.5	3.1	0	0	0	10.2	0	0	0	0	17.2	100.0
stories	0	5	1	0	0	0	2	0	0	0	0	1	9
%	0	55.6	11.1	0	0	0	22.2	0	0	0	0	11.1	100.0
China													
words	0	14,411	19,301	6,160	1,380	2,508	0	0	7,898	444	6,074	2,242	59,968
%	0	24.0	32.2	10.3	2.3	3.4	0	0	13.2	0.7	10.1	3.7	100.0
stories	0	40	32	16	4	5	0	0	16	1	10	5	129
%	0	31.0	24.8	12.4	3.1	3.9	0	0	12.4	0.8	7.8	3.9	100.0
Hong Kong													
words	0	0	427	16,499	0	0	34	727	822	671	23,424	140	42,744
%	0	0	1.0	38.6	0	0	0.1	1.7	1.9	1.6	54.8	0.3	100.0
stories	0	0	1	40	0	0	1	5	2	1	6	1	57
%	0	0	1.8	70.0	0	0	1.8	8.8	3.5	1.8	10.5	1.8	100.0

Table C7 continued

Country	Military, political violence (1)	Foreign relations (2)	Domestic Politics (3)	Economics (4)	Science, Health (5)	Education (6)	Accidents, disasters (7)	Judicial, Crime (8)	Sports (9)	Art, culture (10)	Human interest (11)	Other (12)	Total
India													
words	531	1,280	4,045	2,673	32	0	1,537	1,305	6,768	1,060	0	0	19,231
%	2.8	6.7	21.0	13.9	0.2	0	8.0	6.8	35.2	5.5	0	0	100.0
stories	4	5	16	10	1	0	8	7	18	2	0	0	71
%	5.6	7.0	22.5	14.1	1.4	0	11.3	9.9	25.4	2.8	0	0	100.0
Indonesia													
words	2,858	699	7,164	6,903	70	204	0	397	2,974	1,326	2,573	966	26,104
%	10.9	2.6	27.4	26.4	0.3	0.8	0	1.5	11.4	5.1	9.9	3.7	100.0
stories	8	3	12	9	1	1	0	2	12	2	3	5	58
%	13.8	5.2	20.1	15.5	1.7	1.7	0	3.4	20.1	3.4	5.2	8.6	100.0
Iran													
words	2,368	1,696	320	7,742	2,560	1,906	96	576	7,130	8,288	102	0	32,784
%	7.2	5.2	1.0	23.6	7.8	5.8	0.3	1.8	21.7	25.3	0.3	0	100.0
stories	11	9	2	20	2	5	1	4	17	10	2	0	83
%	13.3	10.8	2.4	24.1	2.4	6.0	1.2	4.8	20.5	12.0	2.4	0	100.0
Laos													
words	1,750	272	374	0	0	0	0	0	0	0	0	0	2,396
%	73.0	11.4	15.6	0	0	0	0	0	0	0	0	0	100.0
stories	2	1	1	0	0	0	0	0	0	0	0	0	4
%	50.0	25.0	25.0	0	0	0	0	0	0	0	0	0	100.0
Malaysia													
words	2,350	6,352	33,044	21,577	0	4,609	78,646	15,910	15,078	2,514	12,902	2,632	195,614
%	1.2	3.2	16.9	11.0	0	2.4	40.2	8.1	7.7	1.3	6.6	1.3	100.0
stories	6	21	44	53	0	7	57	23	16	4	20	8	259
%	2.3	8.1	17.0	20.5	0	2.7	22.0	8.9	6.2	1.5	7.7	3.1	100.0
Nepal													
words	0	3,062	0	402	0	0	0	0	264	0	0	0	3,728
%	0	82.1	0	10.8	0	0	0	0	7.1	0	0	0	100.0
stories	0	7	0	2	0	0	0	0	1	0	0	0	10
%	0	70.0	0	20.0	0	0	0	0	10.0	0	0	0	100.0

Table C7 continued

Country	Military, political violence (1)	Foreign relations (2)	Domestic Politics (3)	Economics (4)	Science, Health (5)	Education (6)	Accidents, disasters (7)	Judicial, Crime (8)	Sports (9)	Art, culture (10)	Human interest (11)	Other (12)	Total
North Korea													
words	0	2,899	1,395	665	0	0	0	280	0	0	0	248	5,487
%	0	52.8	25.4	12.1	0	0	0	5.1	0	0	0	4.5	100.0
stories	0	6	4	1	0	0	0	1	0	0	0	1	13
%	0	46.1	30.8	7.7	0	0	0	7.7	0	0	0	7.7	100.0
Other Asian Countries													
words	2,528	2,291	96	272	992	0	224	32	1,506	528	148	96	8,713
%	29.0	26.3	1.1	3.1	11.4	0	2.6	0.4	17.3	6.1	1.7	1.1	100.0
stories	3	6	1	1	1	0	2	1	3	1	1	1	21
%	14.3	28.6	5.8	4.8	4.8	0	9.5	4.8	14.3	4.8	4.8	4.8	100.0
Pakistan													
words	96	2,003	3,937	3,516	296	0	142	488	18,131	40	275	2,651	31,575
%	0.3	6.3	12.5	11.1	0.9	0	0.4	1.5	57.4	0.1	0.9	8.4	100.0
stories	1	10	17	10	1	0	2	3	29	1	2	17	93
%	1.1	10.8	18.3	10.8	1.1	0	2.2	3.2	31.2	1.1	2.2	18.3	100.0
Philippines													
words	4,787	6,345	16,748	1,166	0	0	438	727	11,662	0	0	32	41,905
%	11.4	15.1	40.0	2.2	0	0	1.0	1.7	27.8	0	0	0.1	100.0
stories	14	16	33	4	0	0	3	2	19	0	0	1	92
%	15.2	17.4	35.9	4.3	0	0	3.3	2.2	20.7	0	0	1.1	100.0
Singapore													
words	672	5,612	1,281	61,754	88	916	13,088	15,452	10,434	5,307	4,006	1,966	120,576
%	0.6	4.7	1.1	51.2	0.1	0.8	10.9	12.8	8.7	4.4	3.3	1.6	100.0
stories	1	6	1	60	1	2	9	18	19	3	8	4	132
%	0.8	4.5	0.8	45.5	0.8	1.5	6.8	13.6	14.4	2.3	6.1	3.0	100.0
South Korea													
words	128	3,212	408	998	0	0	244	496	7,802	124	0	612	14,024
%	0.9	22.9	2.9	7.1	0	0	1.7	3.5	55.6	0.9	0	4.4	100.0
stories	1	15	1	4	0	0	1	1	12	1	0	1	37
%	2.7	40.5	2.7	10.8	0	0	2.7	2.7	32.4	2.7	0	2.7	100.0

Table C7 continued

Country	Military, political violence (1)	Foreign relations (2)	Domestic Politics (3)	Economics (4)	Science, Health (5)	Education (6)	Accidents, disasters (7)	Judicial, Crime (8)	Sports (9)	Art, culture (10)	Human interest (11)	Other (12)	Total
Sri Lanka													
words	96	3,025	826	2,040	0	0	0	0	534	492	175	200	7,388
%	1.3	40.9	11.2	27.6	0	0	0	0	7.2	6.7	2.4	2.7	100.0
stories	1	8	4	3	0	0	0	0	2	2	1	1	22
%	4.5	36.4	18.2	13.6	0	0	0	0	9.1	9.1	4.5	4.5	100.0
Taiwan													
words	744	3,502	3,138	5,424	0	0	0	0	3,314	186	2,895	0	19,203
%	3.9	18.2	16.3	28.2	0	0	0	0	17.3	1.0	15.1	0	100.0
stories	1	8	4	15	0	0	0	0	6	1	5	0	40
%	2.5	20.0	10.0	37.5	0	0	0	0	15.0	2.5	12.5	0	100.0
Thailand													
words	1,340	6,369	1,114	2,736	806	476	185	4,117	6,290	3,696	1,491	0	28,620
%	4.7	22.3	3.9	9.6	2.8	1.7	0.6	14.4	22.0	12.9	5.2	0	100.0
stories	7	19	5	11	2	1	3	10	14	4	4	0	80
%	8.8	23.6	6.3	13.8	2.5	1.3	3.8	12.5	17.5	5.0	5.0	0	100.0
Vietnam													
words	1,825	22,058	648	5,016	192	0	0	1,150	288	0	2,992	1,417	35,586
%	5.1	62.0	1.8	14.1	0.5	0	0	3.2	0.8	0	8.4	4.0	100.0
stories	3	37	2	8	1	0	0	2	1	0	3	2	59
%	5.1	62.7	3.4	13.6	1.7	0	0	3.4	1.7	0	5.1	3.4	100.0
Brazil													
words	1,436	0	0	4,121	0	0	0	74	329	0	0	0	5,960
%	24.1	0	0	69.1	0	0	0	1.2	5.5	0	0	0	100.0
stories	3	0	0	5	0	0	0	1	2	0	0	0	11
%	27.3	0	0	45.5	0	0	0	9.1	18.2	0	0	0	100.0
Columbia													
words	0	0	32	0	0	0	344	0	102	0	0	0	478
%	0	0	6.7	0	0	0	72.0	0	21.3	0	0	0	100.0
stories	0	0	1	0	0	0	2	0	1	0	0	0	4
%	0	0	25.0	0	0	0	50.0	0	25.0	0	0	0	100.0

Table C7 continued

Country	Military, political violence (1)	Foreign relations (2)	Domestic Politics (3)	Economics (4)	Science, Health (5)	Education (6)	Accidents, disasters (7)	Judicial, Crime (8)	Sports (9)	Art, culture (10)	Human interest (11)	Other (12)	Total
Chile													
words	32	0	0	0	0	0	0	0	0	0	0	930	962
%	3.3	0	0	0	0	0	0	0	0	0	0	96.7	100.0
stories	1	0	0	0	0	0	0	0	0	0	0	1	2
%	50.0	0	0	0	0	0	0	0	0	0	0	50.0	100.0
Cuba													
words	914	4,328	0	0	0	0	1,595	296	700	0	1,146	0	8,979
%	10.2	48.2	0	0	0	0	17.8	3.3	7.8	0	12.8	0	100.0
stories	2	9	0	0	0	0	4	1	2	0	2	0	20
%	10.0	45.0	0	0	0	0	20.0	5.0	10.0	0	10.0	0	100.0
Mexico													
words	0	814	430	0	280	0	244	0	4,776	0	0	0	6,544
%	0	12.4	6.6	0	4.3	0	3.7	0	73.0	0	0	0	100.0
stories	0	1	2	0	2	0	1	0	3	0	0	0	9
%	0	11.1	22.2	0	22.2	0	11.1	0	33.3	0	0	0	100.0
Peru													
words	0	0	0	50	0	0	0	0	0	0	0	0	50
%	0	0	0	100.0	0	0	0	0	0	0	0	0	100.0
stories	0	0	0	1	0	0	0	0	0	0	0	0	1
%	0	0	0	100.0	0	0	0	0	0	0	0	0	100.0
Venezuela													
words	0	0	0	1,488	0	0	0	0	590	0	0	0	2,078
%	0	0	0	71.6	0	0	0	0	28.4	0	0	0	100.0
stories	0	0	0	1	0	0	0	0	3	0	0	0	4
%	0	0	0	25.0	0	0	0	0	75.0	0	0	0	100.0
Other Latin Countries													
words	12,000	495	1,054	192	0	0	0	816	3,843	0	0	544	18,944
%	63.3	2.6	5.6	1.0	0	0	0	4.3	20.2	0	0	2.9	100.0
stories	13	3	4	1	0	0	0	1	9	0	0	1	32
%	40.6	9.4	12.5	3.1	0	0	0	3.1	28.1	0	0	3.1	100.0

Table C7 continued

Country	Military, political violence (1)	Foreign relations (2)	Domestic Politics (3)	Economics (4)	Science, Health (5)	Education (6)	Accidents, disasters (7)	Judicial, Crime (8)	Sports (9)	Art, culture (10)	Human interest (11)	Other (12)	Total
Algeria													
words	0	0	868	2,656	0	0	930	0	0	0	427	0	4,881
%	0	0	17.8	54.4	0	0	19.1	0	0	0	8.7	0	100.0
stories	0	0	1	1	0	0	1	0	0	0	1	0	4
%	0	0	25.0	25.0	0	0	25.0	0	0	0	25.0	0	100.0
Egypt													
words	1,462	51,437	2,495	940	68	0	0	0	6,388	886	931	1,072	65,679
%	2.2	78.3	3.8	1.4	0.1	0	0	0	9.7	1.3	1.4	1.6	100.0
stories	6	85	5	4	1	0	0	0	5	2	2	3	113
%	5.3	75.2	4.4	3.5	0.9	0	0	0	4.4	1.8	1.8	2.7	100.0
Iraq													
words	1,679	2,665	0	2,031	0	0	0	245	11,016	0	0	160	17,796
%	9.4	15.0	0	11.4	0	0	0	1.4	61.9	0	0	0.9	100.0
stories	3	6	0	6	0	0	0	1	9	0	0	1	26
%	11.5	23.1	0	23.1	0	0	0	3.8	34.6	0	0	3.8	100.0
Jordan													
words	0	9,398	0	0	0	0	0	0	0	0	0	0	9,398
%	0	100.0	0	0	0	0	0	0	0	0	0	0	100.0
stories	0	13	0	0	0	0	0	0	0	0	0	0	13
%	0	100.0	0	0	0	0	0	0	0	0	0	0	100.0
Libya													
words	358	1,451	0	0	0	0	0	0	0	0	0	0	1,809
%	19.8	80.2	0	0	0	0	0	0	0	0	0	0	100.0
stories	2	5	0	0	0	0	0	0	0	0	0	0	7
%	28.6	71.4	0	0	0	0	0	0	0	0	0	0	100.0
Saudi Arabia													
words	1,525	15,377	0	18,857	0	0	272	64	2,202	855	0	4,997	44,149
%	3.5	34.8	0	42.7	0	0	0.6	0.1	5.0	1.9	0	11.3	100.0
stories	4	21	0	31	0	0	1	1	4	1	0	6	69
%	5.8	30.4	0	44.9	0	0	1.4	1.4	5.8	1.4	0	8.7	100.0

Table C7 continued

Country	Military, political violence (1)	Foreign relations (2)	Domestic Politics (3)	Economics (4)	Science, Health (5)	Education (6)	Accidents, disasters (7)	Judicial, Crime (8)	Sports (9)	Art, culture (10)	Human interest (11)	Other (12)	Total
Syria													
words	800	110,943	3,662	2,146	0	0	0	0	68	0	0	0	117,619
%	0.7	94.3	3.1	1.8	0	0	0	0	0.1	0	0	0	100.0
stories	2	138	3	2	0	0	0	0	1	0	0	0	146
%	1.4	94.5	2.1	1.4	0	0	0	0	0.7	0	0	0	100.0
Other Mideast Countries													
words	4,793	58,256	0	3,609	96	0	1,030	1,771	4,035	624	0	1,797	76,011
%	6.3	76.6	0	4.7	0.1	0	1.4	2.3	5.3	0.8	0	2.4	100.0
stories	8	48	0	9	1	0	4	5	8	2	0	5	90
%	3.3	53.3	0	10.0	1.1	0	4.4	5.6	8.9	2.2	0	5.6	100.0
Kenya													
words	88	0	0	0	0	0	204	0	0	0	0	0	292
%	30.1	0	0	0	0	0	69.9	0	0	0	0	0	100.0
stories	1	0	0	0	0	0	1	0	0	0	0	0	2
%	50.0	0	0	0	0	0	50.0	0	0	0	0	0	100.0
Nigeria													
words	0	0	0	0	0	0	0	0	204	0	0	0	204
%	0	0	0	0	0	0	0	0	100.0	0	0	0	100.0
stories	0	0	0	0	0	0	0	0	1	0	0	0	1
%	0	0	0	0	0	0	0	0	100.0	0	0	0	100.0
Uganda													
words	270	1,011	1,462	574	0	0	32	0	0	1,056	0	1,461	5,866
%	4.6	17.2	24.9	9.8	0	0	0.5	0	0	18.0	0	24.9	100.0
stories	2	5	1	2	0	0	1	0	0	1	0	4	16
%	12.5	31.3	6.3	12.5	0	0	6.3	0	0	6.3	0	25.0	100.0
Other African Countries													
words	10,086	31,731	15,174	5,084	0	0	202	3,098	1,067	1,792	3,934	5,501	77,669
%	13.0	40.9	19.5	6.5	0	0	0.3	4.0	1.4	2.3	5.1	7.1	100.0
stories	20	45	32	21	0	0	2	6	4	4	6	4	144
%	13.9	31.3	22.2	14.6	0	0	1.8	4.2	2.8	2.8	4.2	2.8	100.0

Table C7 continued

Country	Military, political violence (1)	Foreign relations (2)	Domestic Politics (3)	Economics (4)	Science, Health (5)	Education (6)	Accidents, disasters (7)	Judicial, Crime (8)	Sports (9)	Art, culture (10)	Human interest (11)	Other (12)	Total
South Pacific													
words	1,295	751	0	679	0	0	0	0	5,038	0	646	0	8,409
%	15.4	8.9	0	8.1	0	0	0	0	59.9	0	7.7	0	100.0
stories	2	3	0	3	0	0	0	0	6	0	1	0	15
%	13.3	20.0	0	20.0	0	0	0	0	40.0	0	6.7	0	100.0
Total													
words	58,811	380,078	119,397	188,650	6,860	9,965	100,478	48,021	141,253	29,889	64,141	30,944	1,178,537
%	5.0	32.2	10.1	16.0	0.6	0.9	8.5	4.1	12.0	2.5	5.5	2.6	100.0
stories	132	606	231	7	18	10	107	95	245	41	78	74	2,004
%	6.6	30.2	11.5	17.8	0.9	1.0	5.3	4.7	12.2	2.1	3.9	3.7	100.0

TABLE C8

Approximate Number and Percentage of Words and Number and Percentage of Stories for 42 Third World Countries by Area of the World for Each of the Four International News Wires and Hsinhua for Five Days, December 5-9, 1977.

Wire Service	*Third*	*Both*	*Total*
Wire A			
words	53,792	50,307	104,099
%	51.7	48.3	100.0
stories	191	173	364
%	52.5	47.4	100.0
Wire B			
words	45,537	57,233	102,770
%	44.3	55.7	100.0
stories	157	196	353
%	44.5	55.5	100.0
Wire C			
words	91,056	72,198	163,254
%	55.8	44.2	100.0
stories	356	263	619
%	57.5	42.5	100.0
Wire D			
words	88,181	59,508	147,690
%	59.7	40.3	100.0
stories	388	258	646
%	60.1	39.9	100.0
Four Wires			
words	278,567	239,246	517,813
%	53.8	46.2	100.0
stories	1,092	890	1,982
%	55.1	49.9	100.0
Hsinhua			
words	19,230	14,190	33,420
%	57.5	42.5	100.0
stories	83	52	135
%	61.5	38.5	100.0
Total			
words	297,797	253,436	551,233
%	54.0	46.0	100.0
stories	1,175	942	2,117
%	55.5	44.5	100.0

TABLE C9

Approximate Number and Percentage of Words and Number and Percentage of Stories for 42 Third World Countries by Area of the World for Each of 17 Asian Daily Newspapers for Five Days, December 6-10, 1977.

Paper	*Third World*	*Both*	*Total*
Amrita Bazar Patrika			
words	7,038	7,222	14,260
%	49.4	50.6	100.0
stories	25	19	44
%	56.8	43.2	100.0
Bangkok Post			
words	28,594	13,940	42,534
%	67.2	32.8	100.0
stories	62	37	99
%	62.7	37.4	100.0
Ceylon Daily News			
words	15,268	12,320	27,588
%	55.3	44.7	100.0
stories	42	36	78
%	53.3	46.7	100.0
Dong-a Ilbo			
words	22,135	28,975	51,110
%	43.3	56.7	100.0
stories	35	29	64
%	54.7	45.3	100.0
Ettelaat			
words	41,312	73,632	144,944
%	34.9	64.1	100.0
stories	55	97	152
%	36.2	63.8	100.0
Kayhan International			
words	23,648	60,928	84,576
%	30.0	70.0	100.0
stories	64	111	175
%	36.6	63.4	100.0
Kompas			
words	14,688	4,726	19,414
%	75.7	24.3	100.0
stories	29	12	41
%	70.0	29.3	100.0

Table C9 continued

Paper	*Third World*	*Both*	*Total*
Korea Times			
words	17,400	8,480	25,880
%	67.2	32.8	100.0
stories	56	28	84
%	66.7	33.3	100.0
Nanyang Siang Pau			
words	164,639	62,891	227,530
%	72.4	27.6	100.0
stories	142	69	211
%	67.3	32.7	100.0
New Straits Times			
words	34,680	24,140	58,820
%	59.0	41.0	100.0
stories	93	49	142
%	65.6	34.5	100.0
Pilipino Express			
words	3,535	1,085	4,620
%	76.5	23.5	100.0
stories	12	3	15
%	80.0	20.0	100.0
Philippine Daily Express			
words	19,890	15,130	35,020
%	56.8	43.2	100.0
stories	55	27	82
%	67.1	32.9	100.0
Sing Chew Jit Poh			
words	149,625	26,163	175,788
%	85.1	14.9	100.0
stories	148	26	174
%	85.1	14.9	100.0
Sing Tao Jih Pao			
words	55,676	33,728	89,404
%	62.3	37.7	100.0
stories	77	42	119
%	64.7	35.3	100.0
South China Morning Post			
words	54,094	16,095	70,189
%	77.1	22.9	100.0
stories	149	40	189
%	78.8	21.2	100.0

Table C9 continued

Paper	*Third World*	*Both*	*Total*
Statesman			
words	7,350	7,850	15,200
%	48.4	51.6	100.0
stories	38	19	57
%	66.7	33.3	100.0
Straits Times			
words	93,835	27,825	121,660
%	77.1	22.9	100.0
stories	212	59	271
%	78.2	21.8	100.0
Total			
words	753,407	425,130	1,178,537
%	63.9	36.1	100.0
stories	1,294	710	2,004
%	64.4	35.4	100.0

TABLE C10

Approximate Number and Percentage of Words and Number and Percentage of Stories for 42 Third World Countries by World Zones for Each of the Four International News Wires and Hsinhua for Five Days, December 5-9, 1977.

News Wire	*Asia*	*Latin America*	*Middle East*	*Africa*	*Total*
Wire A					
words	43,952	11,152	35,301	13,694	104,009
%	42.2	10.7	33.9	13.2	100.0
stories	198	33	96	37	364
%	54.4	9.1	26.4	10.2	100.0
Wire B					
words	46,741	10,105	34,486	11,438	102,770
%	45.5	9.8	33.6	11.1	100.0
stories	193	35	91	34	353
%	54.7	9.9	25.8	9.6	100.0
Wire C					
words	96,558	9,870	38,818	22,008	167,254
%	57.7	5.9	23.2	13.2	100.0
stories	374	42	128	75	619
%	60.4	6.8	20.7	12.1	100.0
Wire D					
words	90,018	8,856	31,536	17,280	147,690
%	60.9	6.0	21.4	11.7	100.0
stories	387	30	150	79	646
%	59.9	4.6	23.2	12.2	100.0
Four Wires					
words	277,269	39,983	136,141	64,420	517,813
%	53.6	7.7	26.3	12.4	100.0
stories	1,152	140	465	225	1,982
%	58.1	7.1	23.5	11.3	100.0
Hsinhua					
words	17,730	3,060	3,120	9,510	33,420
%	53.1	9.2	9.3	28.4	100.0
stories	71	12	16	36	135
%	52.6	8.9	11.8	26.7	100.0
Total					
words	294,999	43,043	139,261	73,930	511,233
%	53.5	7.8	25.3	13.4	100.0
stories	1,223	152	481	261	2,117
%	57.8	7.2	22.7	12.3	100.0

TABLE C11

Approximate Number and Percentage of Words and Number and Percentage of Stories for 42 Third World Countries by World Zones for Each of 17 Asian Daily Newspapers for Five days, December 6-10, 1977.

Newspaper	*Asia*	*Latin America*	*Middle East*	*Africa*	*Total*
Amrita Bazar Patrika					
words	4,232	368	6,210	3,450	14,260
%	29.7	2.6	43.5	24.2	100.0
stories	17	2	13	12	44
%	38.6	4.5	29.5	27.3	100.0
Bangkok Post					
words	28,832	2,618	6,834	4,250	42,534
%	67.8	6.2	16.1	10.0	100.0
stories	67	7	17	8	99
%	67.7	7.1	17.2	8.1	100.0
Ceylon Daily News					
words	13,992	4,048	7,304	2,244	27,588
%	50.7	14.7	26.5	8.1	100.0
stories	47	2	21	8	78
%	60.3	2.6	26.9	10.2	100.0
Dong-a Ilbo					
words	20,235	1,330	20,235	9,310	51,110
%	39.6	2.6	39.6	18.2	100.0
stories	29	3	27	5	64
%	45.3	4.7	42.2	7.8	100.0
Ettelaat					
words	6,336	1,792	92,832	13,984	114,944
%	5.5	1.5	80.8	12.2	100.0
stories	22	4	109	17	152
%	14.5	2.6	71.7	11.2	100.0
Kayhan International					
words	10,208	1,312	60,736	12,320	84,576
%	12.1	1.6	71.8	14.5	100.0
stories	37	7	103	28	175
%	21.1	4.0	58.9	16.0	100.0
Kompas					
words	10,982	0	5,474	2,958	19,414
%	56.0	0	28.2	15.2	100.0
stories	25	0	13	3	41
%	61.0	0	31.7	7.3	100.0
Korea Times					
words	10,120	920	12,680	2,160	25,880
%	39.0	3.6	49.0	8.4	100.0
stories	38	5	32	9	84
%	45.2	6.0	38.0	10.7	100.0

Table C11 continued

Newspaper	Asia	Latin America	Middle East	Africa	Total
Nanyang Siang Pau					
words	170,739	3,904	44,286	8,610	227,530
%	75.0	1.7	19.5	3.8	100.0
stories	158	4	39	10	211
%	74.9	1.9	18.5	4.7	100.0
New Straits Times					
words	28,628	4,114	17,850	8,228	58,820
%	48.7	7.0	30.3	14.0	100.0
stories	90	8	34	10	142
%	63.4	5.6	23.9	7.0	100.0
Pilipino Express					
words	3,745	630	245	0	4,620
%	81.1	13.6	5.3	0	100.0
stories	13	1	1	0	15
%	86.7	6.7	6.7	0	100.0
Philippine Daily Express					
words	19,142	6,120	8,126	1,632	35,020
%	54.7	17.5	23.2	4.7	100.0
stories	51	7	18	6	82
%	62.2	8.5	22.0	7.3	100.0
Sing Chew Jit Poh					
words	136,003	3,306	34,713	1,767	175,788
%	77.4	1.9	19.7	1.0	100.0
stories	133	5	32	4	174
%	76.4	2.9	18.4	2.3	100.0
Sing Tao Jih Pao					
words	45,880	5,580	35,898	2,046	89,404
%	51.3	6.2	40.2	2.3	100.0
stories	69	8	37	5	119
%	58.0	6.7	31.1	4.2	100.0
South China Morning Post					
words	50,838	4,699	7,178	7,474	70,189
%	72.4	6.7	10.2	10.2	100.0
stories	147	10	18	14	189
%	77.8	5.3	9.5	7.4	100.0
Statesman					
words	5,400	350	4,700	4,750	15,200
%	35.5	2.3	30.9	31.3	100.0
stories	30	3	9	15	57
%	52.6	5.3	15.8	26.3	100.0

Table C11 continued

Newspaper	*Asia*	*Latin America*	*Middle East*	*Africa*	*Total*
Straits Times					
words	97,090	630	21,140	2,800	121,660
%	79.8	0.5	17.4	2.3	100.0
stories	213	4	42	12	271
%	78.6	1.5	15.5	4.4	100.0
Total					
words	662,401	41,721	386,441	87,974	1,178,537
%	56.2	3.5	32.8	7.5	100.0
stories	1,186	80	572	166	2,004
%	56.2	4.0	28.5	8.3	100.0

TABLE C12

Zero-order Correlations[a] (tau) Among Four International News Wires, Hsinhua, and 16 Asian Daily Newspapers[b] (for 42 Third World Countries) for Five Days

	News Wire					16 Asian Daily Newspapers															
	(1)	*(2)*	*(3)*	*(4)*	*(5)*	*(6)*	*(7)*	*(8)*	*(9)*	*(10)*	*(11)*	*(12)*	*(13)*	*(14)*	*(15)*	*(16)*	*(17)*	*(18)*	*(19)*	*(20)*	*(21)*
(1) Wire A	—	78	77	82	34	62	88	74	58	64	68	80	76	66	60	67	67	52	64	54	78
(2) Wire B		—	80	90	34	66	89	68	63	51	55	57	87	56	54	44	73	69	73	56	73
(3) Wire C			—	90	40	61	80	64	70	72	70	53	81	62	66	44	56	49	69	58	77
(4) Wire D				—	39	70	85	63	66	61	66	61	91	60	62	48	68	60	74	60	82
(5) Hsinhua					—	50	30	52	47	48	49	39	41	25	20	20	20	25	29	14	22
(6) Amrita Bazar Patrika						—	59	69	76	59	71	50	81	50	44	37	54	41	65	52	59
(7) Bangkok Post							—	68	67	54	57	66	81	76	71	61	81	61	74	58	83
(8) Ceylon Daily News								—	67	59	60	66	72	49	34	46	50	55	47	34	52
(9) Dong-a Ilbo									—	61	54	37	77	55	59	31	59	39	66	45	60
(10) Ettelaat										—	90	48	58	41	46	45	33	29	41	47	57
(11) Kayhan International											—	56	62	46	47	50	34	39	50	55	58
(12) Kompas												—	56	54	42	64	58	41	45	47	60
(13) Korea Times													—	57	55	42	72	64	77	59	76
(14) Nanyang Siang Pau														—	79	60	64	34	67	46	75
(15) New Straits Times															—	58	58	23	68	57	76
(16) Philippine Daily Express																—	49	16	36	37	57
(17) Sing Chew Jit Poh																	—	53	77	59	70
(18) Sing Tao Jih Pao																		—	48	41	44
(19) South China Morning Post																			—	67	76
(20) Statesman																				—	75
(21) Straits Times																					—

a. Correlations are computed across the 12 content categories. Decimals have been omitted. Underscored coefficients are not significant at the .05 level.
b. Pilipino Express omitted because only 15 stories were published during the five day test period.

APPENDIX D: The Readership Study

12. Number and Proportion of Men and Women in Each Reader Type.

13. Number and Proportion of Readers in Each Type by Occupational Group.

14. Number and Proportion of Readers in Each Type Reading 11 or More Stories.

15. Number and Proportion of Readers in Each Type by Educational Level.

TABLE D1

Recordered Factor Matrix for Oblique Rotation (Oblimax) for 100 News Stories: Dimensions of the News in the *Bulletin Today*, N = 476.

	Headline	*Factor* 1	2	3	4	5	6	h^2
23.	600 refugees trying to escape Cambodia	558	−018	−090	−016	−020	023	638
24.	Ethiopia criticizes China(and CIA)for arming insurgents	570	005	−052	−018	−082	043	620
22.	200 Rhodesian blacks arrested	598	043	−085	044	−040	−063	709
16.	Hanoi rejects China's offer of new plan	510	−023	−045	−111	053	074	604
17.	Somalian officers in coup will die	548	−029	−131	−081	088	−038	604
18.	Saudi Arabia about to decide on oil prices	490	010	−068	−078	129	−028	601
28.	Ambassador discusses Mideast talks	434	081	−066	022	−041	117	561
25.	Indian air force will be used to keep flood victims	525	−152	−030	047	−141	109	619
26.	Carter's anti-inflation programs	470	−060	−090	123	−114	109	637
21.	Boy forced to rape girl	414	027	−070	003	155	−110	505
20.	Opposition calls Iran's imposing martial law illegal	495	−018	−084	−043	175	−167	580
19.	Carter says no to direct talks with North Korea	420	005	−008	−062	−024	216	588
27.	Nixon to write new book	448	050	028	003	−170	237	607
40.	Nine arrested for fraud in coconut business	184	−048	026	052	120	047	302
47.	Civilians given bigger role in crime-busting	194	−103	031	115	060	121	420
35.	Green revolution has not lived up to promise	204	008	−074	062	089	184	456
31.	Who is #1- Borg or Conners?	150	083	119	020	088	144	375
79.	Insurance corporation cleared of fraud	−008	922	−009	025	004	003	945
78.	Saudi Arabians to Quebec	−019	917	−011	018	010	017	933

Table D1 continued

Headline		Factor 1	2	3	4	5	6	h^2
72.	Multilateral trade negotiations to resume	008	<u>904</u>	−001	005	−010	032	905
77.	New crab industry	−021	<u>936</u>	−009	038	−002	008	974
75.	US will begin mining nodules from sea bottom in 1983	−017	<u>912</u>	−015	042	−002	012	934
74.	ASEAN asked to set up pharmaceutical plant	−033	<u>930</u>	−011	030	005	022	962
76.	Egypt planning second Suez canal	−009	<u>893</u>	−013	087	−011	000	934
43.	How to tell whether a worker is 'moonlighting'	150	<u>213</u>	−057	−045	111	200	374
51.	Bowling association schedules tournament	−135	014	<u>774</u>	−051	−012	037	639
54.	Plans collapse for professional track-field meet	003	−063	<u>579</u>	112	−007	019	570
50.	Results of dirt slalom	−098	002	<u>788</u>	−142	043	070	675
53.	Investigating death of Swedish driver	−095	−078	<u>666</u>	035	−001	101	595
58.	Horse racing results	022	−091	<u>524</u>	046	−051	080	431
52.	Results in soccer tournament	−140	004	<u>830</u>	−109	−028	164	749
59.	Leading women players in Tokyo for tennis tournament	−025	−102	<u>495</u>	115	060	−095	414
48.	Jai-alai scores	−044	−084	<u>422</u>	035	101	−084	273
49.	Honda team wins motorbike race	−145	−055	<u>624</u>	178	057	−088	589
61.	Record time in 200 M run	176	140	<u>563</u>	−130	−104	−055	420
57.	Karpov-Korchnoi chess, play by play	061	−031	<u>200</u>	158	−021	−062	157
56.	Trainer thinks Ali will regain title	172	133	<u>308</u>	134	132	−306	466
84.	PESO fund liquid despite troubles	−037	−006	−060	<u>559</u>	021	−027	684
85.	Capital inflow for development vital for Philippines	−019	−079	−045	<u>646</u>	−019	−040	850
82.	US bank rate to rise more	−042	−037	−008	<u>514</u>	035	−065	586
87.	Licensing of foreign technology transferred to industry secretary	−095	009	−010	<u>656</u>	−076	−016	769
69.	Bankers say declining return on investments is causing trouble	058	−006	−087	<u>499</u>	−012	−016	625

Table D1 continued

Headline		Factor 1	2	3	4	5	6	h^2
83.	Finance company, once closed, now back on its feet	−033	119	−041	617	−028	−086	760
71.	SEC creates caretaker committee for brokerage corporations	075	039	−043	558	−037	−105	686
80.	World bank has lent $438 million to Philippines	−063	−027	−093	521	072	−016	623
86.	Will provide technical assistance to sugar planners	−032	−046	001	460	003	110	657
81.	Six minority stockholders of cigar company selling	−065	121	050	539	−051	−021	635
88.	UN meeting considers corporation among developing countries	034	−138	001	586	−106	028	759
70.	Securities and Exchange Commission studying US anomolies to prevent similar troubles here	−003	023	−052	519	063	−166	541
90.	Manila stock exchange	071	−102	066	501	−108	−077	515
89.	Korea will ease import curbs	042	−201	028	545	−111	068	741
68.	Urges local officials to be more 'people oriented'	111	−074	−082	244	127	074	494
37.	Sugar mill denies transfer of ownership	155	−129	000	233	022	090	438
93.	Romulo restates civil rights position	−089	−027	−026	−011	498	001	442
96.	President Marcos inspects university	−017	−014	018	−064	248	−038	086
2.	Lunar eclipse visible Sunday	−016	006	−053	055	490	−140	461
97.	Stay order to close two mining firms for pollution	−097	062	024	050	408	043	436
8.	Measure presented to widen access of media to government information	−051	−139	015	−038	457	021	403
3.	Ministry of Education will regionalize payment of teachers	−036	−048	011	−073	419	131	440
5.	US removes title of 'base commander' from Clark AFB	096	019	063	−129	429	028	504
1.	New weather disturbance forms	−035	−047	−086	105	489	−166	453

Table D1 continued

Headline		Factor 1	2	3	4	5	6	h^2
9.	New regulations on withholding tax	147	052	–019	–024	460	–138	577
4.	Marcos grants clemency to 432	079	017	071	–054	513	–203	535
14.	Flood control projects stopped	–113	–097	031	044	406	106	450
6.	Electricity reaches barrios	082	–027	–074	050	229	054	284
11.	Rebels control northern Nicaragua	183	040	038	–107	352	–000	475
94.	Anti-drug brigade formed for youths	–193	074	043	–030	431	176	450
99.	Premyo savings bond prizes	–035	–033	–072	–032	163	055	051
13.	Weather forecast	–051	015	–090	–218	363	–013	162
12.	Camp David talks enter decisive stage	215	006	019	–070	364	–119	457
10.	Not much news from Camp David meeting	064	035	–111	–091	399	–234	239
66.	Ilocano food prolongs life	–026	–011	–115	182	313	–083	319
63.	Attractive interiors need not cost a fortune	–184	039	–078	001	260	041	101
7.	President brief about cattle dispersal program	036	–104	–012	–115	362	–243	196
92.	One university to be established in every region	–153	118	142	–099	382	170	385
98.	Taclaban City needs fire alarm system	–159	–038	042	–087	377	258	399
34.	Bigornia on government rural service plan	095	137	028	015	223	096	408
64.	Churches and chapels in Pagodian city	009	–112	–064	132	220	058	287
100.	Forum on trademark and copyright	–094	–108	–084	174	258	154	413
91.	To discuss withholding tax law	–087	–016	–051	157	191	110	257
30.	Discussion of oil problem	120	–043	–056	077	190	151	455
15.	Korchnoi wins second chess game	146	067	289	–010	294	–247	467
45.	1,500 get medical aid from team in Cavite	–048	–086	070	030	–045	565	608

Table D1 continued

Headline		Factor 1	2	3	4	5	6	h^2
38.	National quizbee starts	099	135	041	−058	014	472	605
39.	Will hold national seminar on drugs	098	094	114	−107	−066	520	537
42.	Cultural program	204	−023	097	−053	−102	468	591
41.	Philippine trade house opens in Vienna	080	−105	122	090	023	320	528
36.	USSR to conduct earthquake research	060	189	101	−025	034	336	428
46.	UP schedules entrance tests	084	086	144	−018	011	265	309
44.	Teachers will be trained as health guardians	071	−135	031	153	−020	302	462
55.	Ali talks with Spinks	129	−071	051	−012	147	−289	128
62.	Local basketball	138	044	156	186	178	−395	349
95.	President of development bank of Phillipines speaks at Bulletin's correspondents' club	−198	105	031	−103	236	387	356
65.	Committee running utility department charged with incompetence	055	036	−015	214	068	229	490
33.	World will need 6,400 air lines	169	−043	055	149	024	190	516
29.	Ceremony for feast of our Lady of Penafrancia	255	147	061	−233	−116	312	249
32.	Batalla on middle east	137	−080	080	026	134	163	397
60.	Basketball: US and Philippine teams	200	124	104	−095	093	−207	142
67.	Change 'false' recruiter	−030	−150	−017	122	173	180	332
	Eigenvalues	28.57	7.69	4.74	4.43	3.16	2.70	

TABLE D2

Correlations Among the Six Dimensions of the News in the *Bulletin Today*.

News Dimension		*News Dimension*					
		1	*2*	*3*	*4*	*5*	*6*
1.	International violence	1.0	-01	-17	-21	-40	-18
2.	International economics		1.0	11	-16	-09	06
3.	Sports			1.0	-21	-10	12
4.	Finance/ investment				1.0	-23	-40
5.	Philippine general					1.0	-21
6.	Philippine development						1.0

Underscored coefficients are significant at the .05 level.

TABLE D3

Number and Proportion of Stories in Each News Dimension by Standard Content Category.

Dimension		*Military*	*Foreign Relations*	*Domestic*	*Economic*	*Science*	*Education*	*Accident*	*Judicial*	*Sports*	*Culture*	*Human Interest*	*Other*	*Total*
0. Not included[a]	n	0	4	0	6	2	2	1	1	9	1	0	3	29
	%	0.0	13.8	0.0	20.7	6.9	6.9	3.4	3.4	31.0	3.4	0.0	10.3	22.5
1. International violence	n	2	1	0	2	0	0	0	2	1	1	2	6	17
	%	11.8	5.9	0.0	11.8	0.0	0.0	0.0	11.8	5.9	5.9	11.8	35.2	13.2
2. International economics	n	0	0	0	8	0	0	0	1	0	0	0	0	9
	%	0.0	0.0	0.0	88.9	0.0	0.0	0.0	11.1	0.0	0.0	0.0	0.0	7.0
3. Sports	n	0	0	0	0	0	0	1	0	11	0	0	0	12
	%	0.0	0.0	0.0	0.0	0.0	0.0	8.3	0.0	91.7	0.0	0.0	0.0	9.3
4. Finance/ investment	n	0	0	0	16	0	0	0	0	0	0	0	0	16
	%	0.0	0.0	0.0	100.0	0.0	0.0	0.0	0.0	0.0	0.0	0.0	0.0	12.4
5. Philippine general	n	1	3	4	10	2	3	0	0	1	0	0	5	29
	%	3.4	10.3	13.8	34.5	6.9	10.3	0.0	0.0	3.4	0.0	0.0	17.2	22.5
6. Philippine miscellaneous	n	1	0	0	4	2	3	0	1	3	2	0	1	17
	%	5.9	0.0	0.0	23.5	11.8	17.6	0.0	5.9	17.6	11.8	0.0	5.9	13.2
Total	n	4	8	4	46	6	8	2	5	25	4	2	15	129
	%	3.1	6.2	3.1	35.7	4.7	6.2	1.6	3.9	19.4	3.1	1.6	11.6	100.0

a. The 29 stories in this group were each read by fewer than 10 readers and were not included in the factor analysis.

TABLE D4

Number and Proportion of Stories in Each News Dimension by Source of Story.

Dimension			*Wire A*	*Wire B*	*Wire C*	*Wire D*	*Regional Wire*	*Correspondent*	*Local Staff*	*Special Service*	*Total*
0.	Not included[a]	n	2	1	0	1	0	3	21	1	29
		%	6.9	3.4	0.0	3.4	0.0	10.3	72.4	3.4	22.5
1.	International violence	n	5	4	1	3	0	2	2	0	17
		%	29.4	23.5	5.9	17.6	0.0	11.8	11.8	0.0	13.2
2.	International economics	n	0	1	2	4	0	0	2	0	9
		%	0.0	11.0	22.2	44.4	0.0	0.0	22.2	0.0	7.0
3.	Sports	n	0	2	3	1	0	1	5	0	12
		%	0.0	16.7	25.0	8.3	0.0	8.3	41.7	0.0	9.3
4.	Finance/ investment	n	0	0	1	1	0	1	13	0	16
		%	0.0	0.0	6.3	6.3	0.0	6.3	81.3	0.0	12.4
5.	Philippine general	n	2	0	0	1	0	9	15	2	29
		%	6.9	0.0	0.0	3.4	0.0	31.0	51.7	6.9	22.5
6.	Philippine miscellaneous	n	0	1	2	0	1	5	8	0	17
		%	0.0	5.9	11.8	0.0	5.9	29.4	47.1	0.0	13.2
	Total	n	9	9	9	11	1	21	66	3	129
		%	7.0	7.0	7.0	8.5	0.8	16.3	51.2	2.3	100.0

a. The 29 stories in this group were each read by fewer than 10 readers and were not included in the factor analysis.

TABLE D5

Number and Proportion of Stories in Each News Dimension that are Development Stories

Dimension			*Development*		
			No	*Yes*	*Total*
0.	Not included[a]	n	22	7	29
		%	75.9	24.1	22.5
1.	International violence	n	15	2	17
		%	88.2	11.8	13.2
2.	International economics	n	5	4	9
		%	55.6	44.4	7.0
3.	Sports	n	12	0	12
		%	100.0	0.0	9.3
4.	Finance/ investment	n	6	10	16
		%	37.5	62.5	12.4
5.	Philippine general	n	20	9	29
		%	69.0	31.0	22.5
6.	Philippine miscellaneous	n	12	5	17
		%	70.6	29.4	13.2
	Total	n	92	37	129
		%	71.3	28.7	100.0

a. The 29 stories in the group were each read by fewer than 10 readers and were not included in the factor analysis.

TABLE D6

Number and Proportion of Stories in Each News Dimension by Levels of Foreign vs. Domestic Content

Dimension			*Non-Philippine*	*Both*	*Domestic*	*Total*
			Foreign/Domestic			
0.	Not included[a]	n	4	7	18	29
		%	13.8	24.1	62.1	22.5
1.	International violence	n	13	2	2	17
		%	76.5	11.8	11.8	13.2
2.	International economics	n	5	1	3	9
		%	55.6	11.1	33.3	7.0
3.	Sports	n	6	1	5	12
		%	50.0	8.3	41.7	9.3
4.	Finance/ investment	n	2	4	10	16
		%	12.5	25.0	62.5	12.4
5.	Philippine general	n	2	6	21	29
		%	6.9	20.7	72.4	22.5
6.	Philippine miscellaneous	n	4	2	11	17
		%	23.5	11.8	64.7	13.2
	Total	n	36	23	70	129
		%	27.9	17.8	54.3	100.0

a. The 29 stories in this group were read by fewer than 10 readers and were not included in the factor analysis

TABLE D7

Number and Proportion of Stories in Each News Dimension by Levels of Third World Classification

Dimension			*Third World Class*			
			Non-Third World	*Both*	*Third World*	*Total*
0.	Not included[a]	n	2	6	21	29
		%	6.9	20.7	72.4	22.5
1.	International violence	n	4	4	9	17
		%	23.5	23.5	52.9	13.2
2.	International economics	n	3	3	3	9
		%	33.3	33.3	33.3	7.0
3.	Sports	n	2	4	6	12
		%	16.7	33.3	50.0	9.3
4.	Finance/ investment	n	1	4	11	16
		%	6.3	25.0	68.8	12.4
5.	Philippine general	n	0	8	21	29
		%	0.0	27.6	72.4	22.5
6.	Philippine miscellaneous	n	2	3	12	17
		%	11.8	17.6	70.6	13.2
	Total	n	14	32	83	129
		%	10.9	24.8	64.3	100.0

a. The 29 stories in this group were read by fewer than 10 readers and were not included in the factor analysis.

TABLE D8

Number and Proportion of Stories in Each News Dimension by Region of the World.

Dimension			*Region*						
			Asia	*Latin America*	*Africa*	*Middle East*	*North America*	*Non-third*	*Total*
0.	Not included[a]	n	24	0	0	0	3	5	29
		%	82.8	0.0	0.0	0.0	10.3	17.2	22.5
1.	International violence	n	8	0	4	2	3	3	17
		%	47.1	0.0	23.5	11.8	17.6	17.6	13.2
2.	International economics	n	3	0	0	1	3	5	9
		%	33.3	0.0	0.0	11.1	33.3	55.6	7.0
3.	Sports	n	8	0	0	0	1	4	12
		%	66.7	0.0	0.0	0.0	8.3	33.3	9.3
4.	Finance/ investment	n	14	1	0	0	1	1	16
		%	87.5	6.3	0.0	0.0	6.3	6.3	12.4
5.	Philippine general	n	24	1	0	3	1	1	29
		%	82.8	3.4	0.0	10.3	3.4	3.4	22.5
6.	Philippine miscellaneous	n	12	1	0	1	1	3	17
		%	70.6	5.9	0.0	5.9	5.9	17.6	13.2
	Total	n	93	3	4	7	13	22	129
		%	72.1	2.3	3.1	5.4	10.1	17.1	100.0

a. The 29 stories in this group were each read by fewer than 10 readers and were not included in the factor analysis.

Number and Proportion of Readers in Each Type Reading Each Story and Typal Interest Score for Each Story.

Story		Reader Type						
		I	*II*	*III*	*IV*	*V*	*VI*	*Total*
		$(n = 48)$	$(n = 47)$	$(n = 78)$	$(n = 45)$	$(n = 156)$	$(n = 90)$	$(n = 464)$[a]
1. New weather disturbance forms	n	26	20	54	12	76	23	212
	%	54.2	42.6	69.2	26.7	48.7	25.6	44.5
	score[b]	1.2	0.6	7.7	2.3	6.7	-0.3	
2. Lunar eclipse visible Sunday	n	28	21	40	9	54	44	197
	%	58.3	44.7	51.3	20.0	34.6	48.9	41.4
	score	1.5	0.9	6.4	0.9	0.3	1.5	
3. Ministry of Education will regionalize payment of teachers	n	28	17	27	1	9	17	·99
	%	58.3	36.2	34.6	2.2	5.8	18.9	20.8
	score	1.5	0.1	0.3	-0.1	-0.2	-0.3	
4. Marcos grants clemency to 432	n	26	25	60	14	36	62	224
	%	54.2	53.2	76.9	31.1	23.1	68.9	47.1
	score	1.3	2.3	3.4	1.0	-0.2	7.6	
5. U.S. removes title of 'base commander' from Clark AFB	n	33	17	39	2	38	18	147
	%	68.8	36.2	50.0	4.4	24.4	20.0	30.9
	score	2.7	1.5	1.8	-0.3	0.2	-0.3	
6. Electricity reaches barrios	n	14	9	7	4	11	9	54
	%	29.2	19.1	9.0	8.9	7.1	10.0	11.3
	score	0.3	-0.1	-0.3	-0.3	-0.2	-0.3	
7. President brief about cattle dispersal program	n	3	33	4	4	39	2	85
	%	6.3	70.2	5.1	8.9	25.0	2.2	17.9
	score	-1.2	5.7	-0.3	-0.1	0.3	-0.3	

Table D9 continued

Story		Reader Type I	II	III	IV	V	VI	Total
8. Measure presented to widen access of media to government information	n	23	17	21	3	10	34	108
	%	47.9	36.2	26.9	6.7	6.4	37.8	22.7
	score	1.3	0.4	0.8	0.1	-0.2	1.5	
9. New regulations on with-holding tax payments	n	40	35	54	17	102	59	311
	%	83.3	74.5	69.2	37.8	65.4	65.6	65.3
	score	3.8	6.2	1.7	2.7	8.1	0.5	
10. Not much news from Camp David meeting	n	10	29	3	1	39	6	88
	%	20.8	61.7	3.8	2.2	25.0	6.7	18.5
	score	-0.4	5.4	-0.2	-0.3	0.3	-0.3	
11. Rebels control northern Nicaragua	n	30	19	9	9	33	33	133
	%	62.5	40.4	11.5	20.0	21.2	36.7	27.9
	score	1.9	1.5	-0.0	0.9	0.2	2.5	
12. Camp David talks enter decisive stage	n	24	16	23	4	9	33	110
	%	50.0	34.0	29.5	8.9	5.8	36.7	23.1
	score	1.2	0.5	0.6	0.3	-0.2	1.5	
13. Weather forecast	n	4	12	8	1	7	3	35
	%	8.3	25.5	10.3	2.2	4.5	3.3	7.4
	score	-0.9	1.1	0.0	-0.3	-0.2	-0.3	
14. Flood control projects stopped	n	24	10	22	3	9	25	93
	%	50.0	21.3	28.3	6.7	5.8	27.8	19.5
	score	1.7	0.6	0.4	-0.1	-0.2	1.1	
*15. Korchnoi wines second chess game	n	23	19	38	26	61	36	203
	%	47.9	40.4	48.6	57.8	39.1	40.0	42.9
	score	0.8	1.1	0.3	9.3	3.9	0.7	
16. Hanoi rejects China's offer of new plan	n	25	13	3	11	5	4	61
	%	52.1	27.7	3.8	24.4	3.2	4.4	12.8

Story		Reader Type						Total
		I	II	III	IV	V	VI	
17. Somalian officers in coup will die	n	25	16	4	8	4	4	61
	%	52.1	34.0	5.1	17.8	2.6	4.4	12.8
	score	1.5	0.0	-0.3	-0.0	-0.2	-0.3	
18. Saudi Arabia about to decide on oil prices	n	30	16	11	9	8	4	79
	%	62.5	34.0	14.1	20.0	5.1	4.4	16.6
	score	2.1	0.3	0.2	0.3	-0.2	-0.3	
19. Carter says no to direct talks with North Korea	n	24	5	4	8	0	2	43
	%	50.0	10.6	5.1	17.8	0.0	2.2	9.0
	score	1.4	-0.2	-0.3	0.1	-0.2	-0.3	
20. Opposition calls Iran's imposing of marital law illegal	n	29	19	7	14	8	29	106
	%	60.4	40.4	9.0	31.1	5.1	32.2	22.3
	score	1.1	0.4	-0.3	0.9	-0.2	0.2	
21. Boy forced to rape girl	n	25	8	6	10	13	29	91
	%	52.1	17.0	7.7	22.2	8.3	32.2	19.3
	score	1.0	-0.2	-0.2	0.4	-0.2	0.2	
22. 200 Rhodesian blacks arrested	n	24	10	4	6	2	3	49
	%	50.0	21.3	5.1	13.3	1.3	3.3	10.3
	score	1.1	-0.2	-0.2	-0.1	-0.2	-0.3	
23. 600 refugees trying to escape Cambodia	n	21	7	3	3	2	7	43
	%	43.8	14.8	3.8	6.7	1.3	7.8	9.0
	score	0.7	-0.3	-0.3	-0.3	-0.2	-0.3	
24. Protesting Iranians pray in Paris demonstration	n	1	4	0	0	2	3	10
	%	2.1	8.5	0.0	0.0	1.3	3.3	2.1
	score	-1.2	-0.2	-0.3	-0.3	-0.2	-0.3	
25. Ethiopia criticizes China (and CIA) for arming insurgents	n	22	10	1	5	1	2	42
	%	45.8	21.3	1.3	11.3	0.6	2.4	8.8
	score	0.8	0.1	-0.3	0.2	-0.2	-0.3	

Table D9 continued

Story		Reader Type I	II	III	IV	V	VI	Total
26. Indian air force will be used to keep flood victims	n	17	1	0	3	0	3	24
	%	35.4	2.1	0.0	6.7	0.0	3.3	5.0
	score	0.1	-0.3	-0.3	-0.3	-0.2	-0.3	
27. Carter's anti-inflation programs	n	24	4	3	3	1	6	41
	%	50.0	8.5	3.8	6.7	0.6	6.7	8.6
	score	1.0	-0.3	-0.3	-0.3	-0.2	-0.3	
28. Nixon to write new book	n	17	0	0	2	1	3	23
	%	35.4	0.0	0.0	4.4	0.6	3.3	4.8
	score	0.3	-0.3	-0.3	-0.3	-0.2	-0.3	
29. Ambassador discusses Mideast talks	n	23	3	2	3	3	8	42
	%	47.9	6.4	2.6	6.7	1.9	8.9	8.8
	score	1.0	-0.3	-0.3	-0.1	-0.2	-0.3	
30. Ceremony for Feast of Our Lady of Penafrancia	n	6	0	1	3	0	1	11
	%	12.5	0.0	1.3	6.7	0.0	1.0	2.3
	score	-0.2	-0.3	-0.3	0.5	-0.2	-0.3	
31. Discussion of oil problem	n	29	4	9	4	7	13	66
	%	60.4	8.5	11.5	8.9	4.5	14.4	13.9
	score	2.2	-0.3	-0.3	-0.1	-0.2	-0.3	
32. Who is #1-Borg or Conners?	n	17	2	8	2	3	3	35
	%	35.4	4.3	10.3	4.4	1.9	3.3	7.4
	score	0.1	-0.2	-0.3	-0.3	-0.2	-0.3	
33. Batalla on Middle East	n	29	4	10	6	6	8	63
	%	60.4	8.5	12.8	13.3	3.8	8.9	13.2
	score	1.9	-0.2	-0.3	-0.1	-0.2	-0.3	
34. World will need 6,400 air lines	n	21	1	3	2	0	1	29
	%	43.8	2.1	3.8	4.4	0.0	1.0	6.1

Story		Reader Type						Total
		I	II	III	IV	V	VI	
35. Bigornia on government rural service plan	n	25	3	19	4	7	7	66
	%	52.1	6.4	24.4	8.9	4.5	7.8	13.9
	score	1.9	-0.3	0.1	-0.3	-0.2	-0.3	
36. Green revolution has not lived up to promise	n	23	10	2	6	2	4	48
	%	47.9	21.2	2.6	13.3	1.3	4.4	10.2
	score	1.4	0.1	-0.3	0.4	-0.2	-0.3	
37. USSR to conduct earthquake research	n	13	3	3	1	1	2	23
	%	27.1	6.4	3.8	2.2	0.6	2.2	4.8
	score	0.7	-0.3	-0.3	-0.3	-0.2	-0.3	
38. Australian Ambassador traveling in northern Philippines	n	8	1	1	0	1	0	11
	%	16.7	2.1	1.3	0.0	0.6	0.0	2.3
	score	-0.1	-0.3	-0.3	-0.3	-0.2	-0.3	
39. Medical symposium at Quezon City	n	8	0	1	0	0	0	9
	%	16.7	0.0	1.3	0.0	0.0	0.0	1.9
	score	-0.1	-0.3	-0.3	-0.3	-0.2	-0.3	
40. Club starts plan for scholarships	n	2	0	0	1	0	0	3
	%	4.2	0.0	0.0	2.2	0.0	0.0	0.6
	score	-1.2	-0.3	-0.3	-0.3	-0.2	-0.3	
41. Sugar mill denies transfer of ownership	n	13	1	2	2	0	2	20
	%	27.1	2.2	2.2	4.4	0.0	2.2	4.2
	score	-0.2	-0.3	-0.3	-0.3	-0.2	-0.3	
42. National quizbee starts	n	19	1	2	1	2	1	26
	%	39.6	2,1	2.6	2.2	1.1	1.1	5.5
	score	1.1	-0.3	-0.3	-0.3	-0.2	-0.3	
43. Will hold national seminar on drugs	n	13	0	0	0	0	0	13
	%	27.1	0.0	0.0	0.0	0.0	0.0	2.7
	score	0.2	-0.3	-0.3	-0.3	-0.2	-0.3	

Table D9 continued

Story		I	II	III	IV	V	VI	Total
		Reader Type						
44. 9 arested for fraud in coconut business	n	14	4	8	6	5	9	48
	%	29.9	8.5	10.3	13.3	3.2	10.0	10.1
	score	-0.1	-0.3	-0.3	0.4	-0.2	-0.3	
45. 1,500 new graduates of first aid courses	n	2	0	0	1	1	0	4
	%	4.2	0.0	0.0	2.2	0.6	0.0	0.8
	score	-0.9	-0.3	-0.3	-0.3	-0.2	-0.3	
46. Philippine trade house opens in Vienna	n	16	2	3	1	0	2	24
	%	38.3	4.3	3.8	2.2	0.0	2.2	5.0
	score	0.9	-0.3	-0.3	-0.1	-0.2	-0.3	
47. Cultural program	n	13	0	0	1	0	1	15
	%	27.1	0.0	0.0	2.2	0.0	1.0	3.2
	score	0.3	-0.3	-0.3	-0.3	-0.2	-0.3	
48. Manila to hold Red Cross convention	n	8	0	1	0	0	0	9
	%	16.7	0.0	1.3	0.0	0.0	0.0	1.9
	score	-0.9	-0.3	-0.3	-0.3	-0.2	-0.3	
49. How to tell whether a worker is 'moonlighting'	n	16	3	5	1	4	4	33
	%	33.3	6.4	6.4	2.2	2.6	4.4	6.9
	score	0.9	-0.3	-0.3	-0.3	-0.2	-0.3	
50. Association of Philippine-China understanding will hold Seminar	n	5	0	0	0	0	0	5
	%	10.4	0.0	0.0	0.0	0.0	0.0	1.1
	score	-0.9	-0.3	-0.3	-0.3	-0.2	-0.3	
51. Teachers will be trained as health guardians	n	10	1	0	0	1	1	13
	%	20.8	2.1	0.0	0.0	0.6	1.1	2.7
	score	-0.1	-0.3	-0.3	-0.3	-0.2	-0.3	
52. 1,500 get medical aid from team in Cavite	n	11	0	0	0	0	0	11
	%	22.9	0.0	0.0	0.0	0.0	0.0	2.3
	score	0.6	-0.3	-0.3	-0.3	-0.2	-0.3	

Table D9 continued

Story		Reader Type I	II	III	IV	V	VI	Total
53. Lanao resettlement plan	n	2	1	0	0	0	0	3
	%	4.2	2.1	0.0	0.0	0.0	0.0	0.6
	score	-0.9	-0.3	-0.3	-0.3	-0.2	-0.3	
54. UP schedules entrance tests	n	13	1	2	2	3	1	22
	%	27.1	2.1	2.6	4.4	1.9	1.1	4.6
	score	0.5	-0.3	-0.3	-0.1	-0.2	-0.3	
55. Civilians given bigger role in crime-busting	n	22	4	5	1	2	3	38
	%	45.8	8.5	6.4	2.2	1.3	3.3	8.0
	score	0.8	-0.3	-0.3	-0.3	-0.2	-0.3	
56. Fernandez on Asian games	n	10	1	5	3	3	0	25
	%	20.8	2.1	6.4	6.7	1.9	0.0	5.3
	score	-0.5	0.3	-0.2	-0.3	-0.2	-0.3	
57. Rematch of world cup bowlers	n	11	2	7	13	7	5	47
	%	22.9	4.3	9.0	28.9	4.5	5.6	9.9
	score	-0.5	-0.3	-0.2	1.1	-0.2	-0.3	
58. Jai-alai scores	n	5	3	6	12	11	5	44
	%	10.4	6.4	7.7	26.7	7.1	5.6	9.2
	score	-1.2	0.3	-0.3	0.6	-0.2	-0.3	
59. Marcos awards trophy to winning team	n	1	0	0	0	2	0	3
	%	2.1	0.0	0.0	0.0	1.3	0.0	0.6
	score	-1.2	-0.3	-0.3	-0.3	-0.2	-0.3	
60. Honda team wins motorbike races	n	8	2	4	9	3	1	27
	%	16.7	4.3	5.1	20.0	1.9	1.1	5.7
	score	-0.9	0.4	-0.2	0.3	-0.2	-0.3	
61. Results of dirt slalom	n	3	1	2	3	1	0	10
	%	6.3	2.1	2.6	6.7	0.6	0.0	2.1
	score	-1.1	-0.3	-0.3	-0.2	-0.2	-0.3	

Table D9 continued

Story		Reader Type						Total
		I	*II*	*III*	*IV*	*V*	*VI*	
62. Bowling association schedules tournament	n	2	0	3	1	0	0	6
	%	4.2	0.0	3.8	2.2	0.0	0.0	1.3
	score	-1.1	-0.3	-0.3	-0.3	-0.2	-0.3	
63. Results of soccer tournament	n	3	0	2	2	0	0	7
	%	6.3	0.0	2.6	4.4	0.0	0.0	1.5
	score	-1.1	-0.3	-0.3	-0.3	-0.2	-0.3	
64. Investigating death of Swedish driver	n	6	1	2	3	1	1	14
	%	12.5	2.1	2.6	6.7	0.1	1.1	2.9
	score	-1.1	-0.3	-0.3	-0.3	-0.2	-0.3	
65. American baseball	n	3	0	2	1	0	0	6
	%	6.3	0.0	2.6	2.2	0.0	0.0	1.3
	score	-1.1	-0.3	-0.3	-0.3	-0.2	-0.3	
66. Club chess results	n	3	1	3	1	1	0	9
	%	63.	2.1	3.8	2.2	0.6	0.0	1.9
	score	-1.2	-0.2	-0.3	-0.3	-0.2	-0.3	
67. Club tennis championship	n	1	0	2	1	2	0	6
	%	2.1	0.0	2.6	2.2	1.3	0.0	1.3
	score	-1.2	-0.3	-0.3	-0.3	-0.2	0.0	
68. Plans collapse for professional track-field meet	n	8	0	4	4	3	1	20
	%	16.7	0.0	5.1	8.9	1.9	1.1	4.2
	score	-1.2	-0.3	-0.3	-0.1	-0.2	-0.3	
69. Hungarian leads in chess tournament	n	2	1	1	1	1	0	6
	%	4.2	2.1	1.3	2.2	0.6	0.0	1.3
	score	-1.2	-0.2	-0.3	-0.3	-0.2	-0.3	
70. Ali talks with Spinks	n	1	3	2	11	10	3	31
	%	2.1	6.4	2.6	24.4	6.4	3.3	6.5
	score	-1.2	-0.3	-0.3	1.1	-0.2	-0.3	

Table D9 continued

Story		Reader Type						
		I	II	III	IV	V	VI	Total
71. Trainer thinks Ali will regain title	n	19	13	29	19	9	13	103
	%	39.6	27.7	37.2	42.2	5.8	14.4	21.6
	score	0.2	0.0	0.6	0.9	-0.2	-0.2	
72. Karpov-Korchnoi chess play-by-play	n	4	0	3	2	2	1	12
	%	8.0	0.0	3.8	4.4	1.3	1.1	2.5
	score	-1.2	-0.3	-0.3	-0.3	-0.2	-0.3	
73. Horse racing results	n	7	0	2	6	2	1	18
	%	14.6	0.0	2.6	13.3	1.3	1.1	3.5
	score	-1.1	-0.3	-0.2	0.1	-0.2	-0.3	
74. Leading women players in Tokyo for tennis tournament	n	5	2	4	4	3	2	20
	%	10.4	4.3	5.1	8.9	1.9	2.2	4.2
	score	-1.1	-0.3	-0.2	-0.3	-0.2	-0.3	
75. Basketball-US and Philippine teams	n	2	3	2	8	6	3	25
	%	4.2	6.4	2.6	17.8	3.8	3.3	5.3
	score	-0.9	-0.3	-0.3	0.8	-0.2	-0.3	
76. Record time in 200 M. run	n	3	0	4	7	4	0	18
	%	6.3	0.0	5.1	15.6	2.6	0.0	3.8
	score	-1.0	-0.3	-0.3	0.8	-0.2	-0.3	
77. Games today	n	1	0	1	2	2	0	6
	%	2.1	0.0	1.3	4.4	1.3	0.0	1.3
	score	-1.2	-0.3	-0.3	-0.3	-0.2	-0.3	
78. Local basketball	n	20	20	29	28	54	28	181
	%	41.7	42.6	37.2	62.2	34.6	31.1	38.0
	score	0.9	1.8	1.0	3.3	0.5	5.6	
79. Basketball scores	n	1	1	1	1	5	0	9
	%	2.1	2.1	1.3	2.2	3.2	0.0	1.9
	score	-1.2	-0.2	-0.3	-0.3	-0.2	-0.3	

Table D9 continued

Story		I	II	III	IV	V	VI	Total
		Reader Type						
80. Women's organization will conduct toy contest	n	4	0	0	0	2	0	6
	%	8.3	0.0	0.0	0.0	1.3	0.0	1.3
	score	-0.7	-0.3	-0.3	-0.3	-0.2	-0.3	
81. Attractive interiors need not cost a fortune	n	7	1	3	0	8	12	34
	%	14.6	2.1	3.8	0.0	5.1	13.3	7.1
	score	-0.2	-0.3	-0.3	-0.3	-0.2	-0.3	
82. Churches and chapels in Pagodian City	n	9	3	4	0	1	9	27
	%	18.8	6.4	5.1	0.0	0.6	10.0	5.7
	score	-0.2	-0.3	-0.3	-0.3	-0.2	-0.3	
83. Committee running utility charged with incompetence	n	12	0	3	0	1	3	19
	%	25.0	0.0	3.8	0.0	0.6	3.3	4.0
	score	0.3	-0.3	-0.3	-0.3	-0.2	-0.3	
84. US Ambassador guest speaker at Lions	n	1	1	1	0	1	1	5
	%	2.1	2.1	1.3	0.0	0.6	1.1	1.1
	score	-0.9	-0.3	-0.3	-0.3	-0.2	-0.3	
85. Ilocano food prolongs life	n	13	7	4	2	4	20	50
	%	27.1	14.9	5.1	4.4	2.6	22.2	10.5
	score	0.1	-0.3	-0.0	-0.1	-0.2	1.0	
86. Name new police chief	n	4	0	0	0	0	0	4
	%	8.3	0.0	0.0	0.0	0.0	0.0	0.8
	score	-0.7	-0.3	-0.3	-0.3	-0.2	-0.3	
87. Change 'false' recruiter	n	10	2	2	0	3	3	20
	%	20.8	4.3	2.6	0.0	1.9	3.3	4.2
	score	0.0	-0.3	-0.3	-0.3	-0.2	-0.3	
88. Urges local officials to be more 'people oriented'	n	14	3	3	0	2	0	22
	%	29.2	6.4	3.8	0.0	1.3	0.0	4.6
	score	0.3	-0.3	-0.3	-0.3	-0.2	-0.3	

Table D9 continued

Story		*Reader Type*						
		I	*II*	*III*	*IV*	*V*	*VI*	*Total*
89. Bankers say declining return on investments is causing trouble	n	22	1	5	0	2	2	32
	%	45.8	2.1	6.4	0.0	1.3	2.2	6.7
	score	0.7	-0.3	-0.1	-0.3	-0.2	-0.3	
90. Technical assistance for sugar planters	n	1	0	1	0	0	0	2
	%	2.1	0.0	1.3	0.0	0.0	0.0	0.4
	score	-1.1	-0.3	-0.3	-0.3	-0.2	-0.3	
91. Securities and exchange commission studying US anomalies to prevent similar troubles here	n	14	1	8	2	3	3	31
	%	29.2	2.1	10.3	4.4	1.9	3.3	6.5
	score	0.2	-0.3	0.1	-0.3	-0.2	-0.3	
92. SEC creates caretaker committee for brokerage corporation	n	14	1	6	0	1	2	24
	%	29.2	2.1	7.7	0.0	0.6	2.2	5.0
	score	-0.1	-0.3	-0.1	-0.3	-0.2	-0.3	
93. Prices on copra and nuts	n	0	0	0	0	0	2	2
	%	0.0	0.0	0.0	0.0	0.0	2.2	0.4
	score	-1.2	-0.3	-0.3	-0.3	-0.2	-0.3	
94. Multilateral trade negotiations to resume	n	6	0	4	0	1	3	16
	%	12.5	0.0	5.1	0.0	0.6	3.3	3.4
	score	-0.5	-0.3	0.0	-0.3	-0.2	-0.3	
95. English chemist suggests sugar and cassave as alternatives to oil	n	6	0	6	0	1	3	18
	%	12.5	0.0	7.7	0.0	0.6	3.3	3.8
	score	-0.5	-0.3	0.2	-0.3	-0.2	-0.3	
96. ASEAN asked to set up pharmaceutical plant	n	6	0	6	0	1	4	19
	%	12.5	0.0	7.7	7.7	0.6	4.4	4.0
	score	-0.5	-0.3	0.2	-0.3	-0.2	-0.3	
97. US will begin mining nodules from sea bottom in 1983	n	6	0	5	0	1	3	17
	%	12.5	0.0	6.4	0.0	0.6	3.3	3.6
	score	-0.5	-0.3	0.2	-0.3	-0.2	-0.3	

Table D9 continued

Story		Reader Type						Total
		I	*II*	*III*	*IV*	*V*	*VI*	
98. Egypt planning 2nd Suez Canal	n	7	0	5	0	1	4	19
	%	14.6	0.0	6.4	0.0	0.6	4.4	4.0
	score	-0.5	-0.3	0.2	-0.3	-0.2	-0.3	
99. New crab industry	n	6	0	5	0	1	4	18
	%	12.5	0.0	6.4	0.0	0.6	4.4	3.8
	score	-0.5	-0.3	0.2	-0.3	-0.2	-0.3	
100. Saudi Arabians to Quebec	n	6	0	6	0	1	5	20
	%	12.5	0.0	7.7	0.0	0.6	5.6	4.2
	score	-0.5	-0.3	0.2	-0.3	-0.2	-0.3	
101. Insurance corporation cleared of fraud	n	6	0	5	0	1	5	19
	%	12.5	0.0	6.4	0.0	0.6	5.5	4.0
	score	-0.5	-0.3	0.2	-0.3	-0.2	-0.3	
102. World bank has lent $438 million to Philippines	n	20	0	4	2	4	3	35
	%	41.7	0.0	5.1	4.4	2.6	3.3	7.4
	score	0.4	-0.3	-0.1	-0.1	-0.2	-0.3	
103. 6 minority stockholders of cigar company selling	n	9	0	5	0	2	2	18
	%	18.8	0.0	6.4	0.0	1.3	2.2	3.8
	score	-0.2	-0.3	-0.1	-0.3	-0.2	-0.3	
104. US bank rates to rise more	n	12	0	3	0	1	4	21
	%	25.0	0.0	3.8	0.0	0.6	4.4	4.4
	score	0.2	-0.3	-0.3	-0.3	-0.2	-0.3	
105. Finance company, once closed, now back on its feet	n	14	1	3	0	1	5	25
	%	29.2	2.1	3.8	0.0	0.6	5.6	5.3
	score	-0.1	-0.3	-0.1	-0.3	-0.2	-0.3	
106. Peso fund liquid despite troubles	n	17	0	4	1	3	4	29
	%	35.4	0.0	5.1	2.2	1.9	4.4	6.1
	score	0.6	-0.3	-0.1	-0.3	-0.2	-0.3	

Table D9 continued

Story		Reader Type I	II	III	IV	V	VI	Total
107. Capital inflow for development vital for Philippines	n	15	0	1	0	1	2	19
	%	31.5	0.0	1.3	0.0	0.6	2.2	4.0
	score	0.0	-0.3	-0.3	-0.3	-0.2	-0.3	
108. Will provide technical assistance to sugar planners	n	10	0	0	0	0	2	12
	%	20.8	0.0	0.0	0.0	0.0	2.2	2.5
	score	-0.4	-0.3	-0.3	-0.3	-0.2	-0.3	
109. Manufacturing dominates country's corporations	n	4	0	0	1	1	0	6
	%	8.3	0.0	0.0	2.2	0.6	0.0	1.3
	score	-0.1	-0.3	-0.3	-0.3	-0.2	-0.3	
110. Licensing of foreign technology transferred to industry secretary	n	13	0	3	0	1	2	19
	%	27.1	0.0	3.8	0.0	0.6	2.2	4.0
	score	0.0	-0.3	-0.1	-0.3	-0.2	-0.3	
111. UN meeting considers corporation among developing countries	n	10	0	0	0	1	1	12
	%	20.8	0.0	0.0	0.0	0.6	1.1	2.5
	score	-0.6	-0.3	-0.3	-0.3	-0.2	-0.3	
112. Korea will ease import curbs	n	10	0	0	0	0	1	11
	%	20.8	0.0	0.0	0.0	0.0	1.1	2.3
	score	-0.6	-0.3	-0.3	-0.3	-0.2	-0.3	
113. Manila stock exchange	n	10	0	3	1	2	1	17
	%	20.8	0.0	3.8	2.2	1.3	1.1	3.6
	score	-0.1	-0.3	-0.2	-0.3	-0.2	-0.3	
114. To discuss withholding tax law	n	6	1	2	1	2	2	14
	%	12.5	2.1	2.5	2.2	1.3	2.2	2.9
	score	0.2	-0.3	-0.3	-0.1	-0.2	-0.3	
115. QE 2 overcomes violent storms	n	1	0	0	0	1	0	2
	%	2.1	0.0	0.0	0.0	0.6	0.0	0.4
	score	-0.7	-0.3	-0.3	-0.2	-0.2	-0.3	

Table D9 continued

Story		Reader Type I	II	III	IV	V	VI	Total
116. Korean Air Lines computerizing operation in Philippines	n	1	0	0	0	0	0	1
	%	2.1	0.0	0.0	0.0	0.0	0.0	0.2
	score	-0.8	-0.3	-0.3	-0.3	-0.2	-0.3	
117. Philippines Air Lines will resume turbo prop flights	n	2	0	0	0	0	0	2
	%	4.2	0.0	0.0	0.0	0.0	0.0	0.4
	score	-0.8	-0.3	-0.3	-0.3	-0.2	-0.3	
118. One university to be established in every region	n	17	2	7	0	5	12	44
	%	35.4	4.3	9.0	0.0	3.2	13.3	9.2
	score	0.5	-0.2	0.0	-0.3	-0.2	-0.3	
119. Romulo restates civil rights position	n	20	4	19	4	7	21	76
	%	41.7	8.5	24.4	8.9	4.5	23.3	16.0
	score	0.4	-0.3	-0.3	0.1	-0.2	2.7	
120. Philippine Ambassador to Canada presents credentials	n	1	0	0	0	0	0	1
	%	2.1	0.0	0.0	0.0	0.0	0.0	0.2
	score	-0.9	-0.3	-0.3	-0.3	-0.2	-0.3	
121. Anti-drug brigade formed for youth	n	15	0	6	0	4	11	36
	%	31.3	0.0	7.7	0.0	2.6	12.2	7.6
	score	0.5	-0.3	-0.3	-0.3	-0.2	-0.3	
122. President of development bank speaks at Bulletin's correspondent's club	n	7	0	1	1	0	3	12
	%	14.6	0.0	1.3	2.2	0.0	3.3	2.5
	score	-0.3	-0.3	-0.3	-0.3	-0.2	-0.3	
123. No holiday on Sept. 23	n	1	0	0	0	1	3	5
	%	2.1	0.0	0.0	0.0	0.6	3.3	1.1
	score	-0.9	-0.3	-0.3	-0.3	-0.2	-0.3	
124. President Marcos inspects university	n	2	7	1	0	1	1	12
	%	4.2	14.9	1.3	0.0	0.6	1.1	2.5
	score	-0.9	0.6	-0.3	-0.3	-0.2	-0.3	

Table D9 continued

Story		Reader Type I	II	III	IV	V	VI	Total
125. Stay order to close two mining firms for pollution	n	19	2	9	1	7	13	51
	%	39.6	4.3	11.5	2.2	4.5	14.4	10.7
	score	0.4	-0.3	-0.2	-0.3	-0.2	-0.3	
126. Taclaban City needs fire alarm system	n	14	1	5	2	2	6	31
	%	29.2	2.1	6.4	4.4	1.3	6.7	6.5
	score	0.1	-0.3	-0.3	-0.3	-0.2	-0.3	
127. Premyo savings bond prices	n	4	1	3	0	5	2	16
	%	8.3	2.1	3.8	0.0	3.2	2.2	3.4
	score	-0.5	-0.3	0.0	-0.3	-0.2	-0.3	
128. Forum on trademark and copyright	n	10	0	1	1	0	4	17
	%	20.8	0.0	1.3	2.2	0.0	4.4	3.6
	score	-0.5	-0.3	-0.3	-0.3	-0.2	-0.3	
129. Registering pilgrims for Mecca	n	0	0	0	1	0	0	1
	%	0.0	0.0	0.0	2.2	0.0	0.0	0.2
	score	-1.2	-0.3	-0.3	-0.3	-0.2	-0.3	

a. 12 of the 476 respondents did not fit in any reader type and read very little. These 12 did not share among them any observable readership pattern.

b. The score is an index of the extent to which each reader type was interested in the story. High positive scores indicate strong preference, high negative scores indicate strong dislike. Stories with scores between + 0.9 and -0.9 are ones to which the reader is indifferent.

TABLE D10

Number and Proportion of Readers in Each Type by Age Group.

Type		*21—30*	*31—40*	*41—50*	*51 up*	*Total*
I	n	7	12	13	16	48
	%	14.6	25.0	27.1	33.3	10.0
II	n	17	11	13	6	47
	%	36.2	23.4	27.7	12.8	10.1
III	n	27	23	15	13	78
	%	34.6	29.5	19.2	16.7	16.8
IV	n	24	9	8	4	45
	%	53.3	20.0	17.8	8.9	9.7
V	n	72	37	16	31	156
	%	46.2	23.7	10.3	19.9	33.6
VI	n	30	20	15	25	90
	%	33.3	22.2	16.7	27.8	19.4
Total	n	177	112	80	90	464
	%	38.1	24.1	17.3	20.5	100.0

chi square = 35.61, p<.01

TABLE D11

Number and Proportion of Rural and Urban Residents in Each Reader Type

Type		*Urban*	*Rural*	*Total*
I	n	37	11	48
	%	77.1	22.9	10.3
II	n	24	23	47
	%	51.1	48.9	10.1
III	n	43	35	78
	%	55.1	44.9	16.8
IV	n	31	14	45
	%	68.9	31.1	9.7
V	n	91	65	156
	%	58.3	41.7	33.6
VI	n	55	35	90
	%	61.1	38.9	.19.4
Total	n	289	187	464
	%	62.3	37.8	100.0

chi square = 9.93, n. s.

TABLE D12

Number and Proportion of Men and Women in Each Reader Type.

Type		*Men*	*Women*	*Total*
I	n	26	22	48
	%	54.2	45.8	10.4
II	n	22	25	47
	%	46.8	53.2	10.1
III	n	45	33	78
	%	57.7	42.3	16.8
IV	n	35	10	45
	%	77.8	22.2	9.7
V	n	80	75	155
	%	51.6	48.4	33.5
VI	n	38	52	90
	%	42.2	57.8	19.4
Total	n	246	217	463
	%	53.1	46.9	100.0

chi square = 16.1, $p < .01$

TABLE D13

Number and Proportion of Readers in Each Type by Occupational Group.

Type		*Unskilled*	*Skilled*	*White Collar*	*Total*
I	n	1	12	35	48
	%	2.1	25.0	72.9	10.3
II	n	4	15	28	47
	%	8.5	31.9	59.6	10.1
III	n	8	23	47	78
	%	10.3	29.5	60.3	16.8
IV	n	6	17	22	45
	%	13.3	37.8	48.9	9.7
V	n	19	47	90	156
	%	12.2	30.1	57.7	33.6
VI	n	9	26	55	90
	%	10.0	28.9	61.1	19.4
Total	n	48	145	283	464
	%	10.3	29.7	61.0	100.0

chi square = 8.47, n. s.

TABLE D14

Number and Proportion of Readers in Each Type Reading 11 or More Stories

Type		*10 or Less*	*11 or More*	*Total*
I	n	12	36	48
	%	25.0	75.0	10.3
II	n	28	19	47
	%	59.6	40.4	10.1
III	n	47	31	78
	%	60.3	39.7	16.8
IV	n	30	15	45
	%	66.7	33.3	9.7
V	n	139	17	156
	%	89.1	11.9	33.6
VI	n	63	27	90
	%	70.0	30.0	19.4
Total	n	319	145	464
	%	68.8	31.2	100.0

chi square = 77.46, $p<.001$

TABLE D15

Number and Proportion of Readers in Each Type by Educational Level

Type		*Less Than Secondary*	*Secondary*	*College*	*Total*
I	n	0	7	41	48
	%	0.0	14.6	85.4	10.3
II	n	2	12	33	47
	%	4.3	25.5	70.2	10.1
III	n	4	19	55	78
	%	5.1	24.4	70.5	16.8
IV	n	4	18	23	45
	%	8.9	40.0	51.1	9.7
V	n	8	53	95	156
	%	5.1	34.0	60.9	33.6
VI	n	2	29	59	90
	%	2.2	32.9	65.6	19.4
Total	n	20	138	306	464
	%	4.3	29.7	65.9	100.0

chi square = 18.24, $P<.05$

APPENDIX E: Notes on Method

THE CONTENT CODES

Third World

For simplicity's sake we coded the Third World as including:

1. All Asian states except Japan and the Asian part of the USSR.
2. All Pacific states except Australia and New Zealand.
3. All Latin American states except Argentina.
4. All African states except South Africa.
5. All Middle East states except Israel.
6. *No* European states – either East or West Europe – except Albania.
7. *No* states of North America.

Multiple Coding

We did not permit multiple coding. The number of units coded under any heading is therefore always equal to the number of stories coded. In order to avoid some of the potential problems of a decision against multiple coding we adopted conventions like these:

1. A category for "Both." Examples:

    3. Third World news only.
    2. News involving *both* Third World and other countries.
    1. News that does not refer to Third World countries.

    (e.g., the cricket match between India and Australia would be coded 2 because it involves both a Third World and a non-Third World country.)

    1. News of the home country only.
    2. News involving *both* the home country and another country or countries.
    3. News of other countries only.

    (e.g., news in a Philippine paper of a trade treaty between the Philippines and Malaysia would be coded 2 because it involves both the home country and another country.)

2. Coding of country references.

We recorded all countries referred to in a news story, but wherever possible specified the (foreign) country treated most importantly, and, if there were enough references, the *three* countries most important in the story. These were given special treatment. Here, as elsewhere, we asked coders to set down notes on any circumstances about multiple references to countries that we should be aware of in analyzing results.

3. Forced choice.

In situations where a news story obviously falls into more than one category of content, we asked the coder to code the category that seemed most appropriate. For example, a story about an individual being arrested after an accident and brought to trial on a charge of drunken driving, might be coded either as an accident or a crime-judicial story according to where it comes in the sequence of events, and whether the accident or the judicial proceedings are emphasized. The coders recorded every such questionable incidence in the notes.

4. Coding by more than one person.

Most of the cases of doubtful choice disappeared when a second person coded the same content, and the two coders could talk over the choice, and, if necessary, carry the problem to an arbitrator.

Content Categories

We coded 15 categories of news content, as follows:

1. MILITARY, DEFENSE, WAR, INTELLIGENCE OPERATIONS, POLITICAL VIOLENCE

News of actual hostilities between two or more nations, of activities of defense departments of nations, training of personnel, maneuvers, and other military operations. Includes stories on guerrilla and political terrorist actions, and intelligence operations and activities. Includes civil war, widespread violent demonstrations.

2. FOREIGN RELATIONS, POLITICAL

News of formal diplomatic relations between nations; includes news of the official activities of ambassadors and military officials, negotiations between countries.

3. DOMESTIC GOVERNMENT, POLITICAL

News about the internal and domestic acts of a government, city, state, or national, of a nation from which the news originates.

4. ECONOMIC, BUSINESS, LABOR AND AGRICULTURE

News about a country's economic and business life which deals with the management of the economic affairs of a government, private industry or company, with reference to its sources of income, tax, expenditures, prices, banking, trade, commerce, and so on. News of multinational corporations.

Labor relations: news concerned with the conflict element of organized labor in society; strikes, anticipated strikes, the day-to-day activities of organized labor; elections, peaceful settlement of contracts, etc.

Agriculture: news of farming, farm organizations, the technical and business aspects of farming, equipment, and farm prices.

5. SCIENCE, MEDICINE, HEALTH

Articles on scientific, health, medical, space and technological developments and discoveries in these fields.

6. EDUCATION

News of private or public schools, colleges, universities, adult education, and statements by educators.

7. ACCIDENTS, DISASTERS

News involving disasters of nature, explosions, transportation accidents, accidents befalling individuals, property damage, injury and death.

8. JUDICIAL, CRIME

News deals with interpretations by courts, civil suits and laws not political or economic in character. Includes news of criminal trials, acts of crime, arrests, punishment, jail and prison conditions, etc.

9. ENERGY, ENVIRONMENT, CONSERVATION

News involving energy developments, problems; environmental concerns, and conservation developments or concerns.

10. HUMAN RIGHTS

News of general human rights developments, events, activities, problems. Include such rights as speech, travel, press, religion, assembly, and other rights when used in the context of the human rights issues (i.e. human right to a job, food, housing, etc.)

11. SPORTS

12. ART, CULTURE, ENTERTAINMENT

News of the fine arts and entertainment, such as film, television, popular music, literature, painting, drama, architecture, museums. Includes book, drama and other kinds of reviews. This does not include articles about the entertainers and their productions classified as human interest, nor artists and entertainers involvment in political and social causes.

13. SOCIAL AND HUMAN INTEREST

News that is more popular literature than chronicle, social items. Includes prominent people.

14. RELIGION

All religious organizations, processes, issues.

15. OTHER

Because of the few entries in Categories 9, 10, and 14, we found it very easy to collapse the 15 categories into 12, and did so in a number of cases. As a matter of fact, as we have already noted, if a person wants to scan a sample of Third World news content quickly he will not lose too much by using only categories 1 through 4, 7 through 9, 11, and 15.

Development News

We coded "development news" to include all stories of social and economic growth or improvement where human planning and effort are involved. A key concept is "intentional": news of economic and social development involves a government, private organization, group or individual *trying* to improve conditions. For example, the daily grain market reports are not ordinarily codable as development news, but a story of a new way to increase grain production would be. A story about establishment of new literacy training centers would be. A story of a new scientific discovery would be if it is shown to contribute potentially to human and social betterment. Stories about the *failures* of economic and social plans and activities are also development stories.

THE FACTOR ANALYSES

Factor analysis is a statistical technique designed to reduce the complexity of a large data set by helping the investigator describe the large number of variables in terms of a much smaller number of underlying dimensions that represent the relationships among the variables. The variables themselves may be tests, such as our news stories, they may be people, as we use in constructing reader types, or they may be time periods. The purpose of the procedure is to group together those variables—tests, people, or occasions—that are most similar. Members of any one cluster, or factor, are more like other members of that cluster than they are like any variable in any other cluster. The structure is solved for on the basis of the inter-relationships, the correlations, among all of the original items.

The general idea of the factor analysis is to isolate the various components of the common factor variance that exists among the set of variables. Graphically, the variance, or variability, of a variable can be shown as in the figure below.

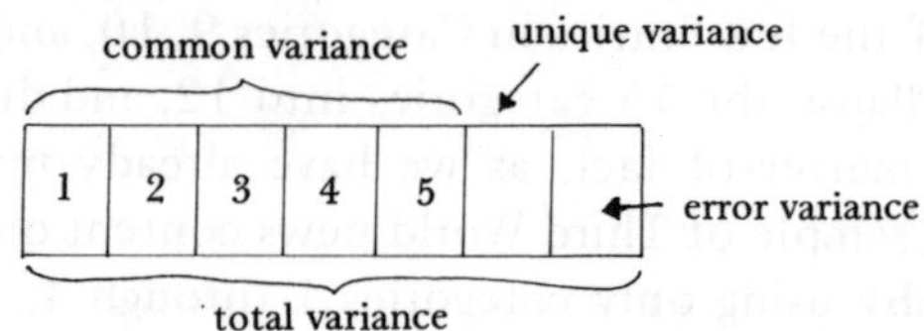

As the graph indicates, each variable has some variance in common with other variables, it has some variance that is unique to itself, and, because of inadequacies of measurement techniques, there is always some error involved in the "scores" we apply to the variable.

There is a wide variety of specific programed techniques available in most computer center libraries. The most popular forms are known as components analysis and principal factors analysis. The difference between the two is based on alteration of the principal diagonal in the correlation matrix for principal factors analysis. The diagonal is left unaltered in components analysis. The most popular procedure for altering the principal diagonal is to substitute the squared multiple correlation *(SMC's)* of each variable with all other variables for the unity that normally appears in the principal diagonal.

We employed components analysis with both sets of data. Following extraction of the desired number of factors the structure was rotated to oblique reference structure to determine if there were correlations between the different factors. We used two different computer programs in the analyses to explore different characteristics of the program's output. Not all programs are equally handy to use, and the printed output provided varies greatly. The program used for the final analysis was written by Dr. Norman Van Tubergen (1975) and is maintained in the Computing Center at Southern Illinois University.

Dimensions of the News Stories

This analysis included only 100 of the original 129 stories appearing in the *Bulletin Today*. Twenty-nine items were found to have been read by fewer than 10 respondents, and since these stories had virtually no associations with the other stories their inclusion in the correlation matrix would have simply introduced unnecessary error variance into the analysis.

Since the data were dichotomous, the story was either read or not read by each respondent, phi coefficients were computed to produce a factorable matrix of association coefficients. The initial solution was designed to extract all factors with latent roots (eigenvalues) equal to or greater than 1.0 (Kaiser, 1960). This rule of thumb permits the investigator to examine a solution in which each included factor must account for at least as much variance as was contributed by one of the original variables (each variable accounts for one unit of variance). The outcomes indicated there were 21 separate dimensions underlying the relationships among the 100 stories. This seemed somewhat unlikely given the kinds of stories included in the analysis, and the 21 rotated factors proved uninterpretable. A second rule of thumb, the common variance test (Rummel, 1970) indicated 10 dimensions that might best represent the structure of these data. The 10-factor solution also turned out to be uninterpretable to us, and a third rule of thumb, Cattell's (1966) scree test was applied. The six factors resulting from the resulting rotation were the ones we have used to describe the dimensions of news based on the reader's selections.

How the Reader Types were Created

The procedures used to create, or isolate, the six "typical" readers of the *Bulletin Today* were more complex. The first step was to draw three random samples of 30 cases each from the total sample of 476 respondents. We begin with small subsamples for two reasons. One is that we had no computer program that will compute a factor analysis on 476 variables. A more important reason, though, is that we have to transpose our data so that the rows become columns and the columns become rows—the matrix is rotated exactly 90 degrees—and the mathematics of factor analysis requires that we have more rows of data than we have columns to give the data the required stability. The transposed matrix has 476 columns and only 129 rows so we must begin with subsamples.

Why three random subsamples? Random samples give us the best chance of obtaining a solution somewhat representative of the total group, and three random subsamples provides more or less instant replication. Note that we are concerned only with the basic patterns of story selection, not all of the possible patterns that we could find. What we want is the minimum number of reading patterns that will describe the story selection behavior of the largest possible number of respondents. Undoubtedly we will miss some reading patterns, and we may never know how many were missed. What we will be quite sure of is that those we do miss are not very important among the total population of newspaper readers, and some of the patterns we miss will represent only a single person.

Next we computed the associations among the 30 respondents in each of the three subsamples using phi coefficients in the same manner as we computed the associations among the 100 news stories as we began the work of determining the psychological dimensions of the news. Since our raw data have been transposed, we will obtain associations among the people, we will discover how the people covary together across the news stories. Each of the three association matrices were then submitted to principal components analysis with rotation to oblique (oblimax) reference structure. In each of the three analyses the common variance test suggested that there were six basic factors or clusters of respondents that would provide a "best" grouping of the respondents into types of readers whose story selection patterns were most similar to each other.

At this point we were ready to create the basic reading patterns. All three subsamples were combined and a single components analysis was computed in which a six factor solution was specified. These factors were then rotated to oblique (oblimax) reference structure. Then the typical reader's score on each story was computed by first calculating a weight for each person that reflected his/her contribution to the group's selection pattern. The higher the individual's factor loading (in the rotated matrix) the higher the individual's weight and the greater his/her contribution to the group score on each story. Once the matrix of weights was assembled it was pre-multipled by the original raw data matrix and the resulting scores for each group were summed for each story. These raw scores were then standardized to produce factor scores.

The concluding step was to determine how many of the 476 respondents "belonged" in each of the six reader types. To do so the story preference scores for each of the six types was dichotomized; the story was assigned a value of "1" if the score was positive and a value of "0" if the score was negative. Roughly, "1" meant that half or more of the respondents read the story and "0" indicated that fewer than half of the respondents in the type read the story. Finally, phi coefficients were computed between each respondent's story selection pattern and each of the six hypothetical reader patterns. The respondents were then assigned to the typal pattern with which they had their highest positive association. As noted above, twelve respondents were not assigned to any of the types as their coefficients of association were less than 0.20. (Coefficients of less than 0.2 indicate less than 4% of the variance in the story selection pattern had been accounted for.)

The mean phi coefficients and the number of respondents in each of the reader types were:

Reader Type	Mean Coefficient	Number of Respondents
0[a]	.103	12
I	.548	48
II	.481	47
III	.473	78
IV	.356	45
V	.454	156
VI	.454	90

a. Respondents with coefficients of less than 0.2 with all types. They do not form a coherent typical reader as do the other groups but are included here for purposes of comparison.

APPENDIX F: References

Adams, J. B. A qualitative analysis of domestic and foreign news on the AP-TA wire. *Gazette,* 10 (1964) 285-295.

Aggarwala, Narinder K. What is development news? *Development Forum,* October 1978, 2-3.

Beltran, Luis Ramiro, and Fox de Cardona, Elizabeth. Latin American mass communication as influenced by the United States: The myth of the free flow of information. Unpublished paper presented at the East-West Communication Institute, March 29-April 3, 1976.

Boyd-Barrett, Oliver. The global news wholesalers. In Gerbner, George, ed. *Mass Media in Changing Cultures.* New York: Wiley, 1978.

Casey, Ralph D., and Copeland, Thomas H., Jr. Uses of foreign news by 19 Minnesota dailies. *Journalism Quarterly,* 35 (1958), 87-89.

Cattell, R. B. *Handbook of Multivariate Experimental Psychology.* Chicago: Rand McNally, 1966.

Chopra, Pran. Asian news values. Unpublished paper presented at Meeting of Experts on Development of News Agencies in Asia, Colombo, Sri Lanka, December 5-9, 1977.

Cooper, Kent. *Barriers Down.* New York: Holt, Rinehart, and Winston, 1942.

Cutlip, Scott M. Content and flow of AP news – From trunk to TTS to reader. *Journalism Quarterly,* 31 (1954), 434-446.

Dajani, Nabil, and Donohue, John. Foreign news in the Arab press: A content analysis of six Arab dailies. *Gazette,* 14 (1973), 155-170.

Deutsch, Karl W., and Merritt, Richard L. Effect of events on national and international images. In Kelman, Herbert, ed., *International Behavior: A Psychological Analysis.* New York: Holt, Rinehart and Winston, 1965.

Dickens, Mary Margaret. Transnational news services: Editors' views in Sri Lanka and Bangladesh. Unpublished paper presented at the East-West Communication Institute, East-West Center, Honolulu, August 6-19, 1978.

Donohew, Lewis. Newspaper gatekeepers and forces in the news channel. *Public Opinion Quarterly,* 31 (1967), 61-68.

El-Sherif, Mahmoud. Reflections on a new international communication order. *Issues in Communication,* 2 (1978), 36-40.

Galtung, Johan, and Ruge, Mari Holmboe. The structure of foreign news. *Journal of Peace Research,* (1965), 64-91.

Gerbner, George, and Marvanyi, George. *The Many Worlds of the World's Press.* Philadelphia: University of Pennsylvania Press, 1975.

Giles, Frank. Obstructions to the free flow of information. Paris: Unesco, Document 52 for the International Commission for the Study of Communication Problems, 1979.

Gunter, Jonathan F. An introduction to the great debate. *Journal of Communication,* 28, 4 (Autumn 1978).

Hart, Jim A. The flow of international news into Ohio. *Journalism Quarterly,* 38 (1961), 541-543.

Hart, Jim A. The flow of news between the U.S. and Canada. *Journalism Quarterly,* 40 (1963), 70-74.

Hart, Jim A. Foreign news in U.S. and English daily newspapers: A comparison. *Journalism Quarterly,* 43 (1966), 443-448.

Hauser, Ernest O. News of the Far East in U.S. dailies. *Public Opinion Quarterly,* 2 (1938), 651-658.

Hester, Albert. An analysis of news flow from developed and developing nations. *Gazette,* 17 (1971), 29-43.

Hester, Albert. *The Associated Press and news from Latin America:* A gatekeeper and news-flow study. Unpublished Ph.D. dissertation, University of Wisconsin, 1972.

Hester, Albert. Theoretical considerations in predicting volume and direction of international information flow. *Gazette,* 19 (1973), 239-247.

Hester, Albert. The news from Latin America via a world news agency. *Gazette,* 20, 2 (1974), 82, 91.

Hicks, Ronald G., and Gordon, Avishag. Foreign news content in Israeli and U.S. newspapers. *Journalism Quarterly,* 51 (1974), 639-644.

International Commission for the Study of Communication Problems. Interim report on communication problems in modern society. Paris: Unesco, 1978.

International Press Institute. *The Flow of the News.* Zurich: International Press Institute, 1953.

International Press Institute. *As Others See Us: Six Studies in Press Relations.* Zurich: International Press Institute, 1954.

International Press Institute. *The News from the Middle East.* Zurich: International Press Institute, 1954.

International Press Institute. *The Press in Authoritarian Countries.* Zurich: International Press Institute, 1959.

Jones, Robert L., Troldahl, Verling G., and Hvistendahl, J. K. News selection patterns from a state TTS-wire. *Journalism Quarterly,* 38 (1961), 303-312.

Kaiser, H.F. The application of electronic computers to factor analysis. *Educational and Psychological Measurement,* 20 (1960), 141-151.

Kawanaka, Yashuhiro. The role of Japan in the flow of news in Asia. Unpublished paper presented to Conference at the East-West Communication Institute, East-West Center, Honolulu, Hawaii, March 29-April 3, 1976.

Kayser, Jacques. *One Week's News: Comparative Study of 17 Major Dailies for a Seven-Day Period.* Paris: Unesco, 1953.

Kayser, Jacques, and Tannenbaum, Percy. A comparative study of foreign news coverage in French and American papers. *IAMCR Bulletin,* October 1962.

Kim, Kyu-Whan. Information imbalance in Asia: A Korean case. Paper presented to AMIC Sri Lanka conference, 1975.

Kirkpatrick, Clayton. Remarks on news agencies and the flow of information. To symposium of International Communication Division, Association for Education in Journalism, Madison, Wisconsin, March 1979.

Kulkarni, V. G. News flow: An East Asian overview. Paper for meeting on development of news agencies in Asia. Colombo, December 5-9, 1977.

Lee, John, International news flow in the expatriate English-language press. *Journalism Quarterly,* 42 (1965), 632-638.

Lent, John A. Foreign news content of United States and Asian print media: A literature review and problem analysis. Unpublished paper, Temple University, Philadelphia, n.d.

Lewis, Howard L. The Cuban revolt story: AP, UPI, and three papers. *Journalism Quarterly,* 37 (1960), 573-578.

Liu, Alan C., and Gunaratne, Shelton A. Foreign news in two Asian dailies. *Gazette,* 18 (1972), 38-41.

McNelly, John T. Intermediary communicators in the international flow of news. *Journalism Quarterly,* 36 (1959), 23-26.

Markham, James W. *A Comparative Analysis of Foreign News in Newspapers of the United States and South America.* University Park, Pennsylvania: Penn State Press, 1959.

Masmoudi, Mustapha. The new world information order. *Journal of Communication,* 29, 2 (Spring 1979), 172-188.

Merrill, John C. The image of the United States in ten Mexican dailies. *Journalism Quarterly,* 39 (1962), 203-209.

Nam, Sunwoo. The flow of international news into Korea. *Gazette,* 16 (1970), 14-26.

Nordenstreng, Kaarle, and Varis, Tapio. Television Traffic – A one-way street? A survey and analysis of the international flow of television programme material. *Unesco Papers and Reports on Mass Communication,* No. 70, 1974.

Olasope, Biola. News flow and African broadcasters. Paper presented to Conference on the Third World and Press Freedom, May 11-13, 1977.

Pinch, Edward T. A brief study on news patterns in sixteen Third World countries. Paper commissioned by the Edward R. Murrow Center, Tufts University, for Conference on the International News Agencies and the Developing World, Cairo, April 2-5, 1978.

Rachty, Gehan. Foreign news in nine Arab countries. Commissioned by the Edward R. Murrow Center, Tufts University, for the Conference on the International News Agencies and the Developing World, Cairo, April 2-5, 1978.

Rowlands, D. G. H. Is the complaint of news imbalance overstated? Unpublished paper, Thompson Foundation, Cardiff, Wales, 1978.

Rummel, R. J. *Applied Factor Analysis.* Evanston, Illinois: Northwester University Press, 1970.

Schiller, Herbert I. Freedom from the 'free flow.' *Journal of Communication* (1974), 110-117.

Schiller, Herbert I. Transnational media and national development. Unpublished paper presented at the East-West Communication Institute, East-West Center, Honolulu, Hawaii, March 29-April 3, 1976.

Schiller, Herbert I. The Free flow of information – for whom? In Gerbner, George, ed., *Mass Media in Changing Cultures,* New York: John Wiley, 1977.

Schramm, Wilbur. *One Day in the World's Press: Fourteen Great Newspapers on a Day of Crisis.* Stanford, California: Stanford University, 1959.

Shastri, Raj Kumar. Communication challenges in the developing world. Unpublished paper prepared for Conference at East-West Communication Institute, East-West Center, Honolulu, August 6-10, 1978.

Sommerlad, E. Lloyd. Free flow of information, balance, and the right to communicate. Unpublished paper prepared for Conference at East-West Communication Institute, East-West Center, Honolulu, Hawaii, March 29-April 3, 1976.

Swanson, Charles E. What they read in 130 daily newspapers. *Journalism Quarterly,* 32 (1956), 411-421.

Tharoon, Roger. News flow and press freedom. Paper for Conference of Edward R. Murrow Center, New York, May 11-13, 1977.

Tinbergen, Jon. Rio – reshaping the international order. Report of Rio de Janeiro Conference, Paris, Unesco, 1977.

Tuchman, Gaye. *Making News: A Study in the Construction of Reality.* New York: The Free Press, 1978.

Tuchman, Gaye. Professionalization as an agent of legitimization. *Journal of Communication,* 28, 2 (Spring 1978), 106-113.

Tunstall, Jeremy. Some dilemmas of mass media exporters. Paper prepared for East-West Communication Institute, East-West Center, Honolulu, Hawaii, August 6-19, 1978.

Unesco. Intergovernmental conference on communication policies in Asia and Oceania. Report of conference, Kuala Lumpur, Malaysia, February 4-14, 1979.

Unesco. *News Agencies, Their Structure and Operation.* Paris: Unesco, 1953.

Unesco. The world of news agencies. Document prepared for International Commission for the Study of Communication Problems. Paris: Unesco, 1979.

Unesco. *World Press, Newspapers and News Agencies.* Paris: Unesco, 1975.

Van Horn, G. A. Analysis of AP news on trunk and Wisconsin state wires. *Journalism Quarterly,* 29 (1952), 426-432.

Van Tubergen, N. QUANAL users guide. Carbondale, Illinois: Southern Illinois University, 1975. Mimeo.

Vilanilam, John V. Foreign news in two U.S. newspapers and Indian newspapers during selected periods. *Gazette,* 18 (1972).

White, Llewellyn, and Leigh, Robert D. The international news-gatherers. In Schramm, Wilbur, ed., *Mass Communications,* Urbana: University of Illinois Press, 1960.

Wolfe, Wayne. Images of the U.S. in the Latin American press. *Journalism Quarterly,* 40 (1963), 83-86.

Yu, Frederick T. C. Treatment of the Little Rock incident in selected foreign newspapers. Unpublished paper, University of Montana, 1958.

Yu, Frederick T. C., and Luter, John. The foreign correspondent and his work. *Columbia Journalism Review,* 3, 4 (Spring 1964), 5-12.